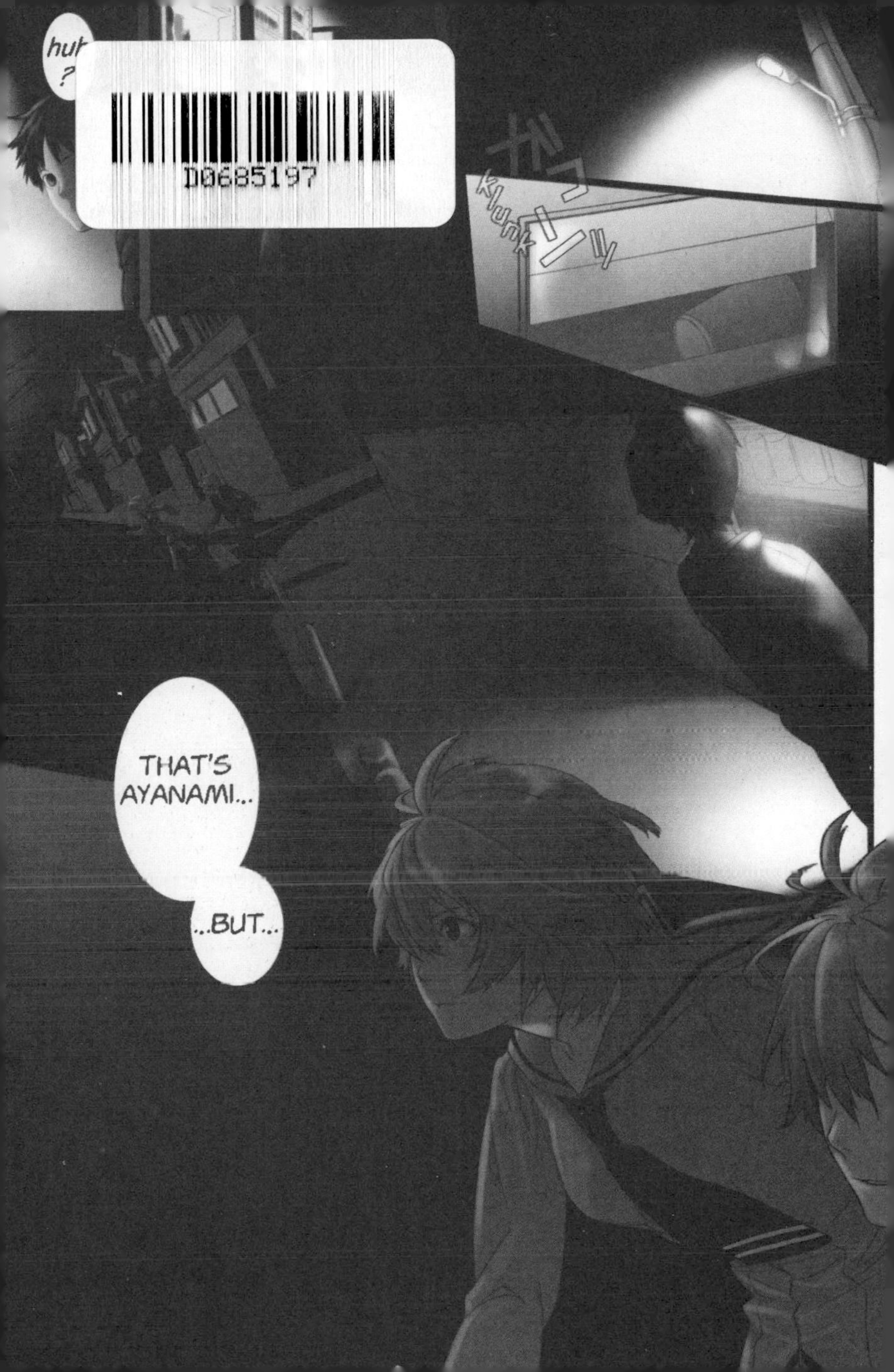
klunk
hu
?
THAT'S AYANAMI...
...BUT...

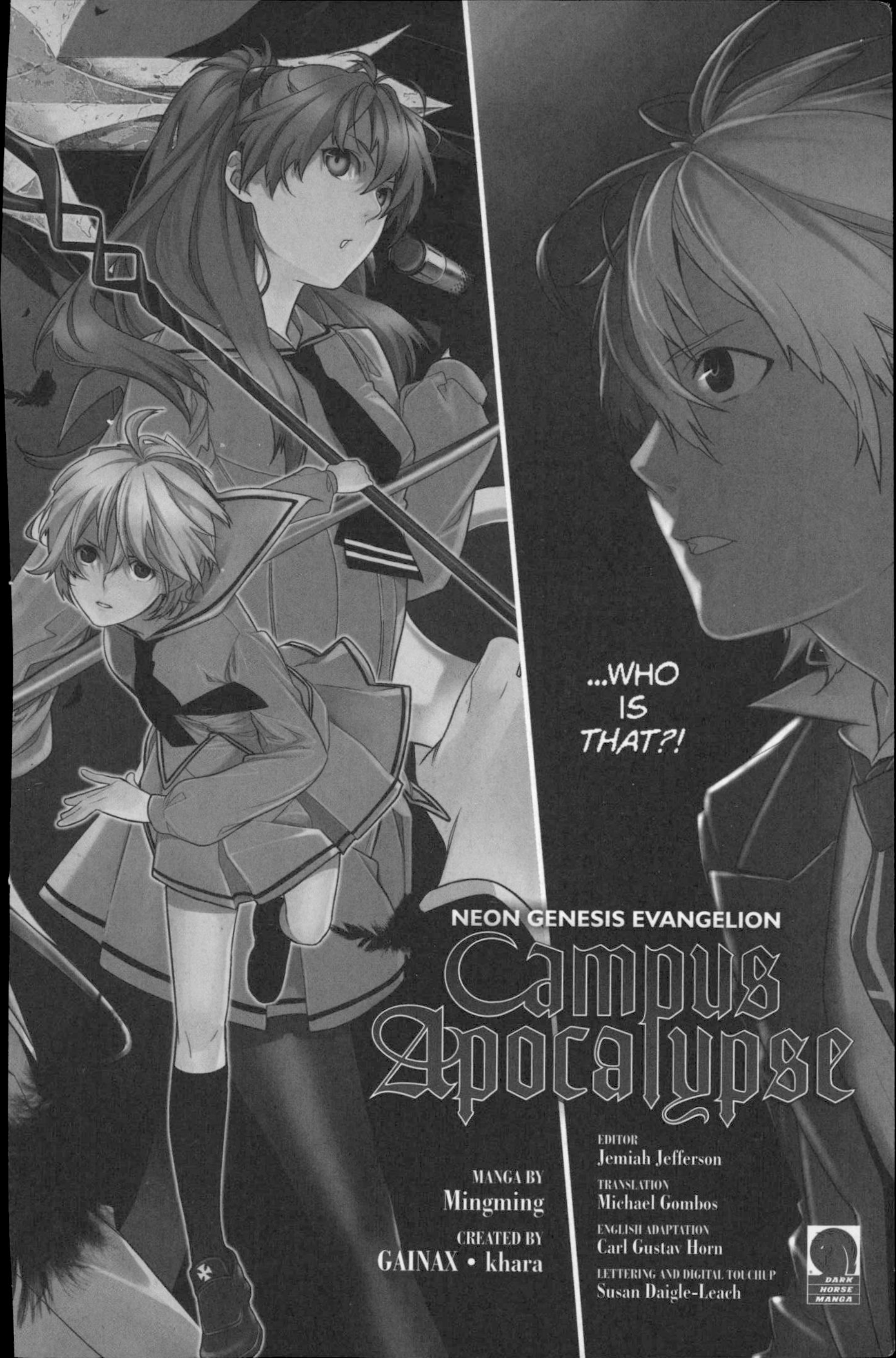
...WHO IS THAT?!

NEON GENESIS EVANGELION

Campus Apocalypse

MANGA BY
Mingming

CREATED BY
GAINAX • khara

EDITOR
Jemiah Jefferson

TRANSLATION
Michael Gombos

ENGLISH ADAPTATION
Carl Gustav Horn

LETTERING AND DIGITAL TOUCHUP
Susan Daigle-Leach

DARK HORSE MANGA

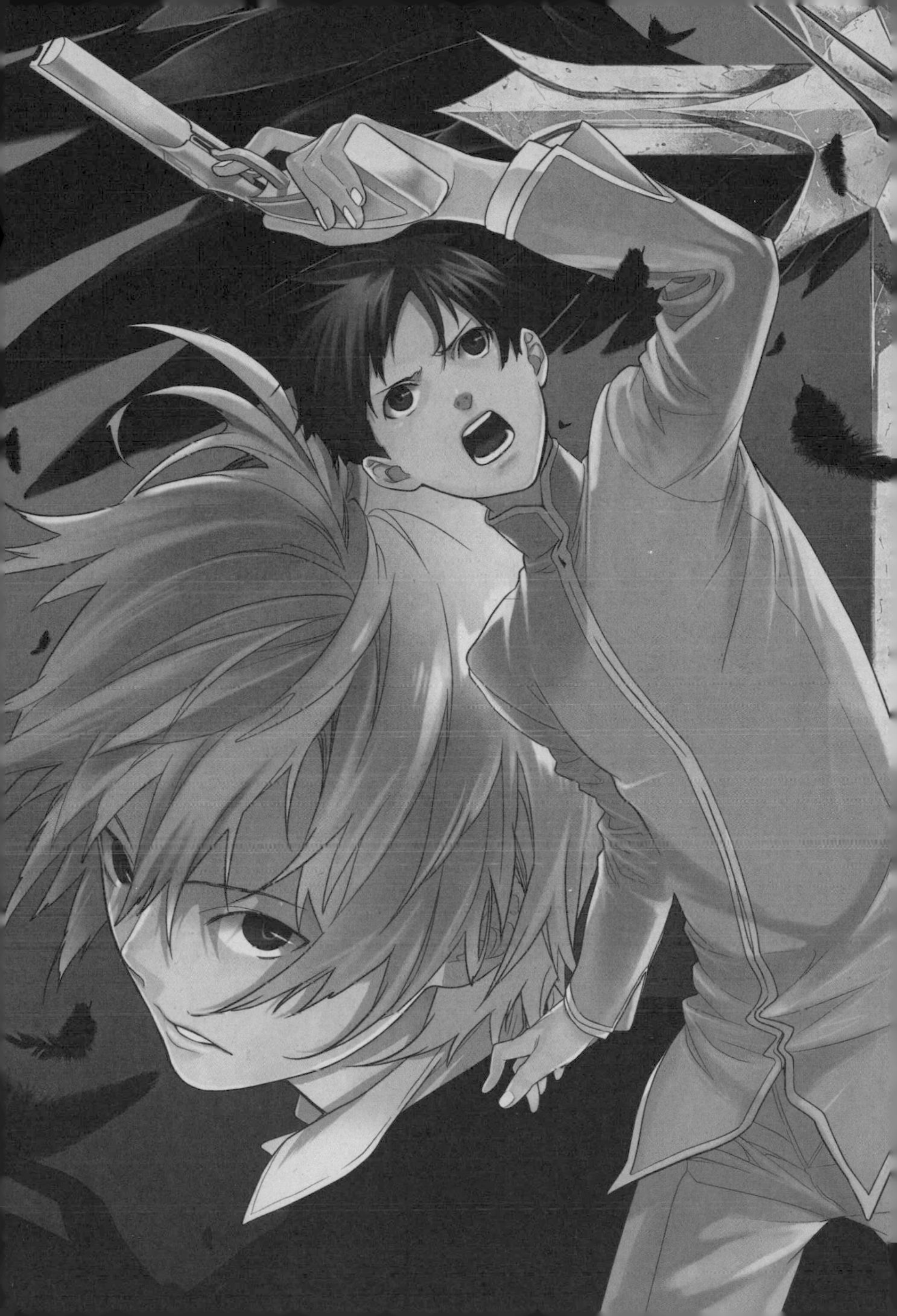

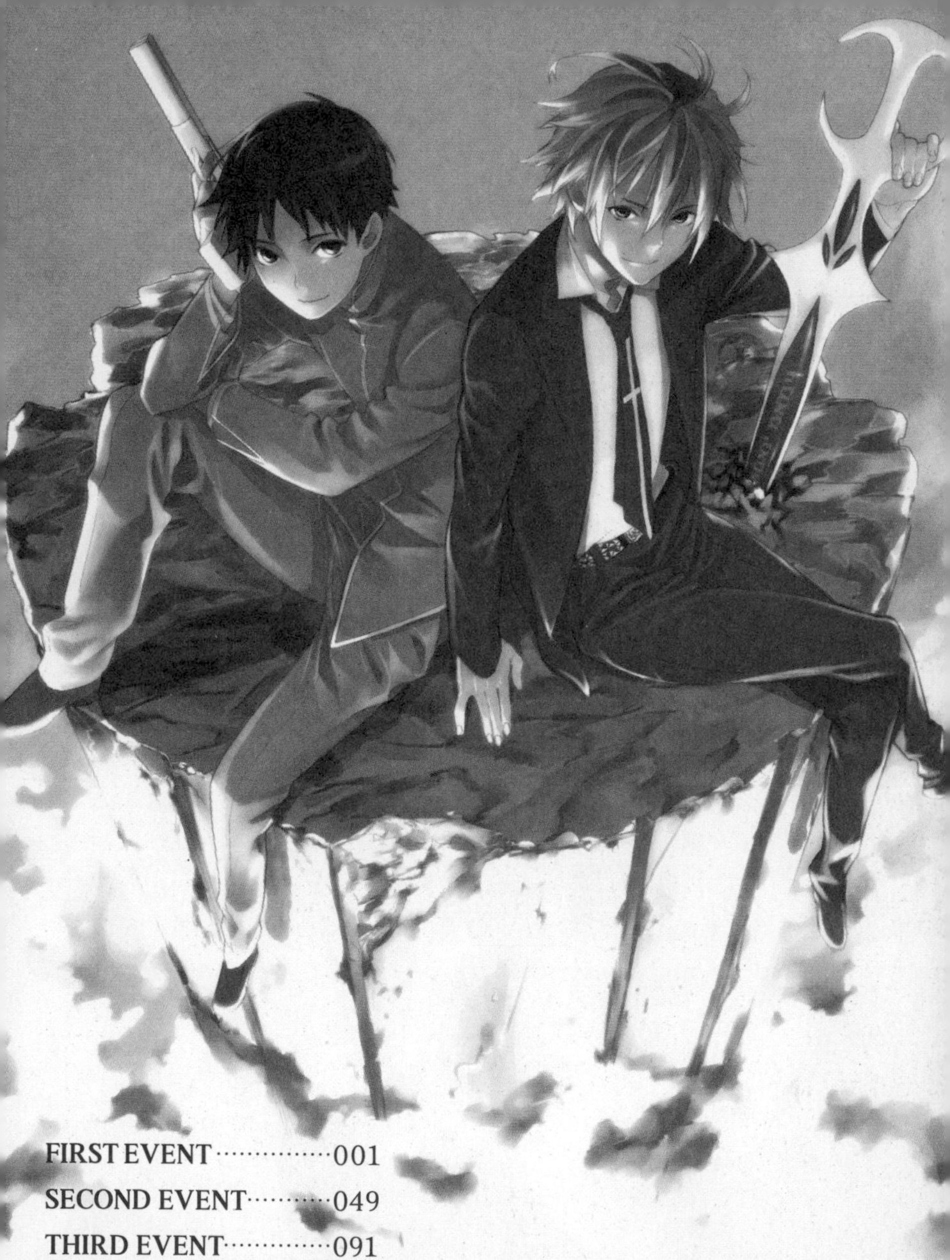

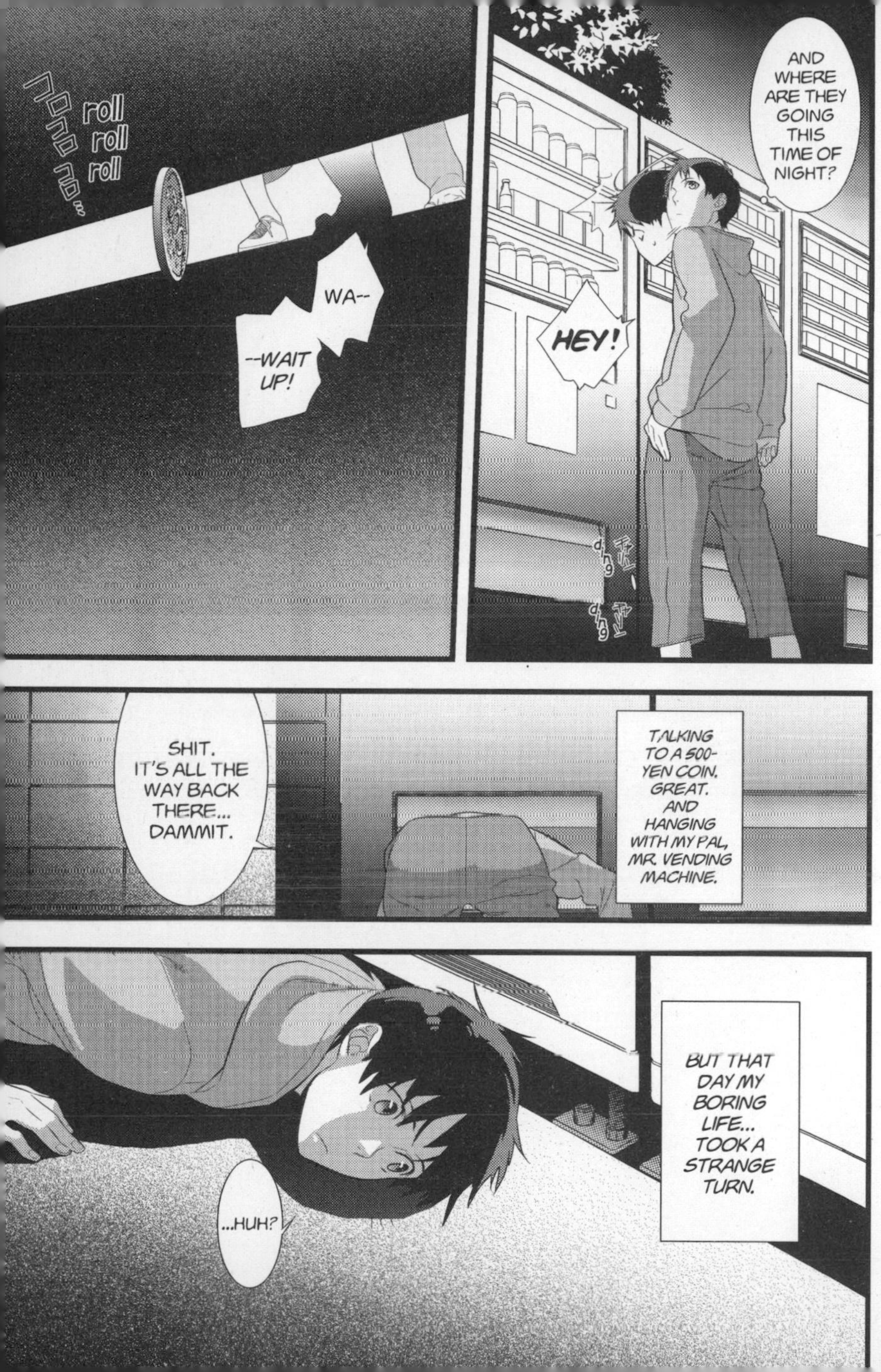
AND WHERE ARE THEY GOING THIS TIME OF NIGHT?
HEY!
ding ding
roll roll roll
WA--
--WAIT UP!
TALKING TO A 500-YEN COIN. GREAT. AND HANGING WITH MY PAL, MR. VENDING MACHINE.
SHIT. IT'S ALL THE WAY BACK THERE... DAMMIT.
BUT THAT DAY MY BORING LIFE... TOOK A STRANGE TURN.
...HUH?

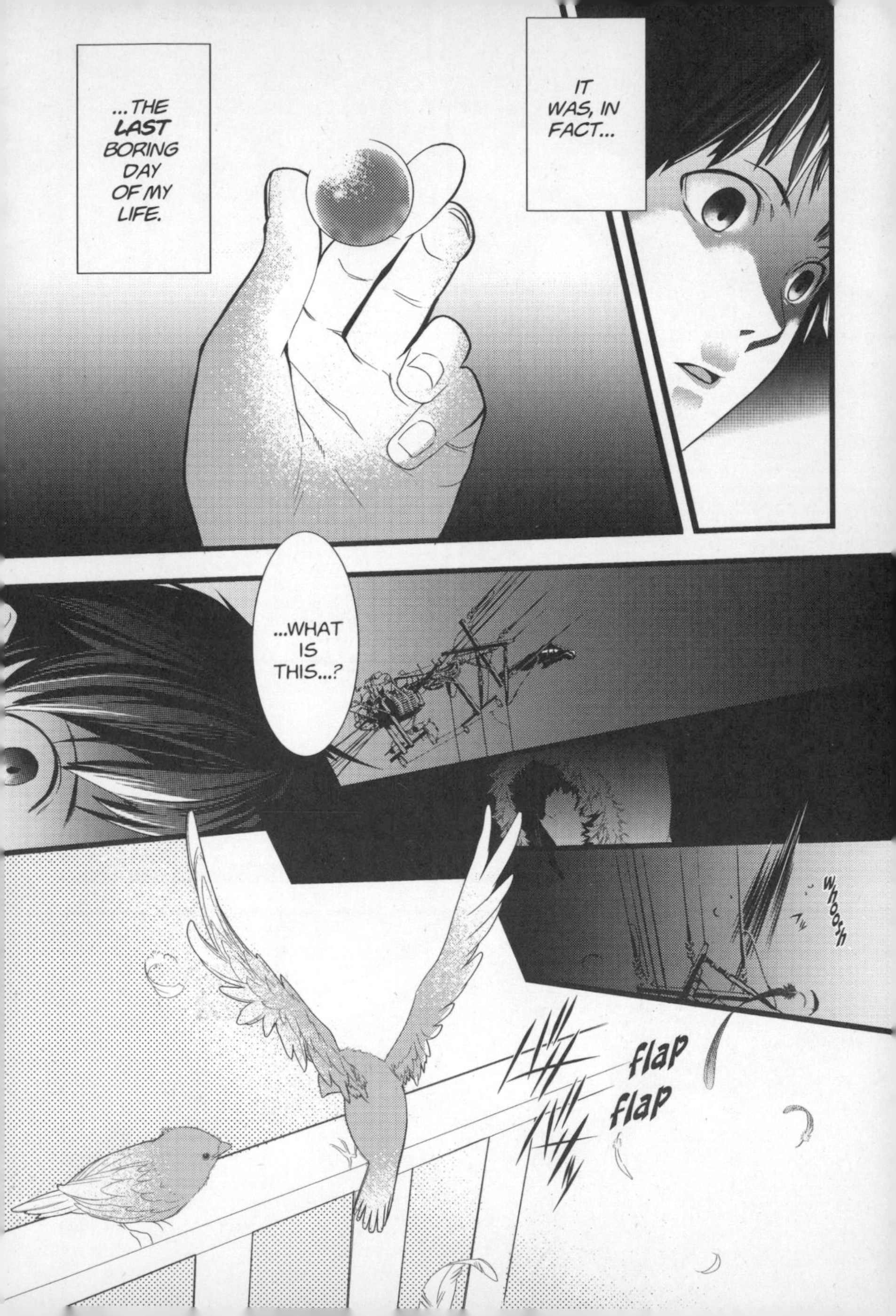
IT WAS, IN FACT...
...THE LAST BORING DAY OF MY LIFE.
...WHAT IS THIS...?
WHOOSH
flap
flap

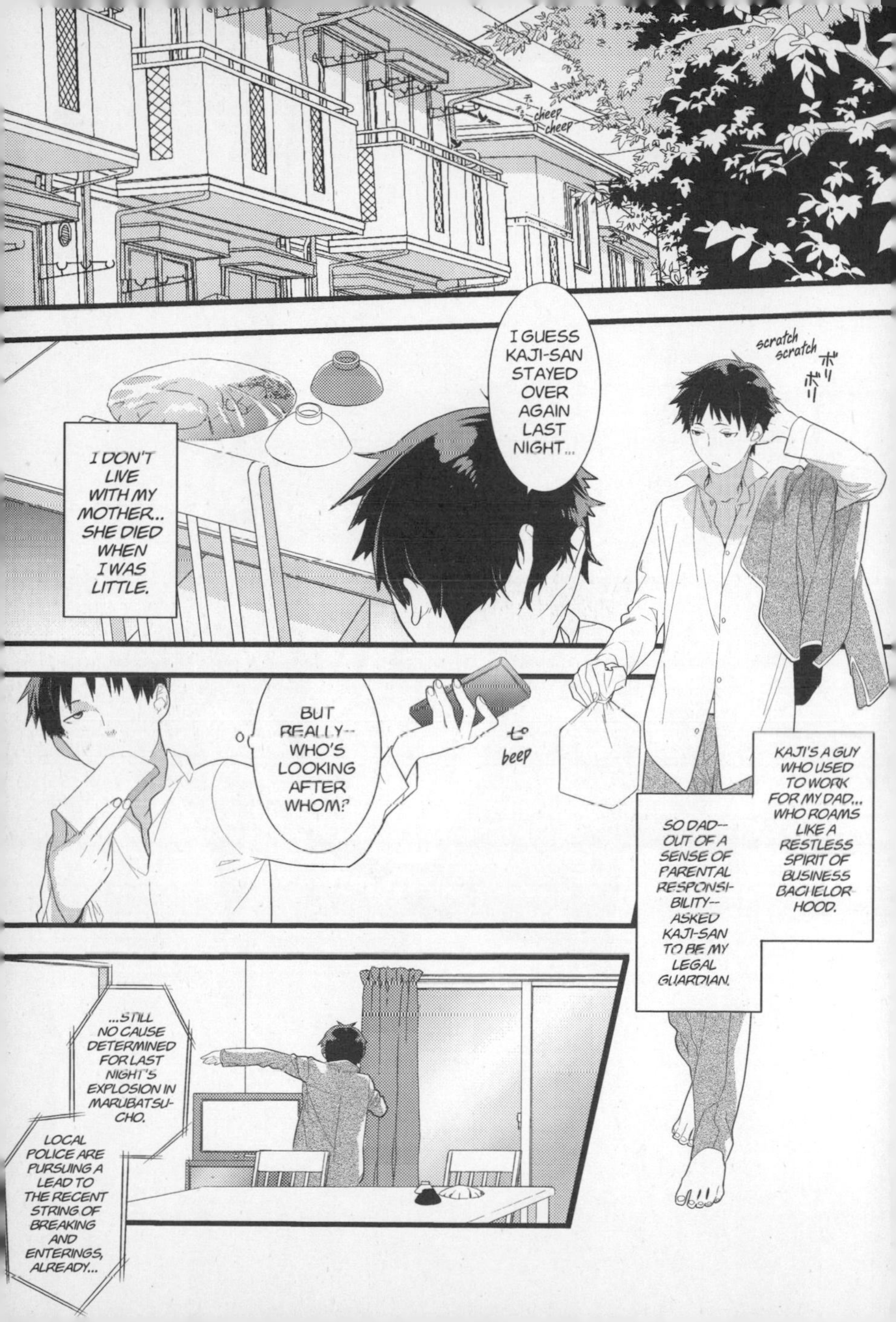

チュ
チュ
cheep
cheep
scratch
scratch
ボリ
ボリ
I GUESS KAJI-SAN STAYED OVER AGAIN LAST NIGHT...
I DON'T LIVE WITH MY MOTHER... SHE DIED WHEN I WAS LITTLE.
KAJI'S A GUY WHO USED TO WORK FOR MY DAD... WHO ROAMS LIKE A RESTLESS SPIRIT OF BUSINESS BACHELORHOOD.
SO DAD-- OUT OF A SENSE OF PARENTAL RESPONSIBILITY-- ASKED KAJI-SAN TO BE MY LEGAL GUARDIAN.
ピ
beep
BUT REALLY-- WHO'S LOOKING AFTER WHOM?
...STILL NO CAUSE DETERMINED FOR LAST NIGHT'S EXPLOSION IN MARUBATSU-CHO.
LOCAL POLICE ARE PURSUING A LEAD TO THE RECENT STRING OF BREAKING AND ENTERINGS, ALREADY...

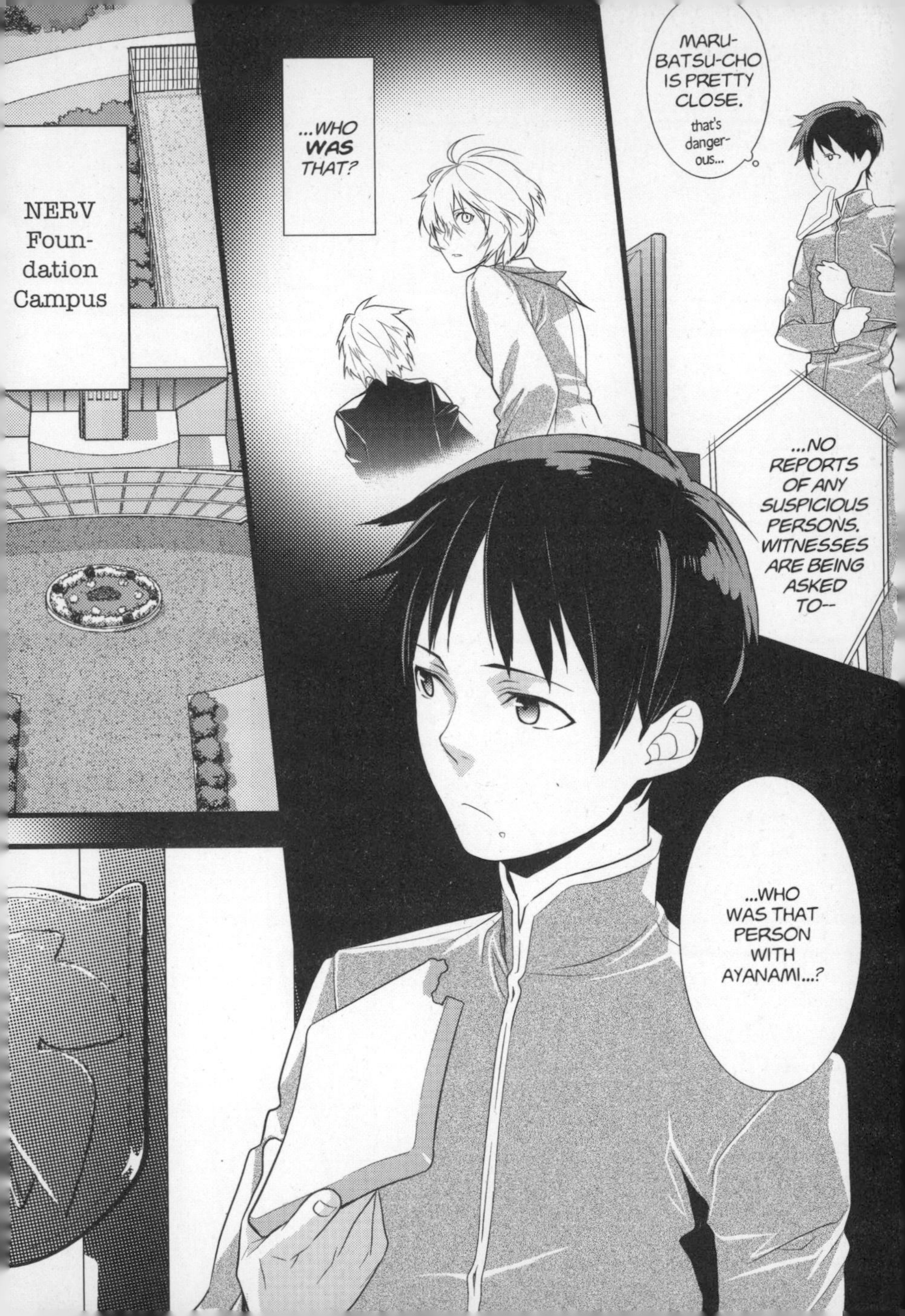
MARU-BATSU-CHO IS PRETTY CLOSE.
that's danger-ous...
...NO REPORTS OF ANY SUSPICIOUS PERSONS. WITNESSES ARE BEING ASKED TO--
...WHO WAS THAT?
NERV Foun-dation Campus
...WHO WAS THAT PERSON WITH AYANAMI...?

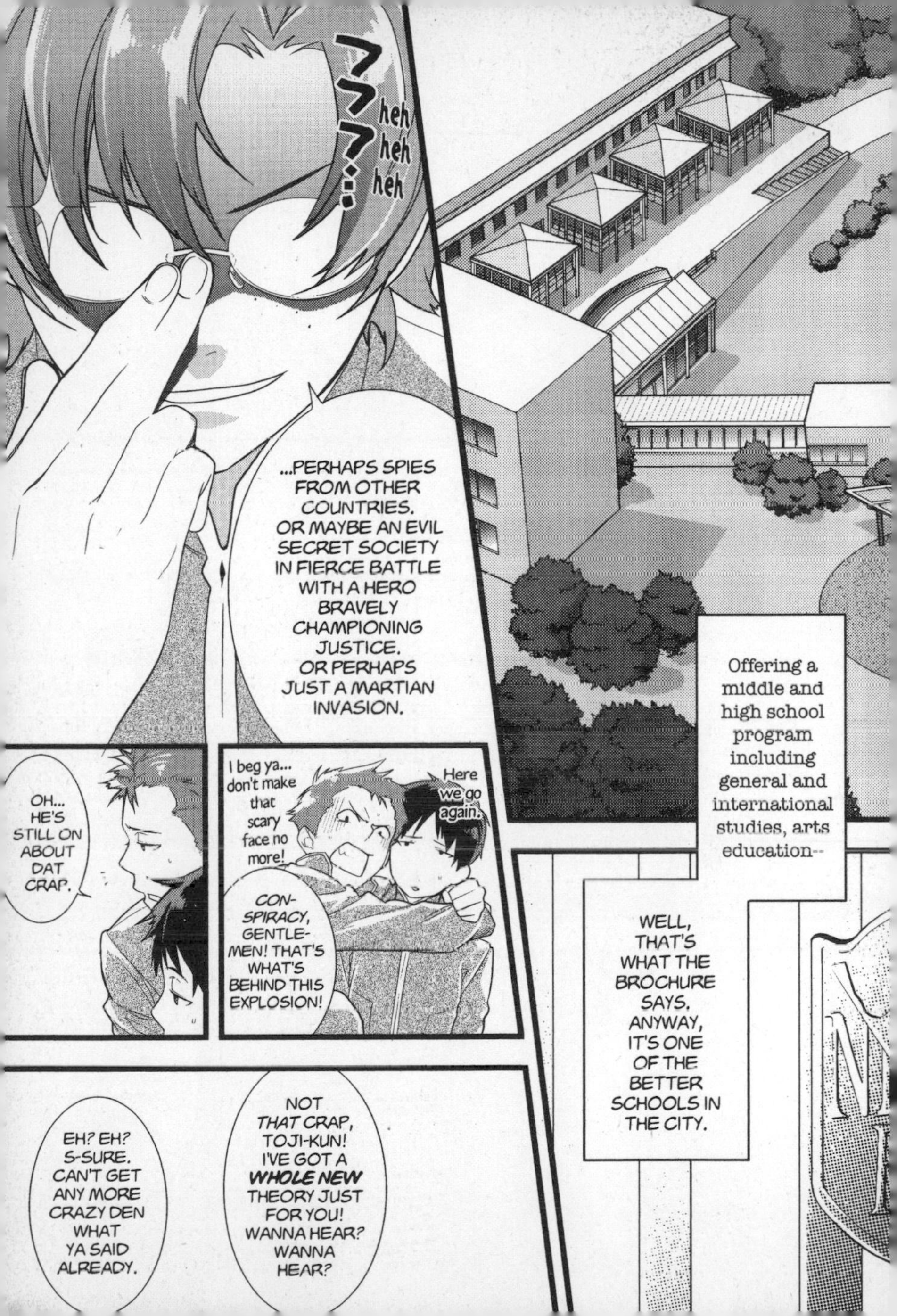
Offering a middle and high school program including general and international studies, arts education--
WELL, THAT'S WHAT THE BROCHURE SAYS. ANYWAY, IT'S ONE OF THE BETTER SCHOOLS IN THE CITY.
フフフ...
heh heh heh
...PERHAPS SPIES FROM OTHER COUNTRIES. OR MAYBE AN EVIL SECRET SOCIETY IN FIERCE BATTLE WITH A HERO BRAVELY CHAMPIONING JUSTICE. OR PERHAPS JUST A MARTIAN INVASION.
Here we go again.
I beg ya... don't make that scary face no more!
CON-SPIRACY, GENTLE-MEN! THAT'S WHAT'S BEHIND THIS EXPLOSION!
OH... HE'S STILL ON ABOUT DAT CRAP.
NOT *THAT* CRAP, TOJI-KUN! I'VE GOT A ***WHOLE NEW*** THEORY JUST FOR YOU! WANNA HEAR? WANNA HEAR?
EH? EH? S-SURE. CAN'T GET ANY MORE CRAZY DEN WHAT YA SAID ALREADY.

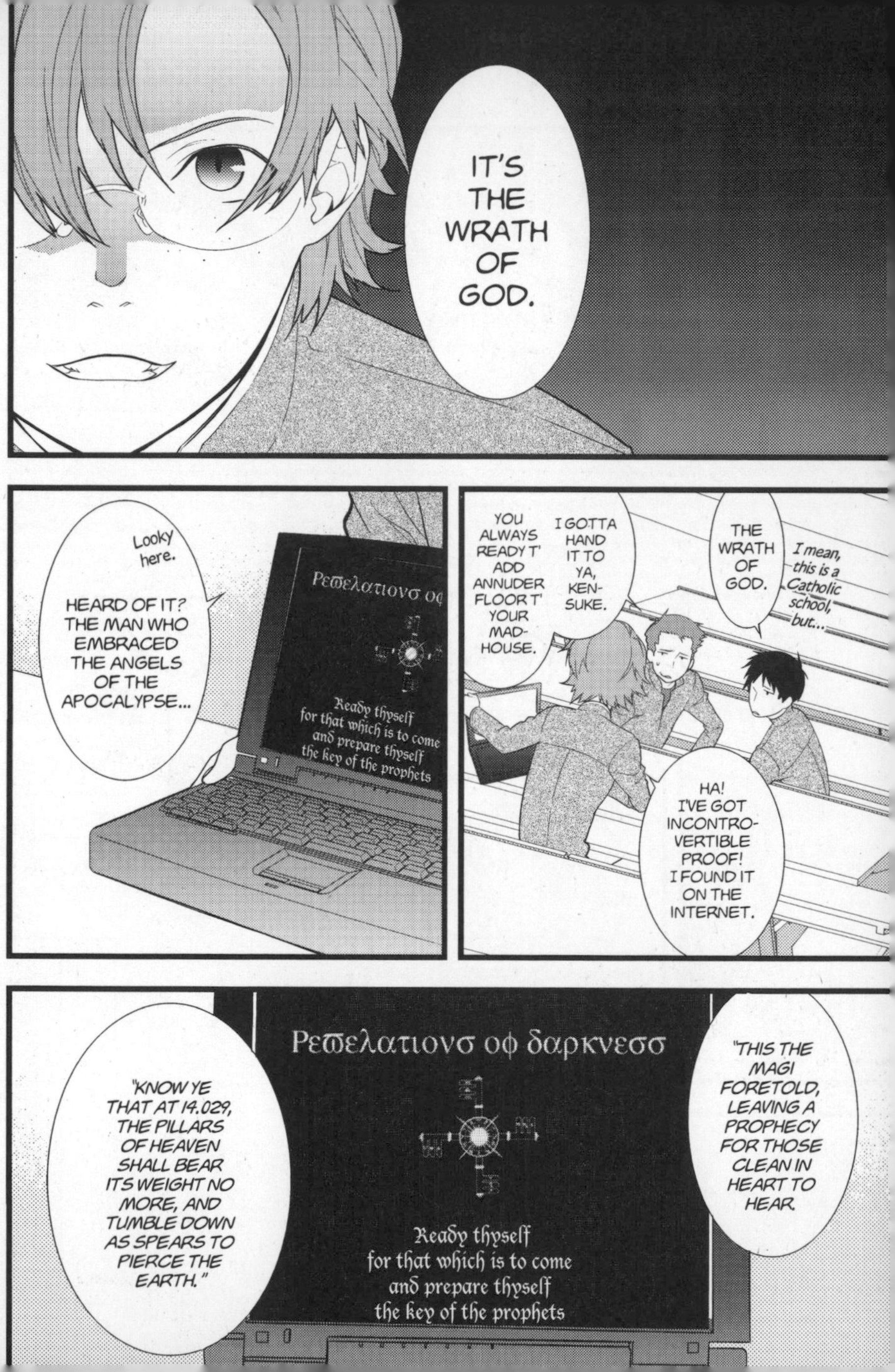
IT'S THE WRATH OF GOD.
I mean, this is a Catholic school, but...
THE WRATH OF GOD.
I GOTTA HAND IT TO YA, KEN-SUKE.
YOU ALWAYS READY T' ADD ANNUDER FLOOR T' YOUR MAD-HOUSE.
HA! I'VE GOT INCONTRO-VERTIBLE PROOF! I FOUND IT ON THE INTERNET.
Looky here.
HEARD OF IT? THE MAN WHO EMBRACED THE ANGELS OF THE APOCALYPSE...
Ρεϖελατιονσ οφ
Ready thyself for that which is to come and prepare thyself the key of the prophets
"THIS THE MAGI FORETOLD, LEAVING A PROPHECY FOR THOSE CLEAN IN HEART TO HEAR.
Ρεϖελατιονσ οφ δαρκνεσσ
Ready thyself for that which is to come and prepare thyself the key of the prophets
"KNOW YE THAT AT 14.029, THE PILLARS OF HEAVEN SHALL BEAR ITS WEIGHT NO MORE, AND TUMBLE DOWN AS SPEARS TO PIERCE THE EARTH."

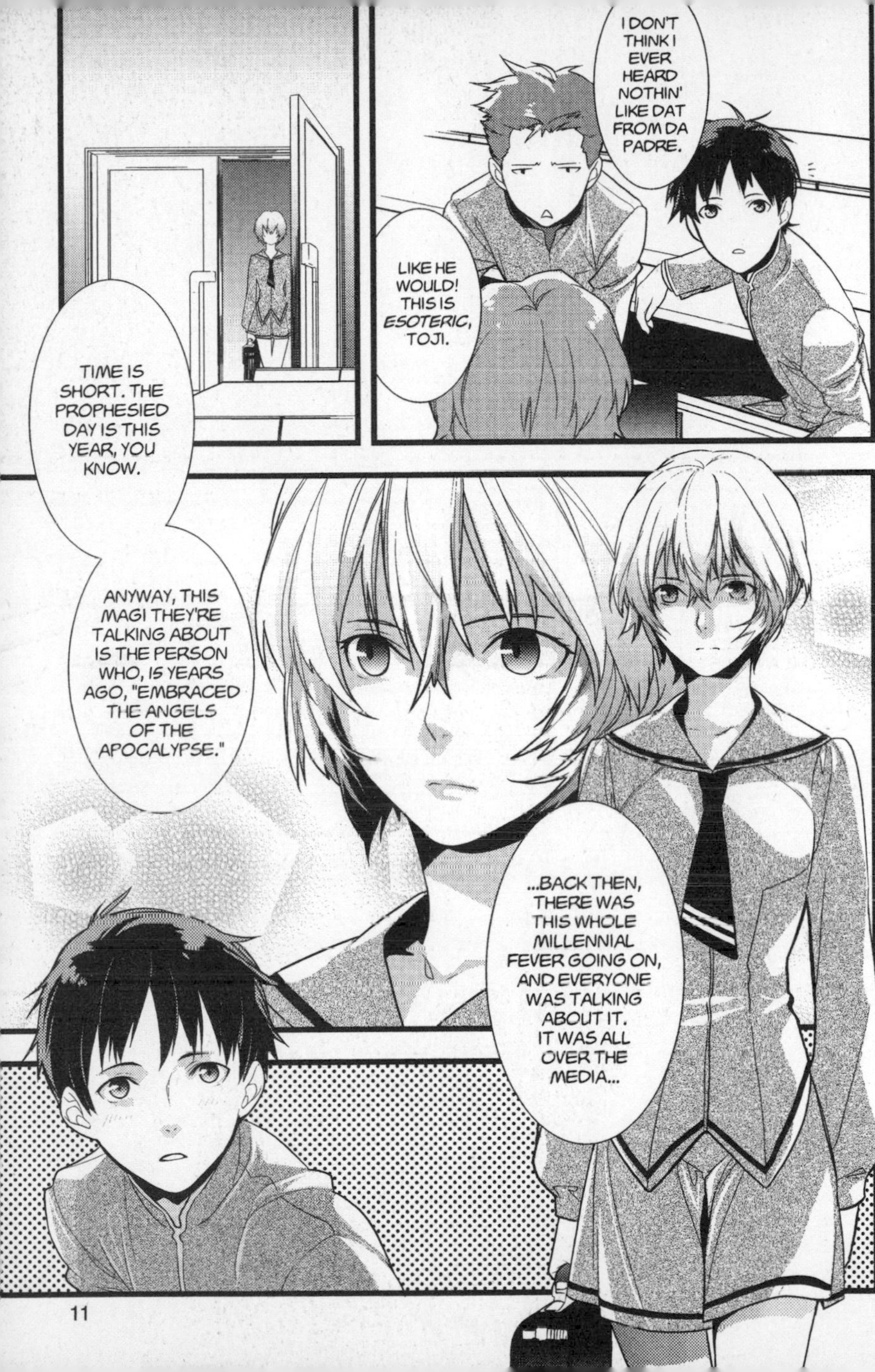
I DON'T THINK I EVER HEARD NOTHIN' LIKE DAT FROM DA PADRE.
LIKE HE WOULD! THIS IS *ESOTERIC*, TOJI.
TIME IS SHORT. THE PROPHESIED DAY IS THIS YEAR, YOU KNOW.
ANYWAY, THIS MAGI THEY'RE TALKING ABOUT IS THE PERSON WHO, 15 YEARS AGO, "EMBRACED THE ANGELS OF THE APOCALYPSE."
...BACK THEN, THERE WAS THIS WHOLE MILLENNIAL FEVER GOING ON, AND EVERYONE WAS TALKING ABOUT IT. IT WAS ALL OVER THE MEDIA...

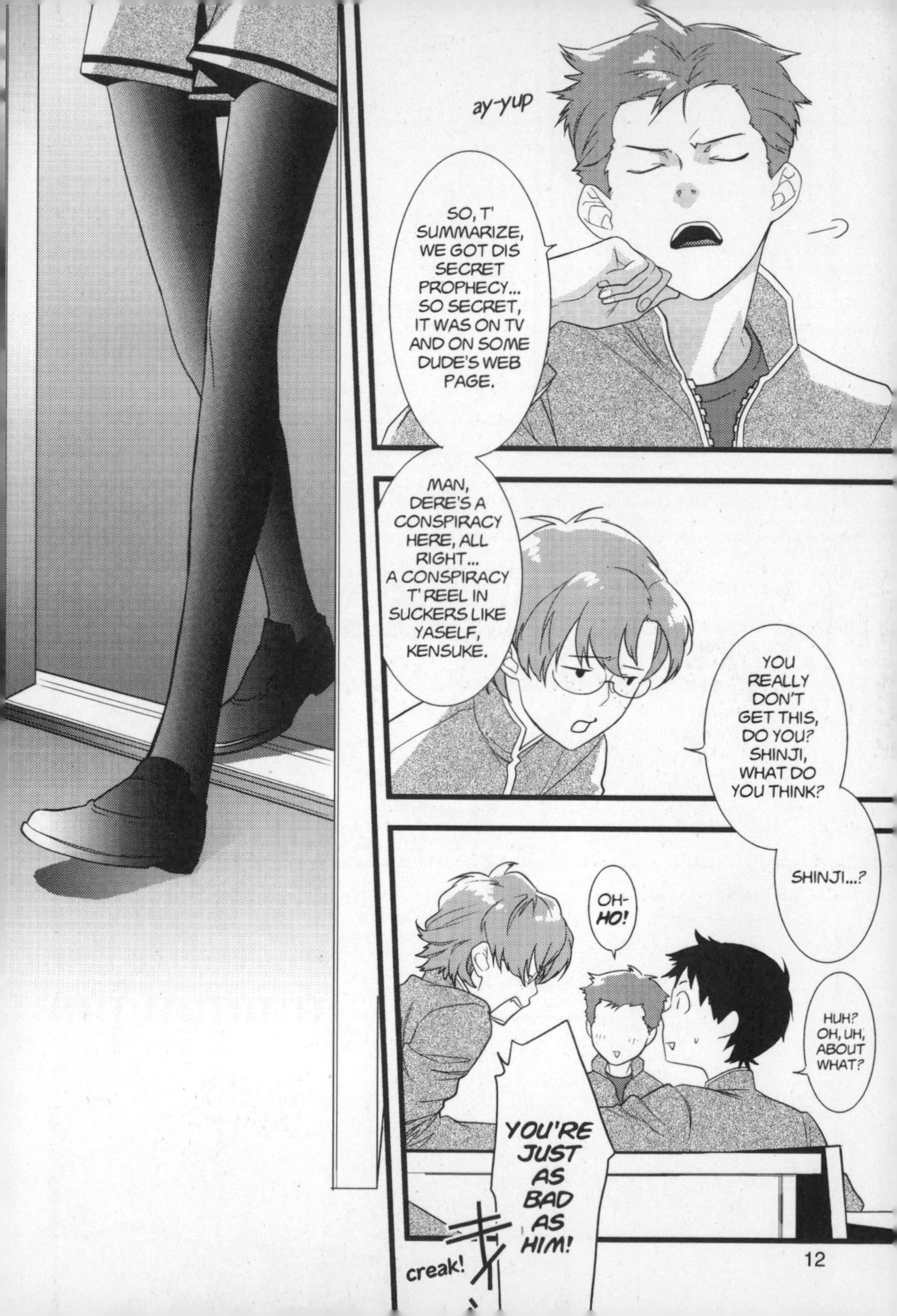
ay-yup
SO, T' SUMMARIZE, WE GOT DIS SECRET PROPHECY... SO SECRET, IT WAS ON TV AND ON SOME DUDE'S WEB PAGE.
MAN, DERE'S A CONSPIRACY HERE, ALL RIGHT... A CONSPIRACY T' REEL IN SUCKERS LIKE YASELF, KENSUKE.
YOU REALLY DON'T GET THIS, DO YOU? SHINJI, WHAT DO YOU THINK?
SHINJI...?
OH-HO!
HUH? OH, UH, ABOUT WHAT?
YOU'RE JUST AS BAD AS HIM!
creak!

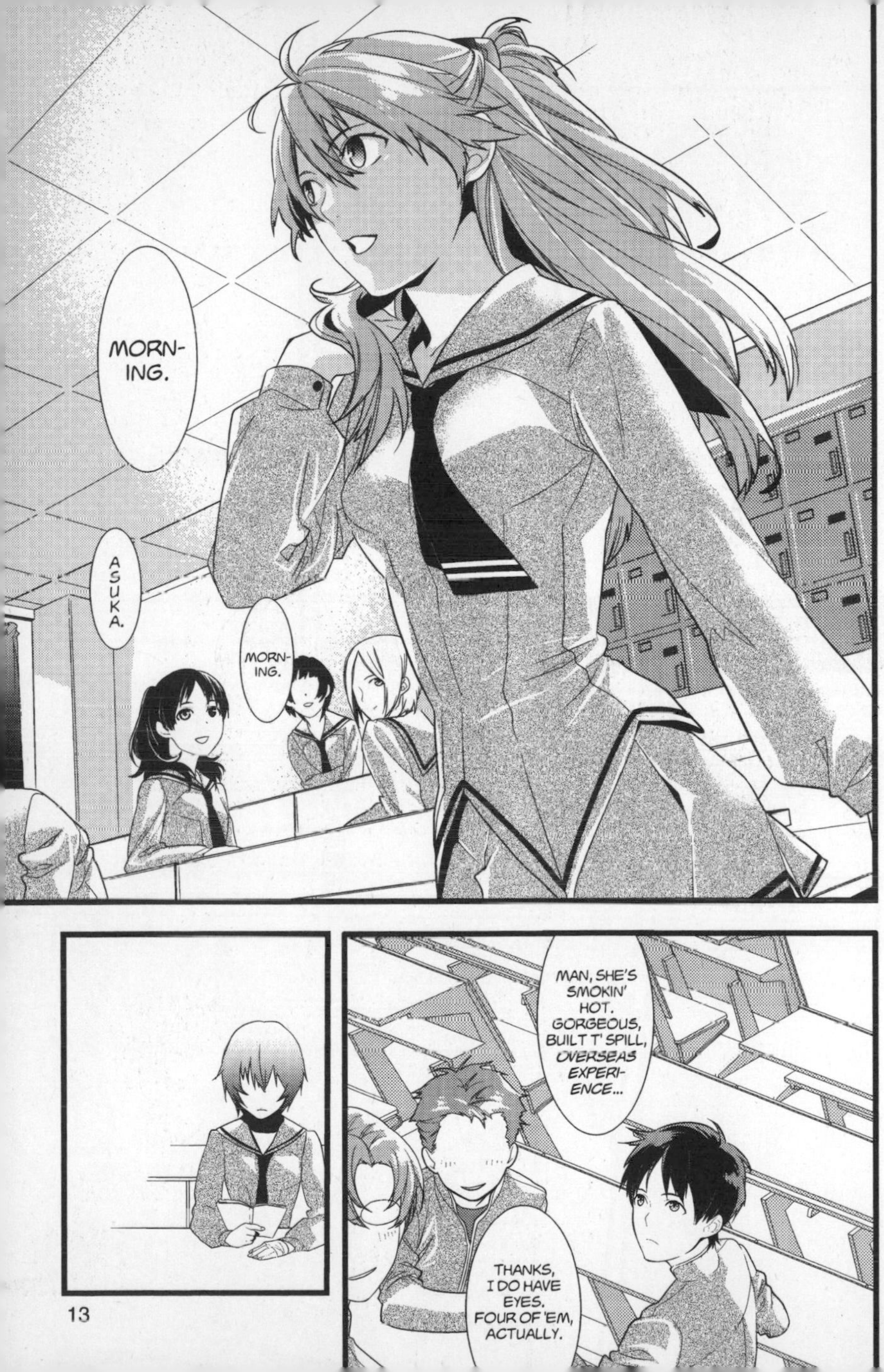
MORN-ING.
ASUKA.
MORN-ING.
MAN, SHE'S SMOKIN' HOT. GORGEOUS, BUILT T' SPILL, OVERSEAS EXPERI-ENCE...
THANKS, I DO HAVE EYES. FOUR OF 'EM, ACTUALLY.

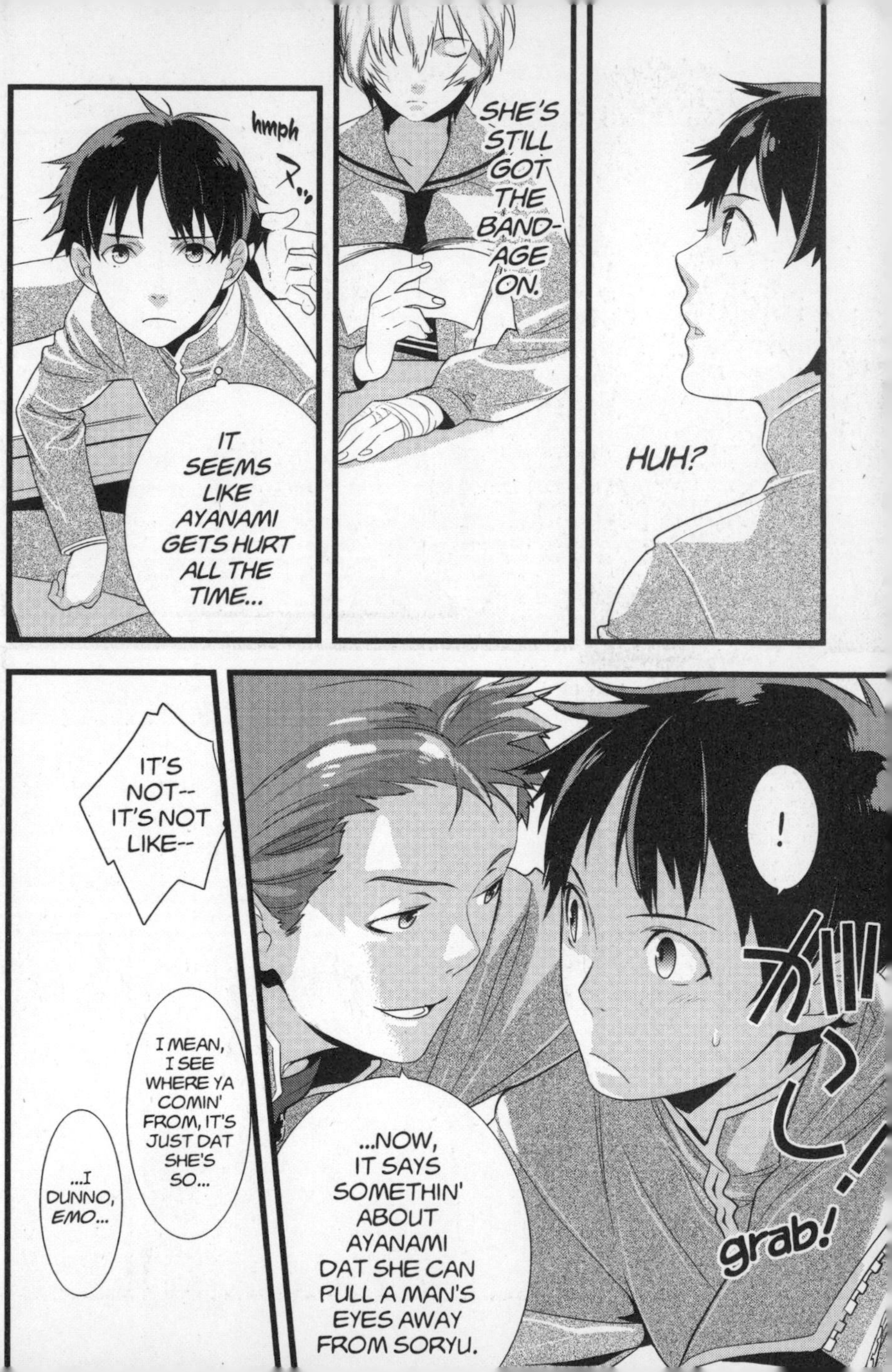
HUH?
SHE'S STILL GOT THE BAND-AGE ON.
hmph
IT SEEMS LIKE AYANAMI GETS HURT ALL THE TIME...
!
grab!
...NOW, IT SAYS SOMETHIN' ABOUT AYANAMI DAT SHE CAN PULL A MAN'S EYES AWAY FROM SORYU.
I MEAN, I SEE WHERE YA COMIN' FROM, IT'S JUST DAT SHE'S SO...
...I DUNNO, EMO...
IT'S NOT-- IT'S NOT LIKE--

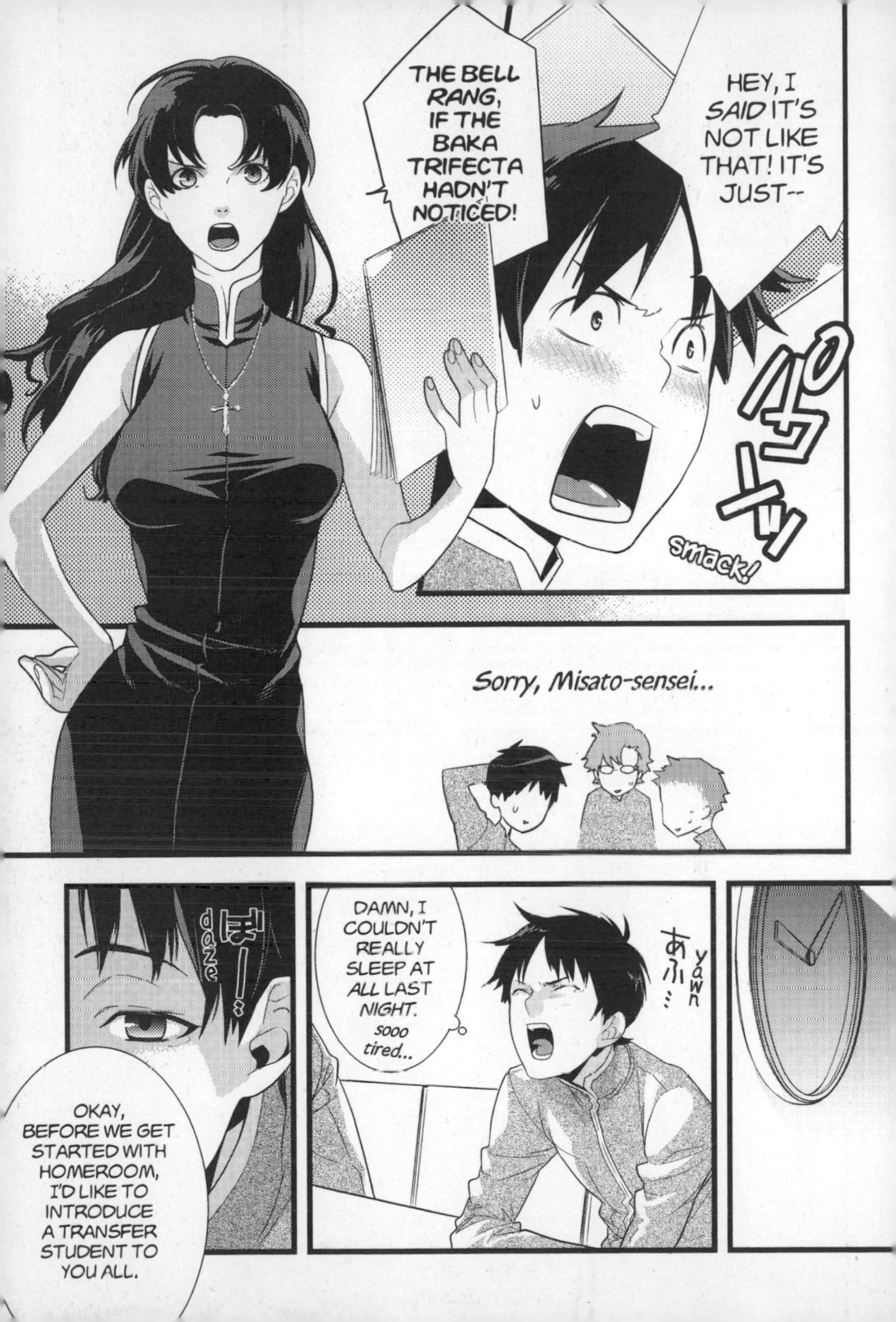

HEY, I SAID IT'S NOT LIKE THAT! IT'S JUST--
THE BELL RANG, IF THE BAKA TRIFECTA HADN'T NOTICED!
パコッ
smack!
Sorry, Misato-sensei...
あふ…
yawn
DAMN, I COULDN'T REALLY SLEEP AT ALL LAST NIGHT.
sooo tired...
ぽー…
daze
OKAY, BEFORE WE GET STARTED WITH HOMEROOM, I'D LIKE TO INTRODUCE A TRANSFER STUDENT TO YOU ALL.

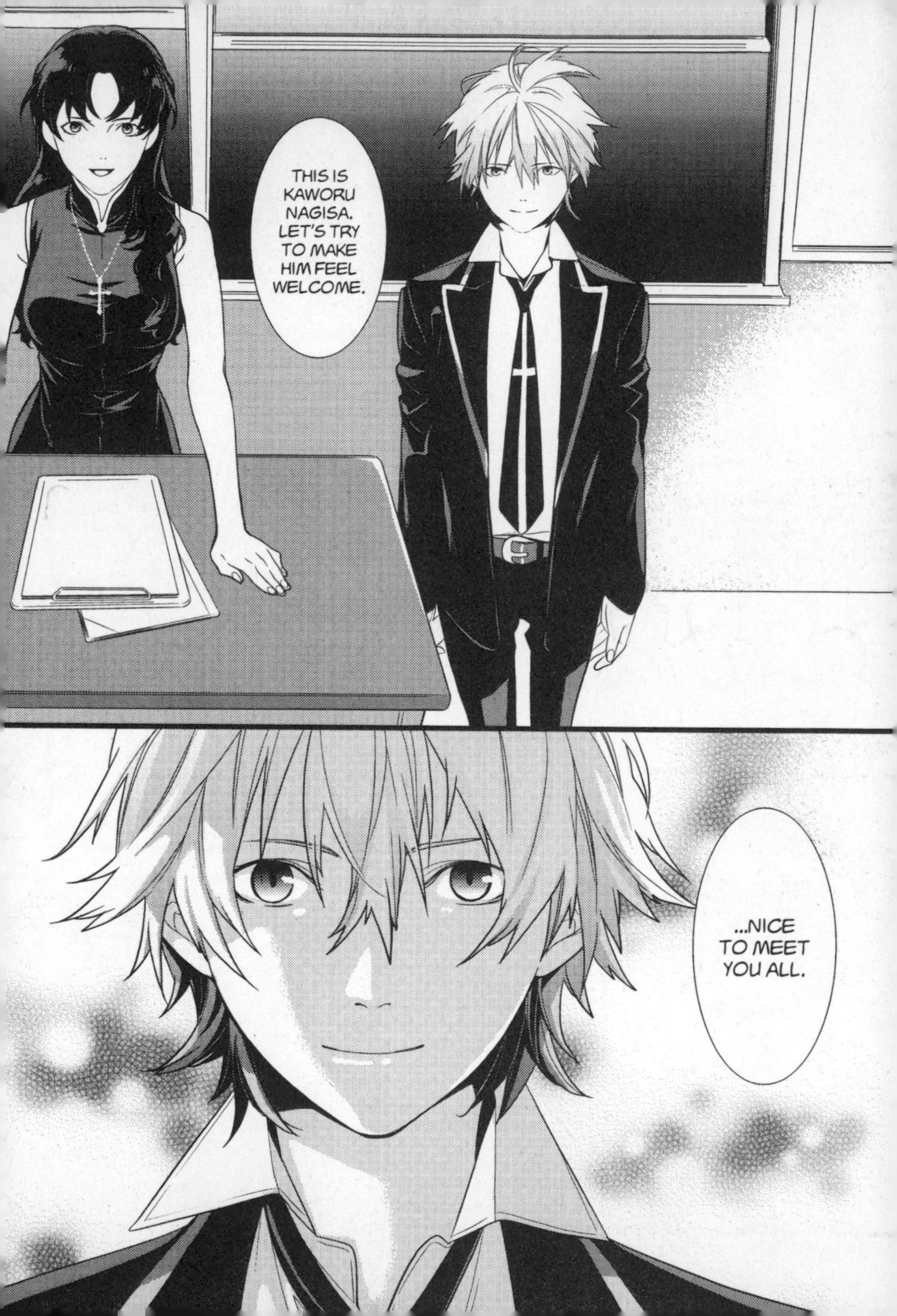
THIS IS KAWORU NAGISA. LET'S TRY TO MAKE HIM FEEL WELCOME.
...NICE TO MEET YOU ALL.

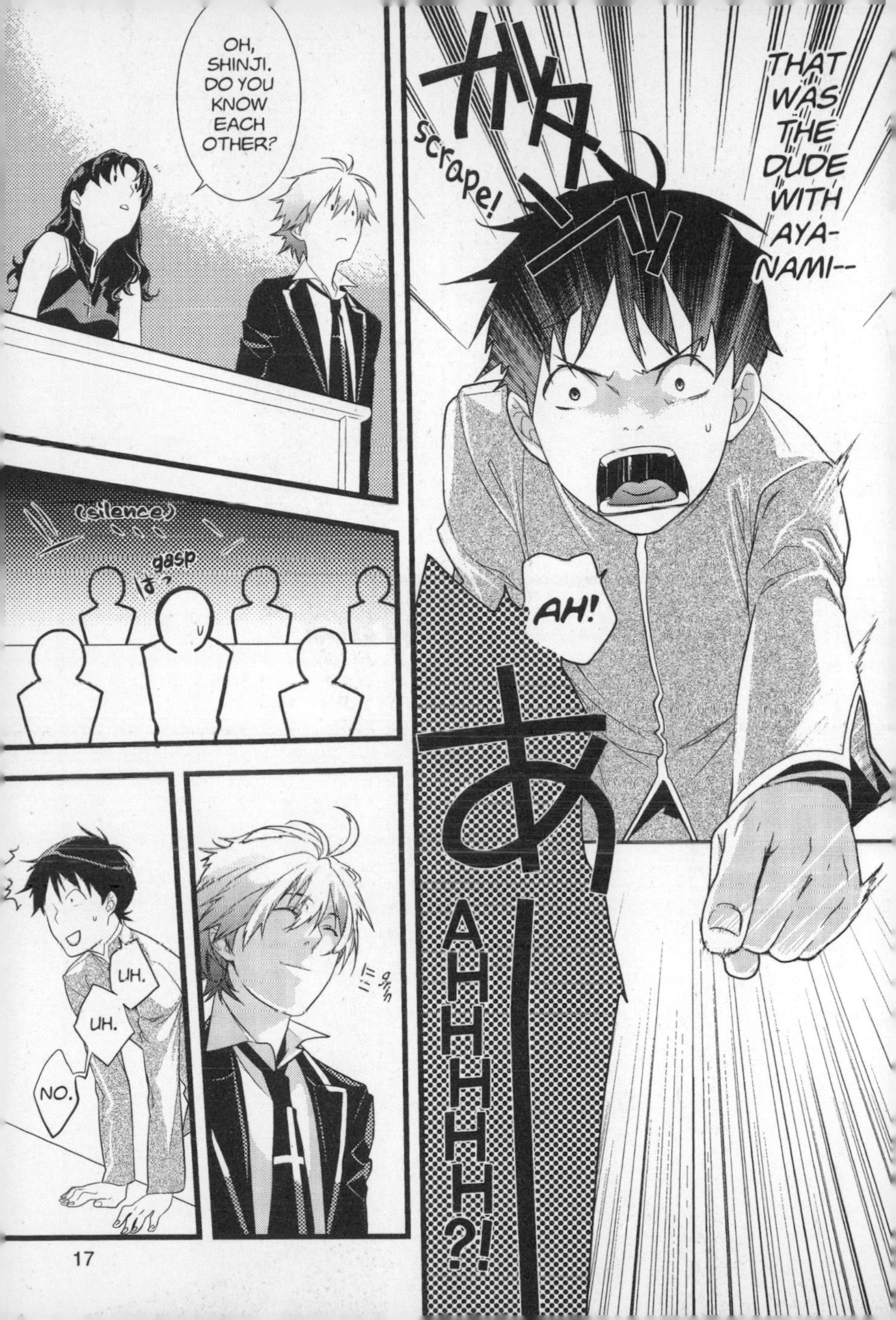
THAT WAS THE DUDE WITH AYA-NAMI--
scrape!
AH!
AHHHHH?!
OH, SHINJI. DO YOU KNOW EACH OTHER?
(silence)
gasp
grin
UH.
UH.
NO.

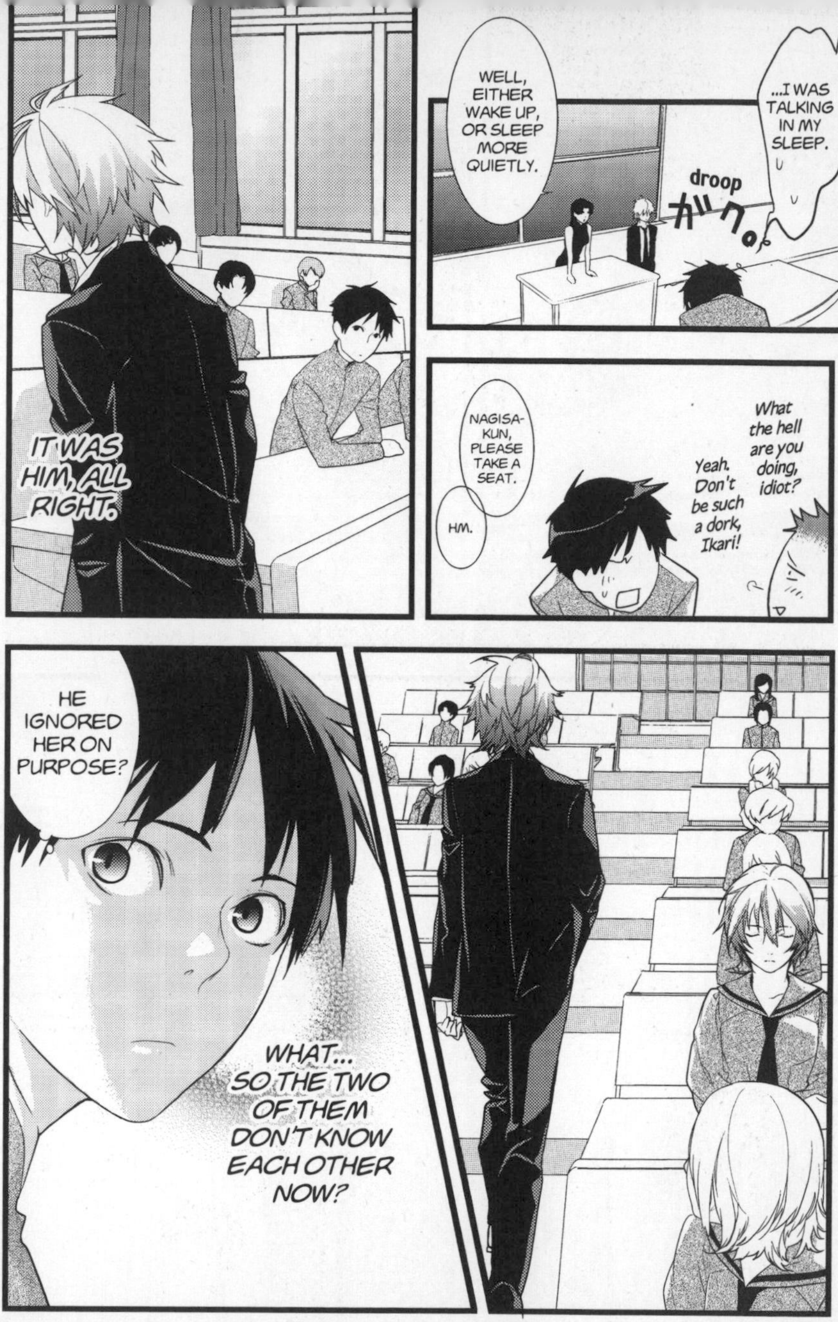
SOR-RY...
...I WAS TALKING IN MY SLEEP.
WELL, EITHER WAKE UP, OR SLEEP MORE QUIETLY.
droop
What the hell are you doing, idiot?
Yeah. Don't be such a dork, Ikari!
NAGISA-KUN, PLEASE TAKE A SEAT.
HM.
IT WAS HIM, ALL RIGHT.
HE IGNORED HER ON PURPOSE?
WHAT... SO THE TWO OF THEM DON'T KNOW EACH OTHER NOW?

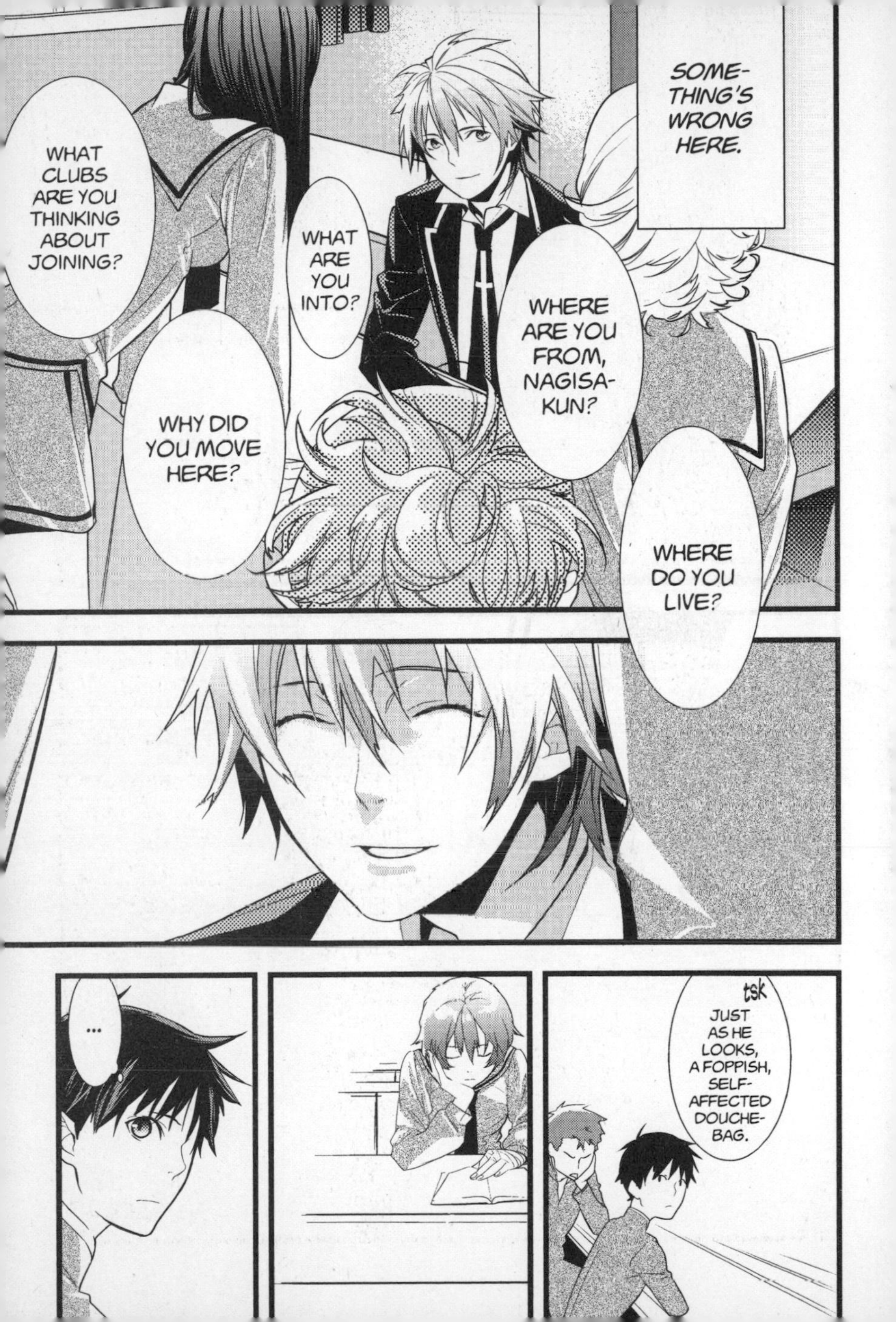
SOMETHING'S WRONG HERE.
WHERE ARE YOU FROM, NAGISA-KUN?
WHAT ARE YOU INTO?
WHAT CLUBS ARE YOU THINKING ABOUT JOINING?
WHERE DO YOU LIVE?
WHY DID YOU MOVE HERE?
tsk
JUST AS HE LOOKS, A FOPPISH, SELF-AFFECTED DOUCHE-BAG.
...

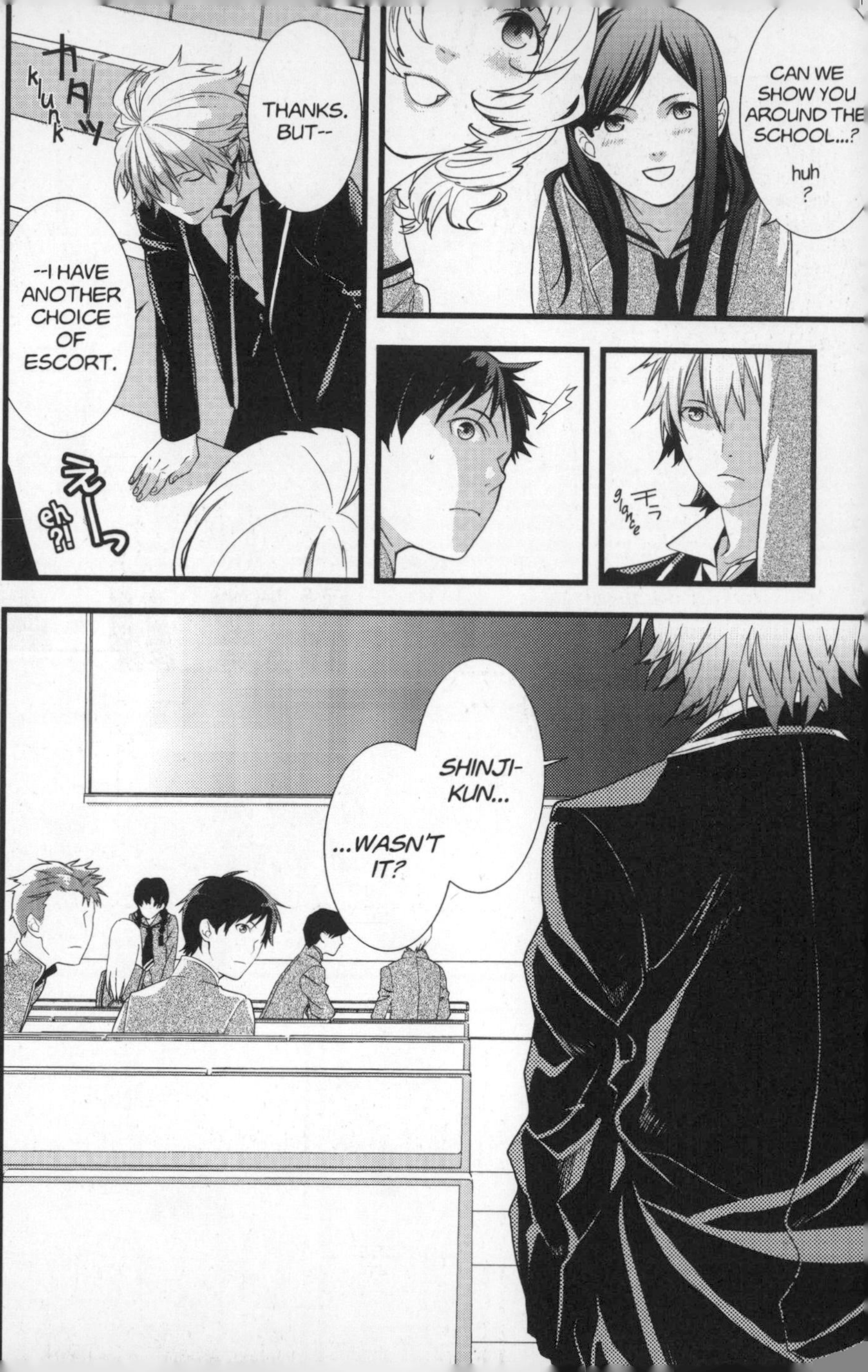
CAN WE SHOW YOU AROUND THE SCHOOL...?
huh ?
チラ
glance
カタッ
klunk
THANKS. BUT--
--I HAVE ANOTHER CHOICE OF ESCORT.
えっ
eh?!
SHINJI-KUN...
...WASN'T IT?

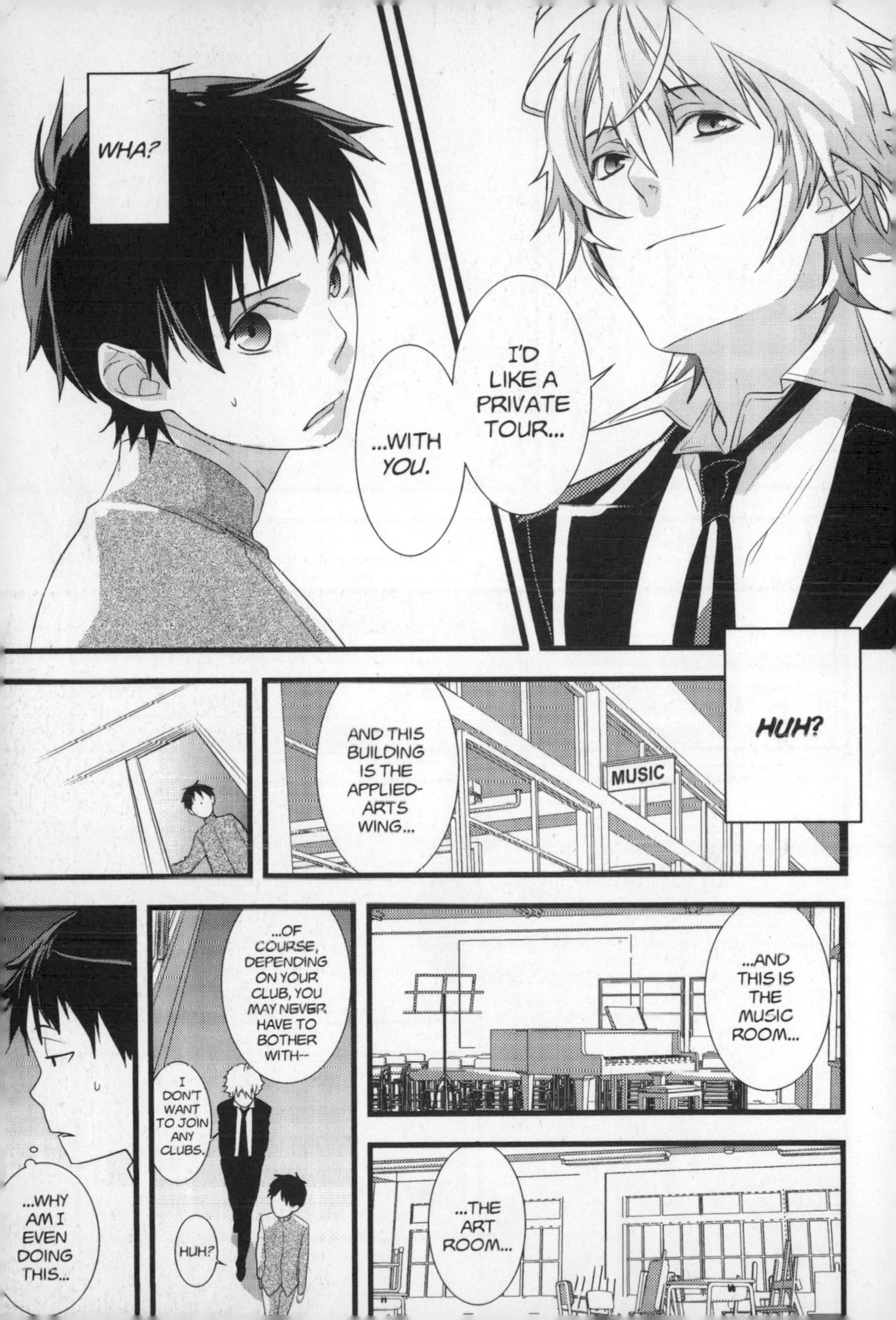
I'D LIKE A PRIVATE TOUR...
...WITH YOU.
WHA?
HUH?
AND THIS BUILDING IS THE APPLIED-ARTS WING...
MUSIC
...AND THIS IS THE MUSIC ROOM...
...THE ART ROOM...
...OF COURSE, DEPENDING ON YOUR CLUB, YOU MAY NEVER HAVE TO BOTHER WITH--
I DON'T WANT TO JOIN ANY CLUBS.
HUH?
...WHY AM I EVEN DOING THIS...

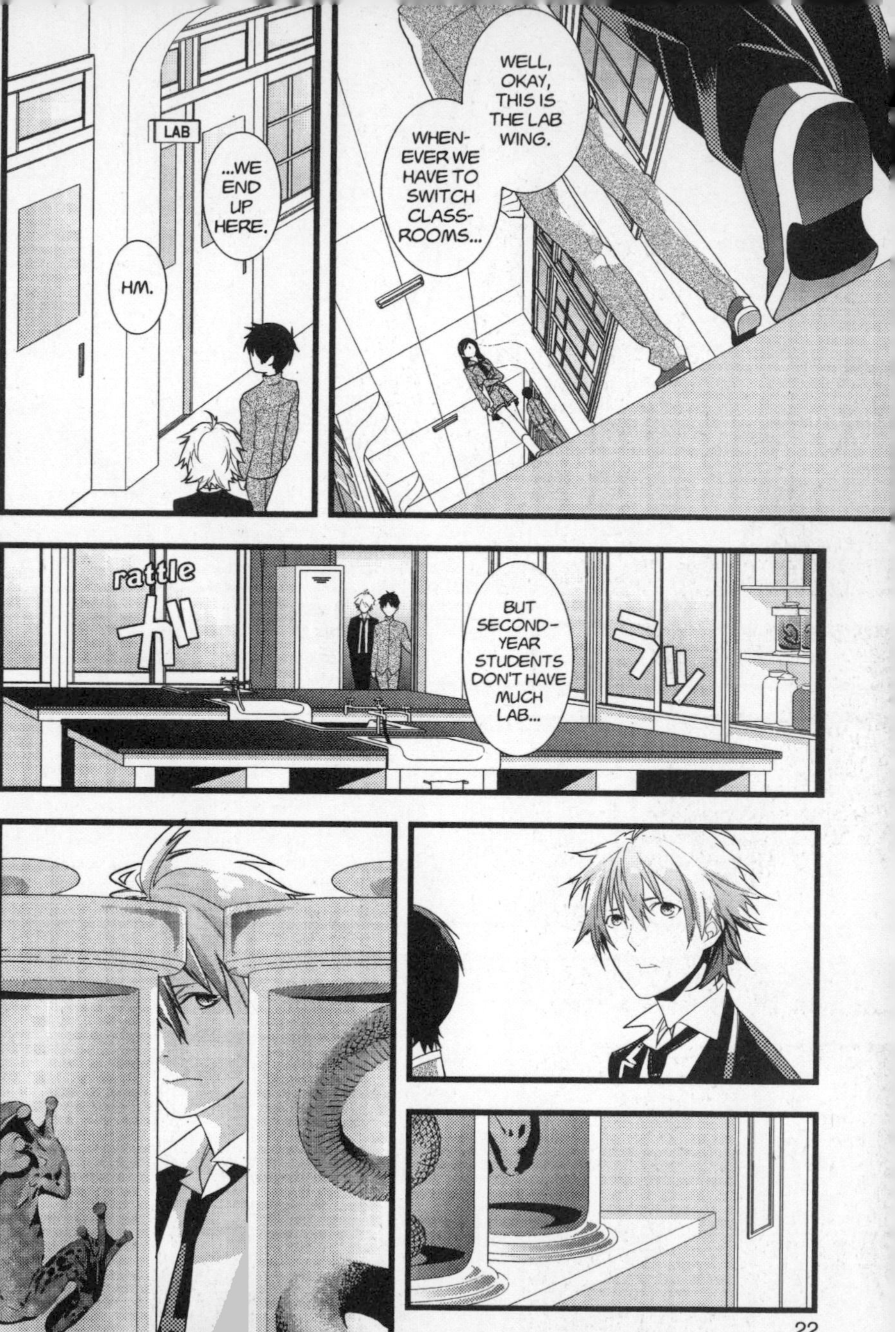
WELL, OKAY, THIS IS THE LAB WING.
WHENEVER WE HAVE TO SWITCH CLASSROOMS...
LAB
...WE END UP HERE.
HM.
rattle
ガラッ
BUT SECOND-YEAR STUDENTS DON'T HAVE MUCH LAB...

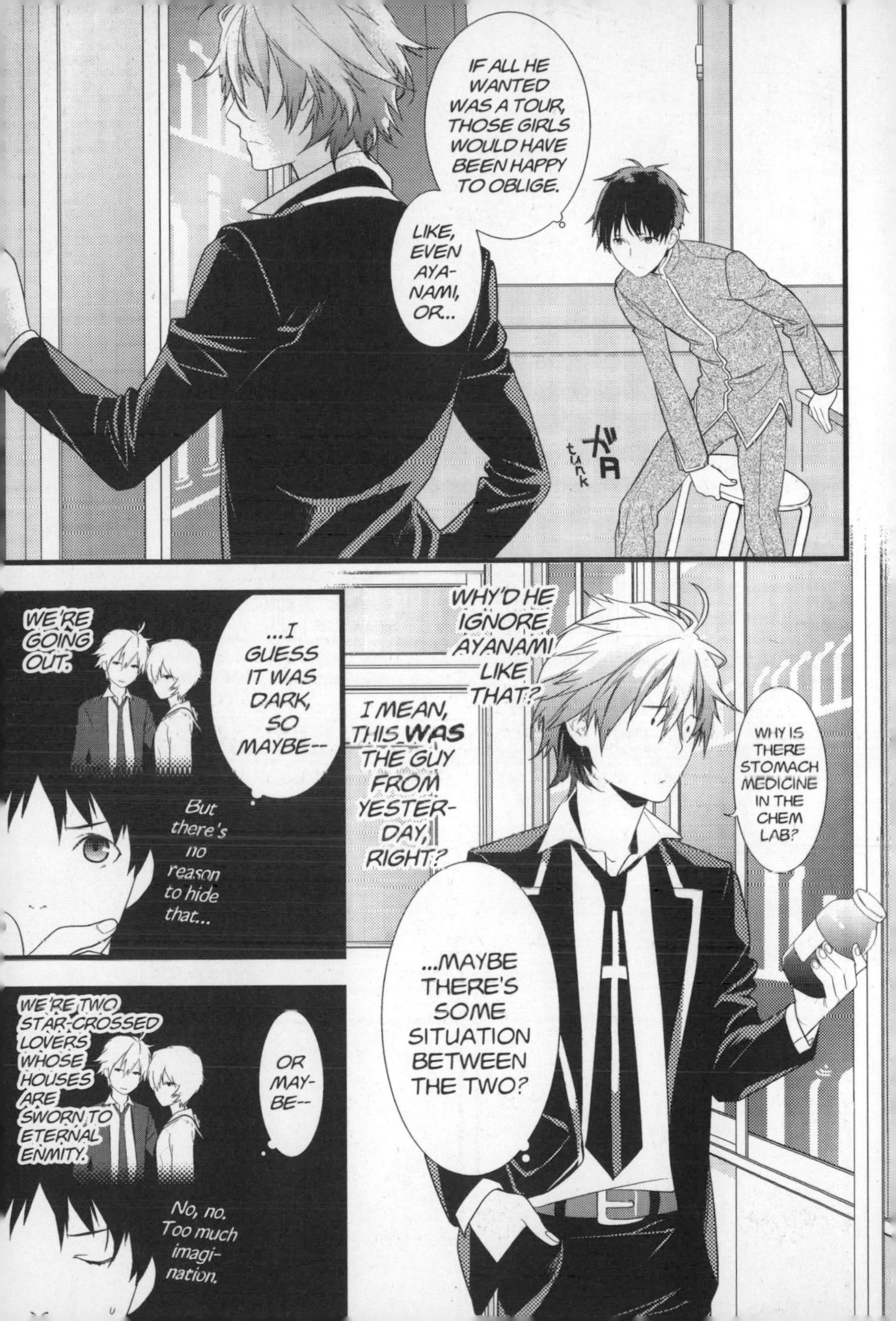
IF ALL HE WANTED WAS A TOUR, THOSE GIRLS WOULD HAVE BEEN HAPPY TO OBLIGE.
LIKE, EVEN AYANAMI, OR...
ガタ
tunk
WHY'D HE IGNORE AYANAMI LIKE THAT?
I MEAN, THIS WAS THE GUY FROM YESTERDAY, RIGHT?
WHY IS THERE STOMACH MEDICINE IN THE CHEM LAB?
...MAYBE THERE'S SOME SITUATION BETWEEN THE TWO?
...I GUESS IT WAS DARK, SO MAYBE--
WE'RE GOING OUT.
But there's no reason to hide that...
OR MAYBE--
WE'RE TWO STAR-CROSSED LOVERS WHOSE HOUSES ARE SWORN TO ETERNAL ENMITY.
No, no. Too much imagination.

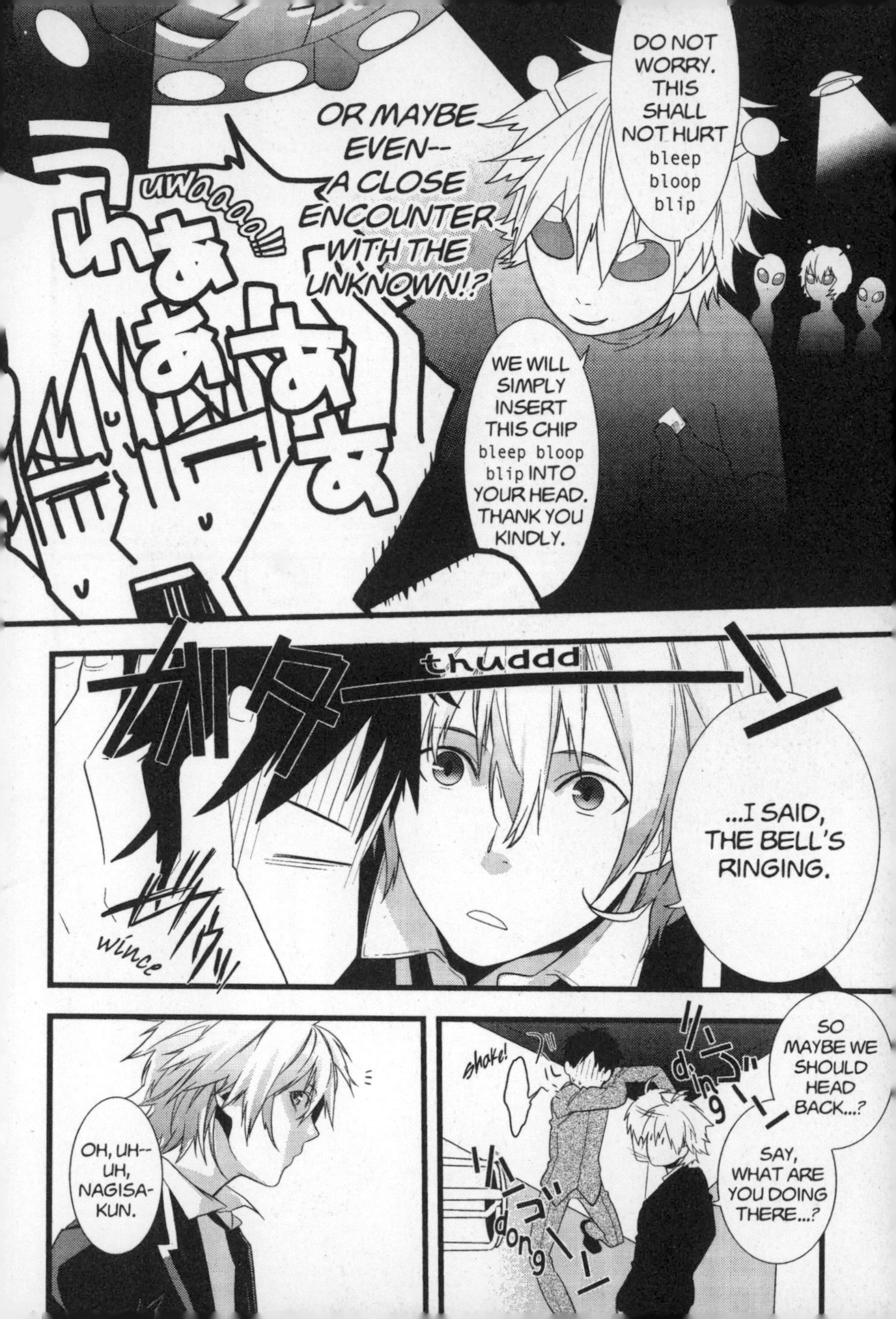
DO NOT WORRY. THIS SHALL NOT HURT bleep bloop blip
OR MAYBE EVEN-- A CLOSE ENCOUNTER WITH THE UNKNOWN!?
uwaaaaa!!
WE WILL SIMPLY INSERT THIS CHIP bleep bloop blip INTO YOUR HEAD. THANK YOU KINDLY.
thuddd
...I SAID, THE BELL'S RINGING.
wince
SO MAYBE WE SHOULD HEAD BACK...?
ding
shake!
SAY, WHAT ARE YOU DOING THERE...?
dong
OH, UH-- UH, NAGISA-KUN.

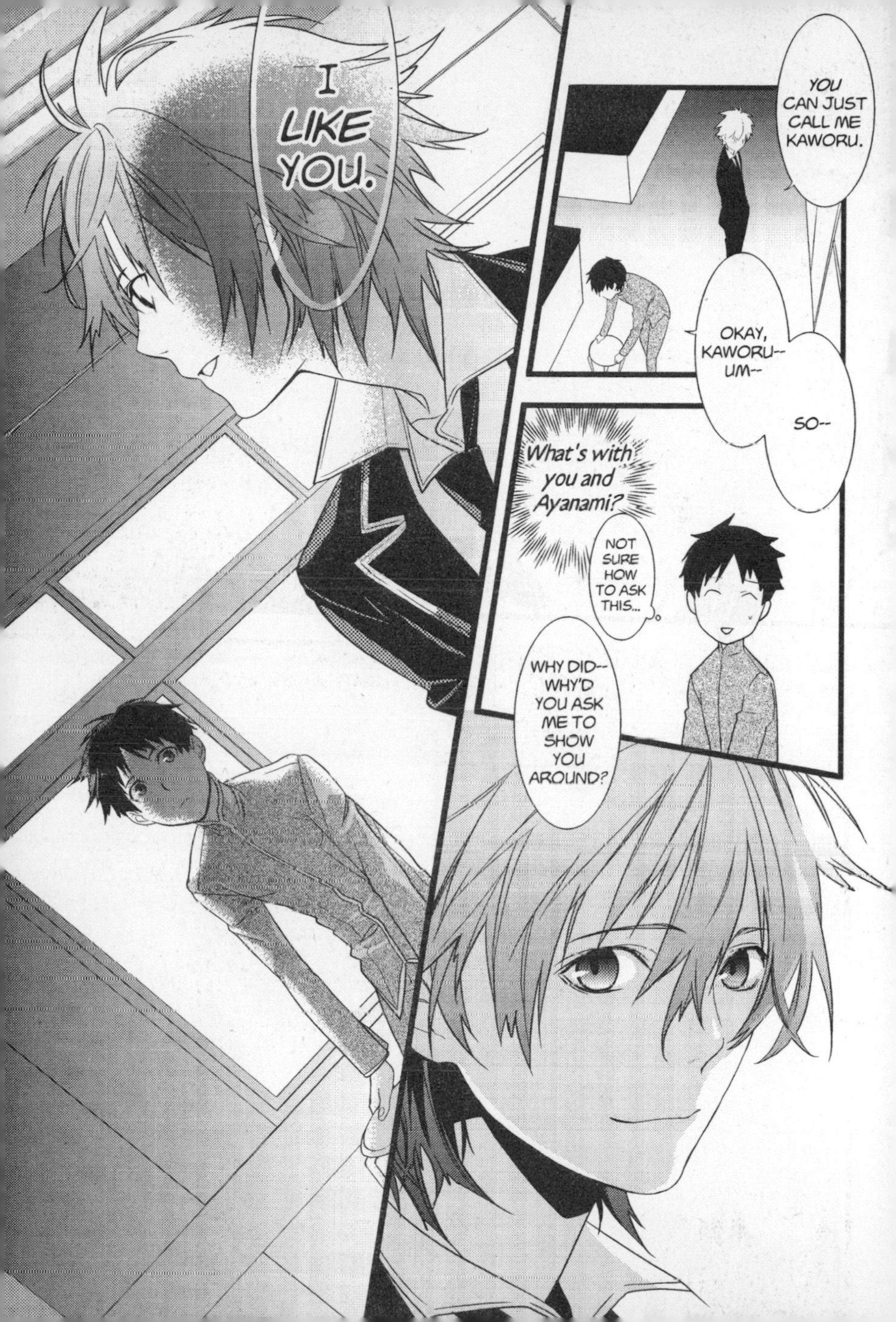
YOU CAN JUST CALL ME KAWORU.
OKAY, KAWORU-- UM--
SO--
What's with you and Ayanami?
NOT SURE HOW TO ASK THIS...
WHY DID-- WHY'D YOU ASK ME TO SHOW YOU AROUND?
I LIKE YOU.

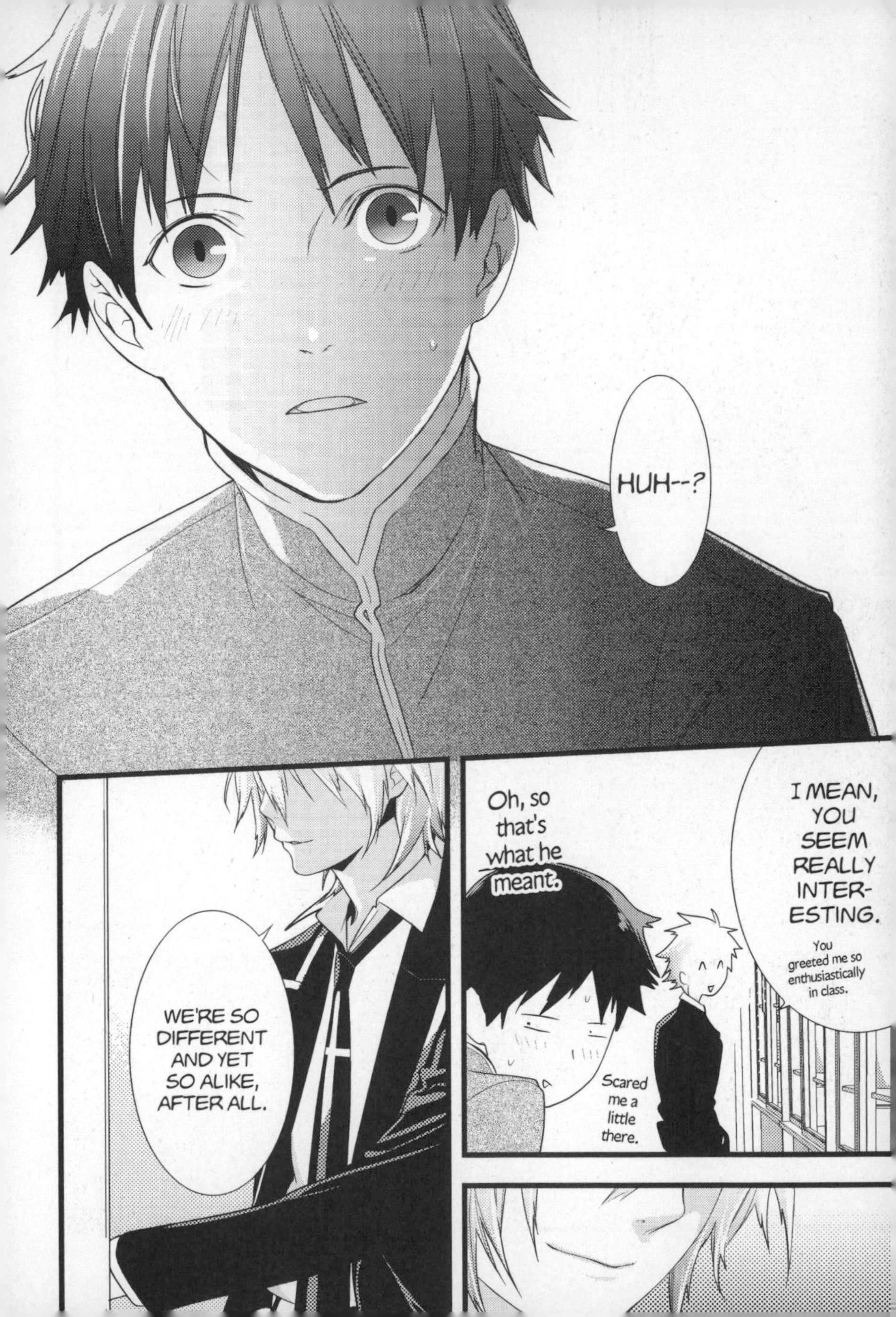
HUH--?
I MEAN, YOU SEEM REALLY INTER-ESTING.
You greeted me so enthusiastically in class.
Oh, so that's what he meant.
Scared me a little there.
WE'RE SO DIFFERENT AND YET SO ALIKE, AFTER ALL.

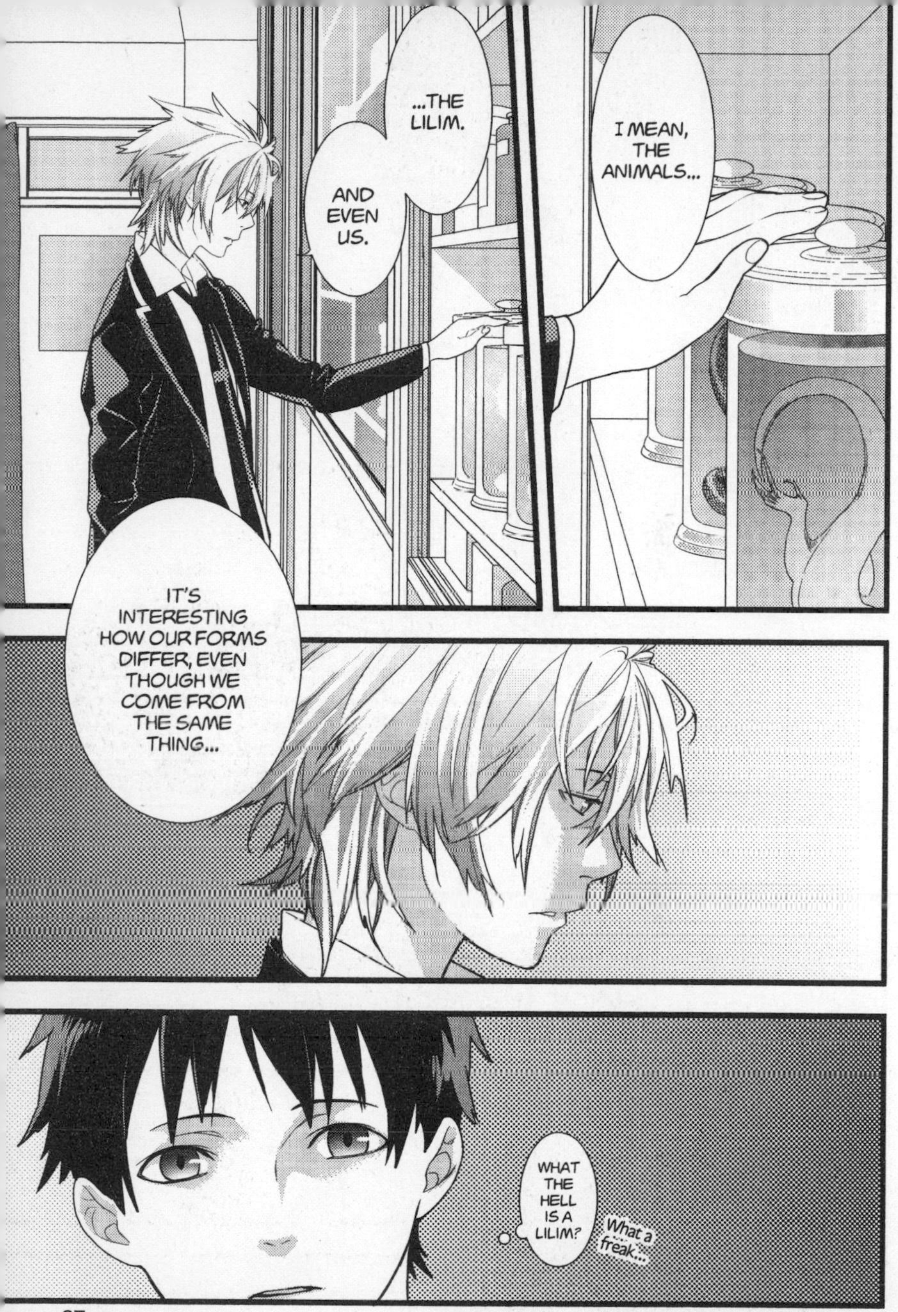
I MEAN, THE ANIMALS...
...THE LILIM.
AND EVEN US.
IT'S INTERESTING HOW OUR FORMS DIFFER, EVEN THOUGH WE COME FROM THE SAME THING...
WHAT THE HELL IS A LILIM?
What a freak...

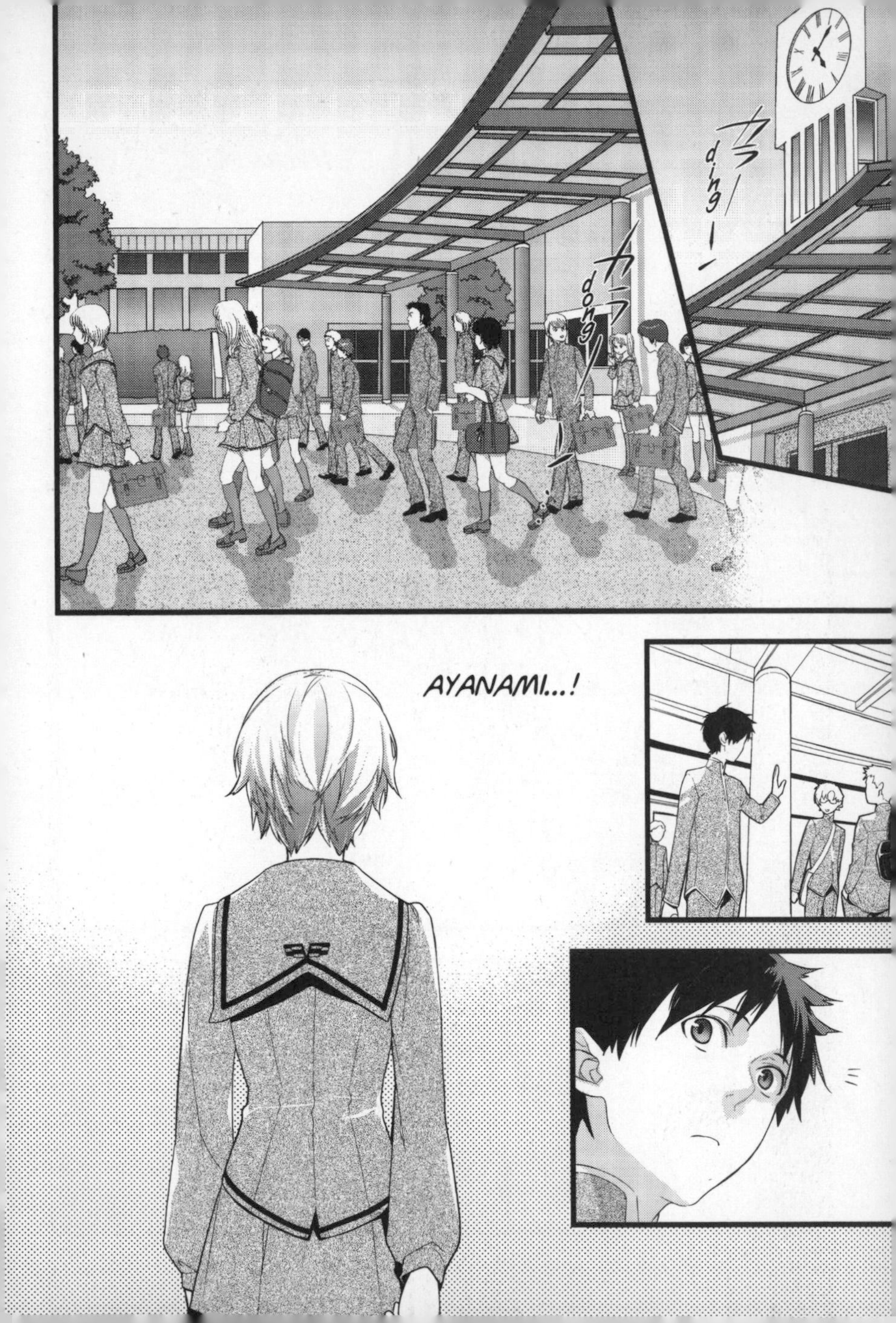
ding!
dong!
AYANAMI...!

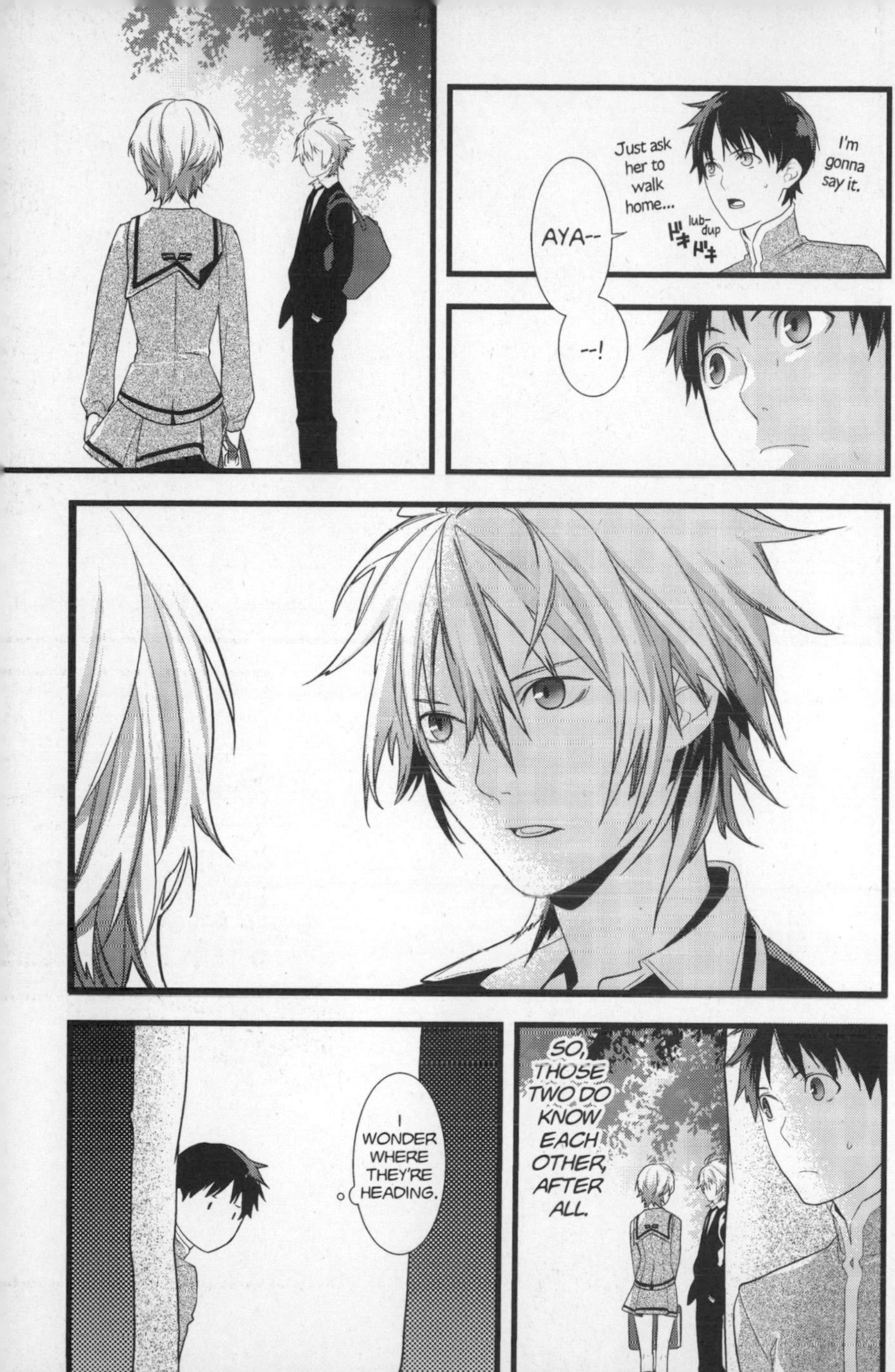
I'm gonna say it.
Just ask her to walk home...
ドキドキ lub-dup
AYA--
--!
SO, THOSE TWO DO KNOW EACH OTHER, AFTER ALL.
I WONDER WHERE THEY'RE HEADING.

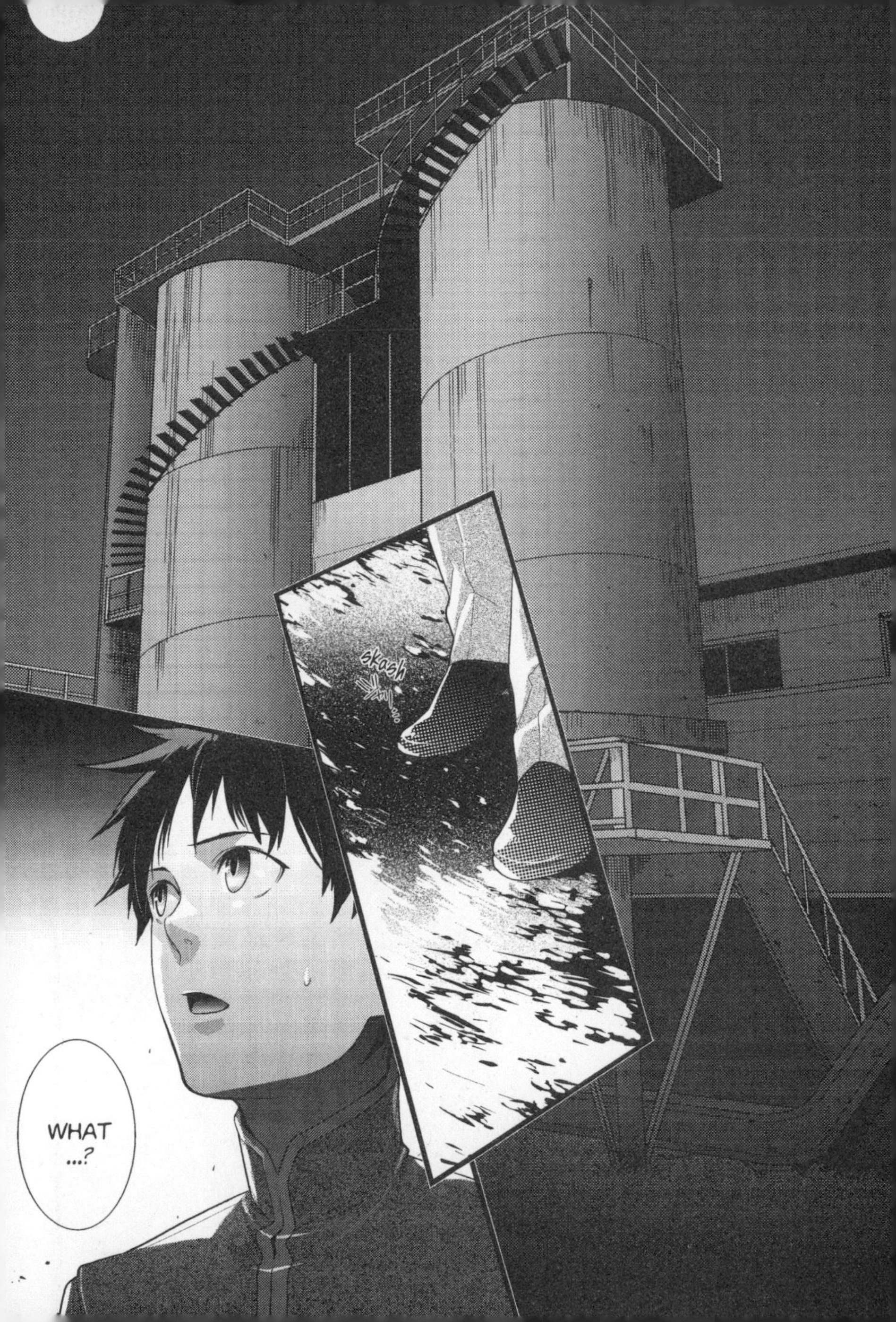
skash
WHAT ...?

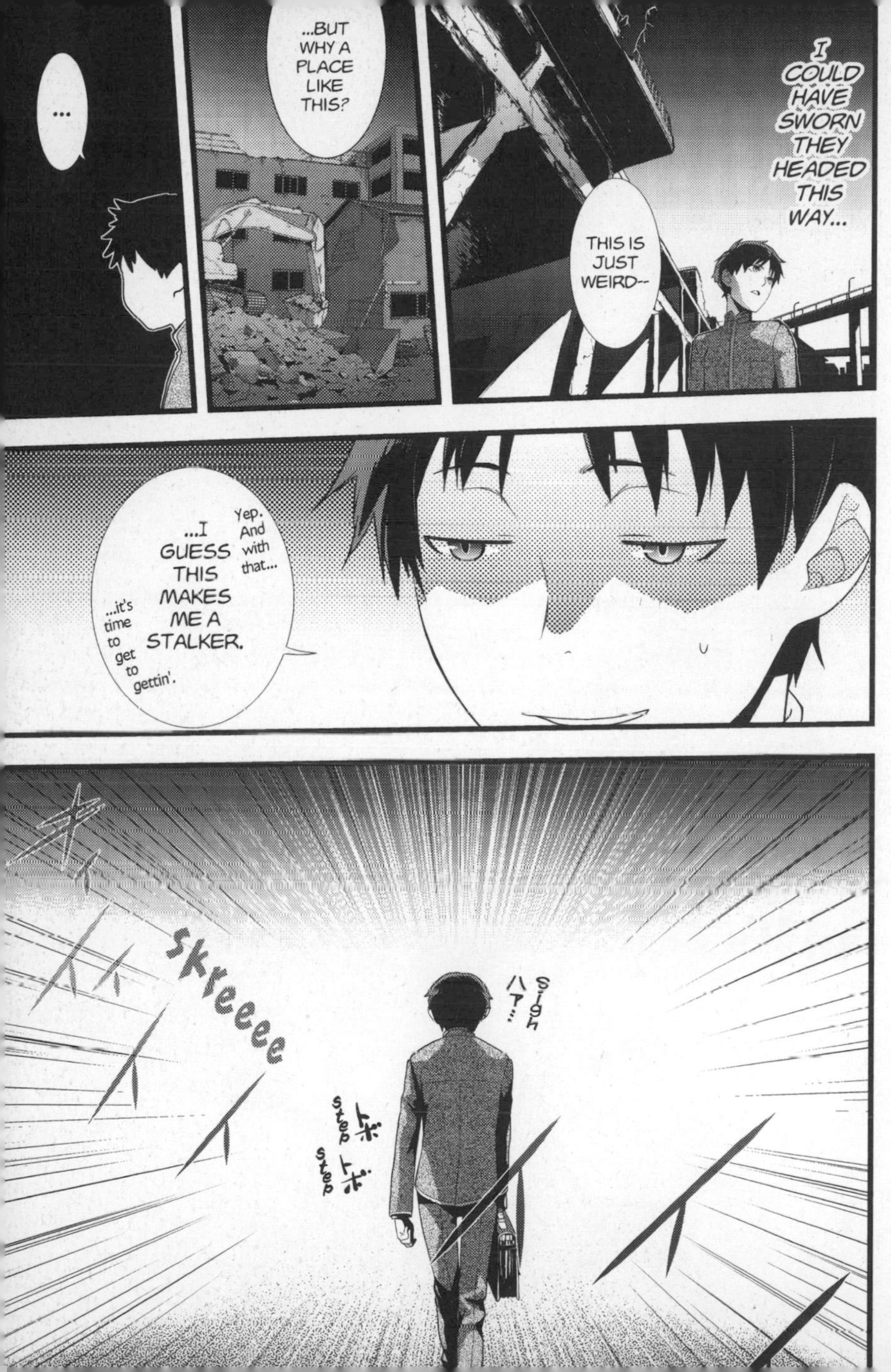
I COULD HAVE SWORN THEY HEADED THIS WAY...
THIS IS JUST WEIRD--
...BUT WHY A PLACE LIKE THIS?
...
...I GUESS THIS MAKES ME A STALKER.
Yep. And with that...
...it's time to get to gettin'.
Sigh
ハァ…
step トボ
step トボ
skreeeee

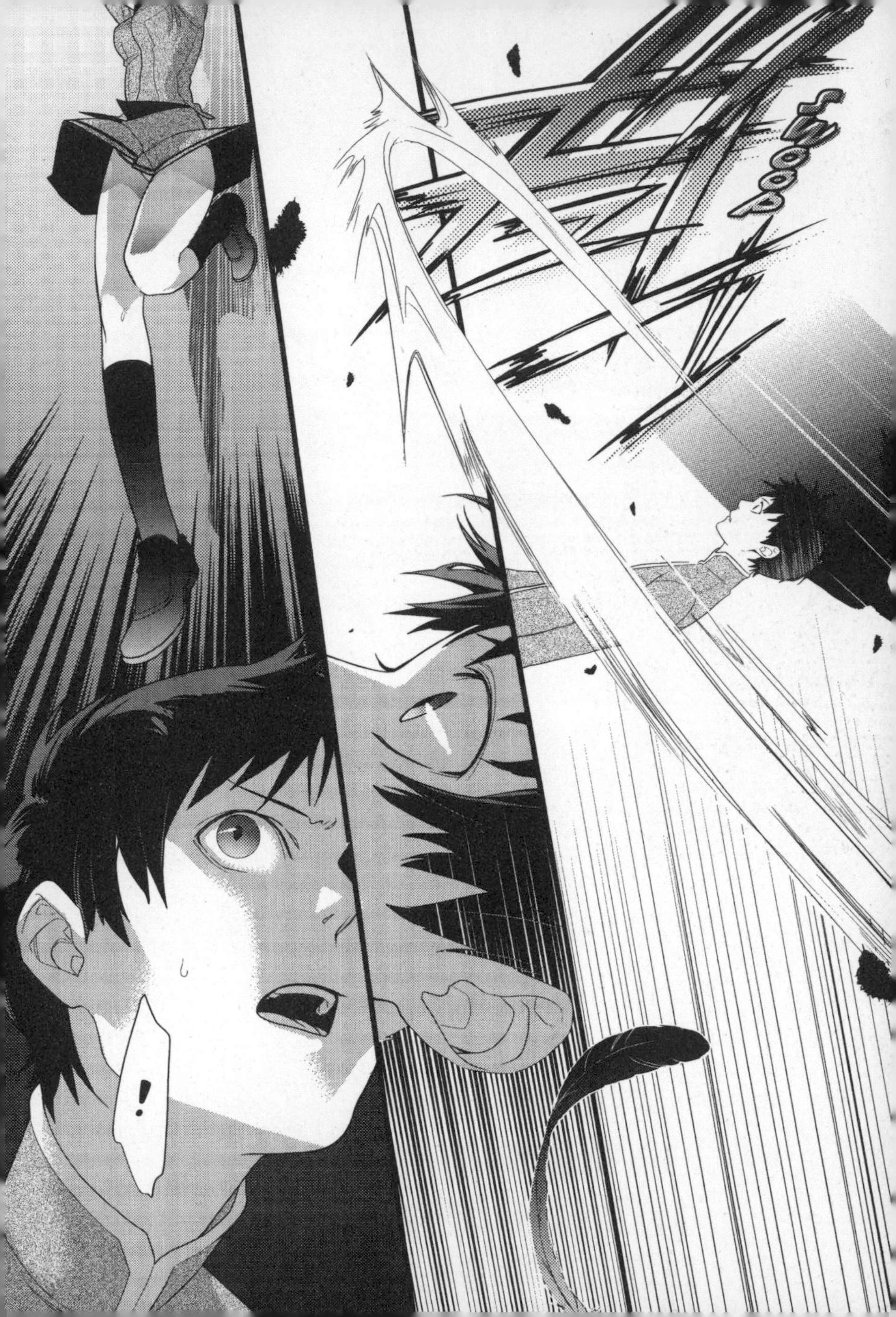
WHOOP
!

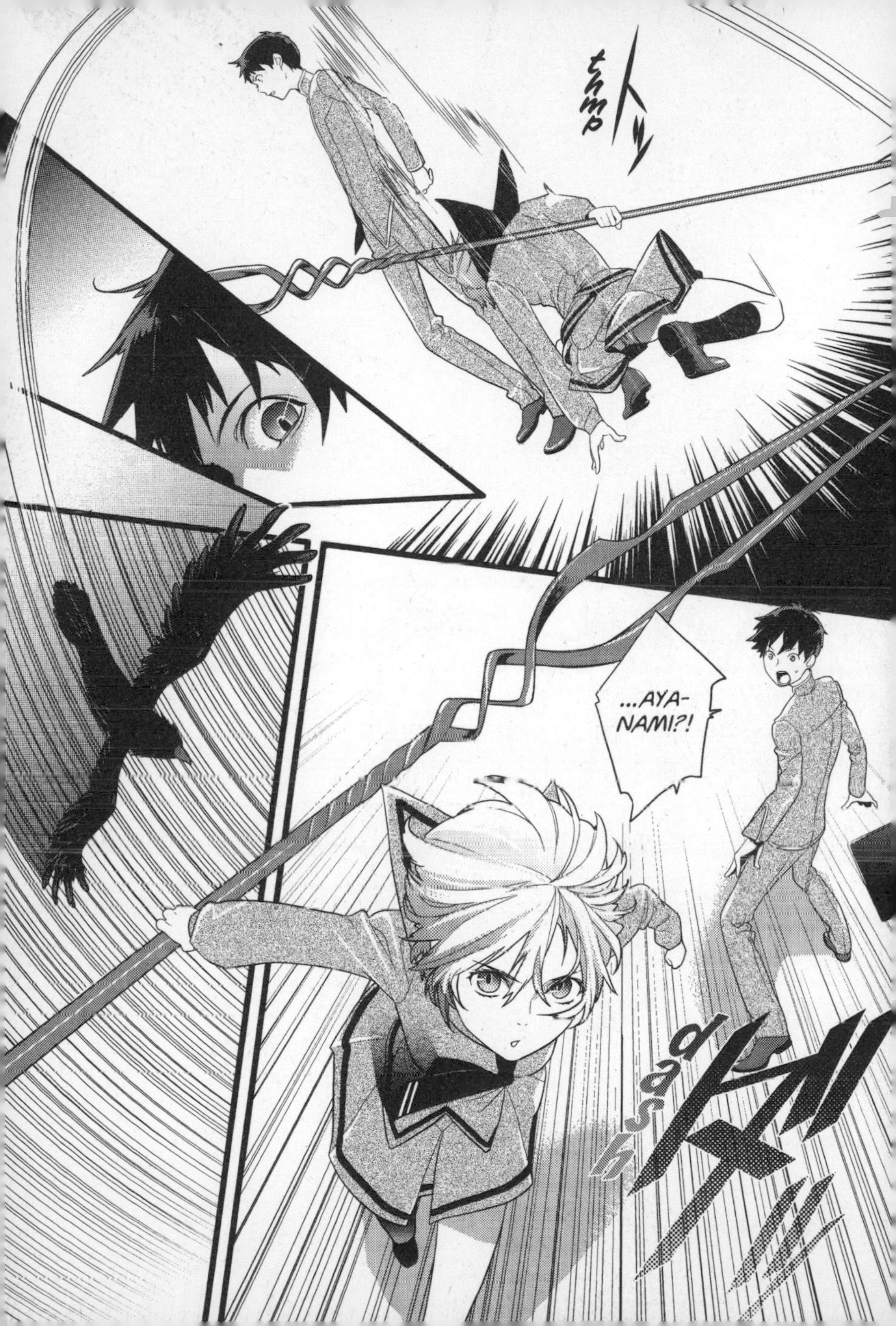
tmp
...AYA-
NAMI?!
dash

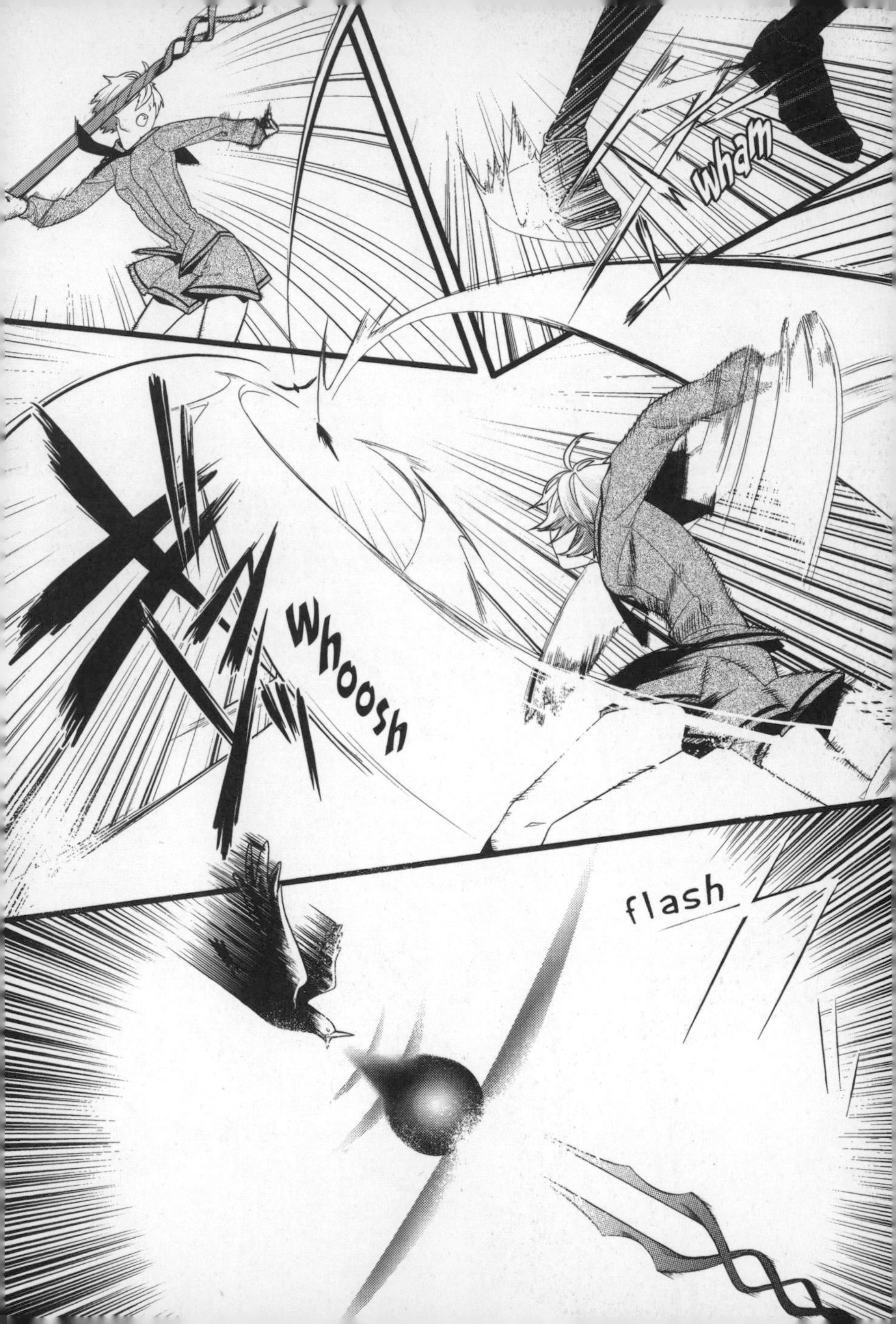
wham
whoosh
flash

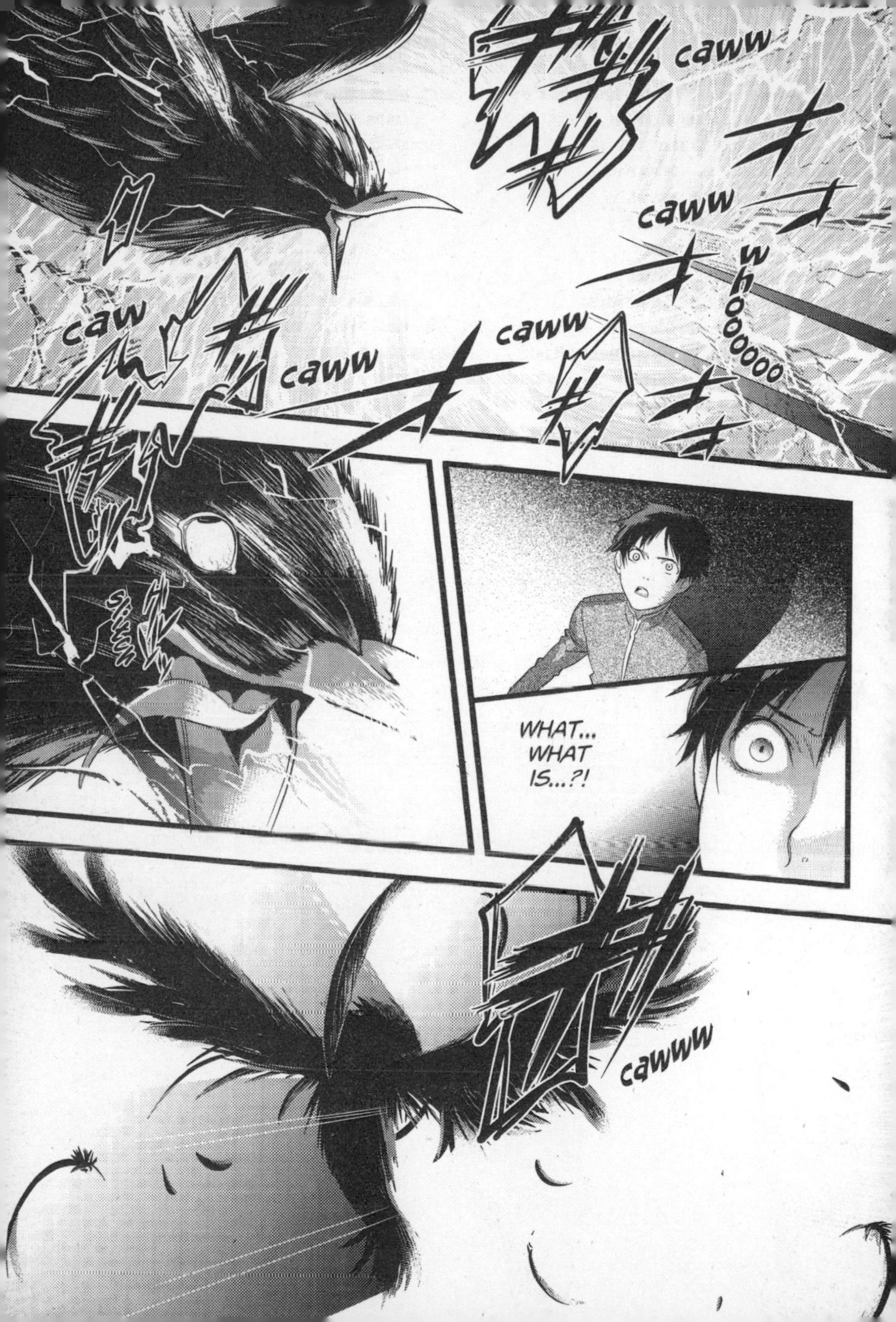
caww
caww
whoooooo
caww
caww
caw
WHAT... WHAT IS...?!
cawww

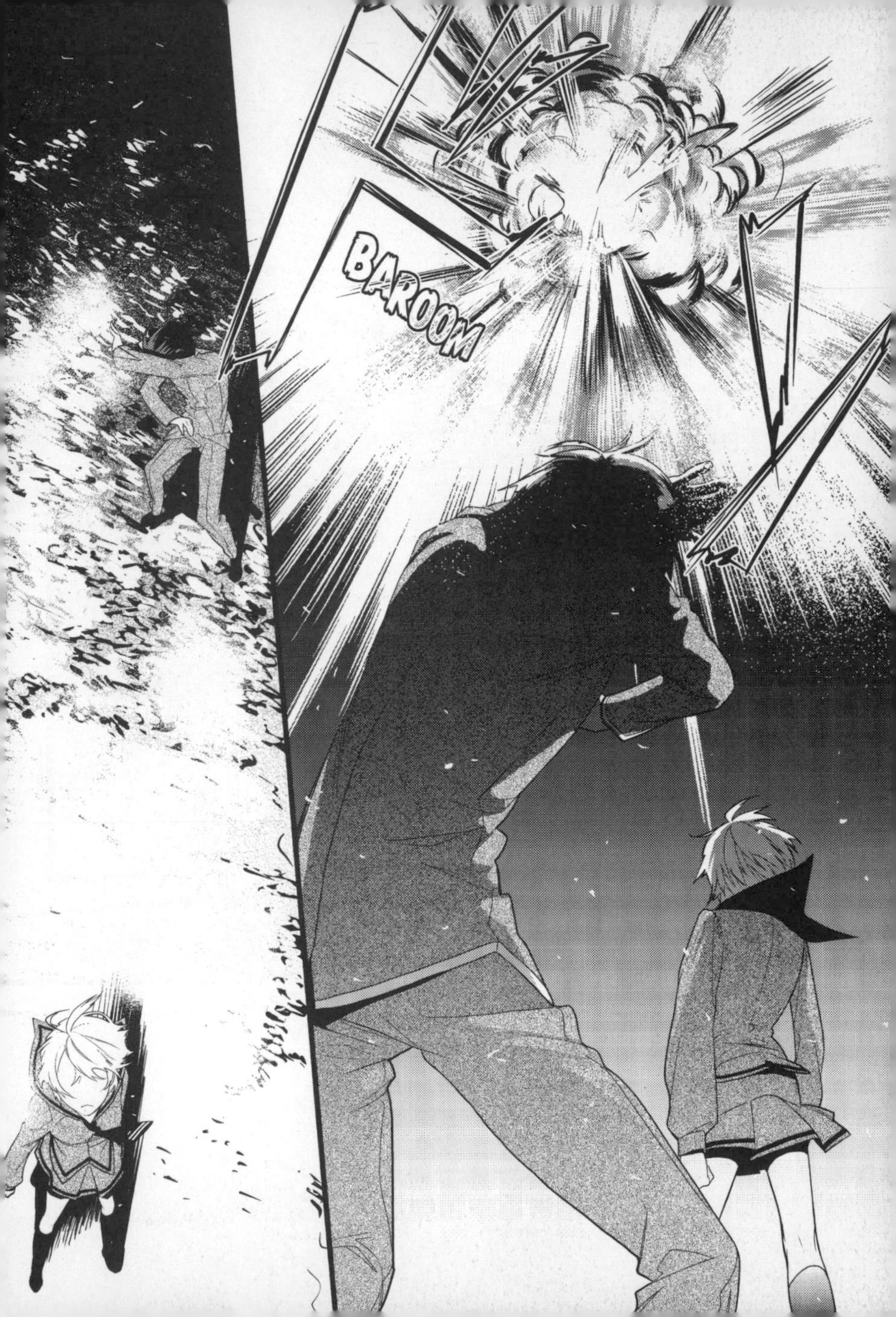
BAROOM

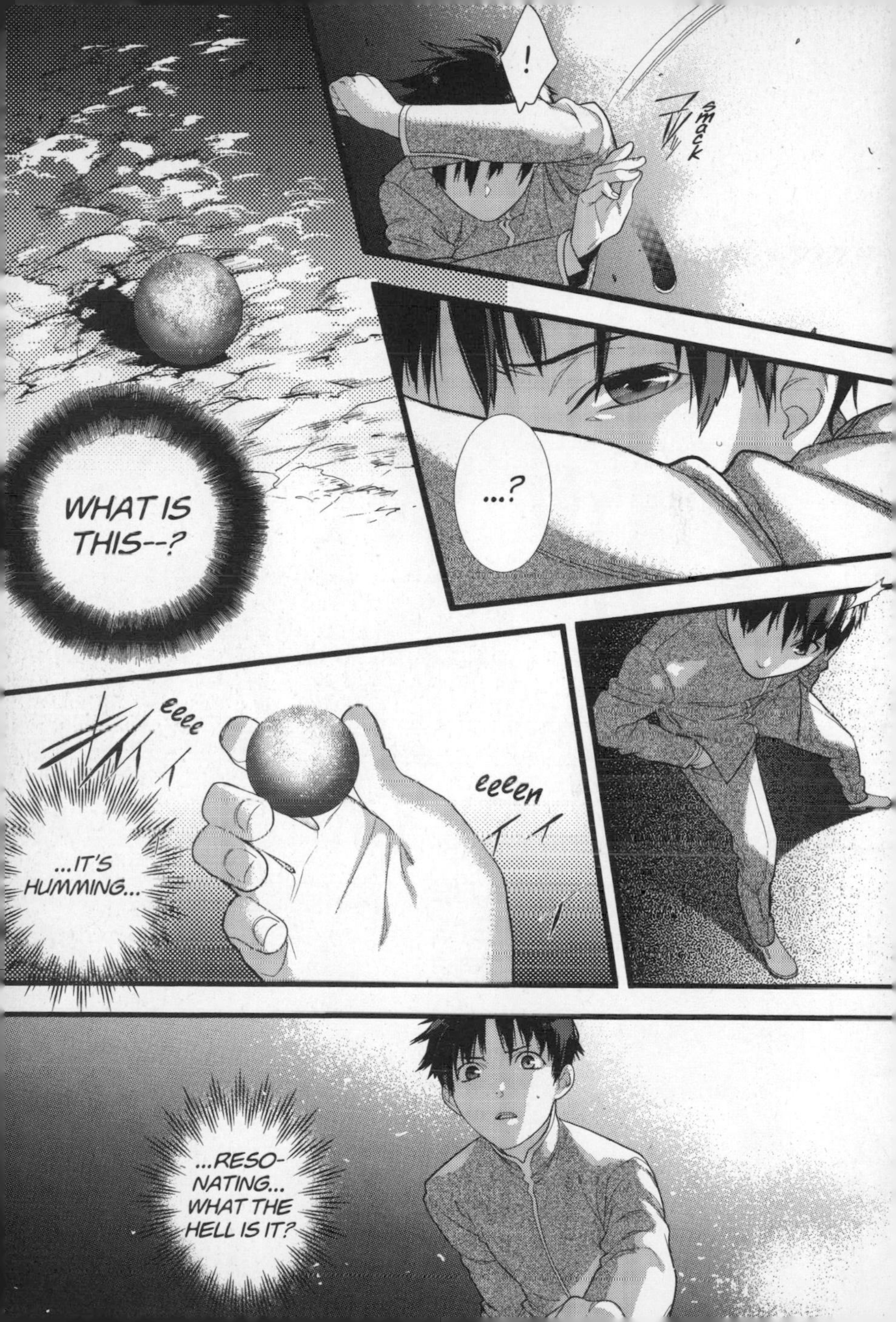
!
smack
...?
WHAT IS THIS--?
eeee
eeeen
...IT'S HUMMING...
...RESONATING... WHAT THE HELL IS IT?

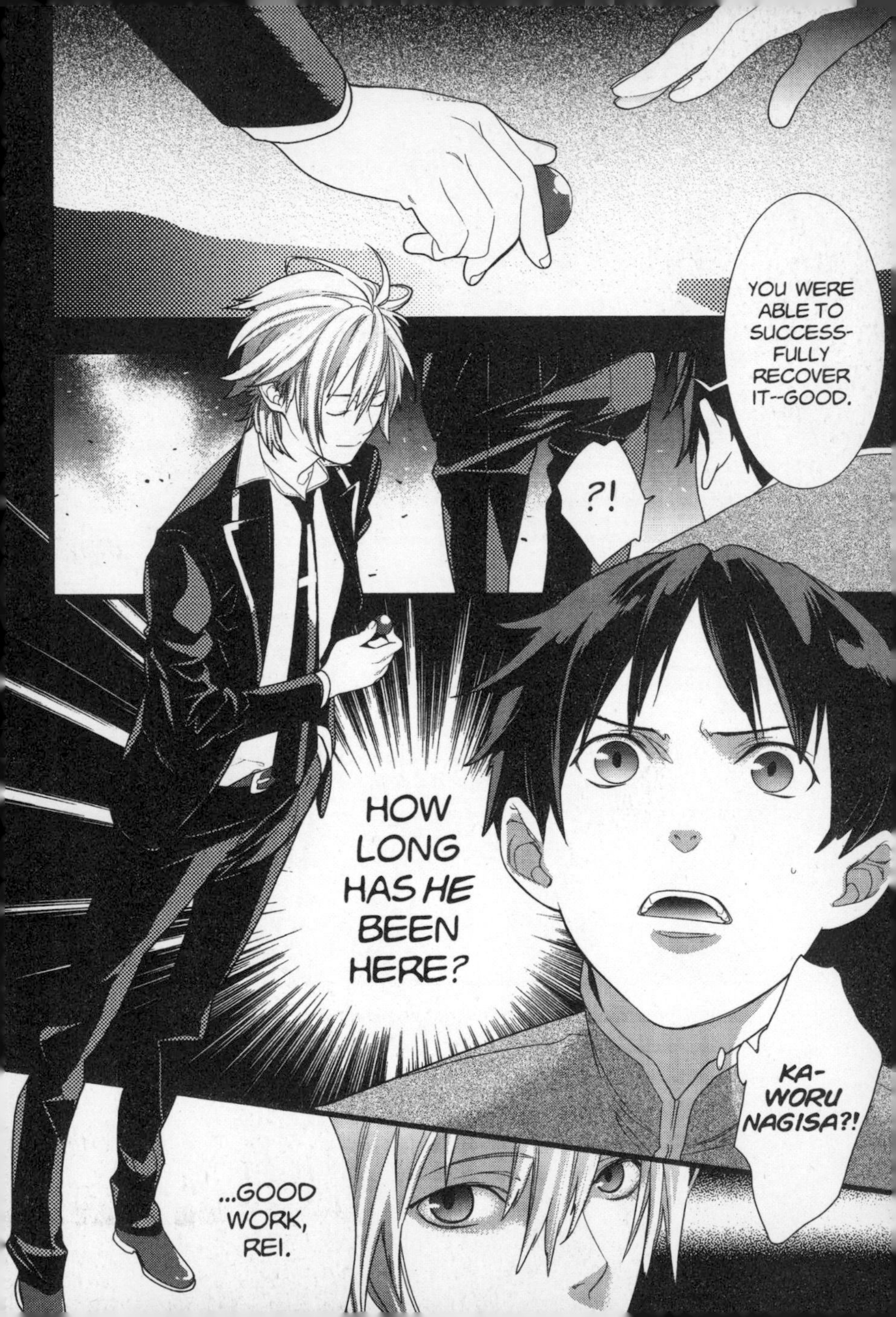
YOU WERE ABLE TO SUCCESSFULLY RECOVER IT--GOOD.
?!
HOW LONG HAS HE BEEN HERE?
KAWORU NAGISA?!
...GOOD WORK, REI.

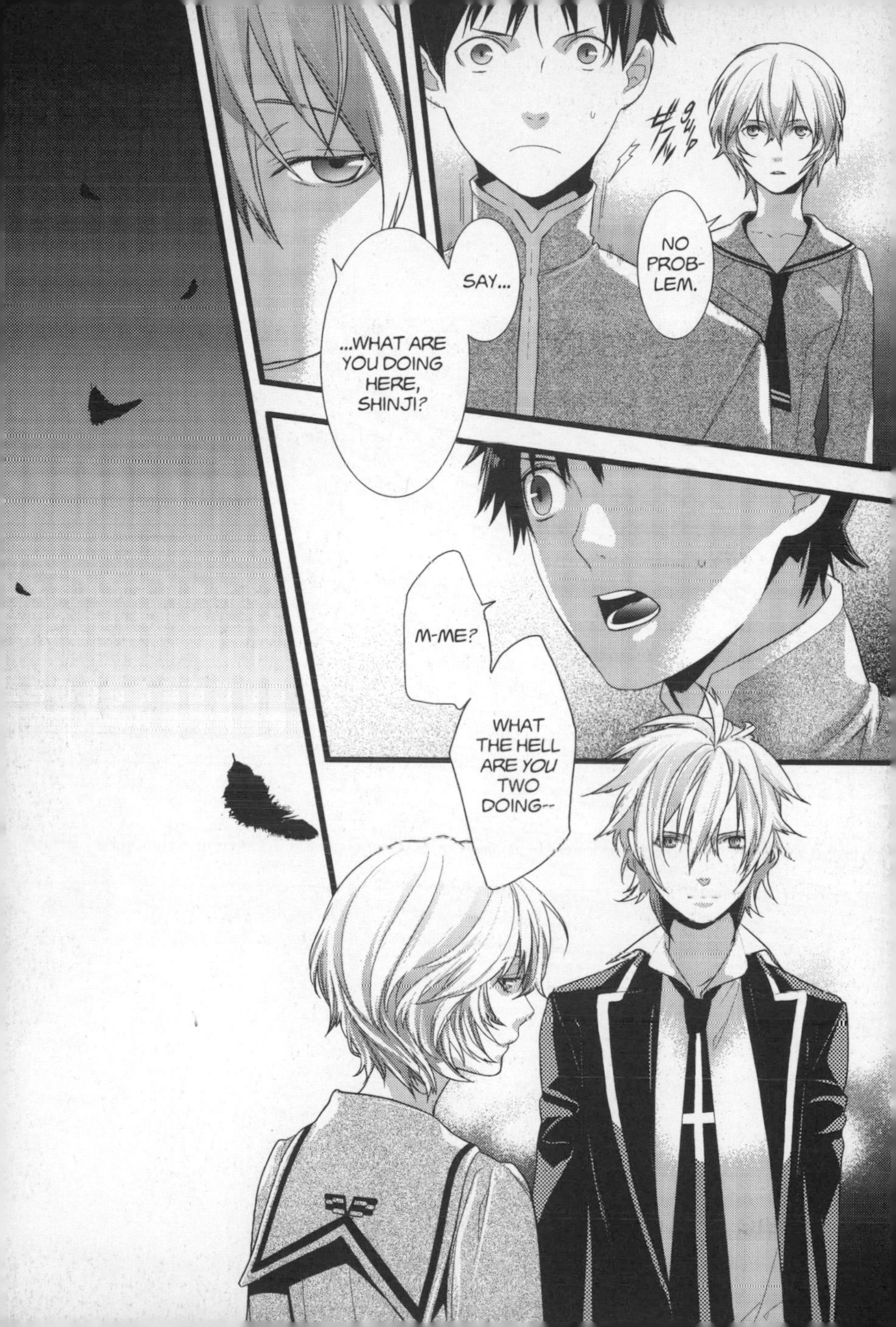
NO PROBLEM.
SAY...
...WHAT ARE YOU DOING HERE, SHINJI?
M-ME?
WHAT THE HELL ARE YOU TWO DOING--

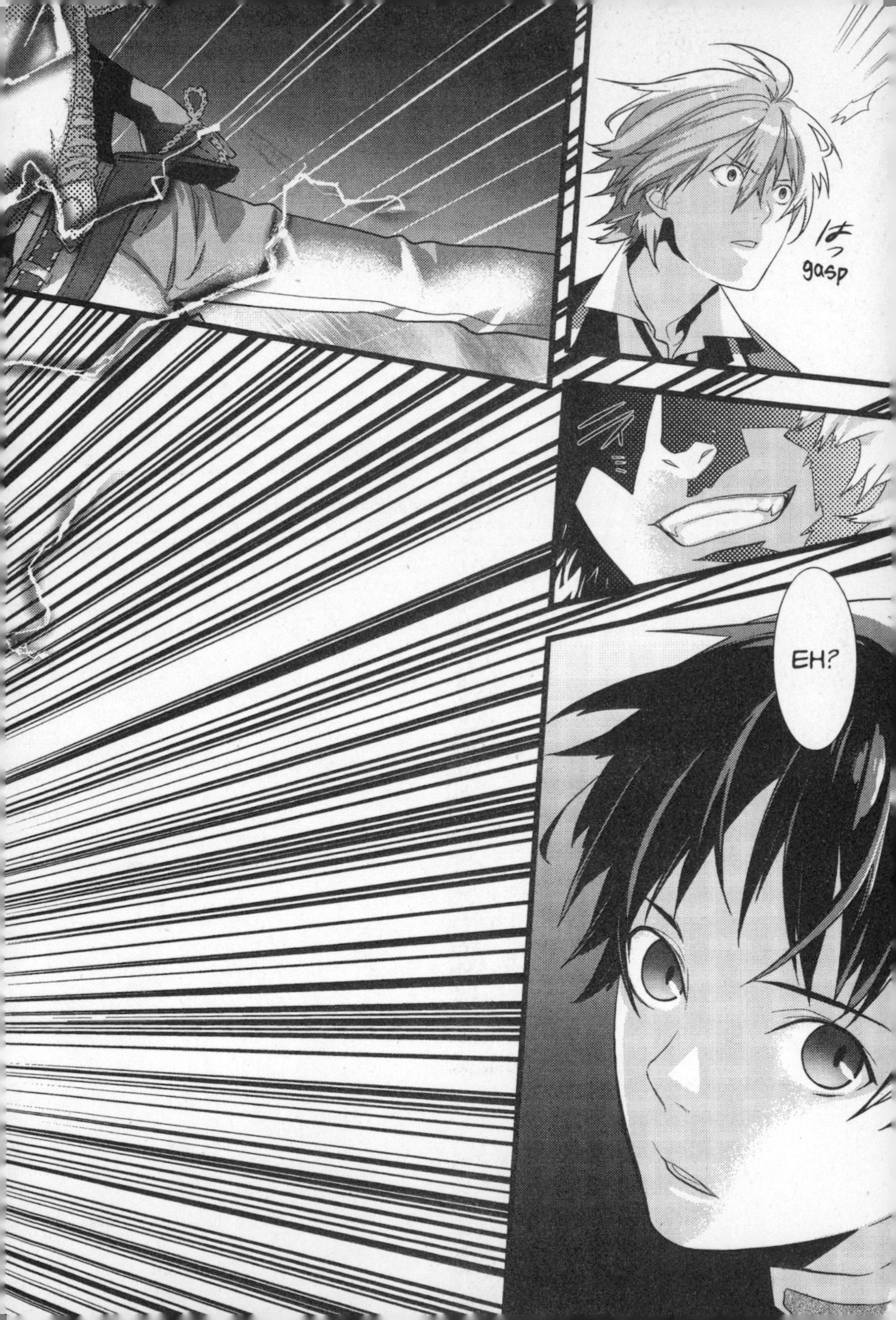
はっ
gasp
EH?

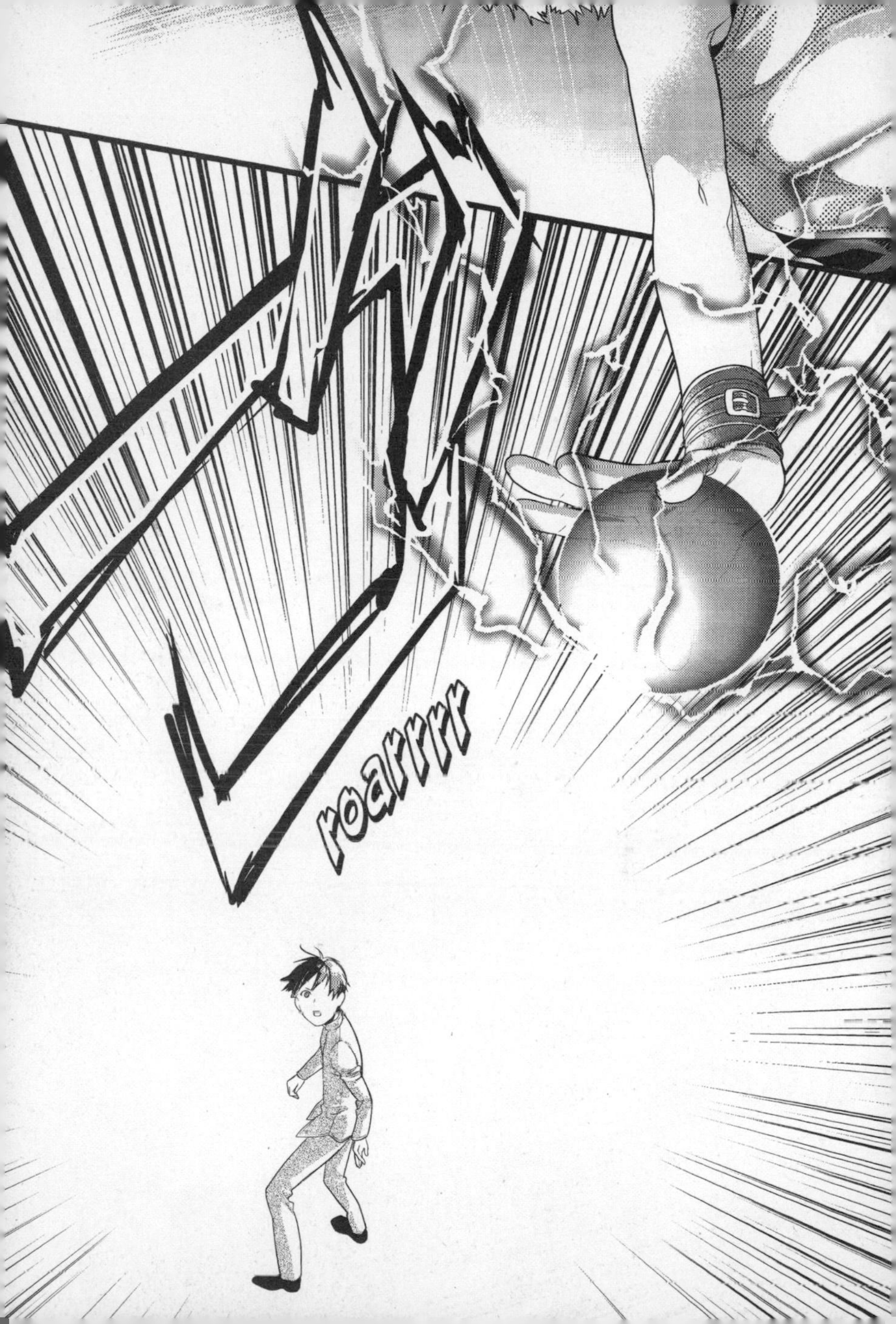
roarrrr

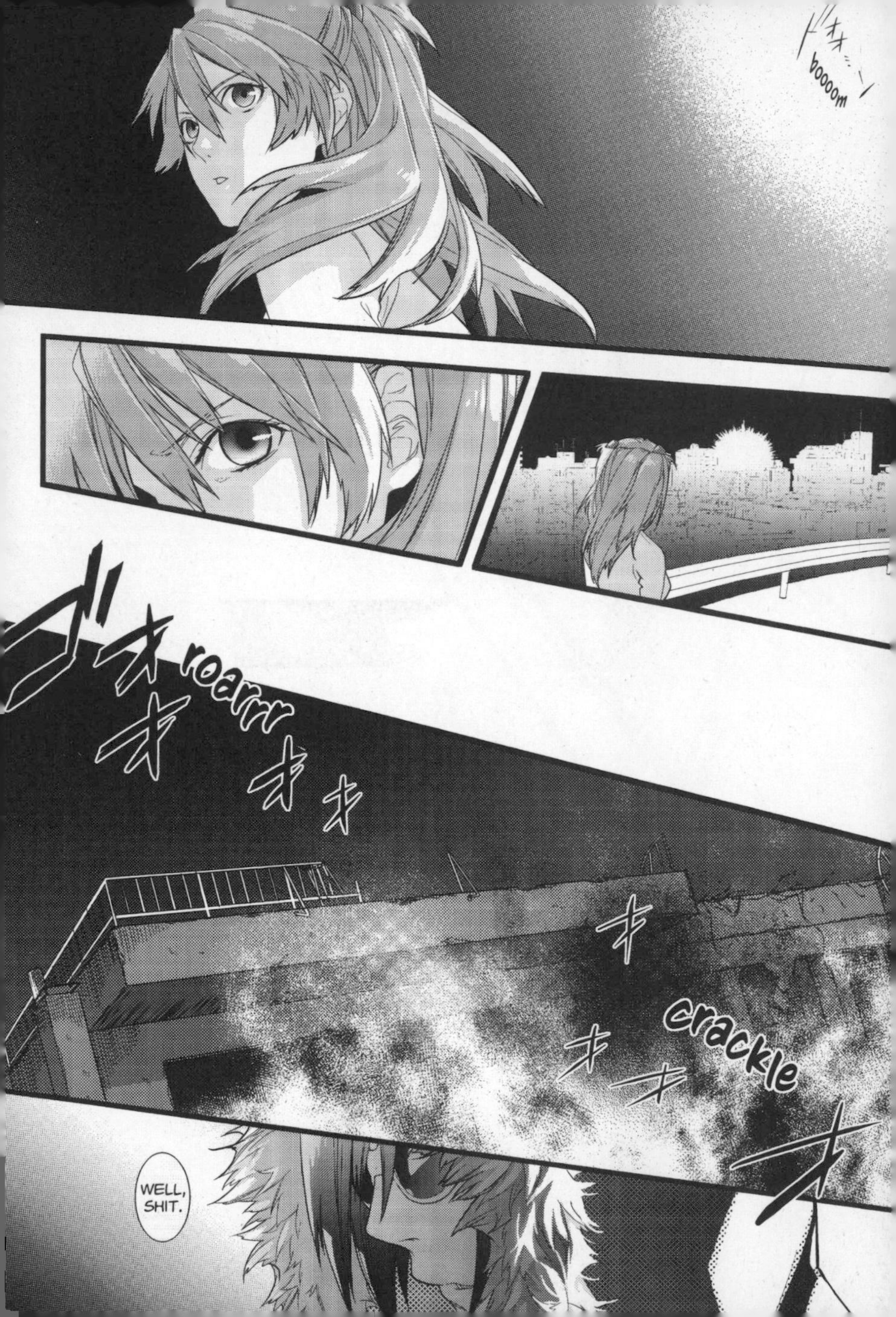
ドオオ…ン
booooom
ゴオオオオオオオオオオ
roarrr
crackle
WELL, SHIT.

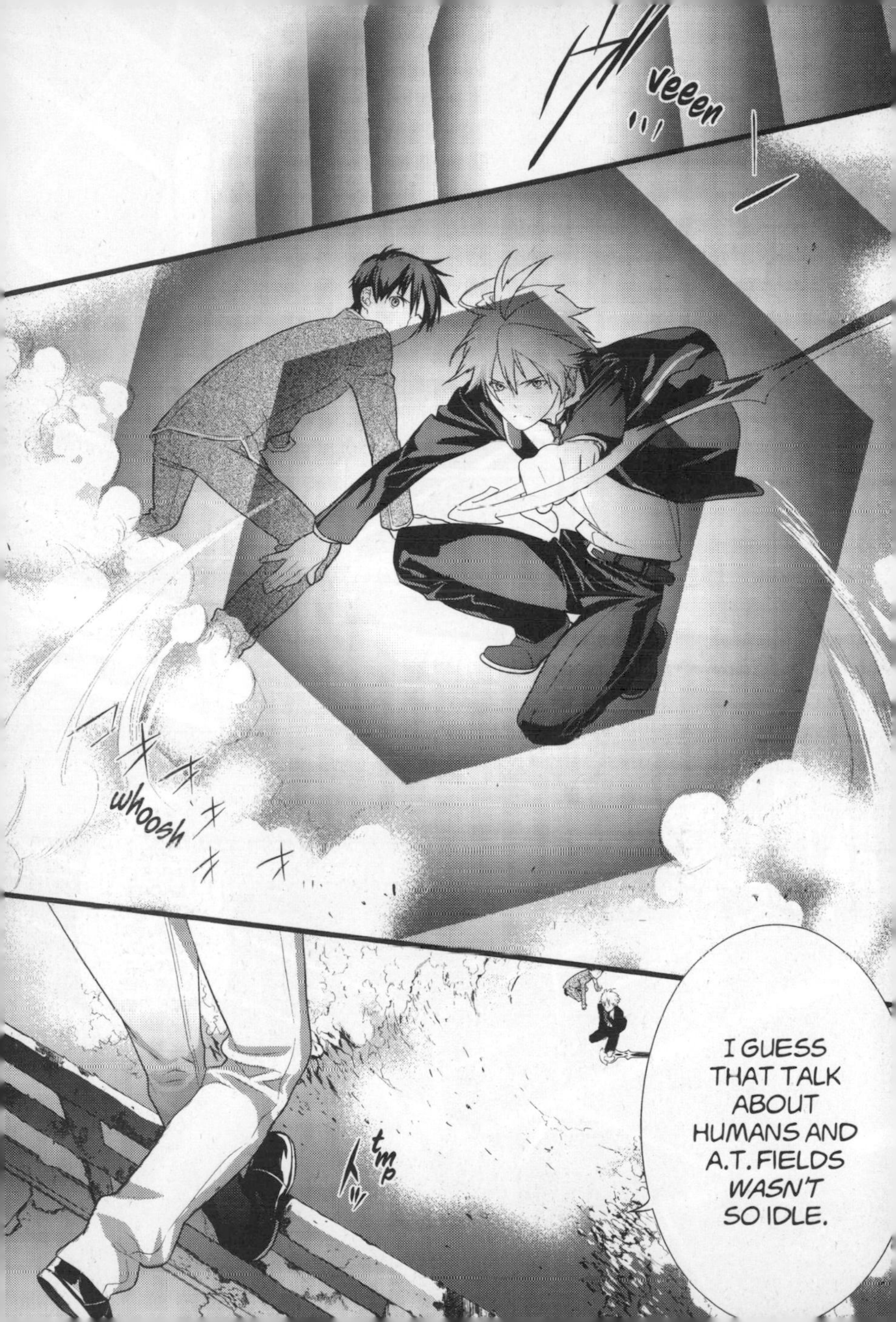
veeen
whoosh
tmp
I GUESS THAT TALK ABOUT HUMANS AND A.T. FIELDS WASN'T SO IDLE.

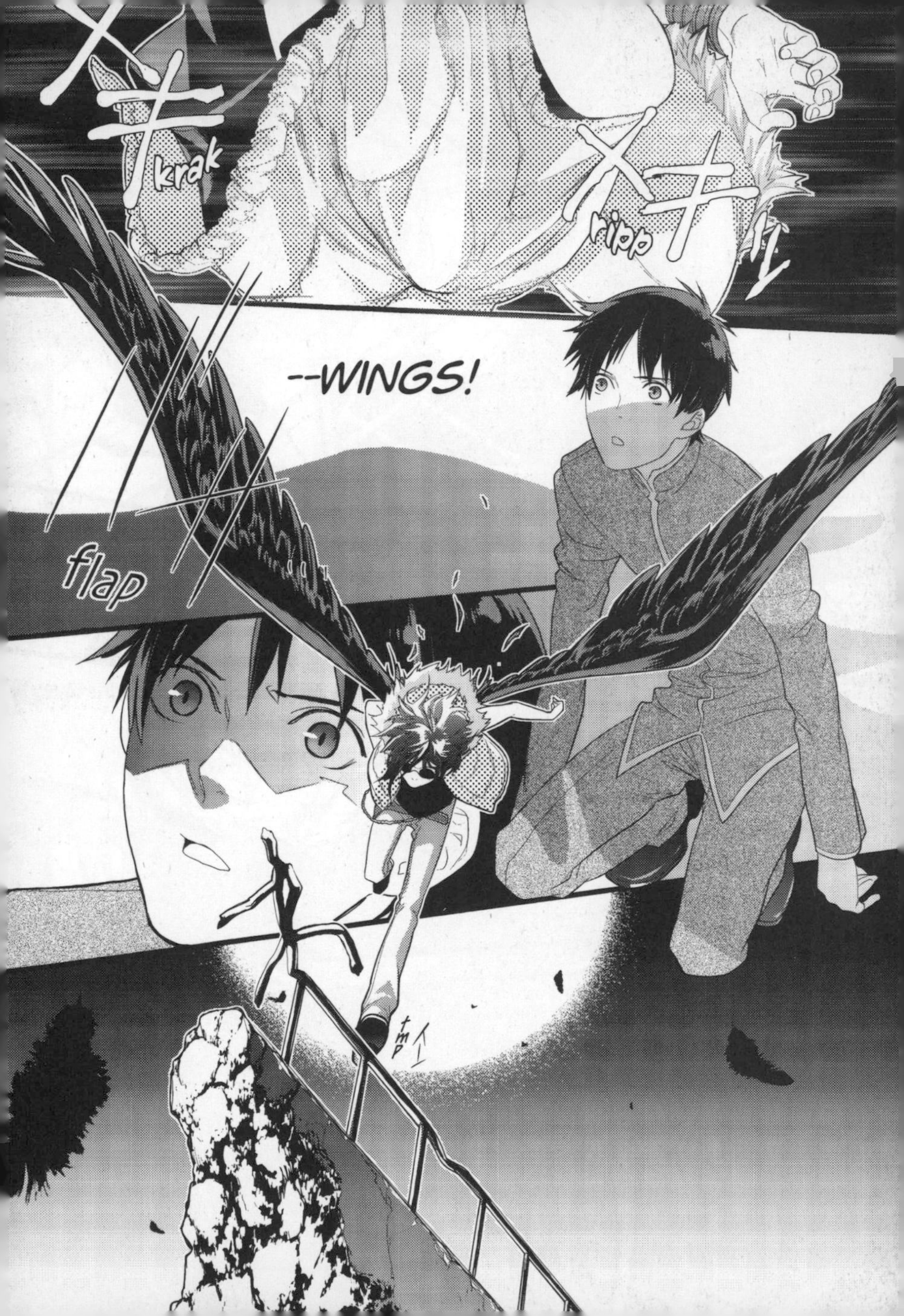
ripp
krak
--WINGS!
flap
tmp

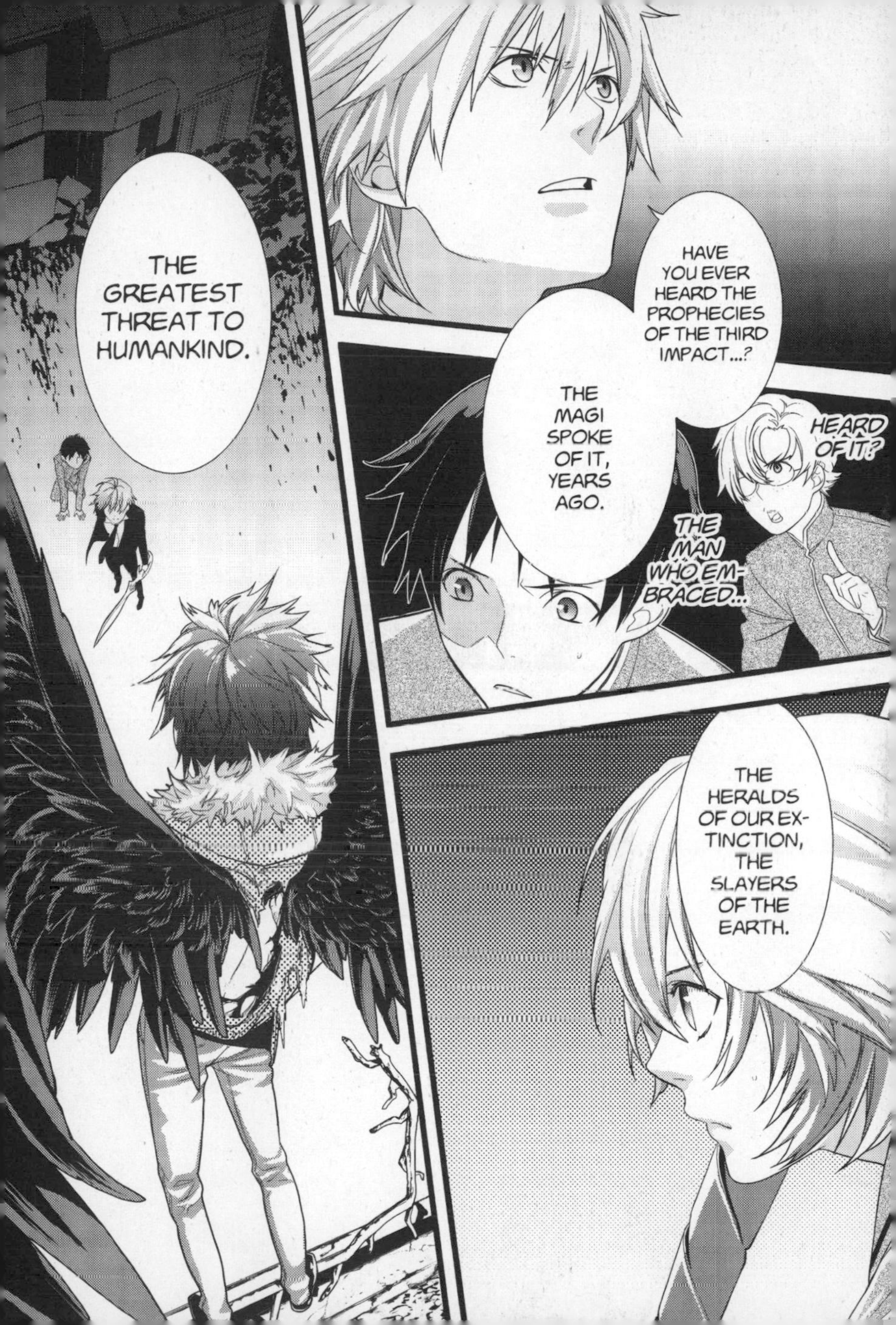
HAVE YOU EVER HEARD THE PROPHECIES OF THE THIRD IMPACT...?
HEARD OF IT?
THE MAN WHO EM-BRACED...
THE MAGI SPOKE OF IT, YEARS AGO.
THE HERALDS OF OUR EX-TINCTION, THE SLAYERS OF THE EARTH.
THE GREATEST THREAT TO HUMANKIND.

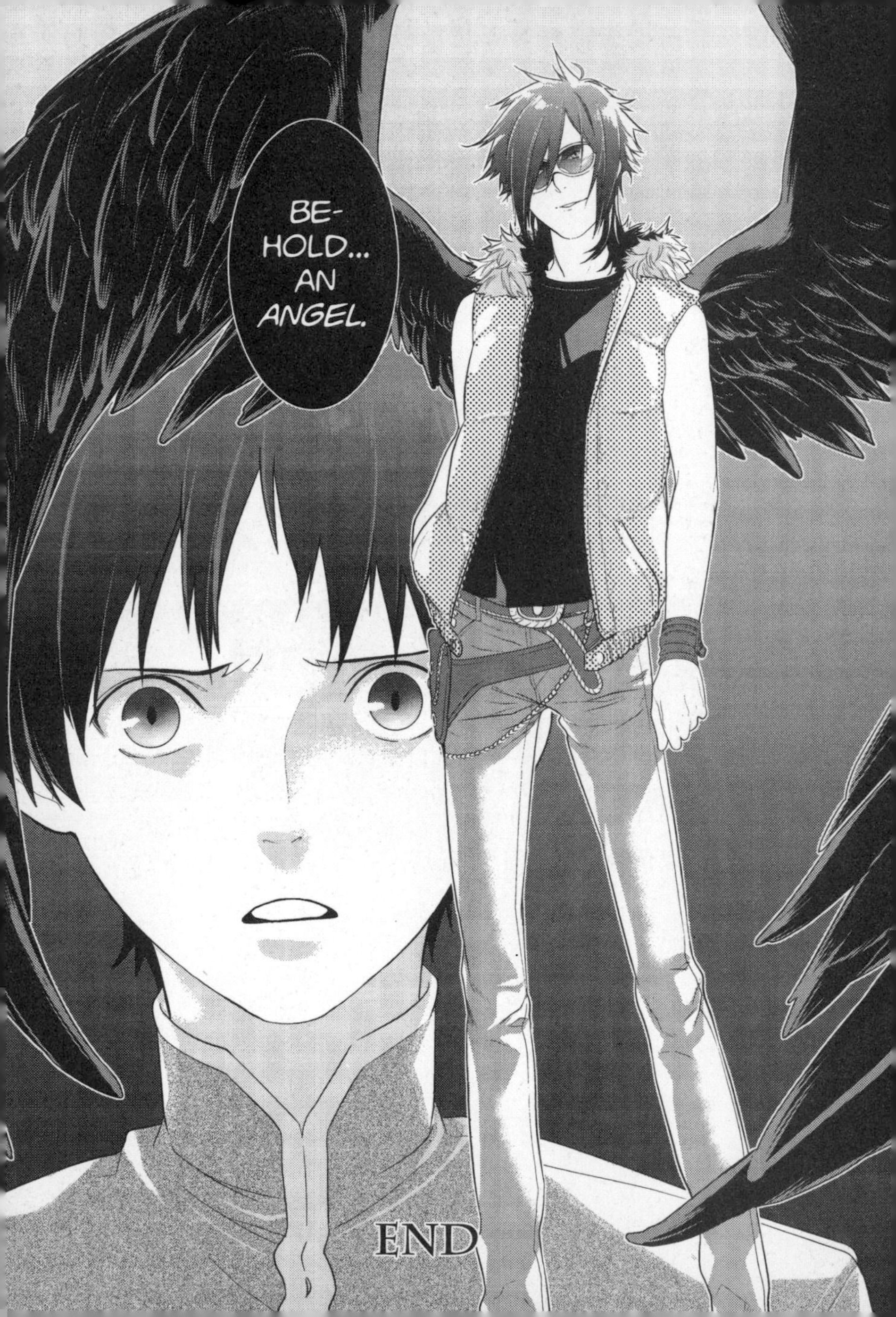
BE-HOLD... AN ANGEL.
END

SECOND EVENT

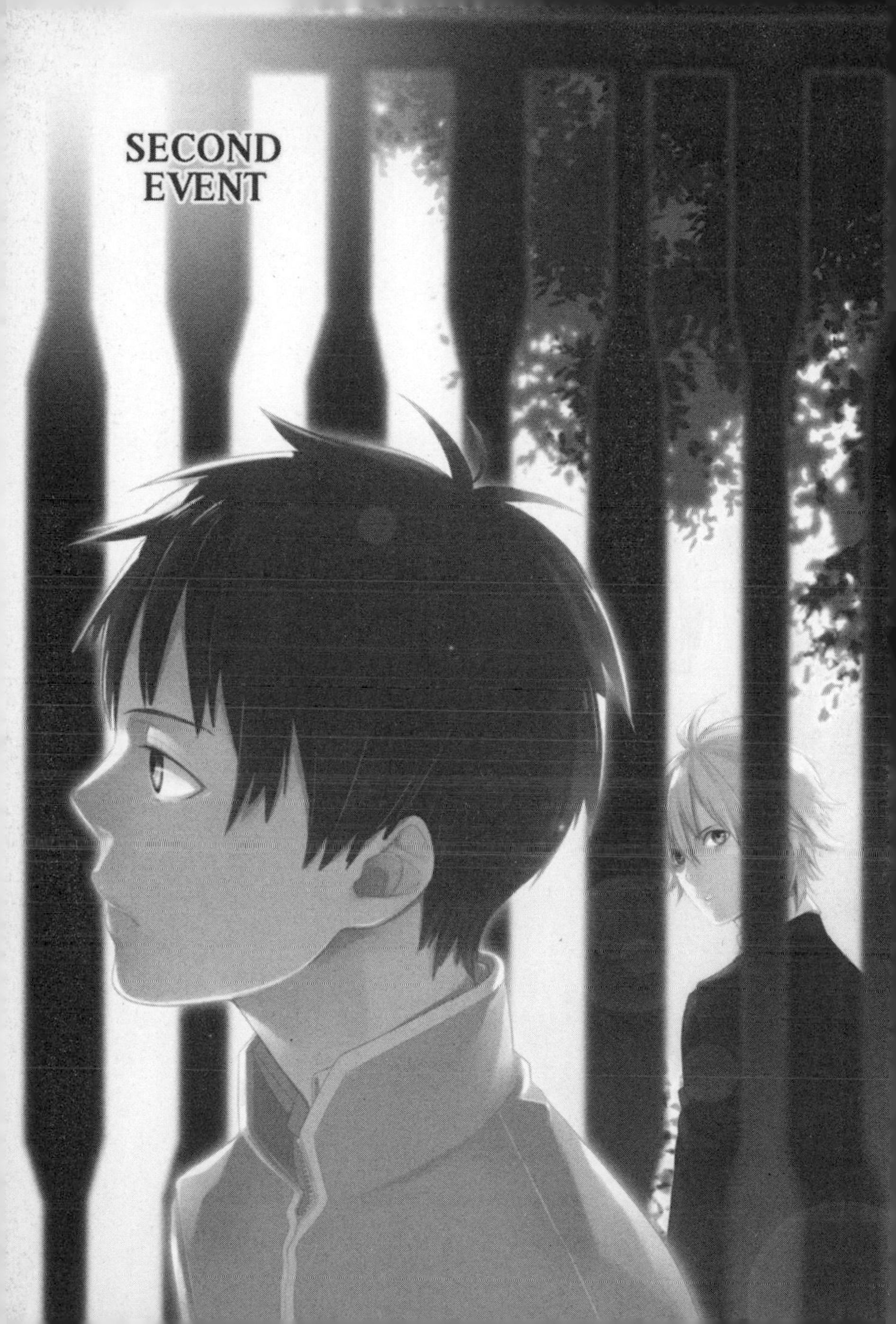

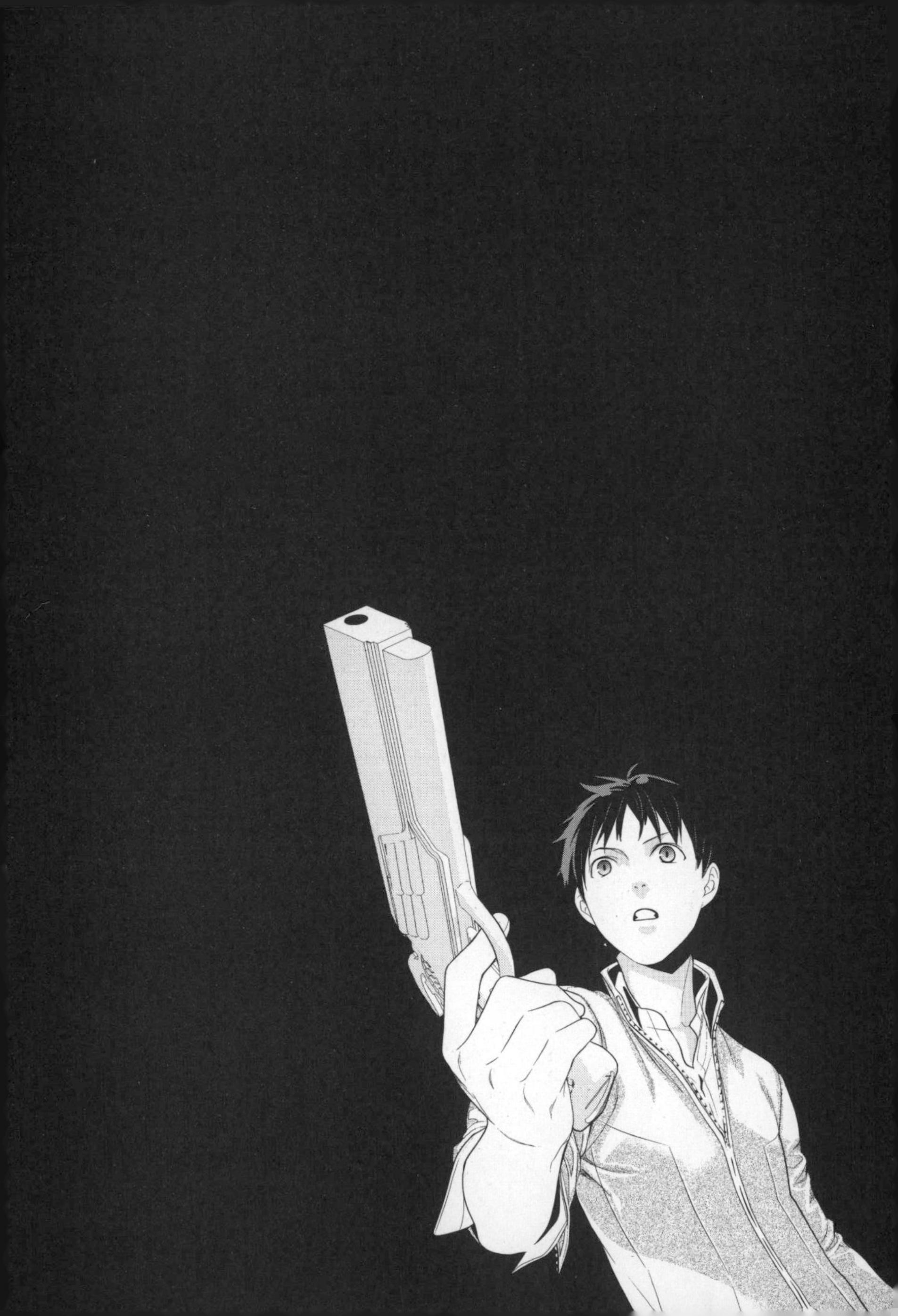

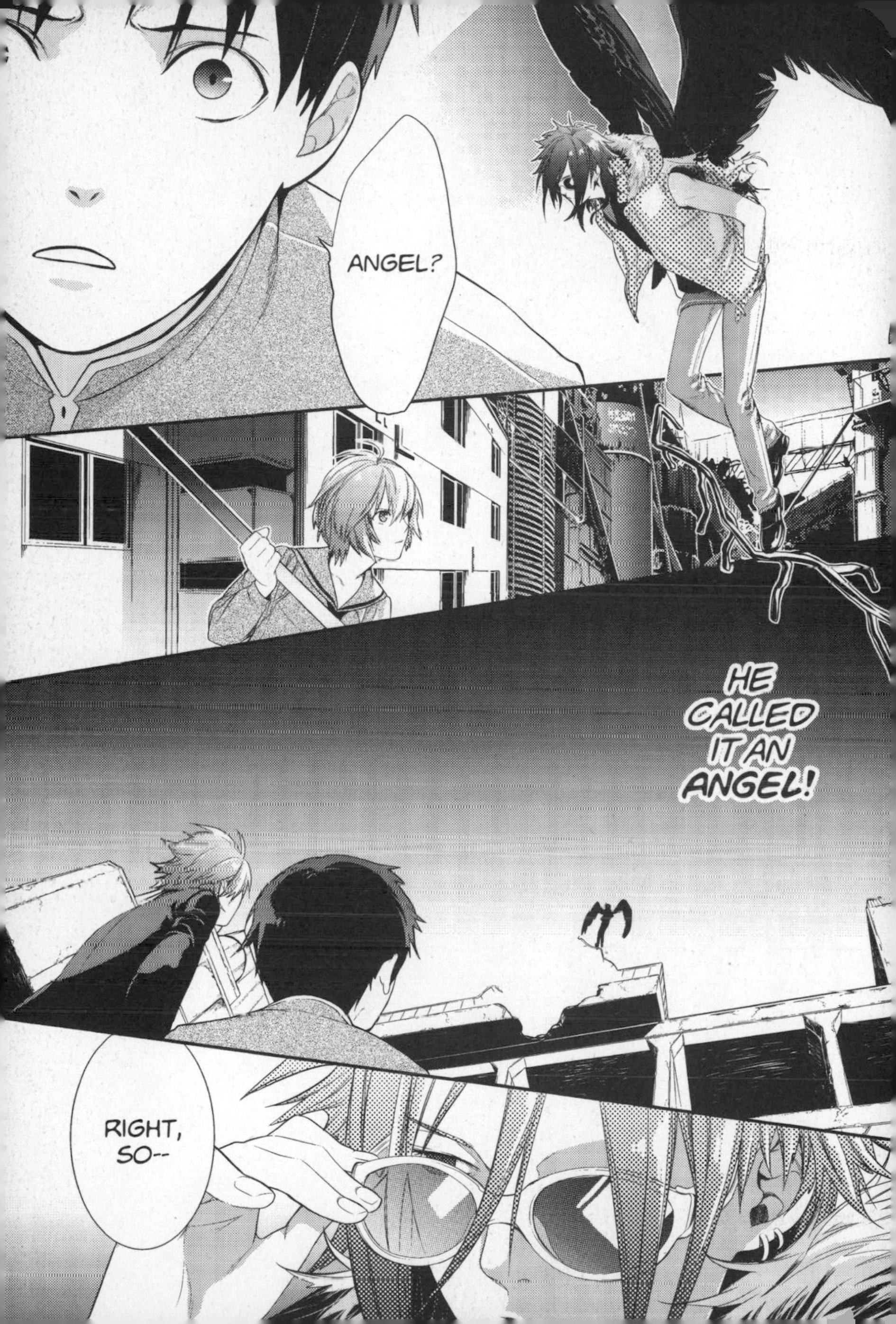
ANGEL?
HE CALLED IT AN ANGEL!
RIGHT, SO--

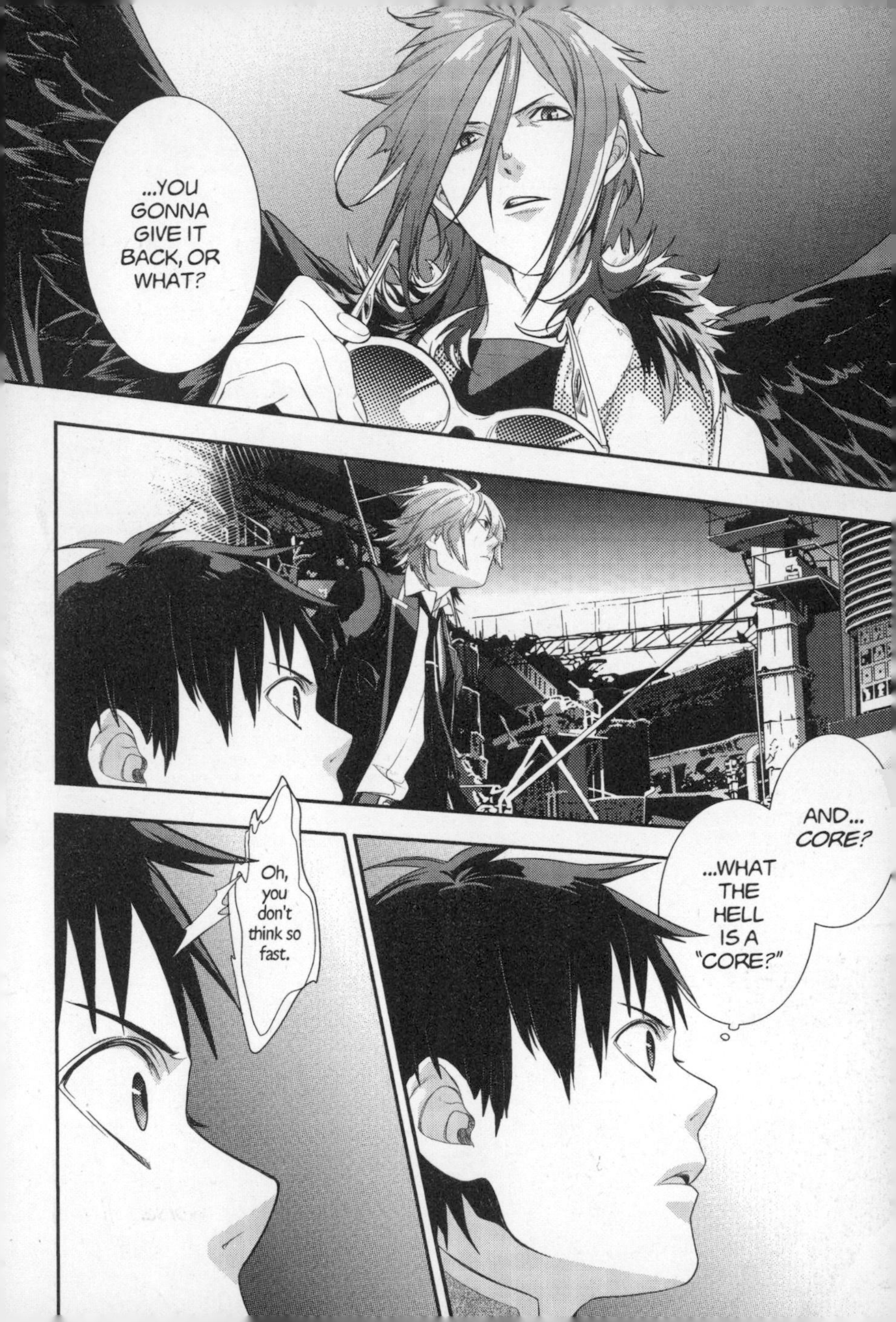
...YOU GONNA GIVE IT BACK, OR WHAT?
AND... *CORE?*
...WHAT THE HELL IS A "CORE?"
Oh, you don't think so fast.

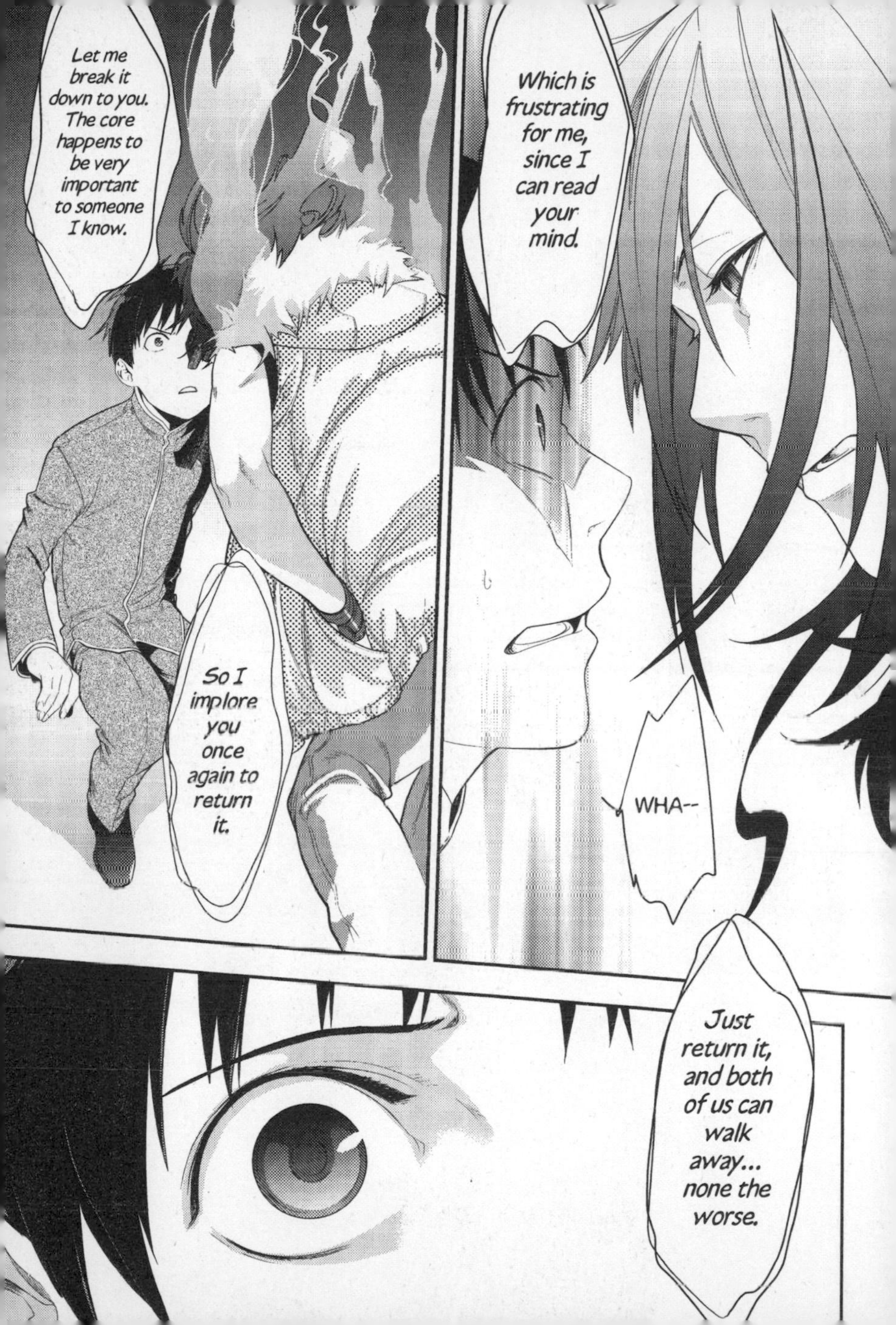
Which is frustrating for me, since I can read your mind.
WHA--
Let me break it down to you. The core happens to be very important to someone I know.
So I implore you once again to return it.
Just return it, and both of us can walk away... none the worse.

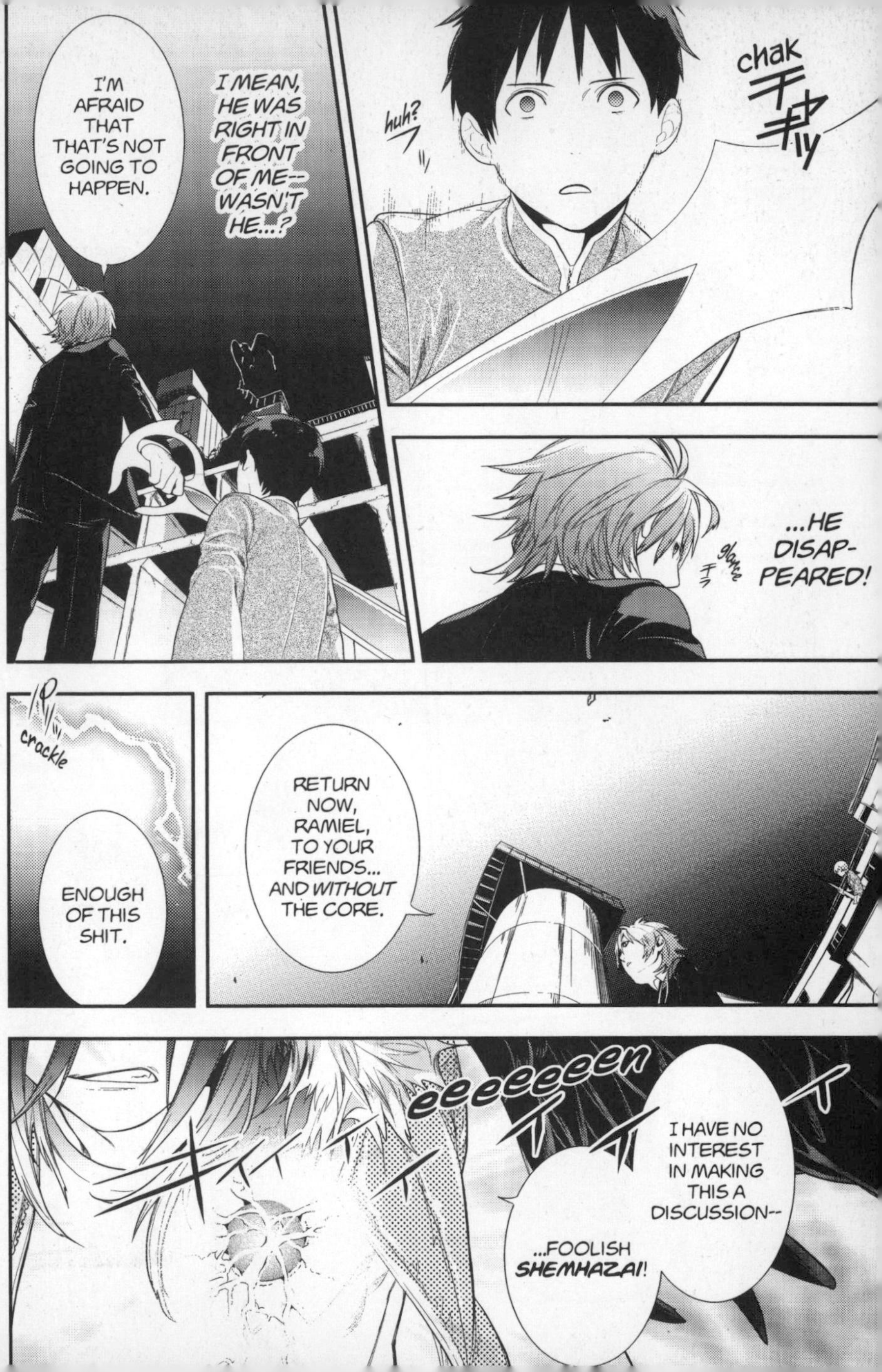
chak
huh?
glance
...HE DISAPPEARED!
I MEAN, HE WAS RIGHT IN FRONT OF ME--WASN'T HE...?
I'M AFRAID THAT THAT'S NOT GOING TO HAPPEN.
RETURN NOW, RAMIEL, TO YOUR FRIENDS... AND *WITHOUT* THE CORE.
crackle
ENOUGH OF THIS SHIT.
eeeeeeeen
I HAVE NO INTEREST IN MAKING THIS A DISCUSSION--
...FOOLISH **SHEMHAZAI**!

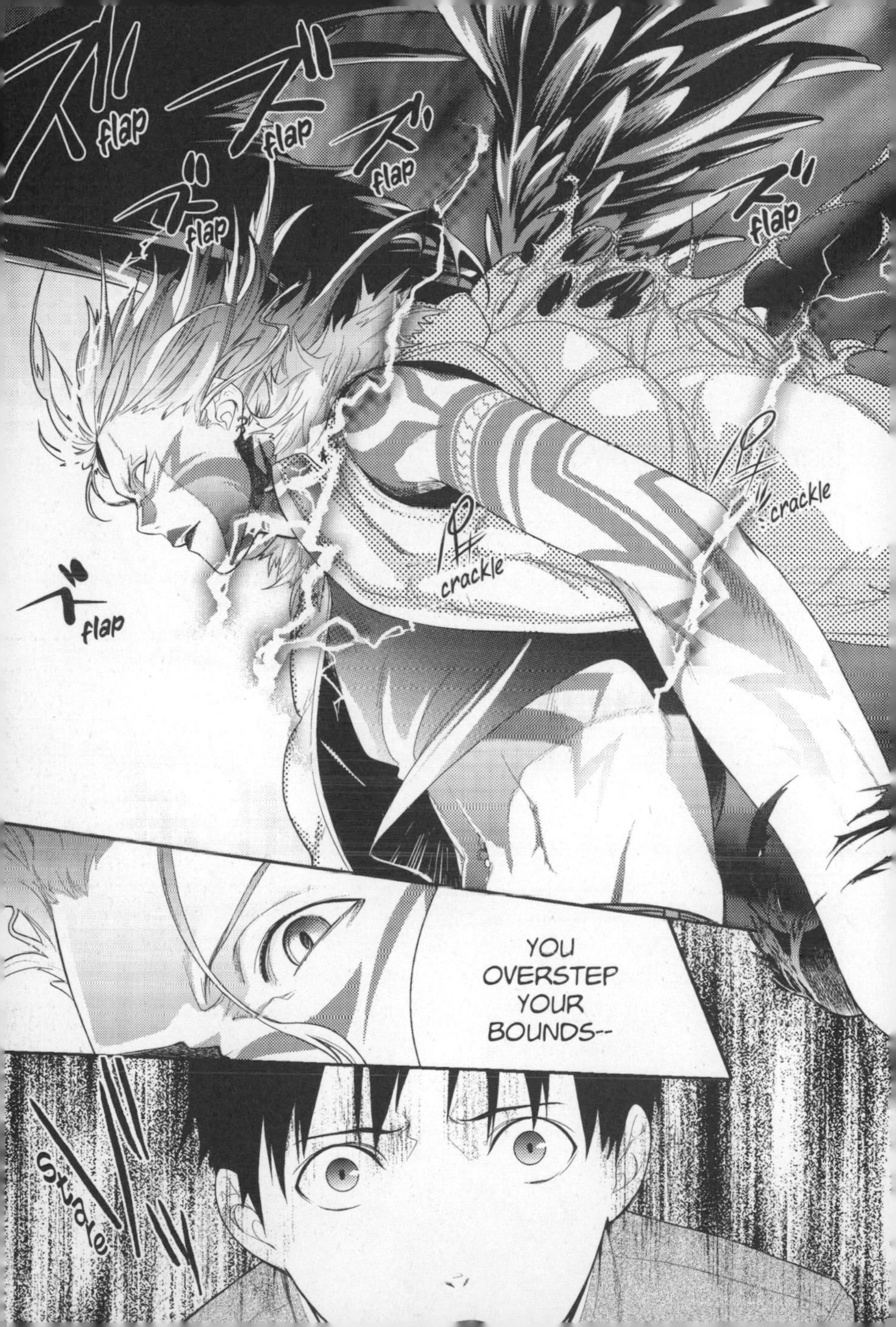
flap
flap
flap
flap
flap
crackle
crackle
flap
YOU OVERSTEP YOUR BOUNDS--
Stare

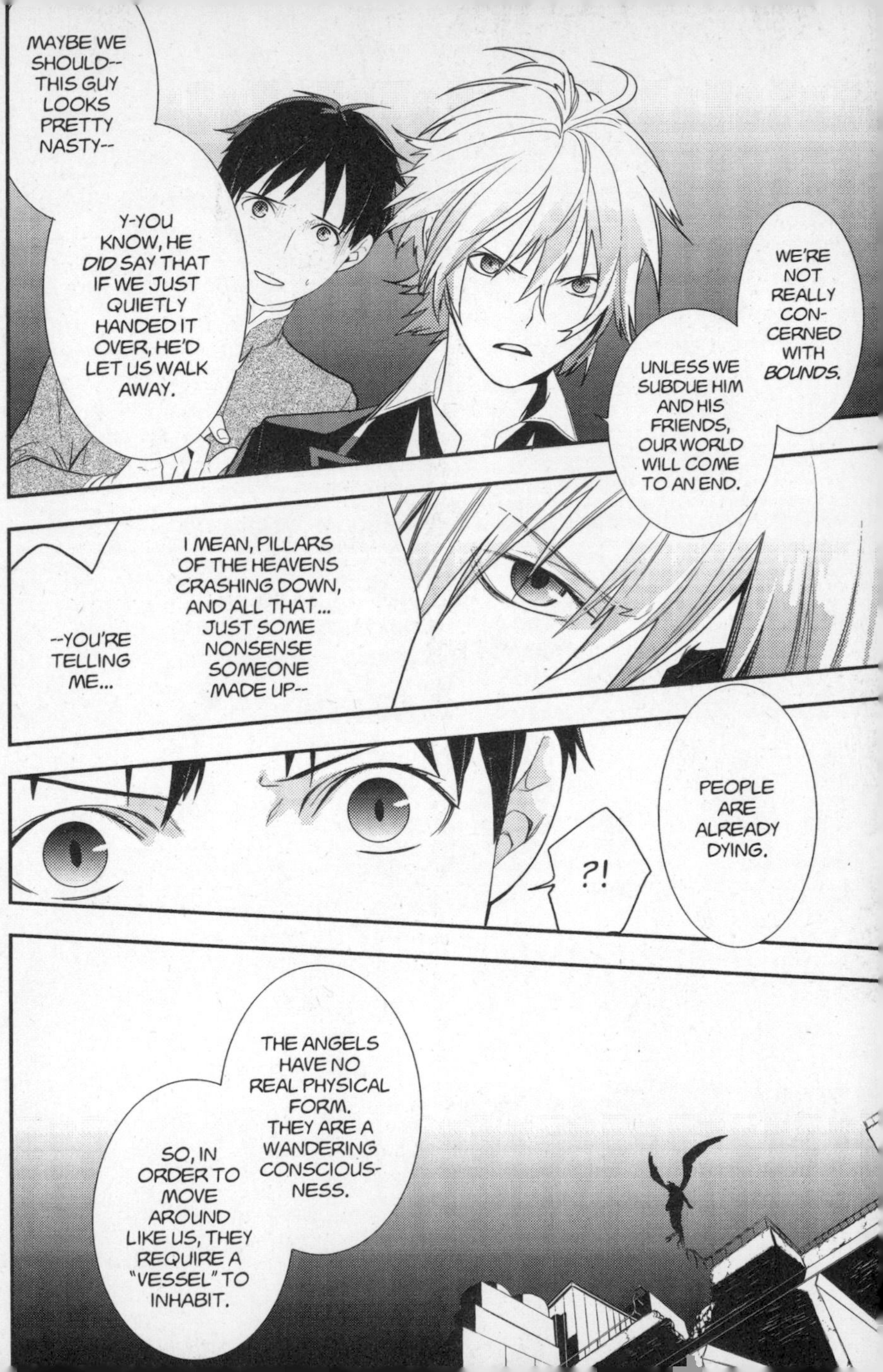
MAYBE WE SHOULD-- THIS GUY LOOKS PRETTY NASTY--
Y-YOU KNOW, HE *DID* SAY THAT IF WE JUST QUIETLY HANDED IT OVER, HE'D LET US WALK AWAY.
WE'RE NOT REALLY CON-CERNED WITH *BOUNDS.*
UNLESS WE SUBDUE HIM AND HIS FRIENDS, OUR WORLD WILL COME TO AN END.
I MEAN, PILLARS OF THE HEAVENS CRASHING DOWN, AND ALL THAT... JUST SOME NONSENSE SOMEONE MADE UP--
--YOU'RE TELLING ME...
PEOPLE ARE ALREADY DYING.
?!
THE ANGELS HAVE NO REAL PHYSICAL FORM. THEY ARE A WANDERING CONSCIOUS-NESS.
SO, IN ORDER TO MOVE AROUND LIKE US, THEY REQUIRE A "VESSEL" TO INHABIT.

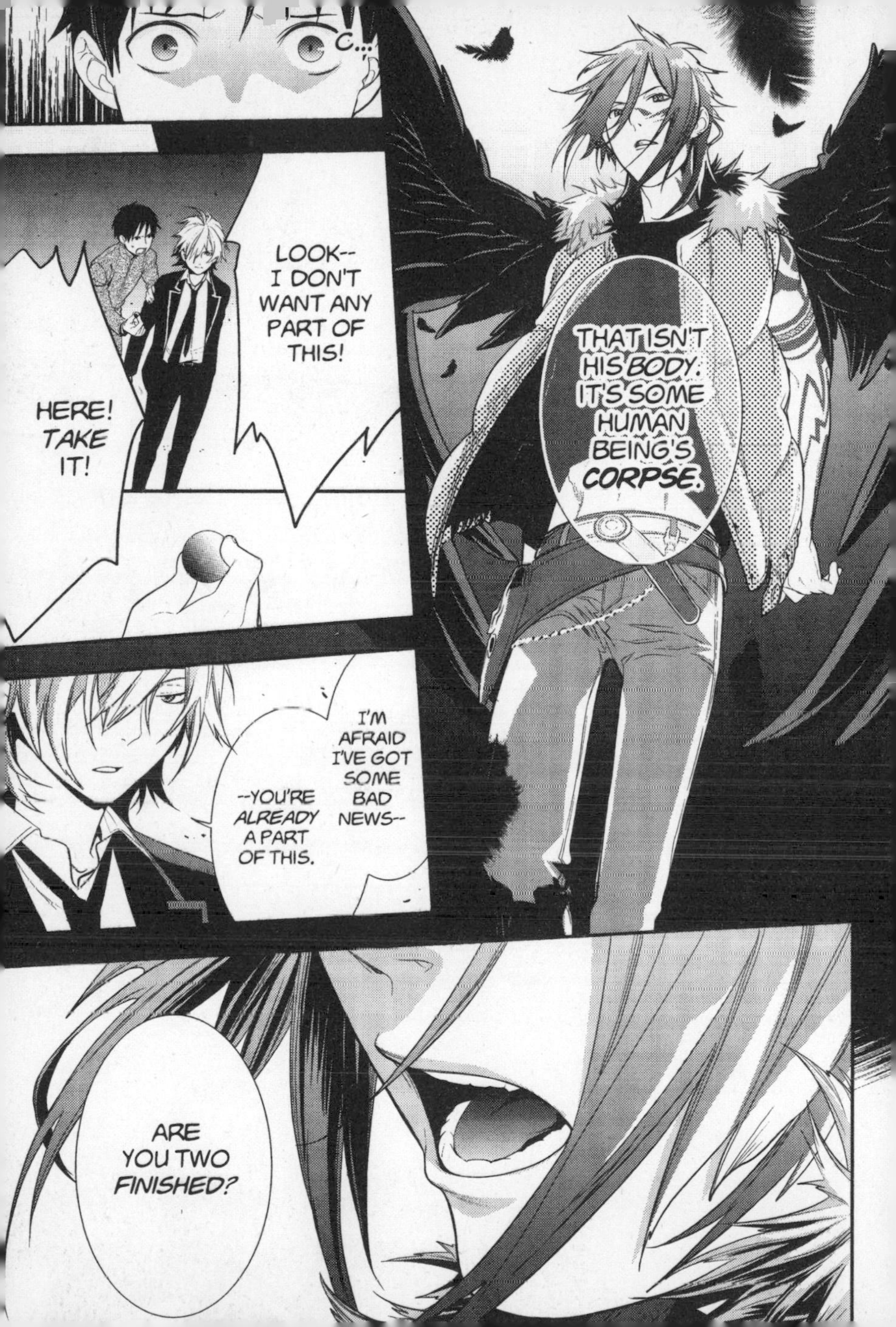
THAT ISN'T HIS *BODY*. IT'S SOME HUMAN BEING'S ***CORPSE***.
C...!
LOOK-- I DON'T WANT ANY PART OF THIS!
HERE! *TAKE* IT!
I'M AFRAID I'VE GOT SOME BAD NEWS--
--YOU'RE *ALREADY* A PART OF THIS.
ARE YOU TWO ***FINISHED?***

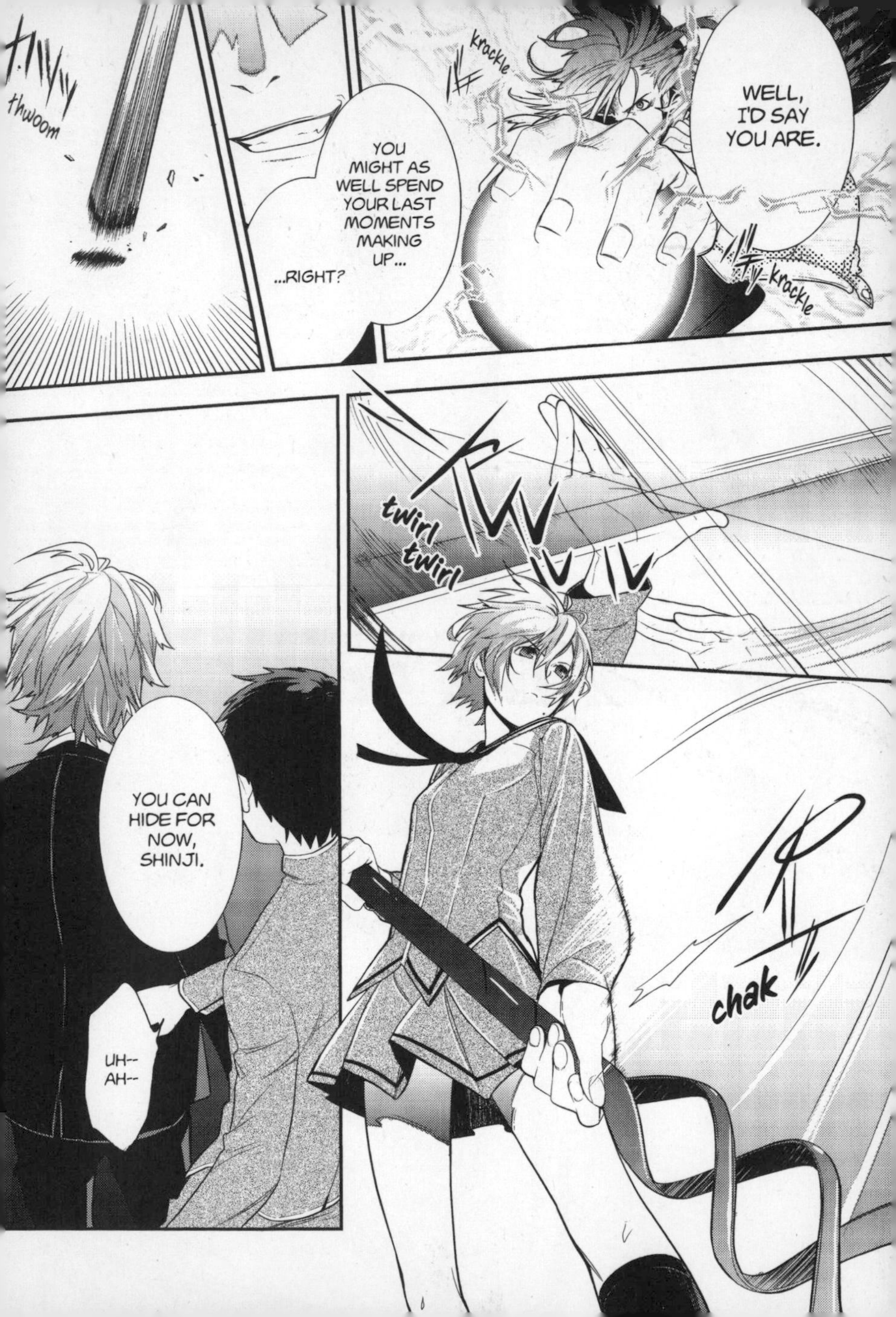
krackle
WELL, I'D SAY YOU ARE.
krackle
YOU MIGHT AS WELL SPEND YOUR LAST MOMENTS MAKING UP...
...RIGHT?
thwoom
twirl twirl
chak
YOU CAN HIDE FOR NOW, SHINJI.
UH-- AH--

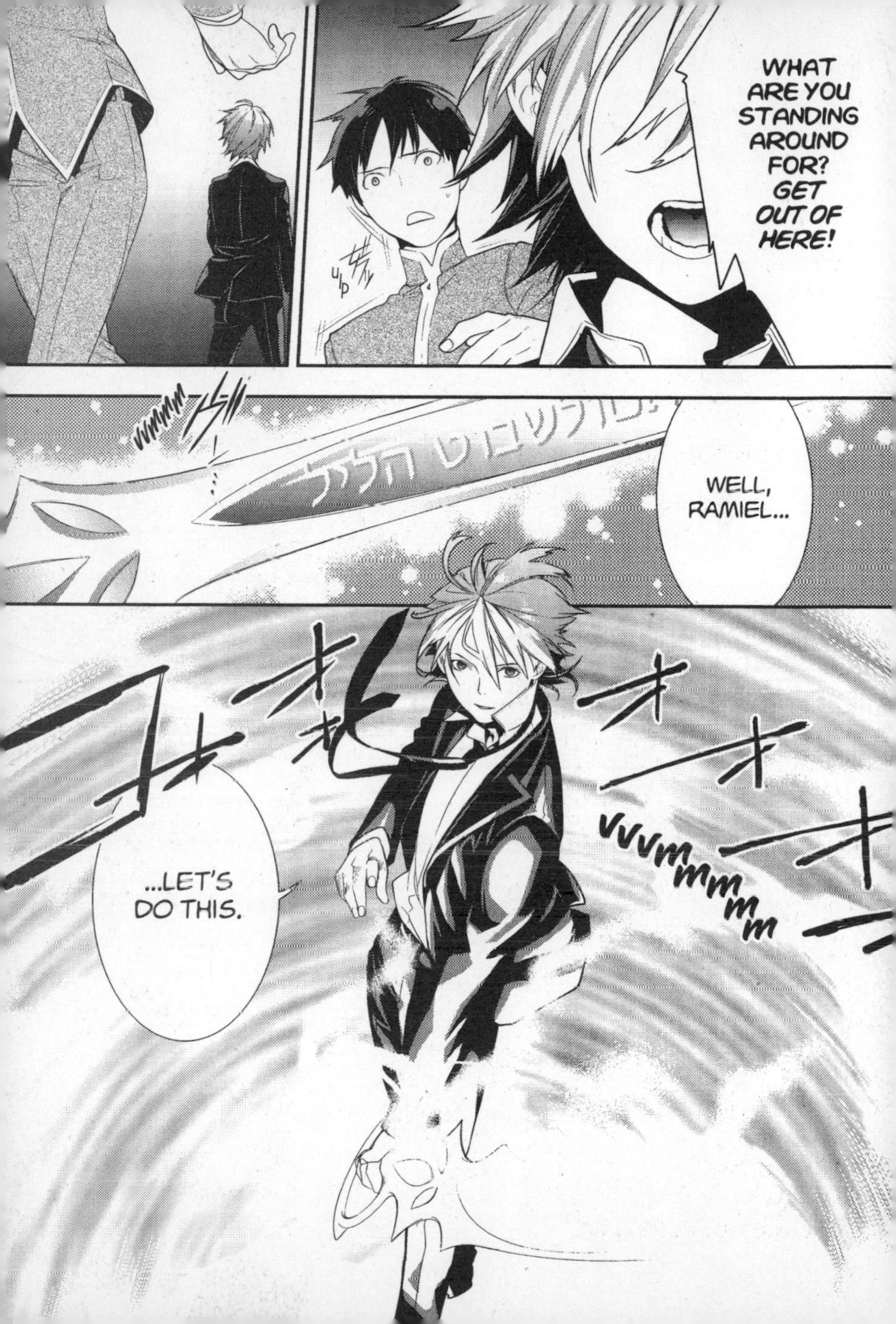
WHAT ARE YOU STANDING AROUND FOR? GET OUT OF HERE!
ulp
WELL, RAMIEL...
vvmmm
VVVMMMMMM
...LET'S DO THIS.

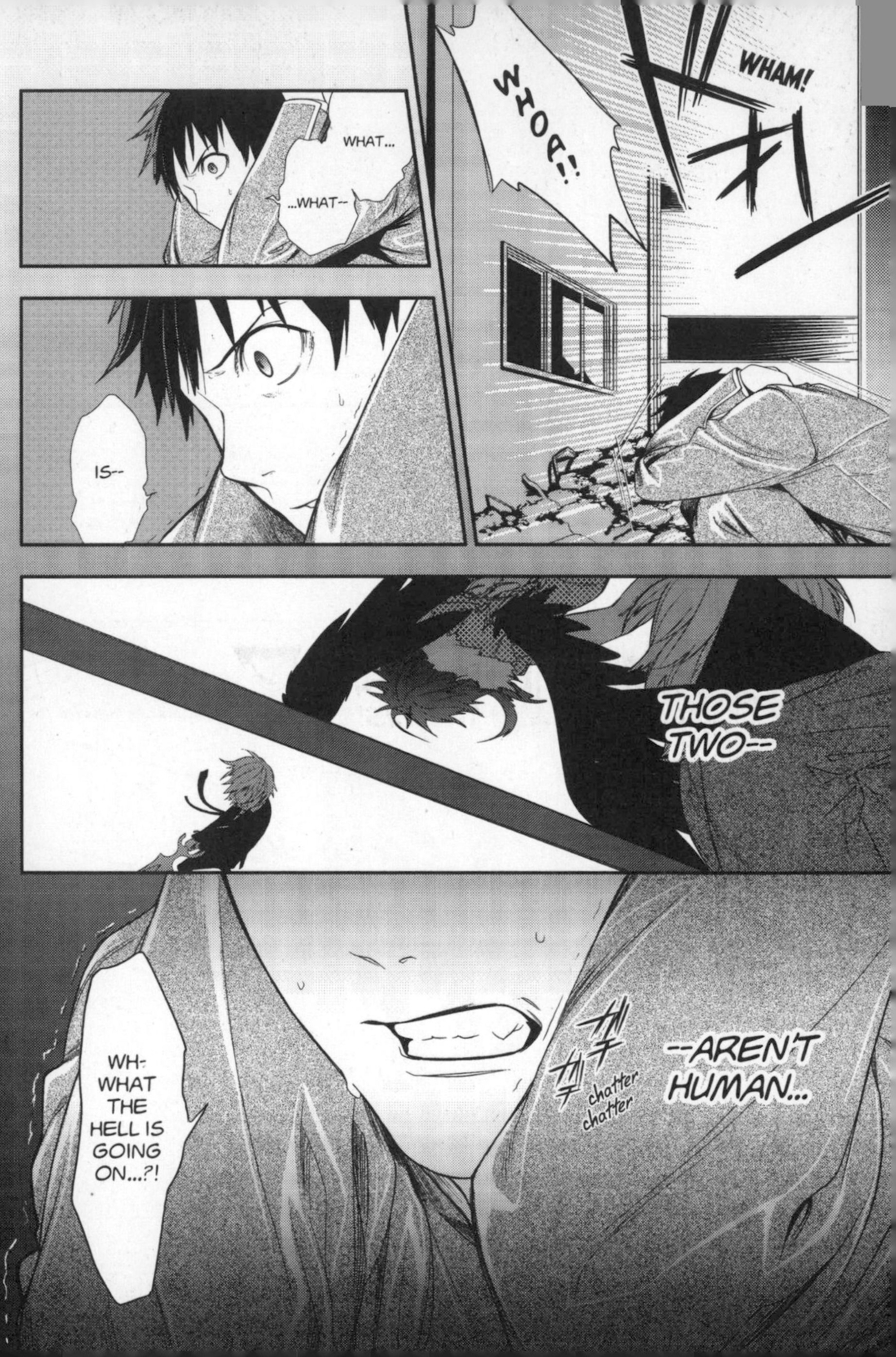
WHAM!
WHOA!!
WHAT...
...WHAT--
IS--
THOSE TWO--
chatter chatter
--AREN'T HUMAN...
WH- WHAT THE HELL IS GOING ON...?!

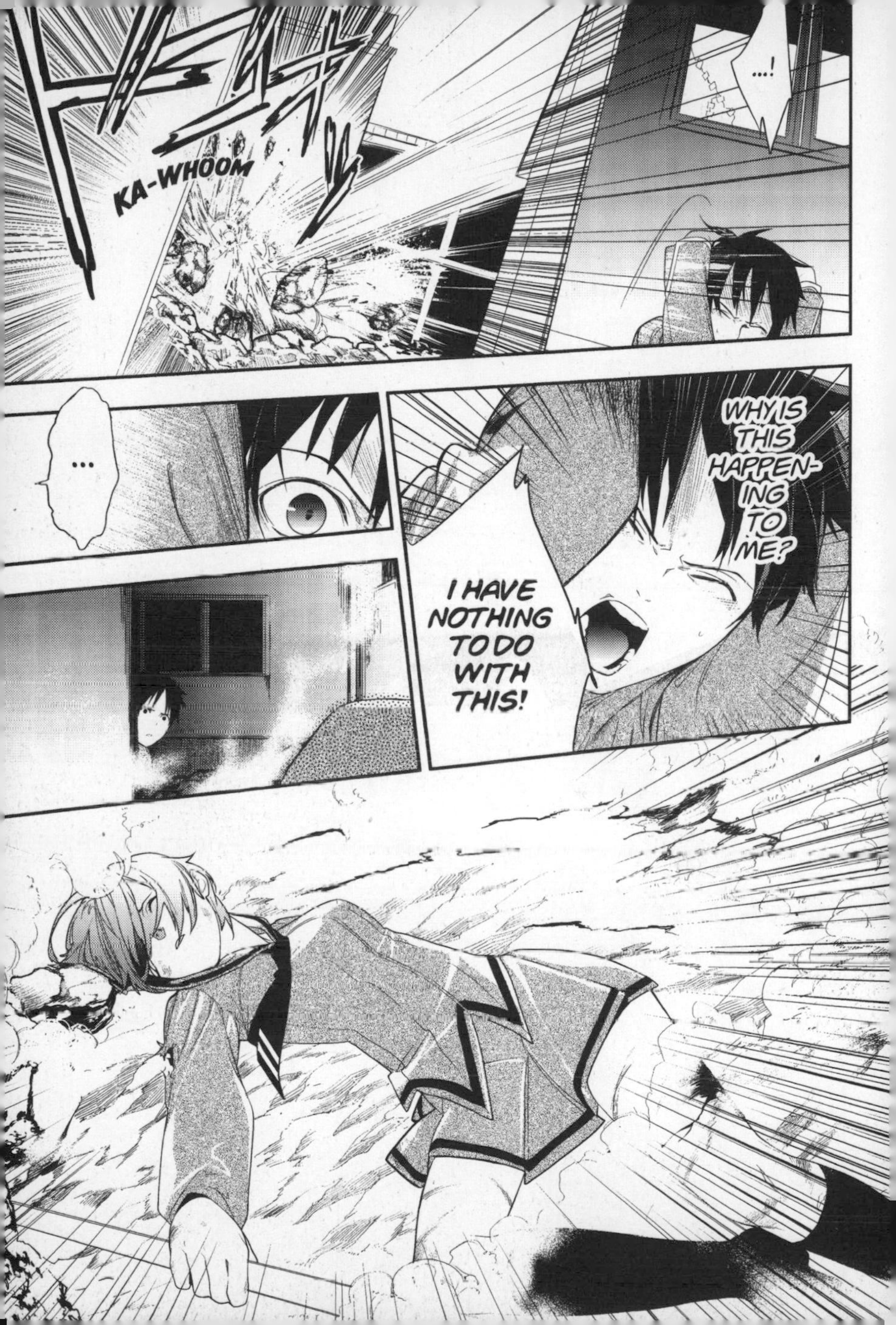
...!
KA-WHOOM
WHY IS THIS HAPPENING TO ME?
I HAVE NOTHING TO DO WITH THIS!
...

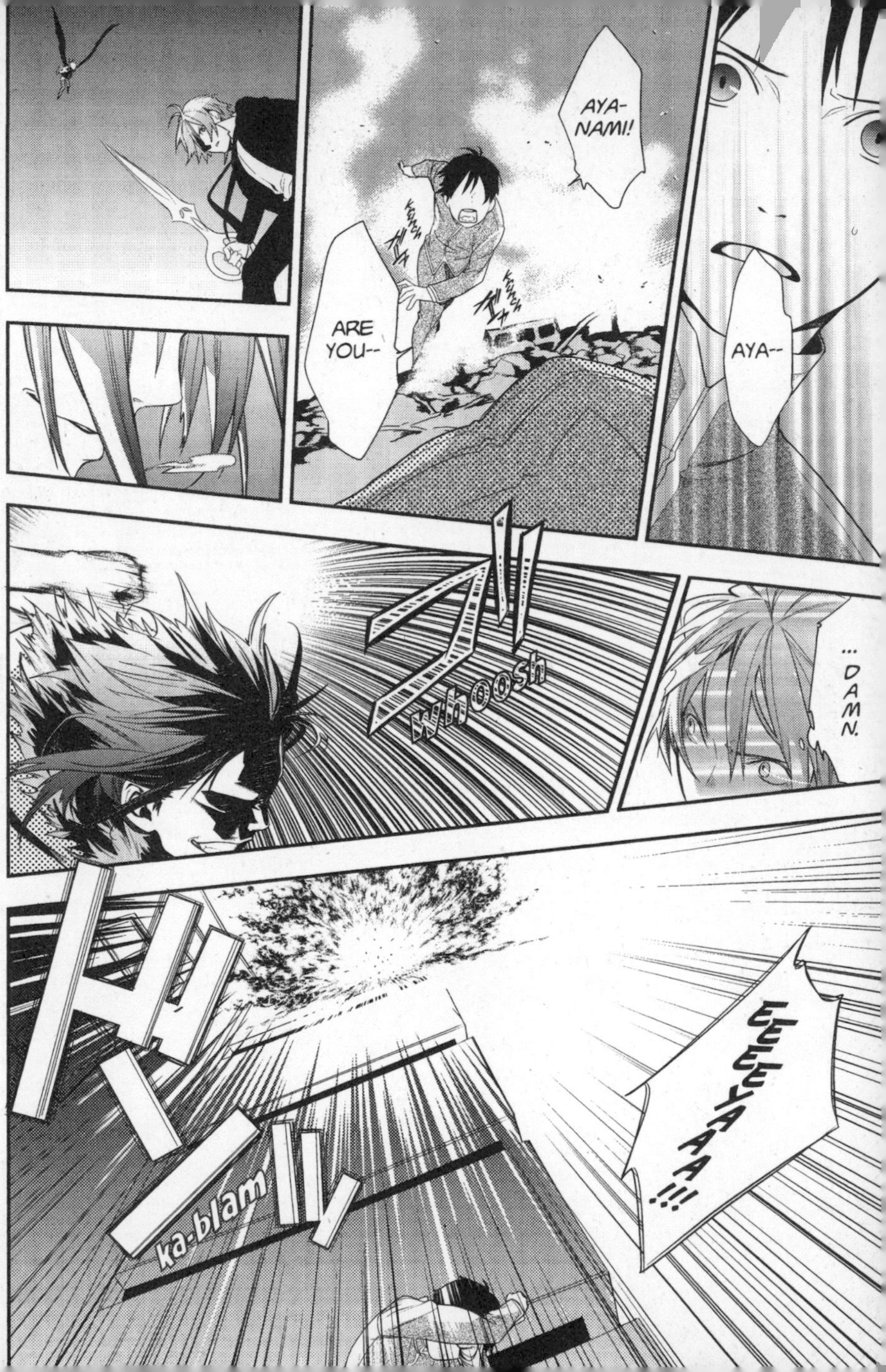
AYA--
AYA-NAMI!
ARE YOU--
...DAMN.
whoosh
EEEEYAAAA!!!
ka-blam

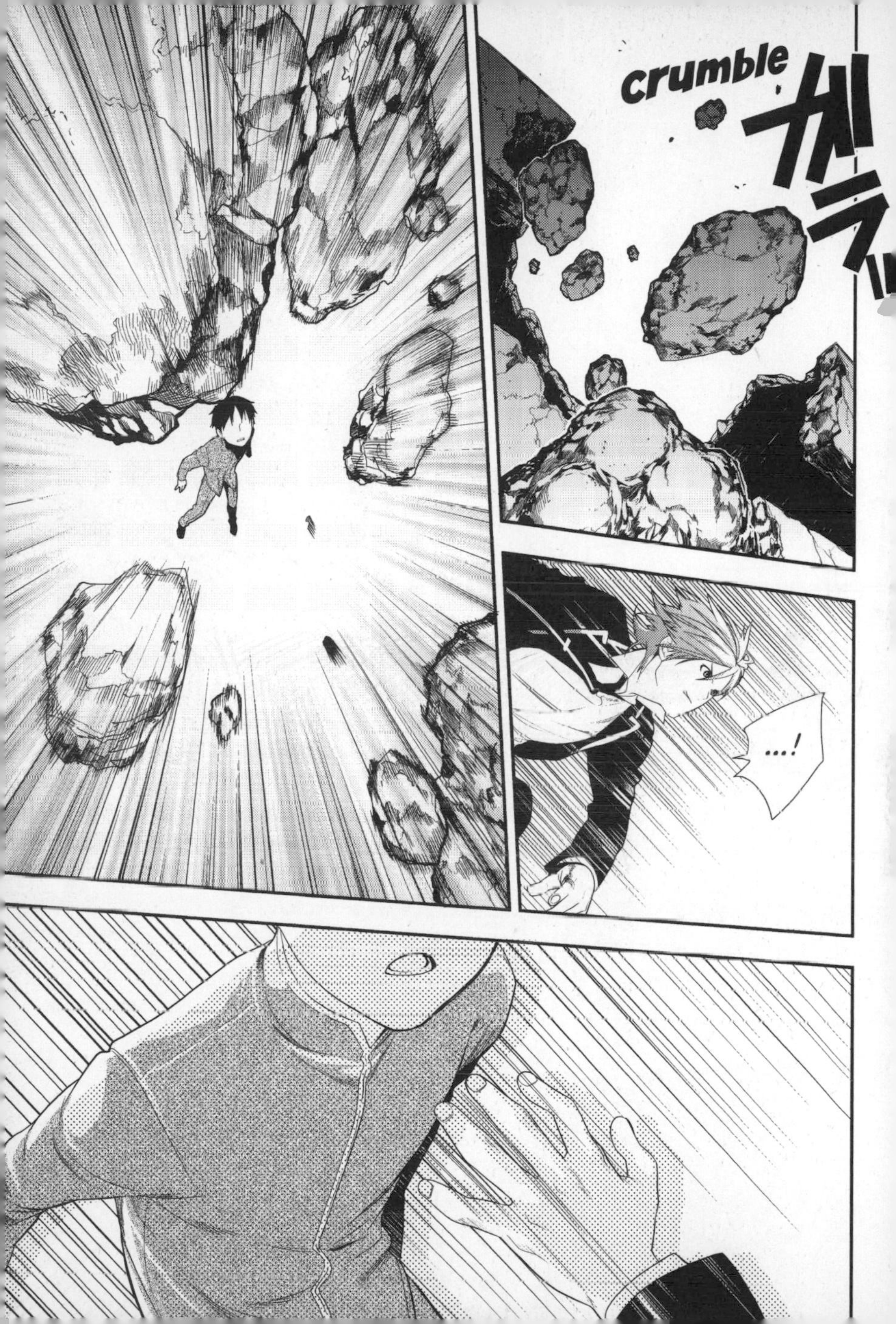
crumble
ガラッ
...!

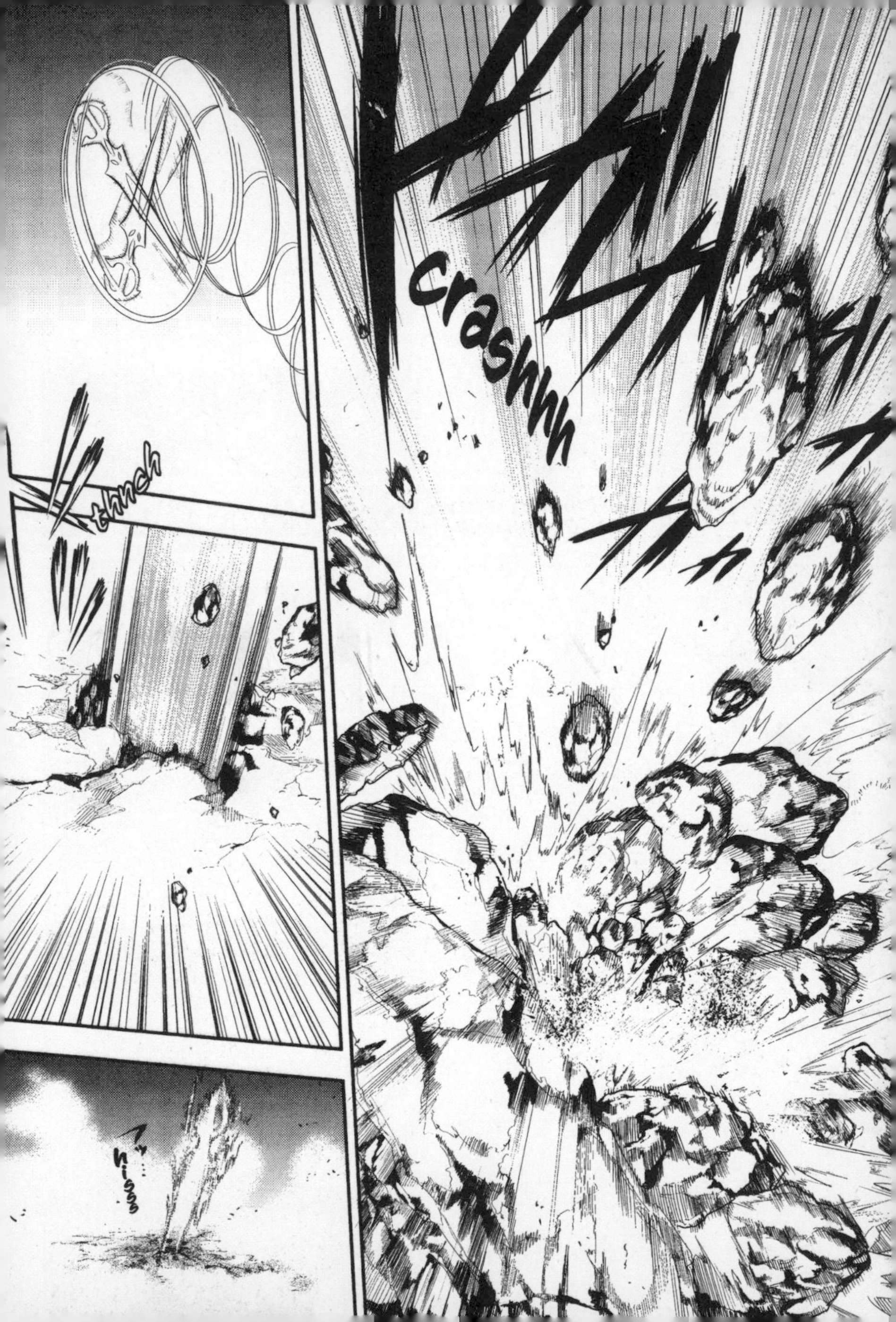
Crashhhh
thnch
hisss...

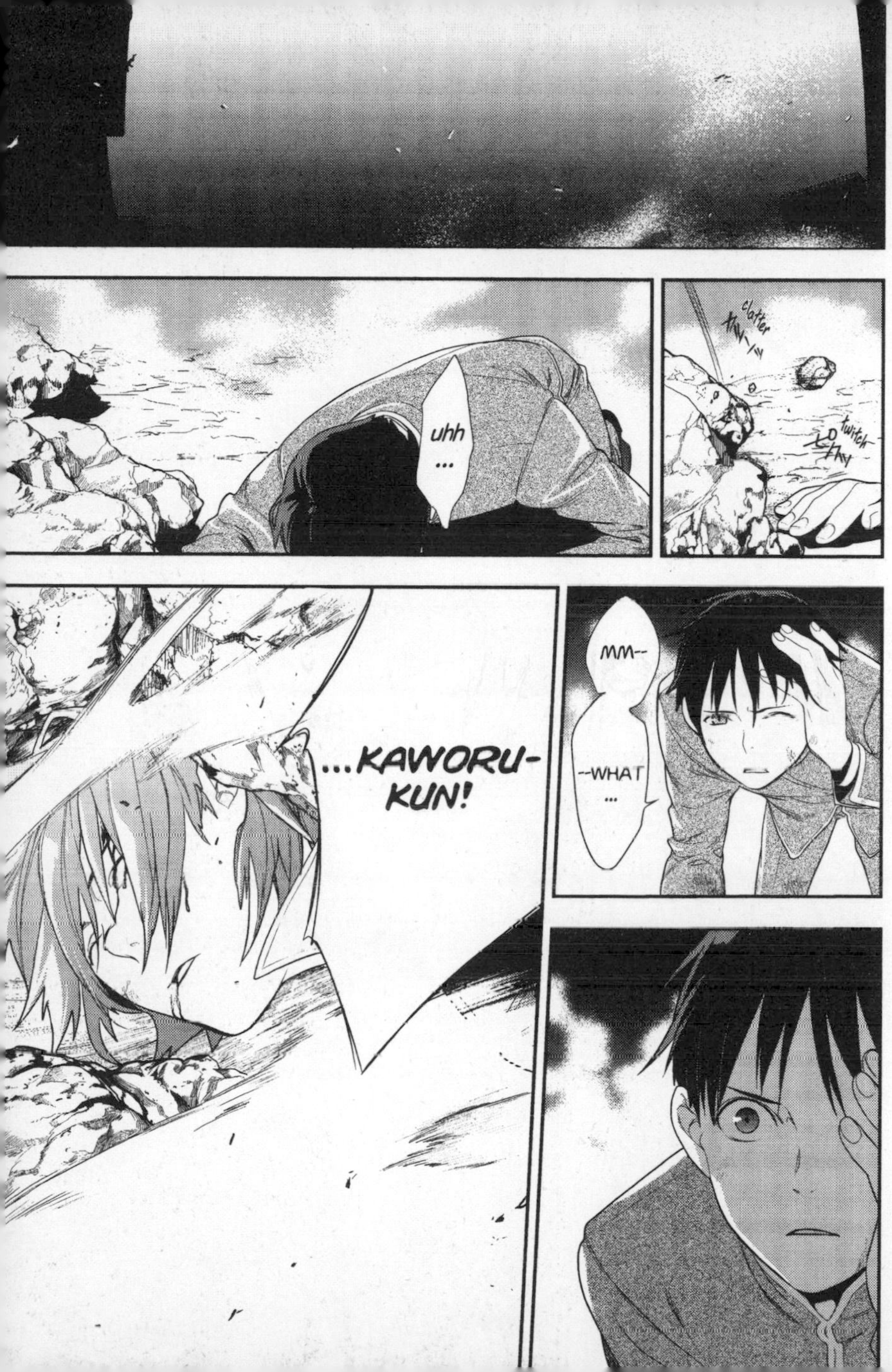
clatter
twitch
uhh ...
MM--
--WHAT ...
...KAWORU-KUN!

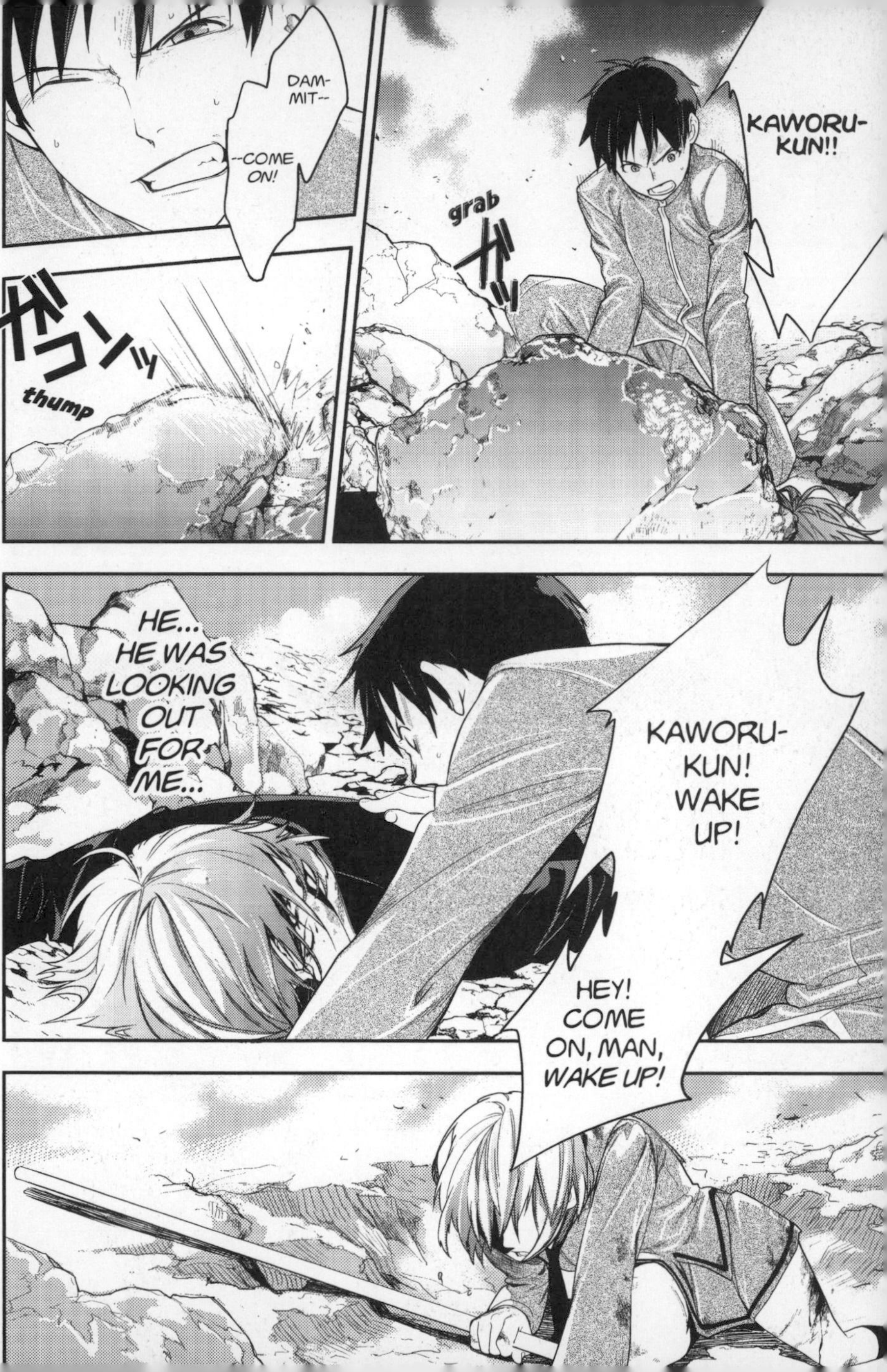
KAWORU-KUN!!
grab
ガッ
DAM-MIT--
--COME ON!
ガコンッ
thump
KAWORU-KUN! WAKE UP!
HE... HE WAS LOOKING OUT FOR ME...
HEY! COME ON, MAN, WAKE UP!

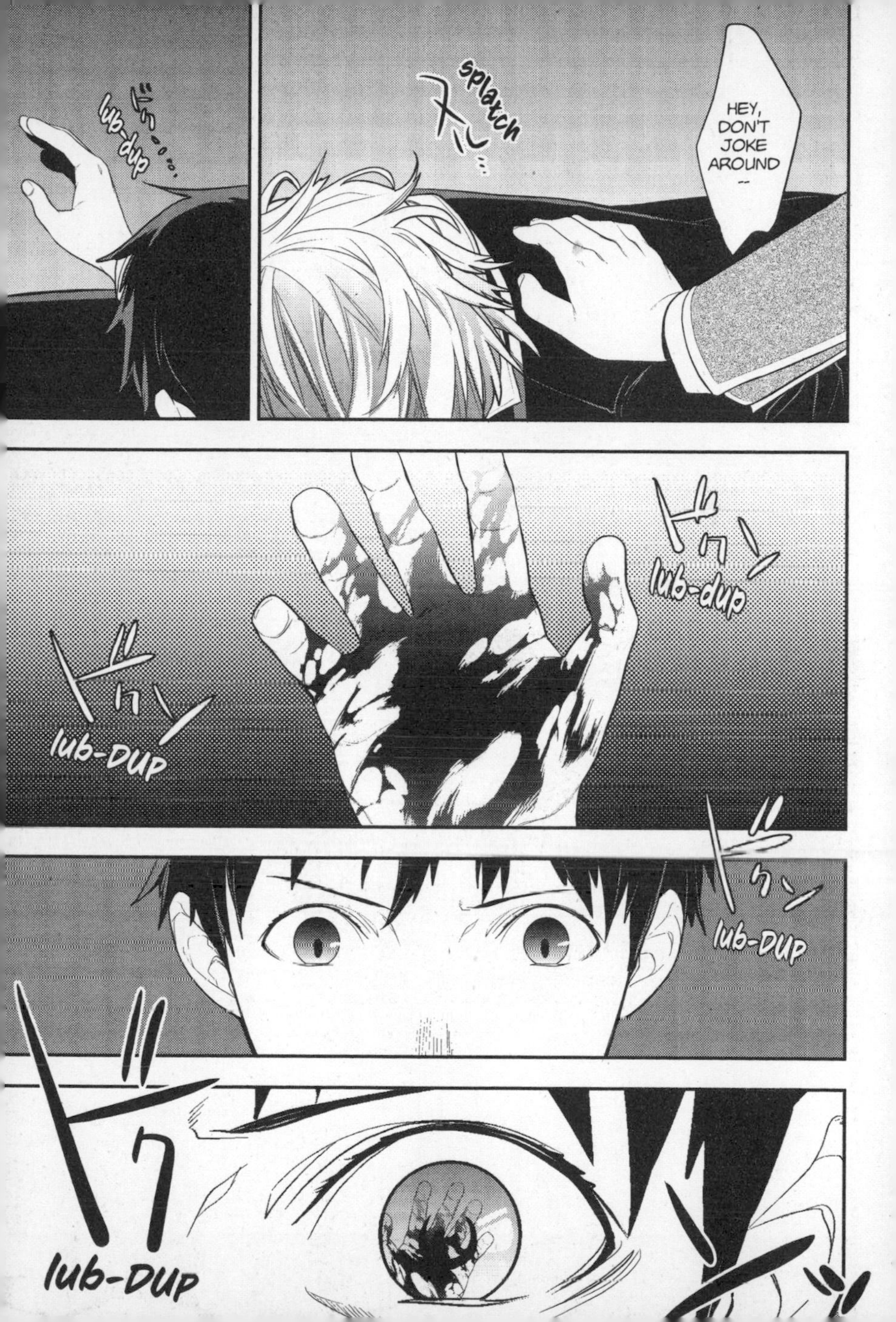
HEY, DON'T JOKE AROUND --
splatch
lub-dup
lub-dup
lub-DUP
lub-DUP
lub-DUP

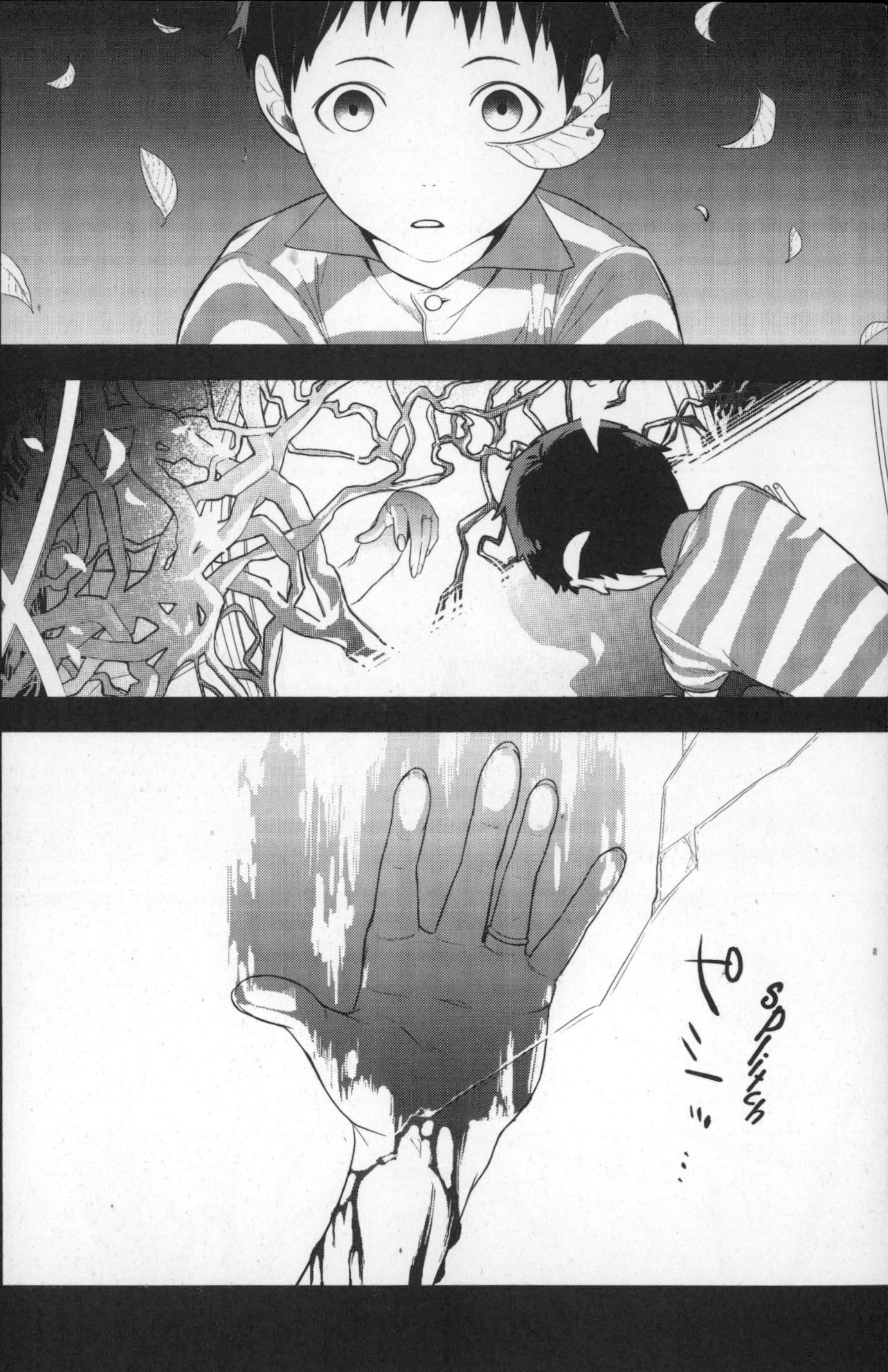
SPLITCH

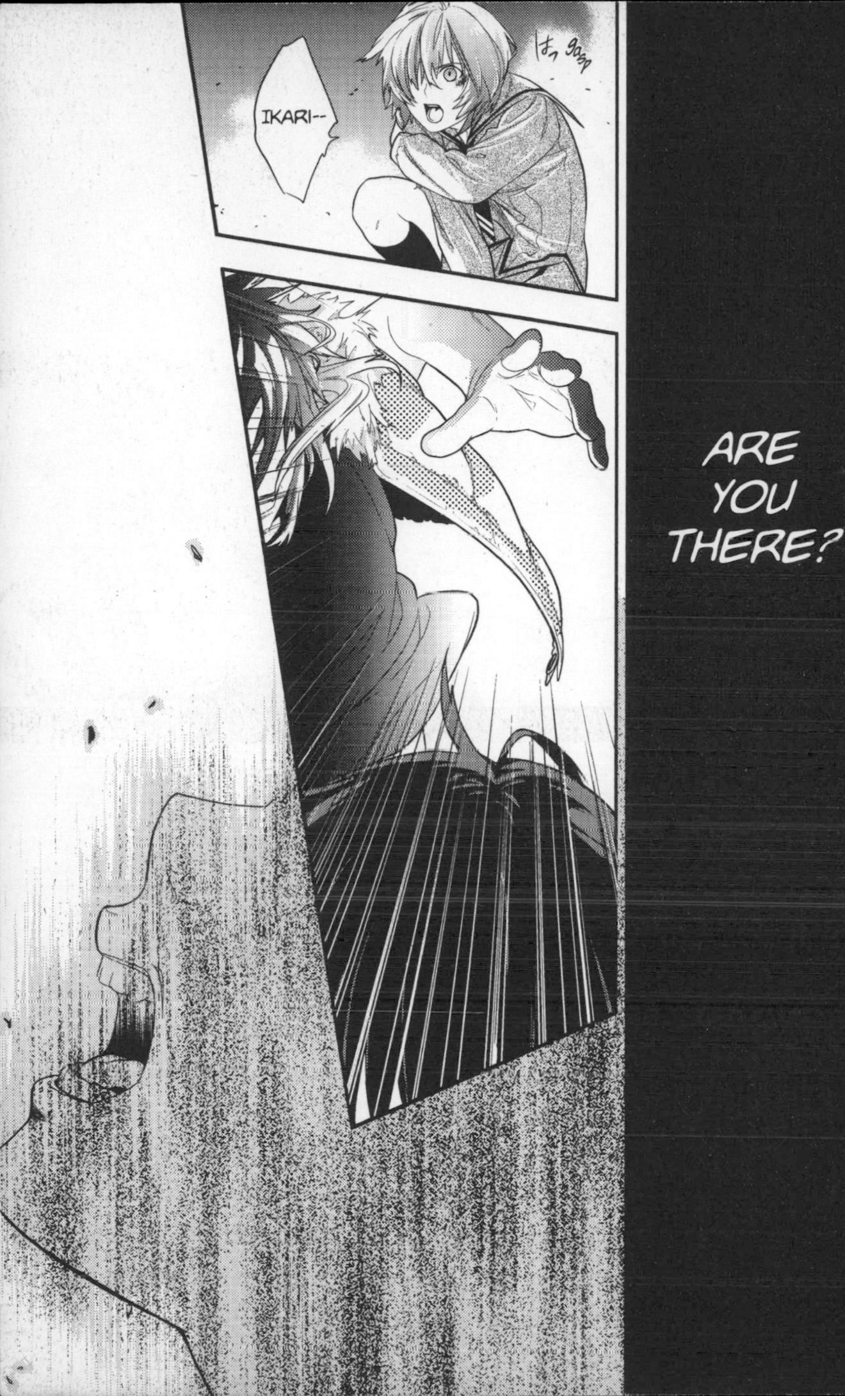

ARE YOU THERE?
はっ gasp
IKARI--

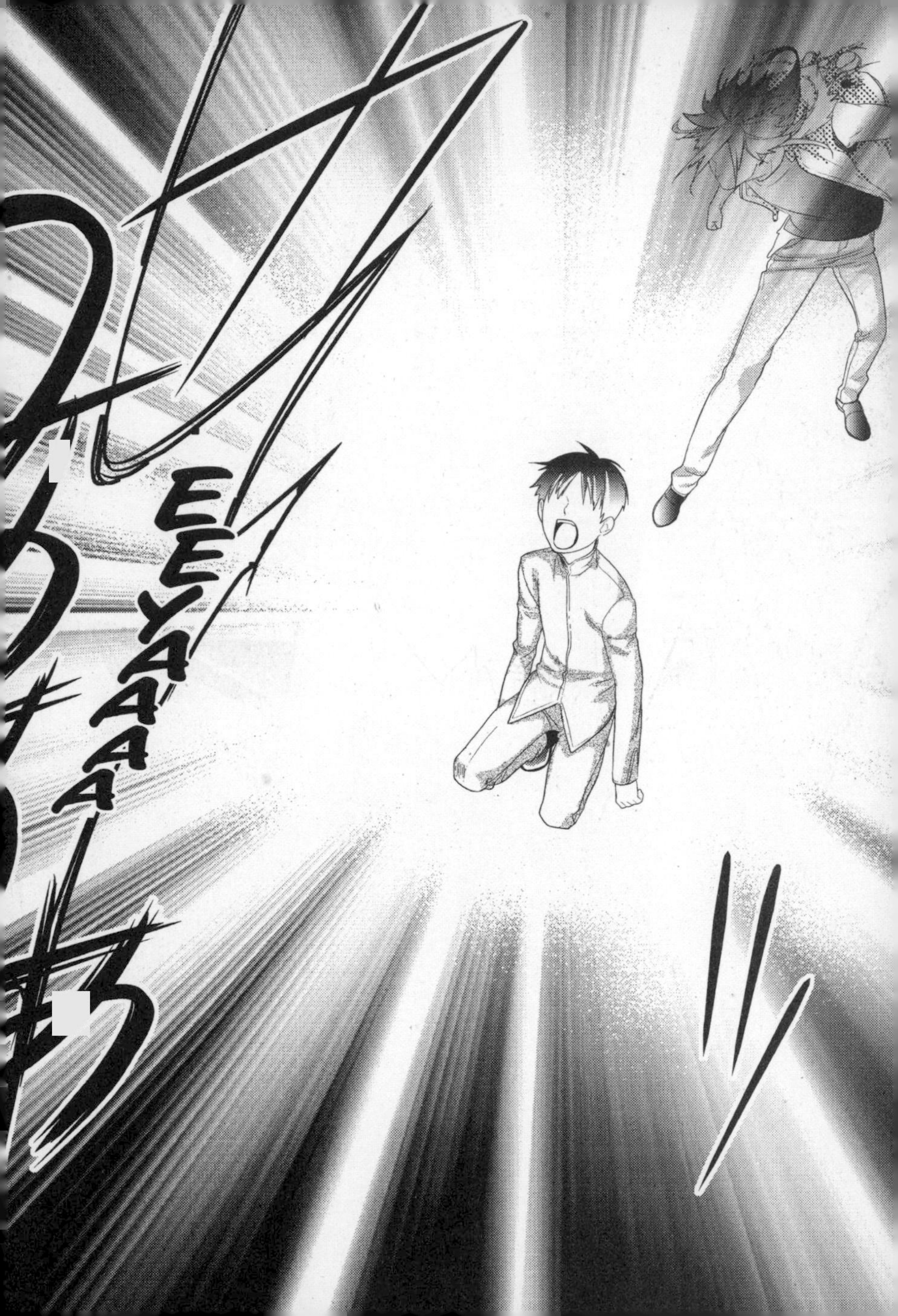
EEYAAAA

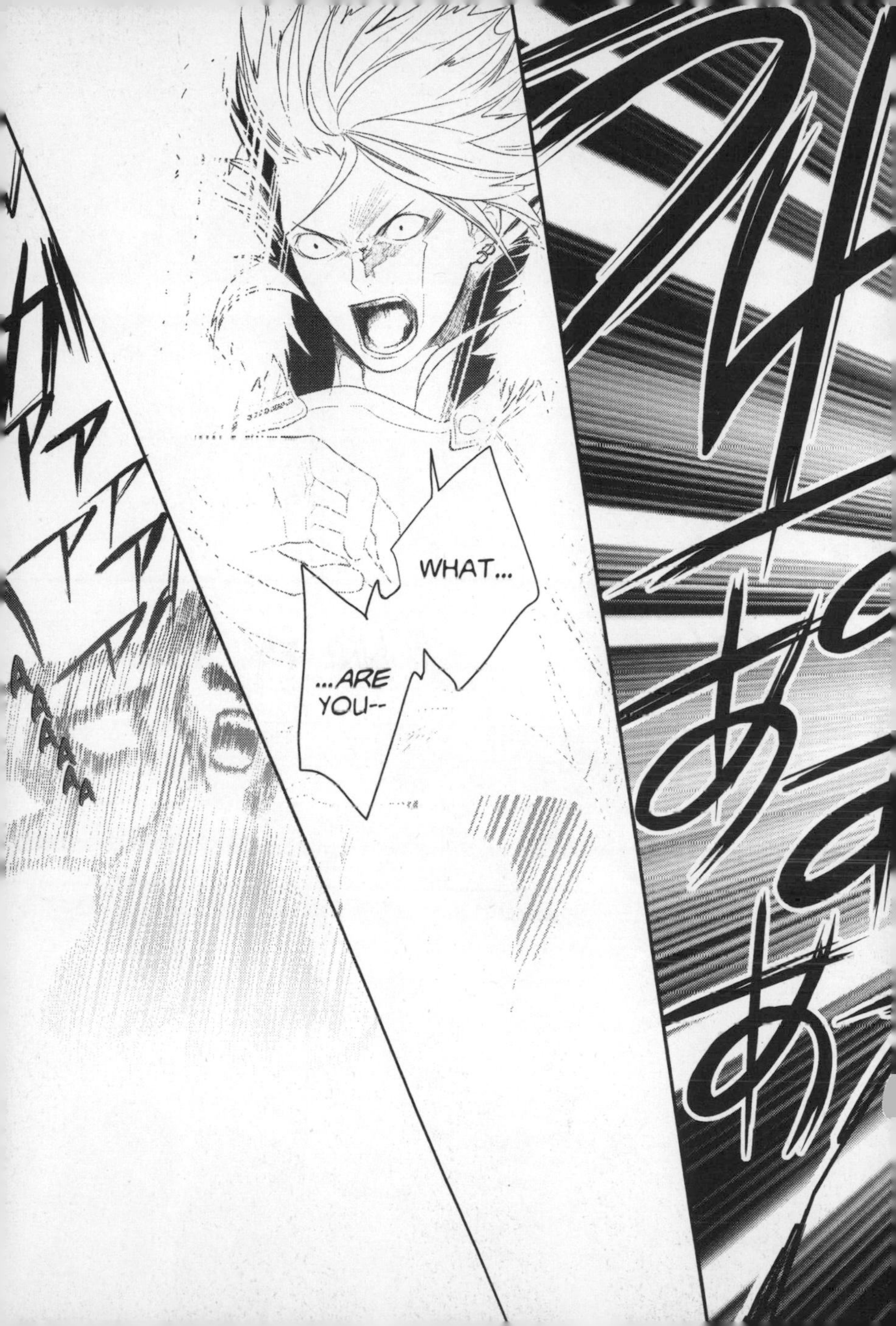
WHAT...
...ARE YOU--

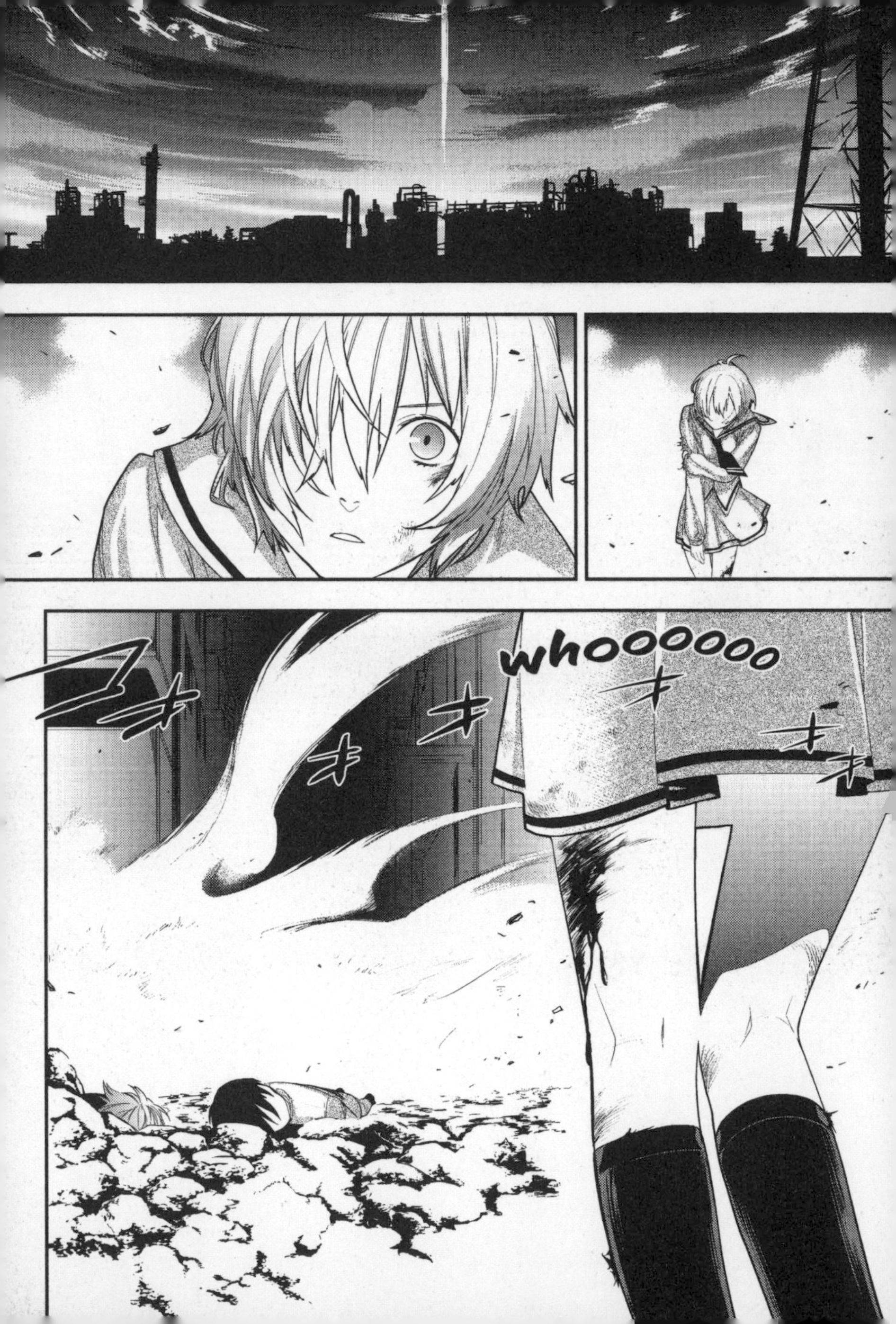
whooooooo

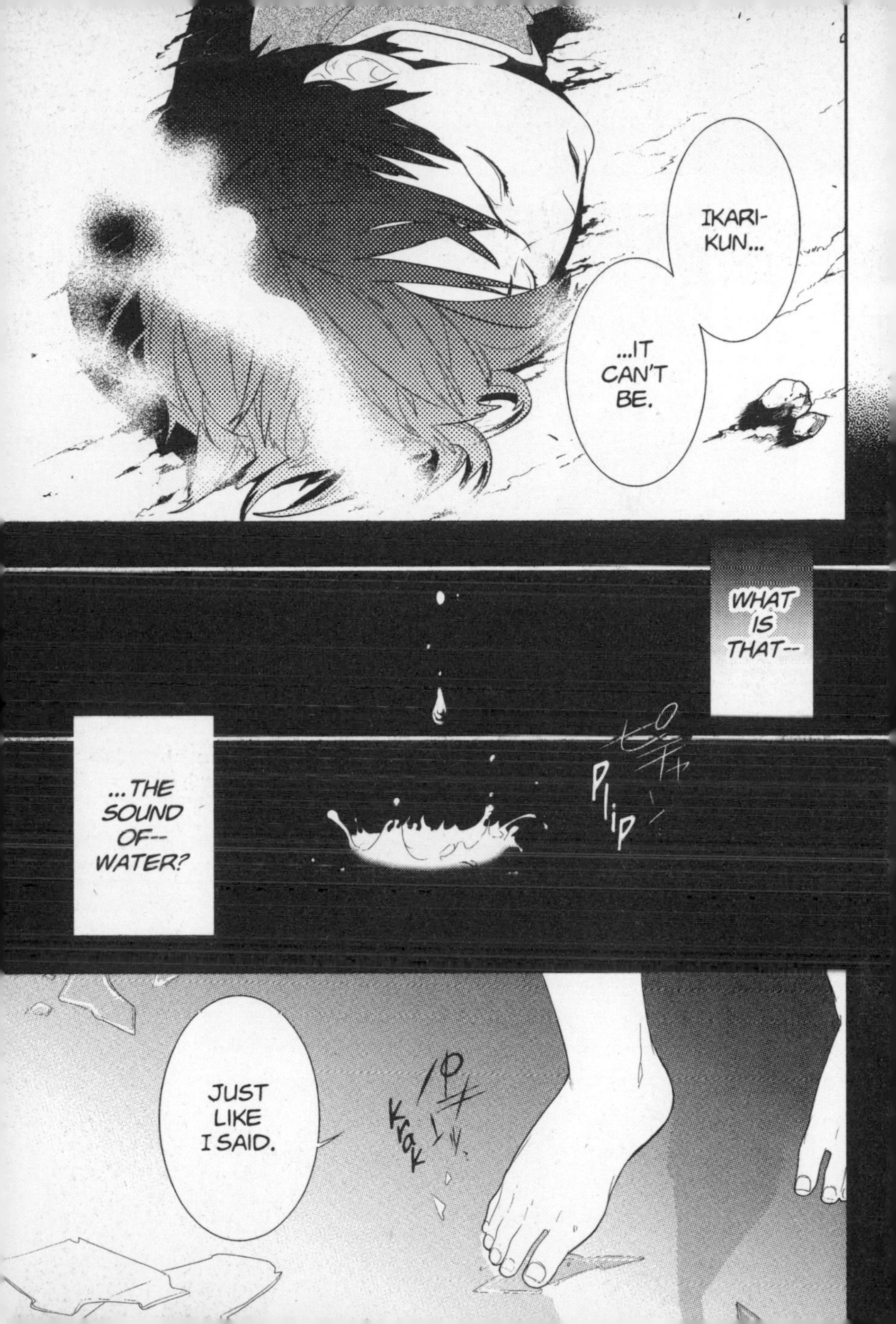
IKARI-KUN...
...IT CAN'T BE.
WHAT IS THAT--
...THE SOUND OF-- WATER?
Plip
JUST LIKE I SAID.
Krak

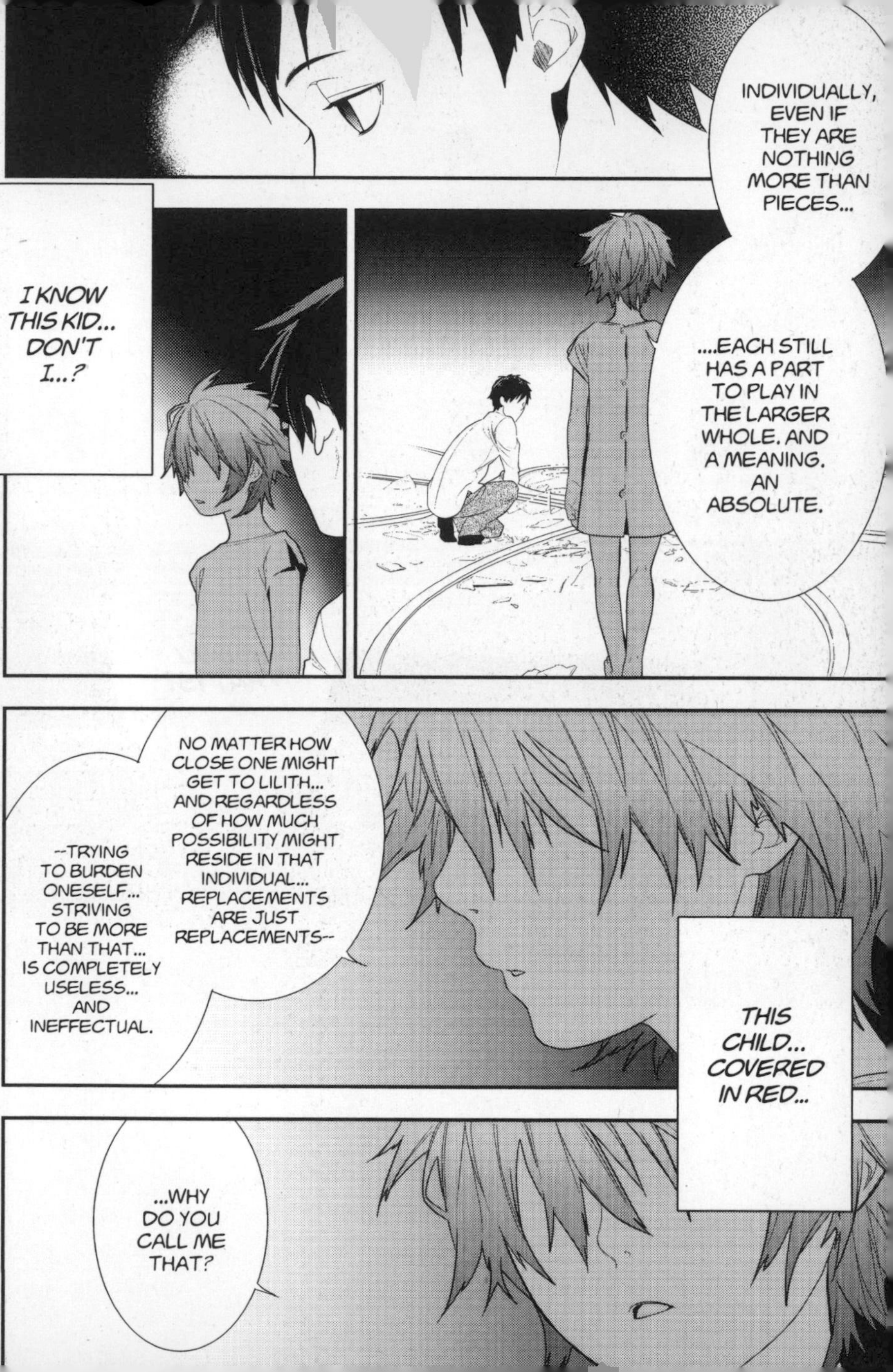
INDIVIDUALLY, EVEN IF THEY ARE NOTHING MORE THAN PIECES...
....EACH STILL HAS A PART TO PLAY IN THE LARGER WHOLE. AND A MEANING. AN ABSOLUTE.
I KNOW THIS KID... DON'T I...?
NO MATTER HOW CLOSE ONE MIGHT GET TO LILITH... AND REGARDLESS OF HOW MUCH POSSIBILITY MIGHT RESIDE IN THAT INDIVIDUAL... REPLACEMENTS ARE JUST REPLACEMENTS--
--TRYING TO BURDEN ONESELF... STRIVING TO BE MORE THAN THAT... IS COMPLETELY USELESS... AND INEFFECTUAL.
THIS CHILD... COVERED IN RED...
...WHY DO YOU CALL ME THAT?

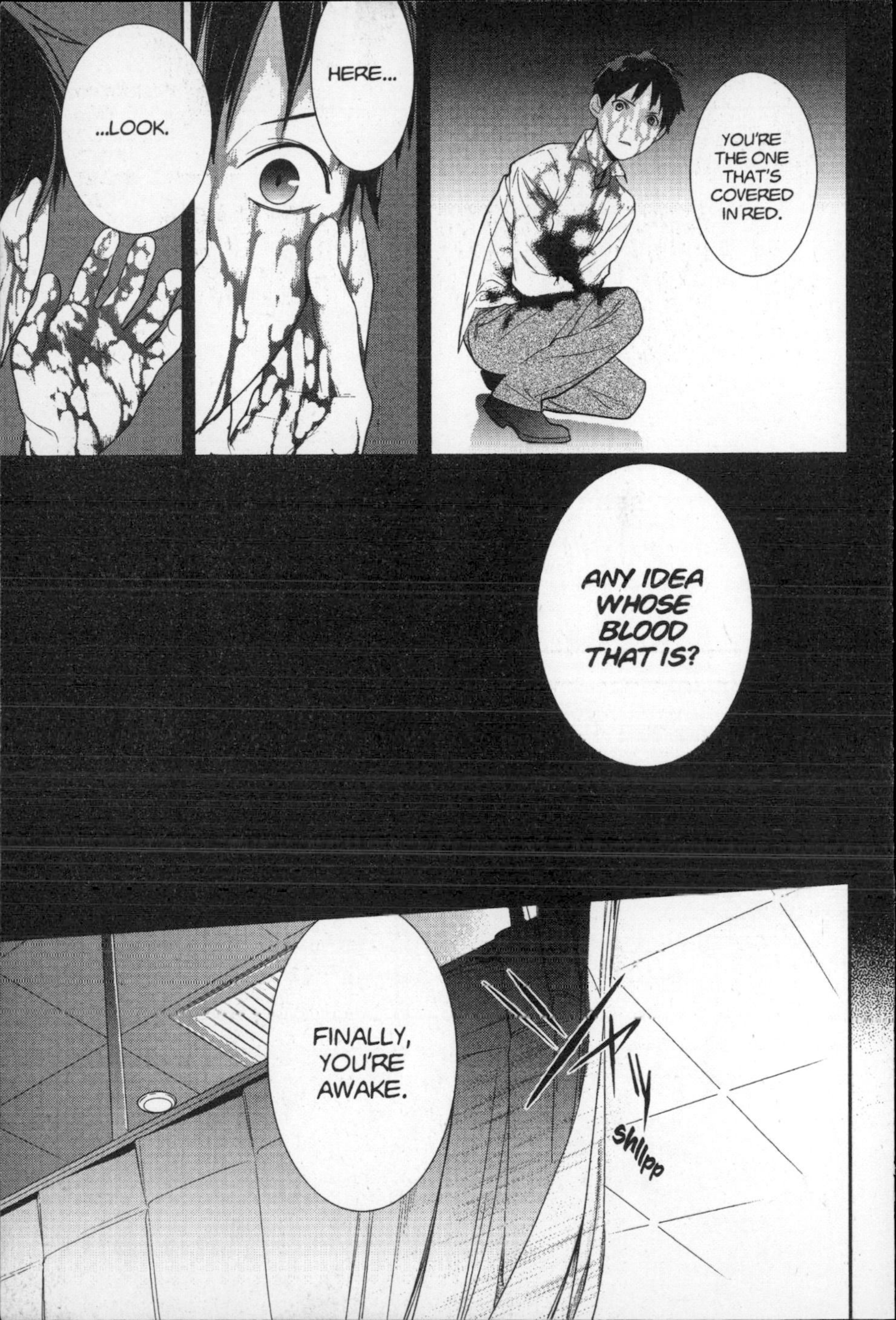
YOU'RE THE ONE THAT'S COVERED IN RED.
HERE...
...LOOK.
ANY IDEA WHOSE BLOOD THAT IS?
FINALLY, YOU'RE AWAKE.
shllpp

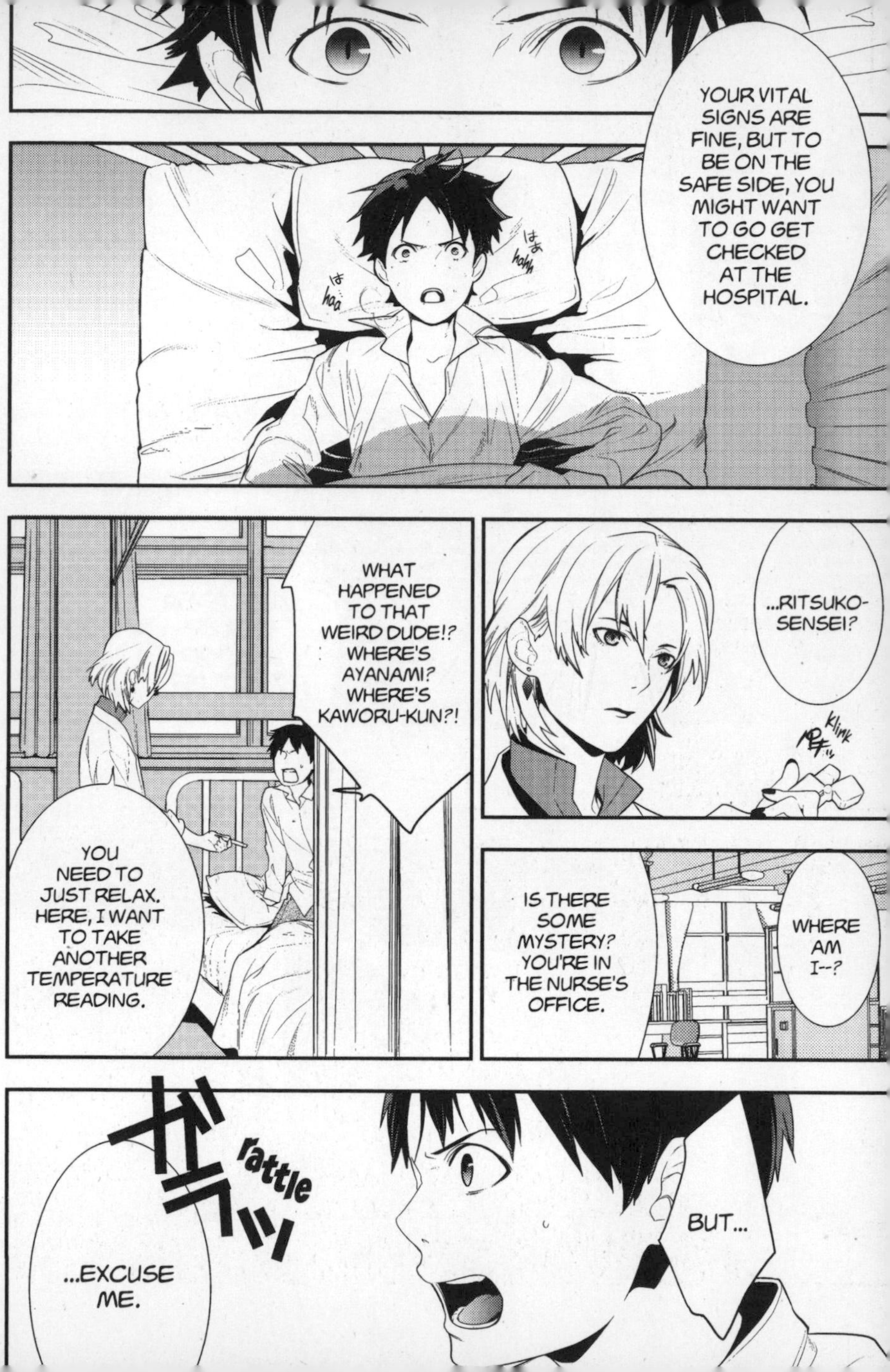
YOUR VITAL SIGNS ARE FINE, BUT TO BE ON THE SAFE SIDE, YOU MIGHT WANT TO GO GET CHECKED AT THE HOSPITAL.
はぁ hahh
は… haa
...RITSUKO-SENSEI?
Klink
WHERE AM I--?
IS THERE SOME MYSTERY? YOU'RE IN THE NURSE'S OFFICE.
WHAT HAPPENED TO THAT WEIRD DUDE!? WHERE'S AYANAMI? WHERE'S KAWORU-KUN?!
YOU NEED TO JUST RELAX. HERE, I WANT TO TAKE ANOTHER TEMPERATURE READING.
BUT...
rattle
...EXCUSE ME.

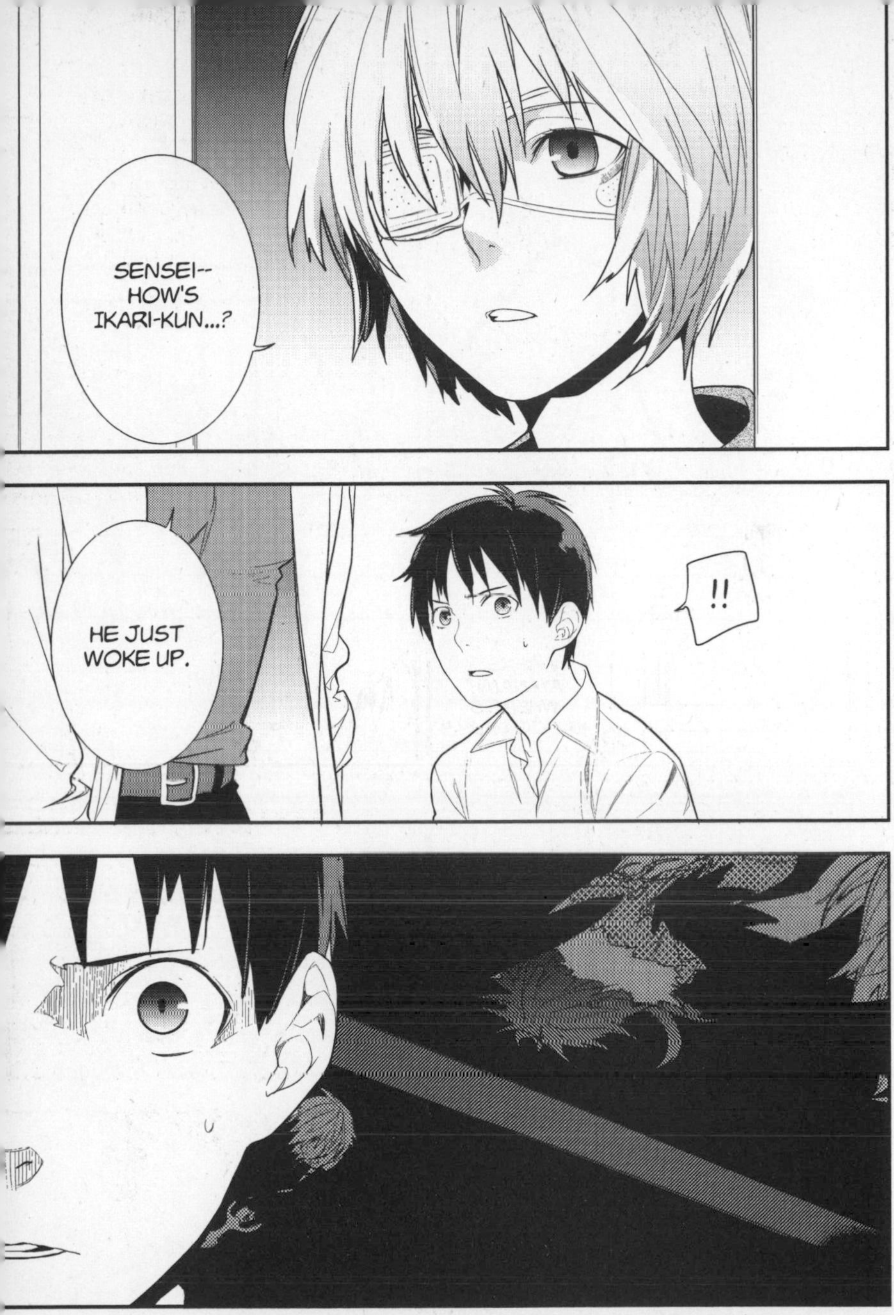
SENSEI-- HOW'S IKARI-KUN...?
!!
HE JUST WOKE UP.

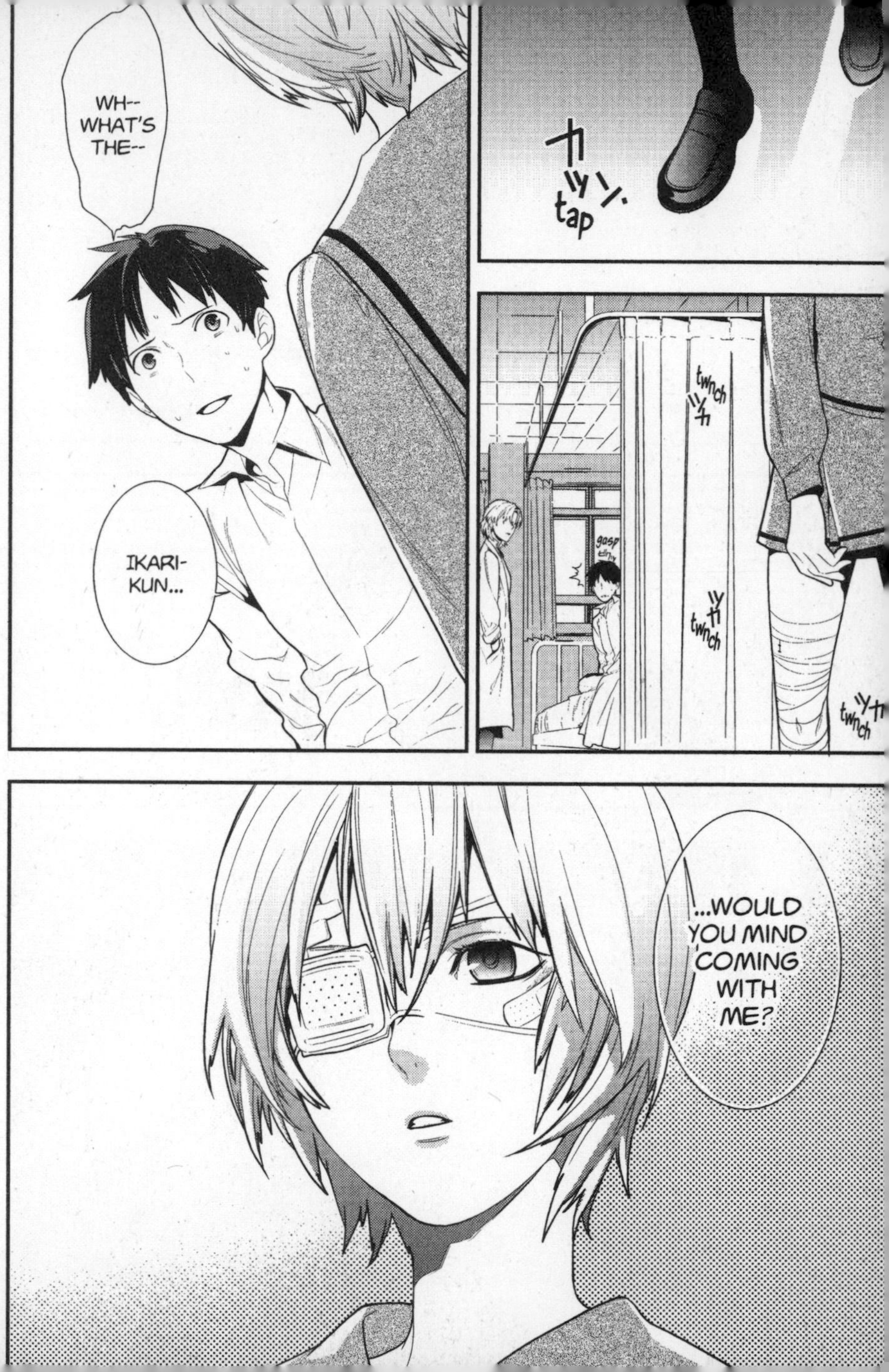
カッン
tap
twnch
ツカ
gasp
ツカ
twnch
ツカ
twnch
WH-- WHAT'S THE--
IKARI-KUN...
...WOULD YOU MIND COMING WITH ME?

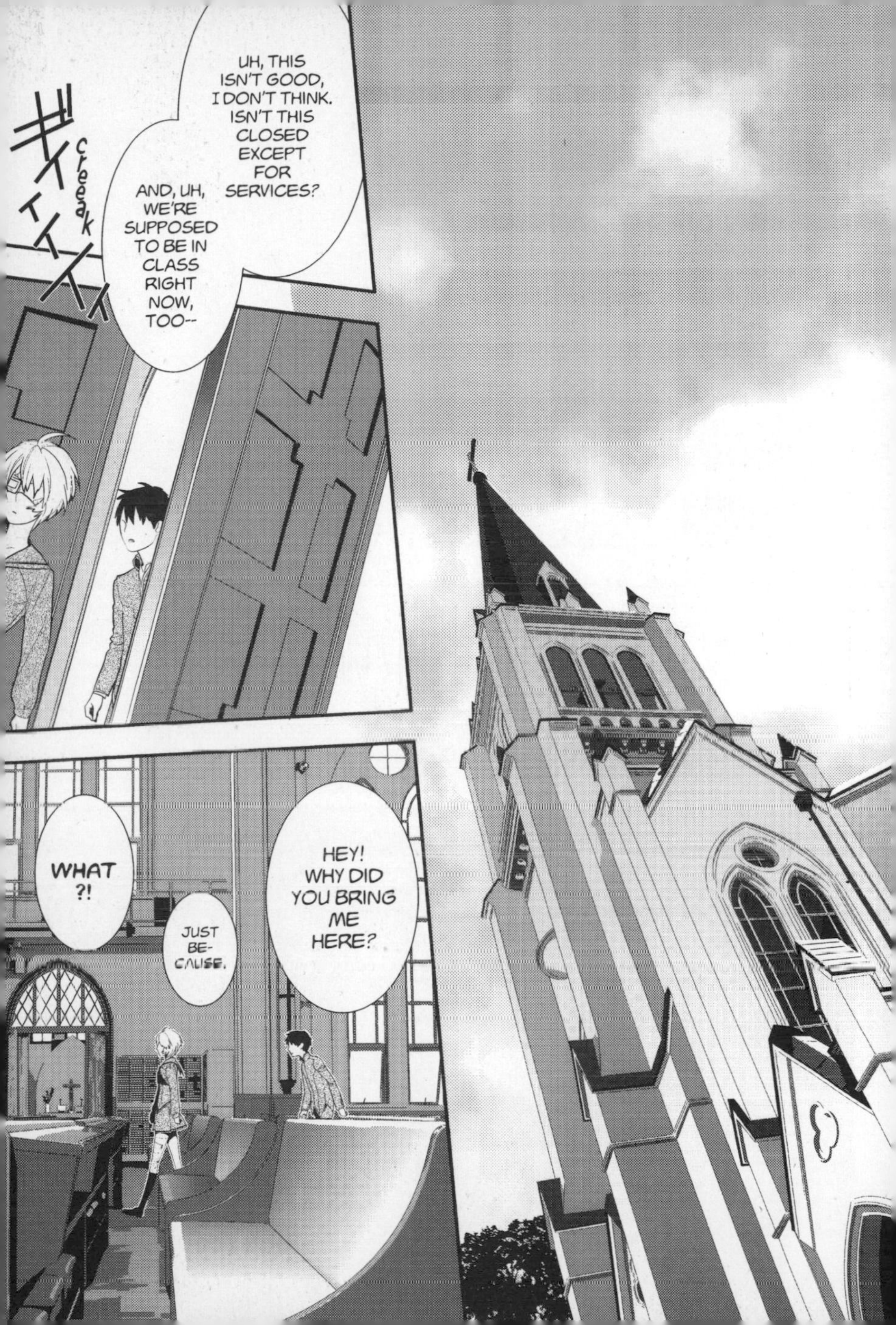
UH, THIS ISN'T GOOD, I DON'T THINK. ISN'T THIS CLOSED EXCEPT FOR SERVICES?
AND, UH, WE'RE SUPPOSED TO BE IN CLASS RIGHT NOW, TOO--
ギイイイイ
creeak
HEY! WHY DID YOU BRING ME HERE?
JUST BE-CAUSE.
WHAT?!

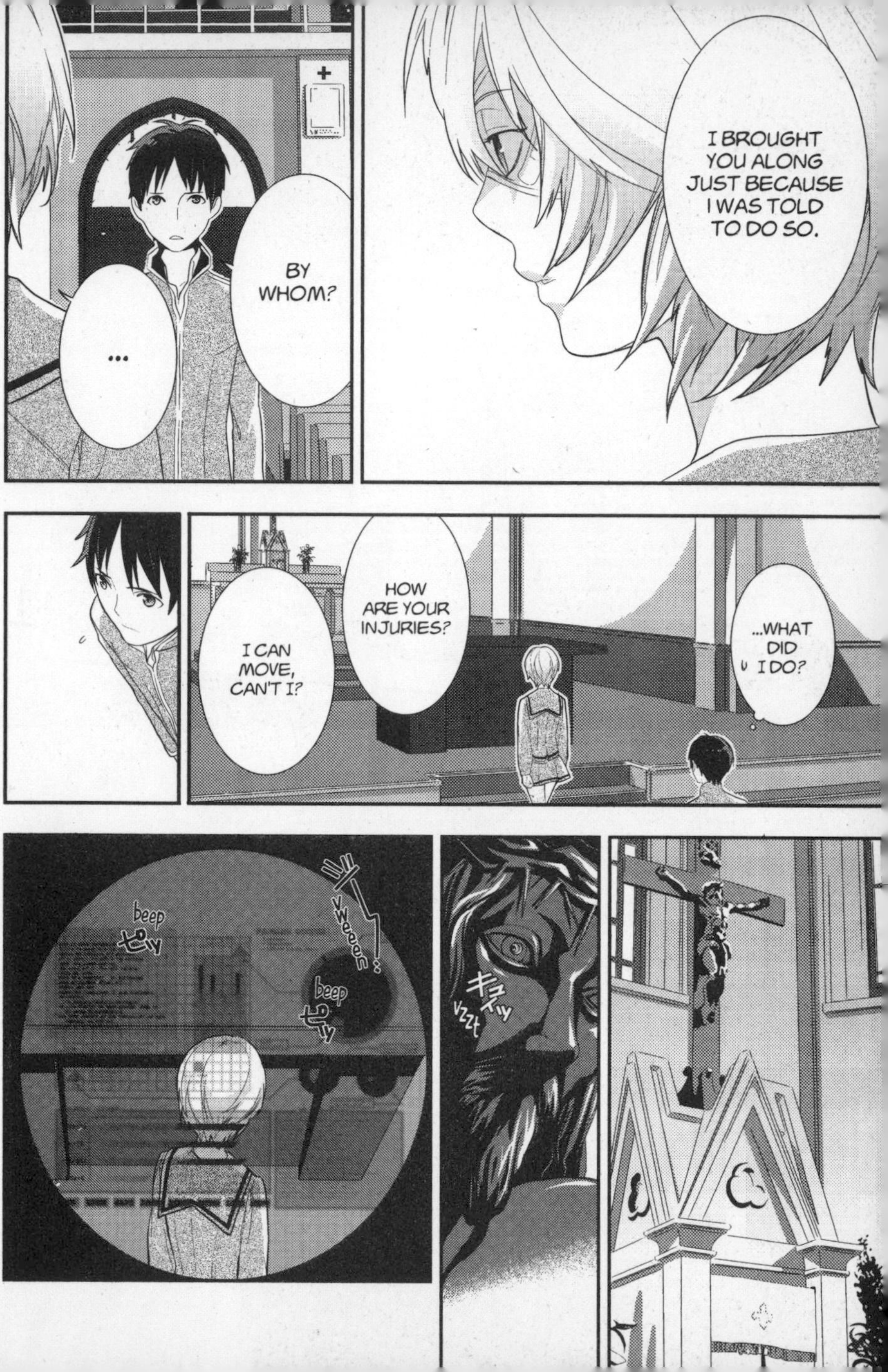
I BROUGHT YOU ALONG JUST BECAUSE I WAS TOLD TO DO SO.
BY WHOM?
...
...WHAT DID I DO?
HOW ARE YOUR INJURIES?
I CAN MOVE, CAN'T I?
キュイッ
vzzt
vweeen
beep
ピッ
beep
ピッ

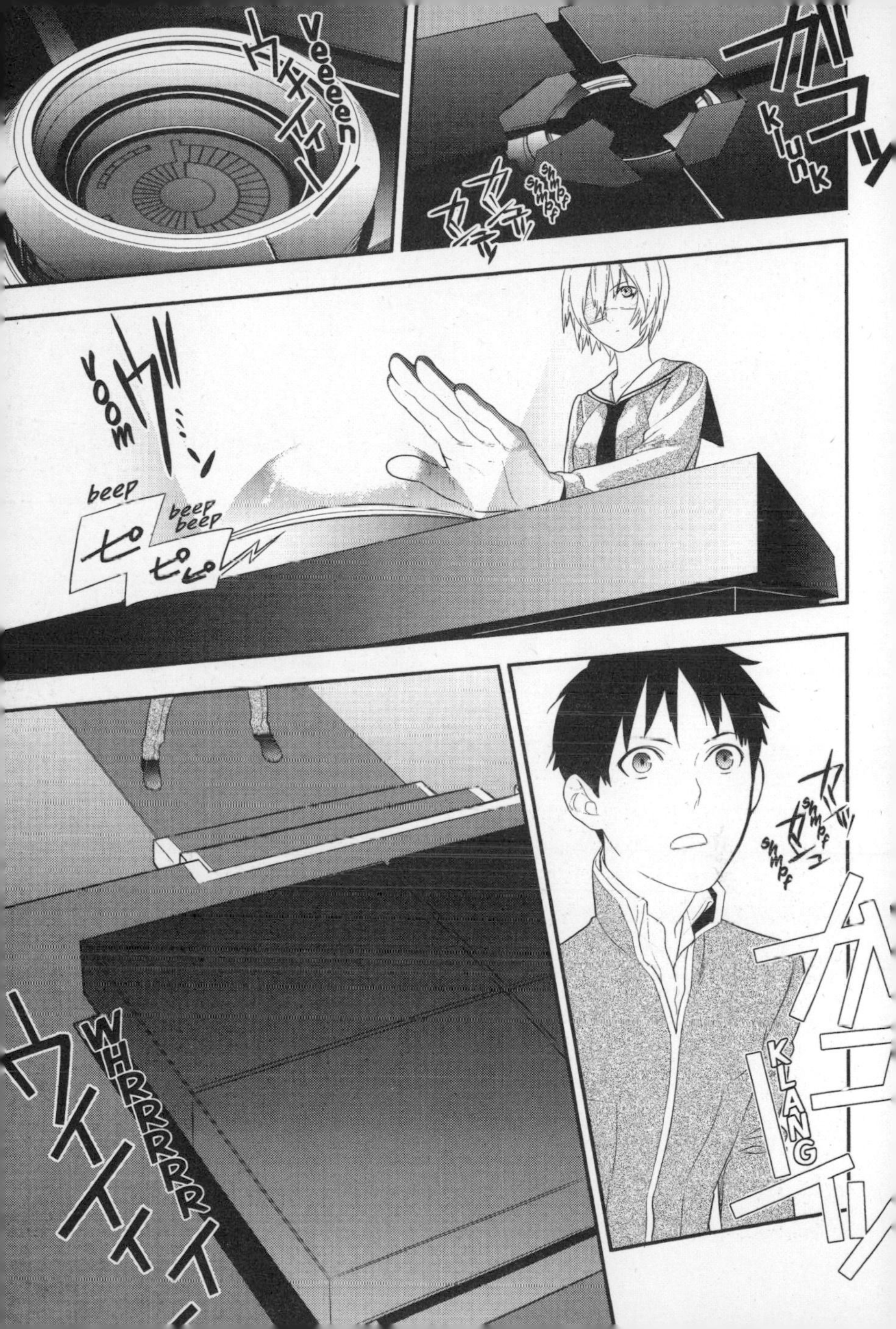
ガコッ
klunk
smmpf smmpf
veeeeen
voom
beep
beep beep
ピ ピピ
smmpf smmpf
KLANG
WHRRRRRR
ウィイイイ

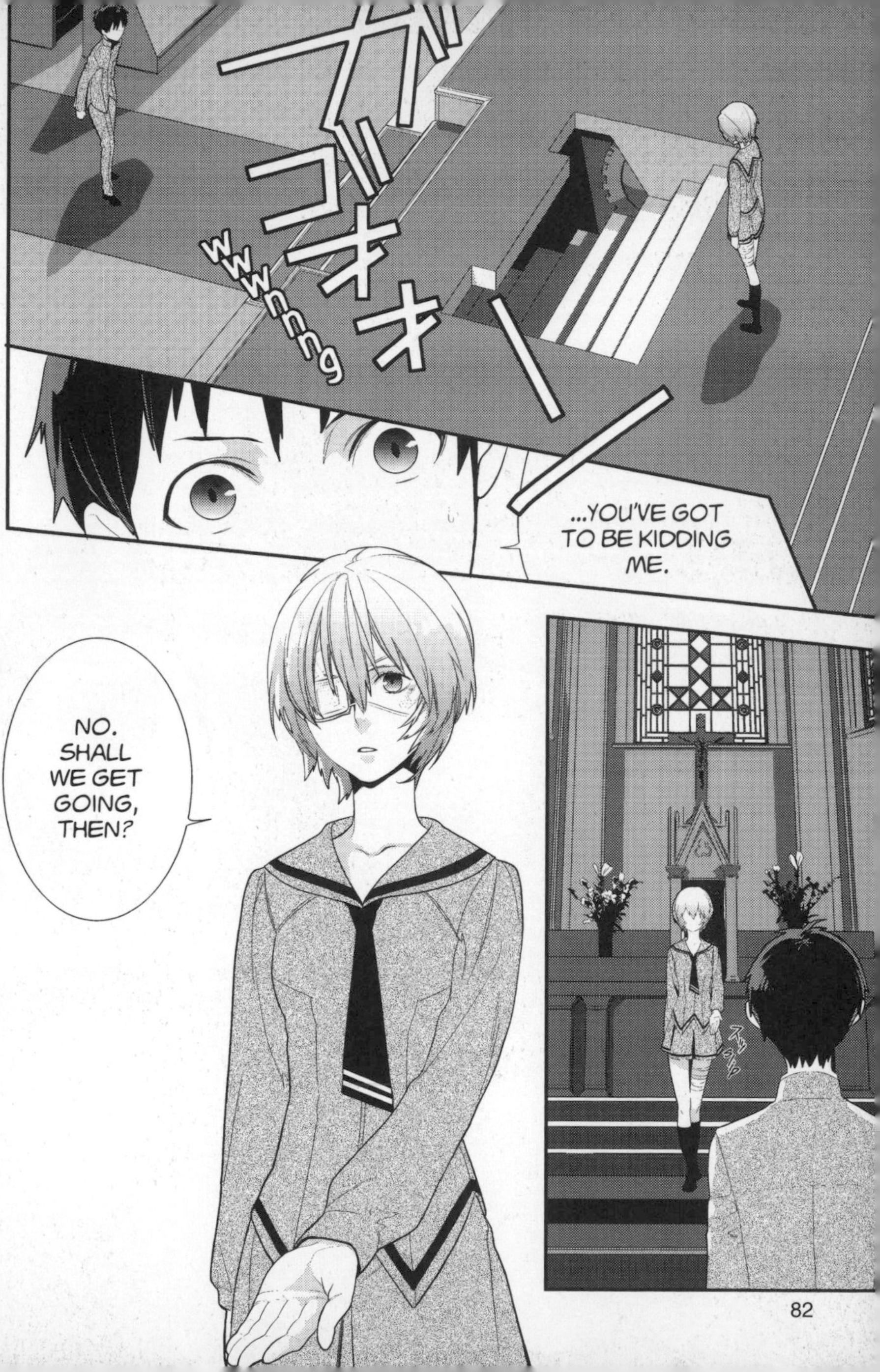
ガコォォー
WWWNNNG
...YOU'VE GOT TO BE KIDDING ME.
NO. SHALL WE GET GOING, THEN?

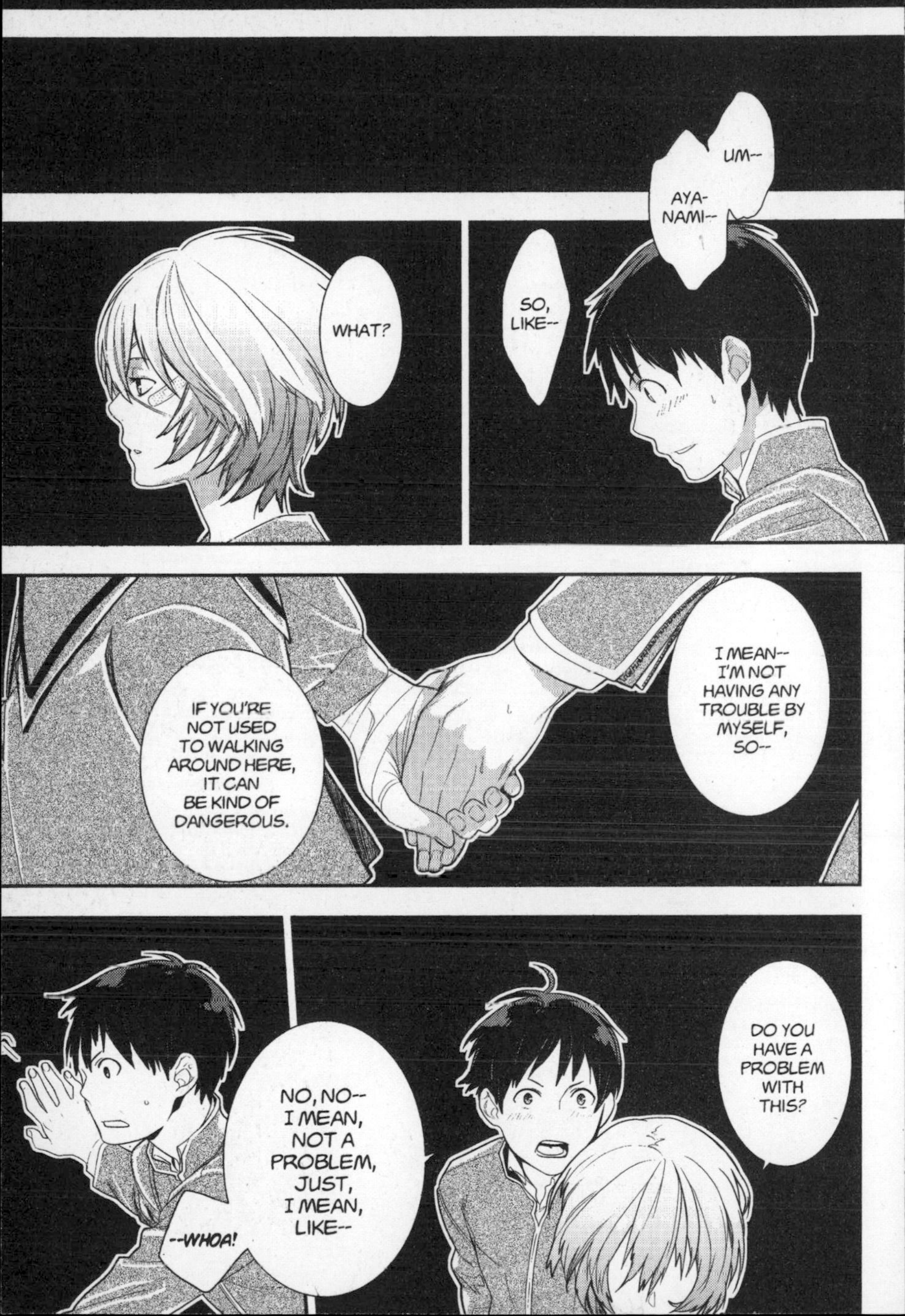
UM--
AYA-NAMI--
SO, LIKE--
WHAT?
I MEAN-- I'M NOT HAVING ANY TROUBLE BY MYSELF, SO--
IF YOU'RE NOT USED TO WALKING AROUND HERE, IT CAN BE KIND OF DANGEROUS.
DO YOU HAVE A PROBLEM WITH THIS?
NO, NO-- I MEAN, NOT A PROBLEM, JUST, I MEAN, LIKE--
--WHOA!

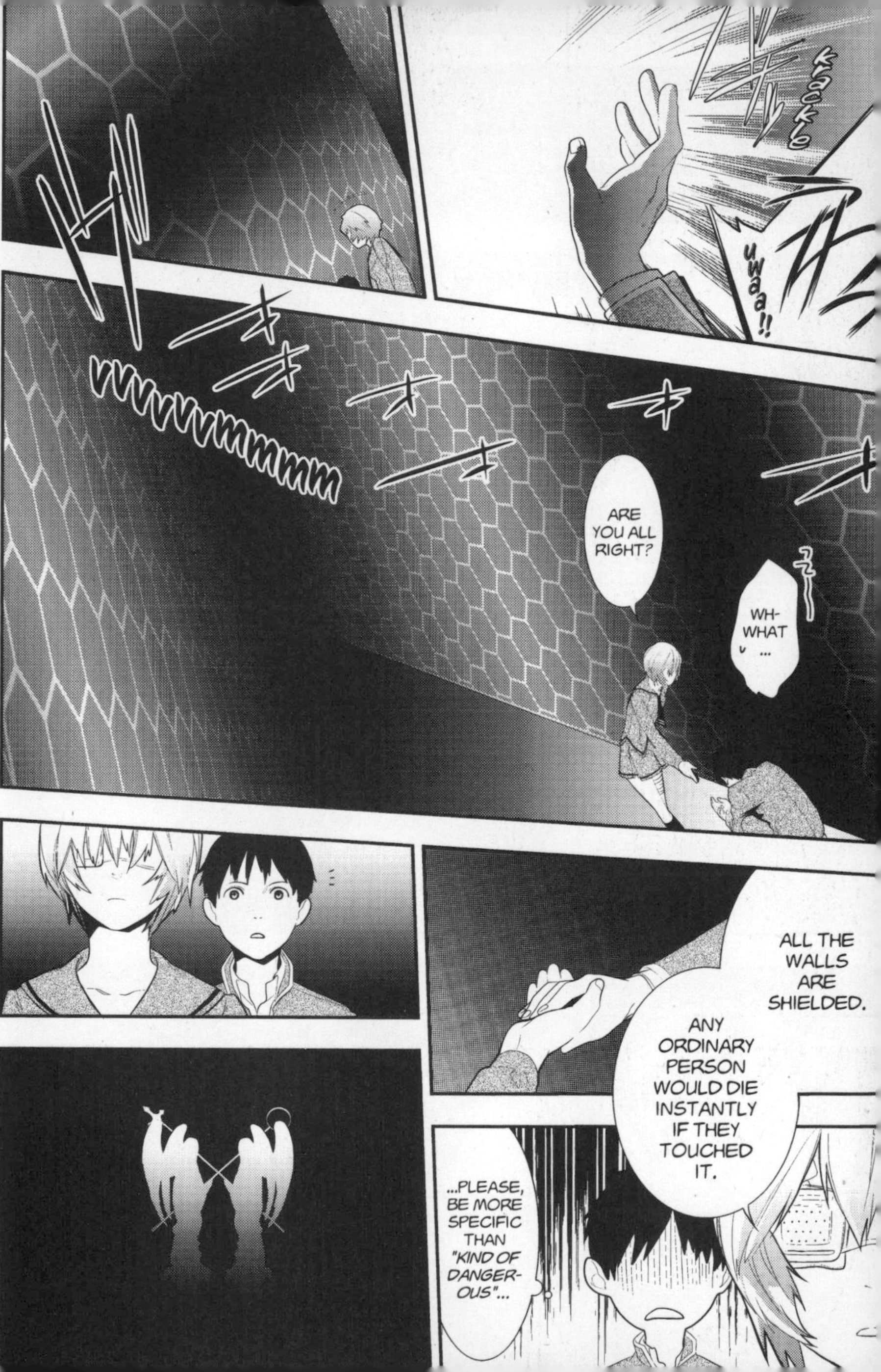
krackle
uwaa!!
vvvvvvmmmmm
ARE YOU ALL RIGHT?
WH-WHAT...
ALL THE WALLS ARE SHIELDED.
ANY ORDINARY PERSON WOULD DIE INSTANTLY IF THEY TOUCHED IT.
...PLEASE, BE MORE SPECIFIC THAN "KIND OF DANGEROUS"...

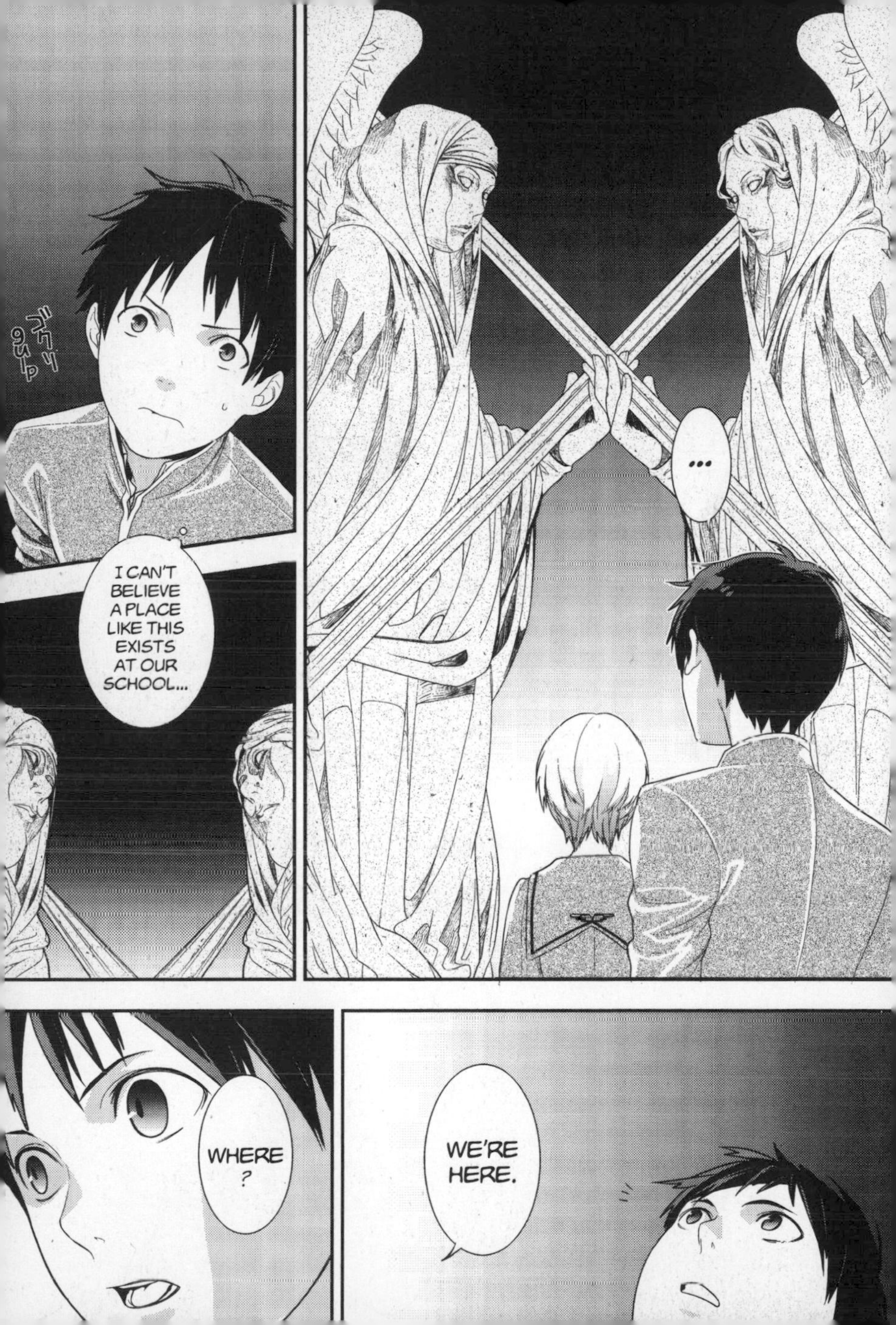
...
ゴクリ
gulp
I CAN'T BELIEVE A PLACE LIKE THIS EXISTS AT OUR SCHOOL...
WE'RE HERE.
WHERE ?

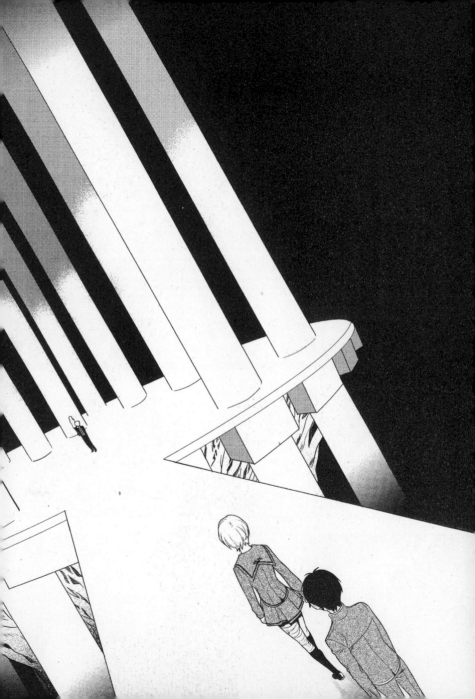

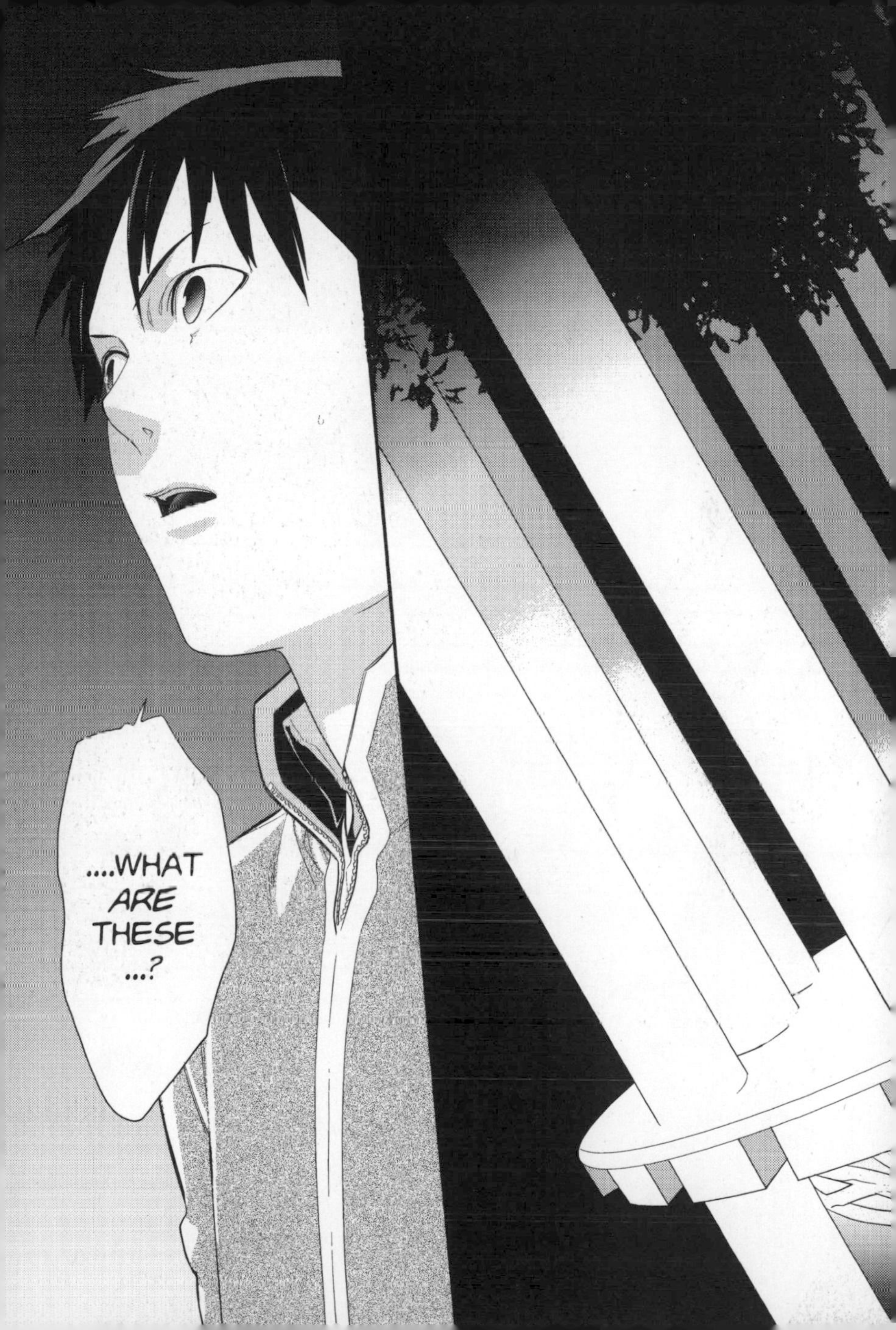
....WHAT ARE THESE ...?

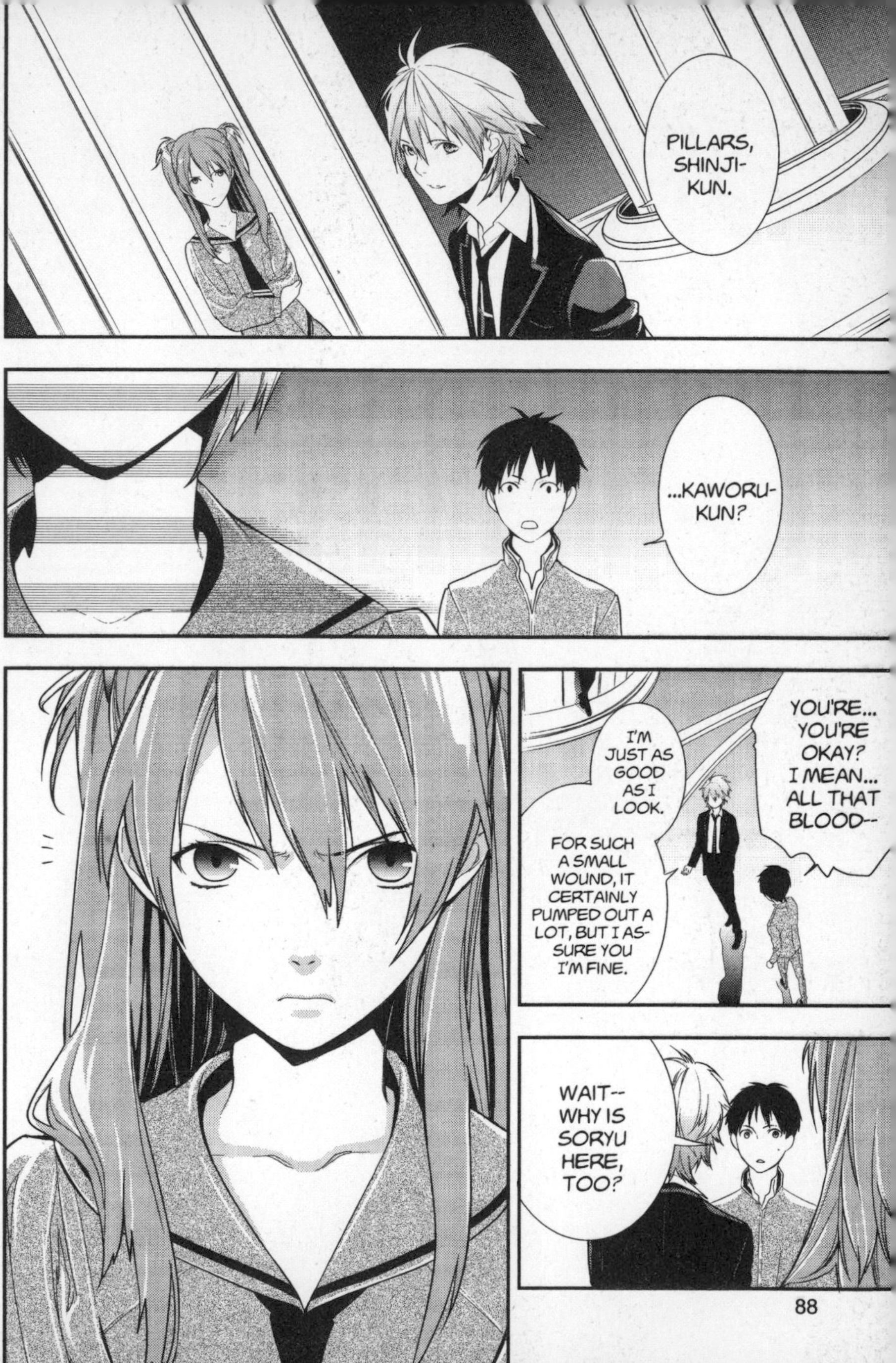
PILLARS, SHINJI-KUN.
...KAWORU-KUN?
YOU'RE... YOU'RE OKAY? I MEAN... ALL THAT BLOOD--
I'M JUST AS GOOD AS I LOOK.
FOR SUCH A SMALL WOUND, IT CERTAINLY PUMPED OUT A LOT, BUT I AS-SURE YOU I'M FINE.
WAIT-- WHY IS SORYU HERE, TOO?

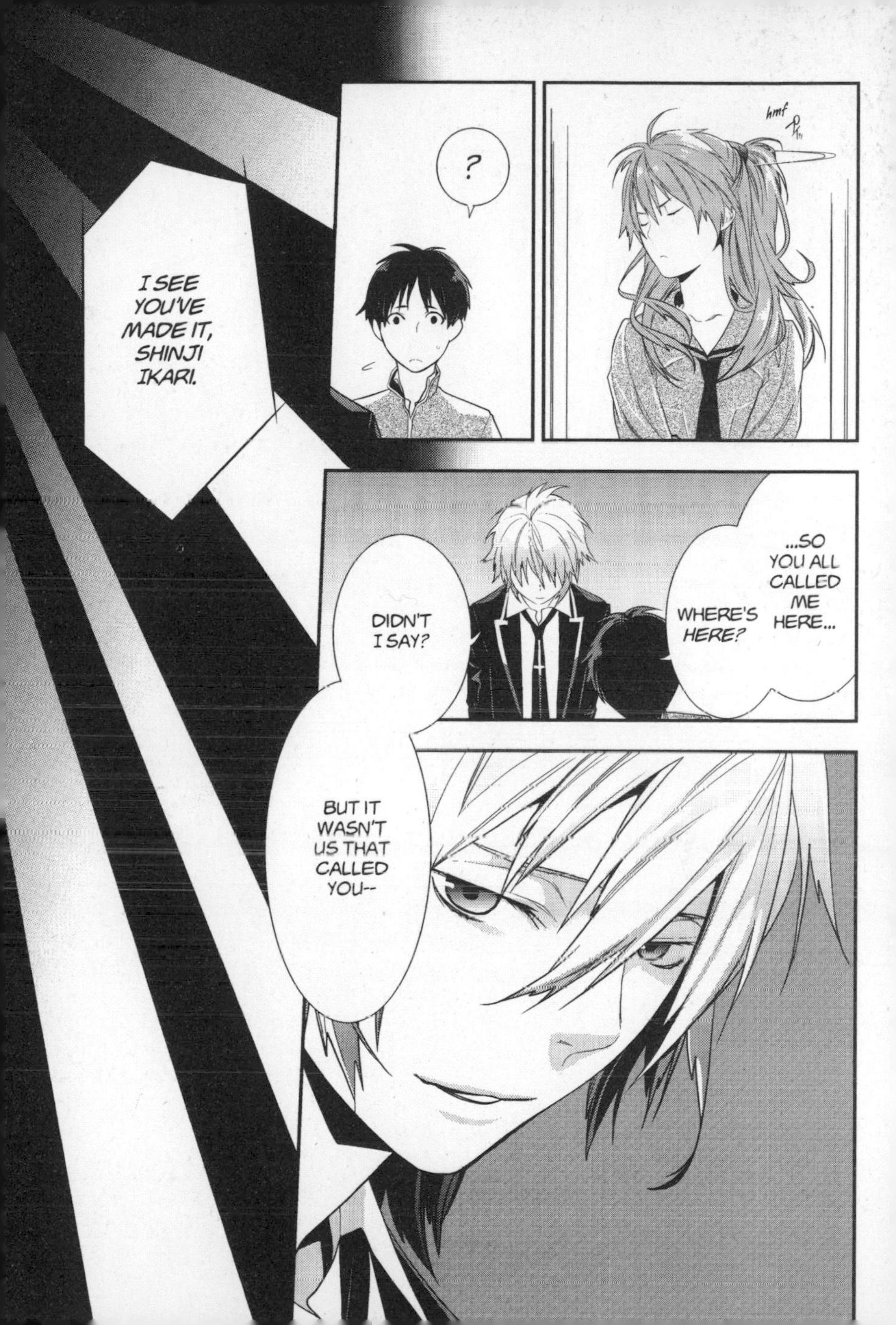
hmf
?
I SEE YOU'VE MADE IT, SHINJI IKARI.
...SO YOU ALL CALLED ME HERE...
WHERE'S HERE?
DIDN'T I SAY?
BUT IT WASN'T US THAT CALLED YOU--

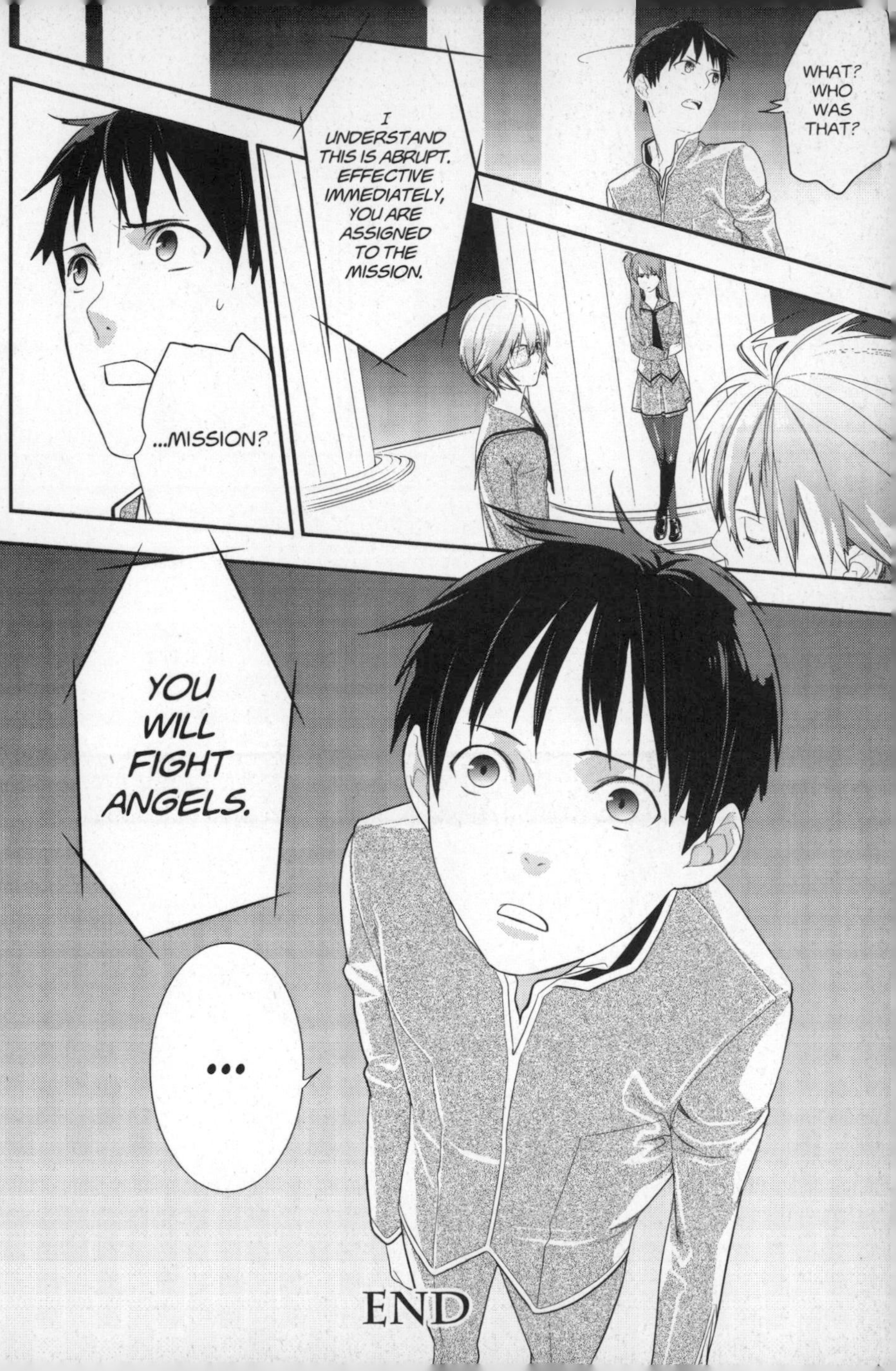
WHAT? WHO WAS THAT?
I UNDERSTAND THIS IS ABRUPT. EFFECTIVE IMMEDIATELY, YOU ARE ASSIGNED TO THE MISSION.
...MISSION?
YOU WILL FIGHT ANGELS.
...
END

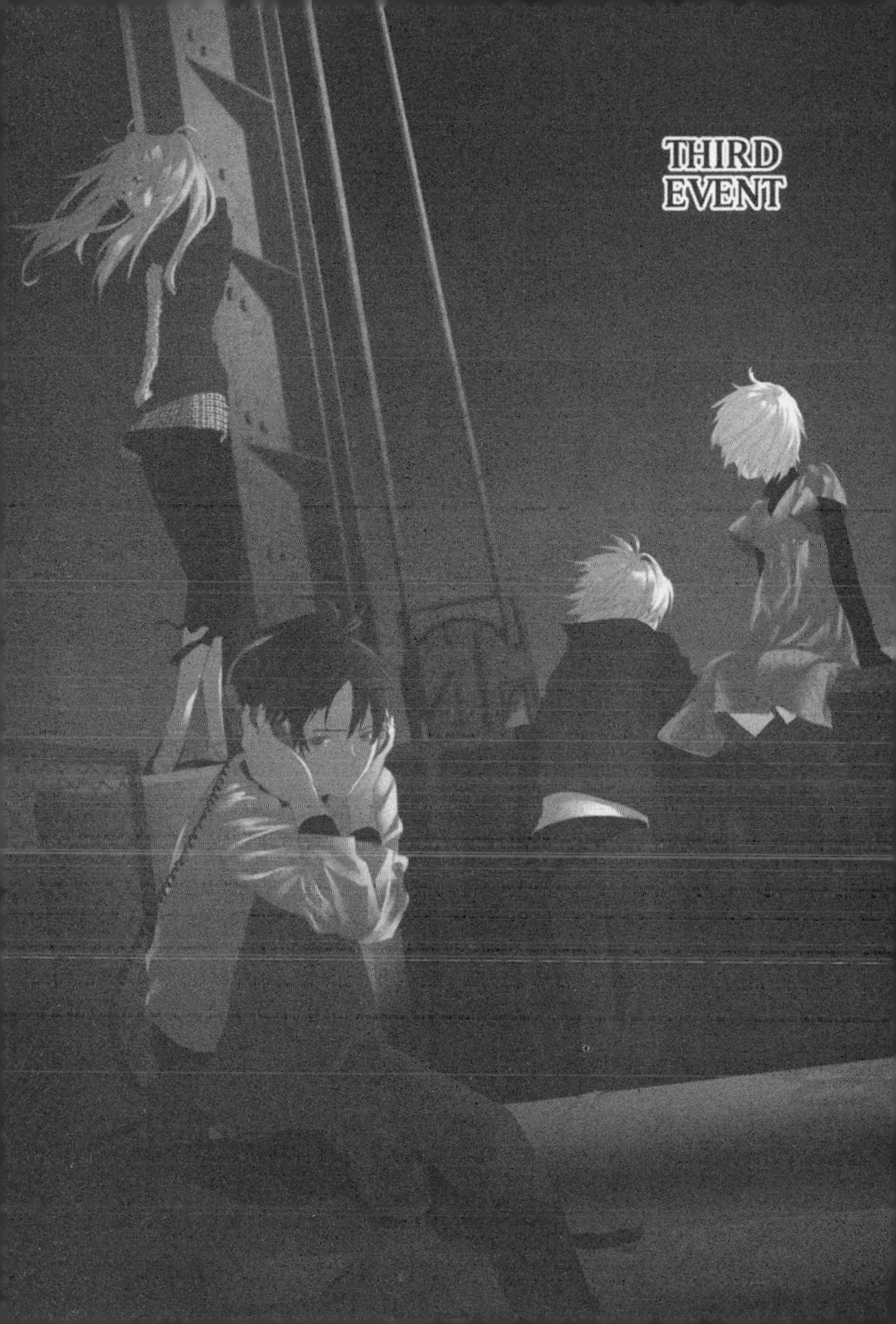
THIRD
EVENT

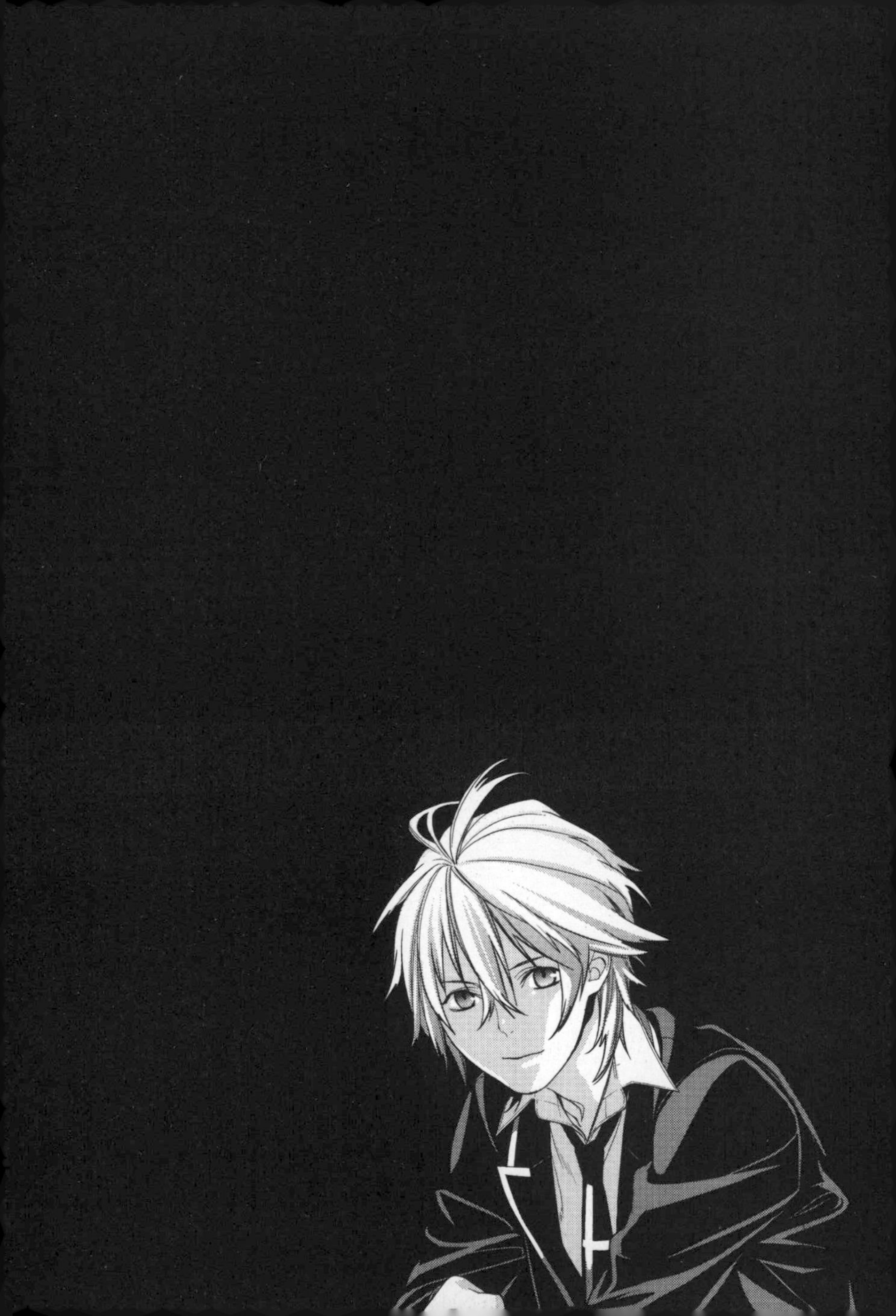

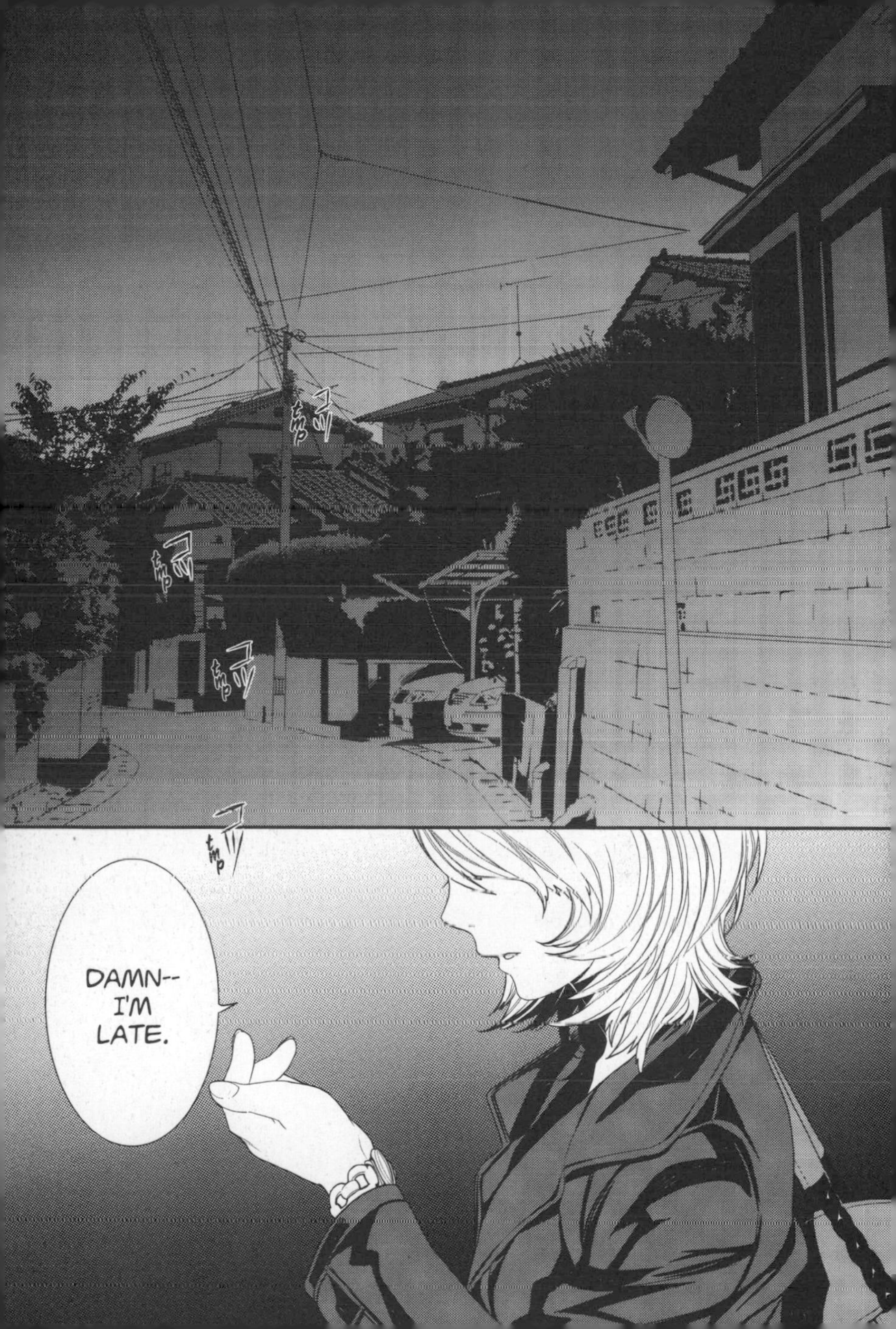
tmp
tmp
tmp
tmp
DAMN-- I'M LATE.

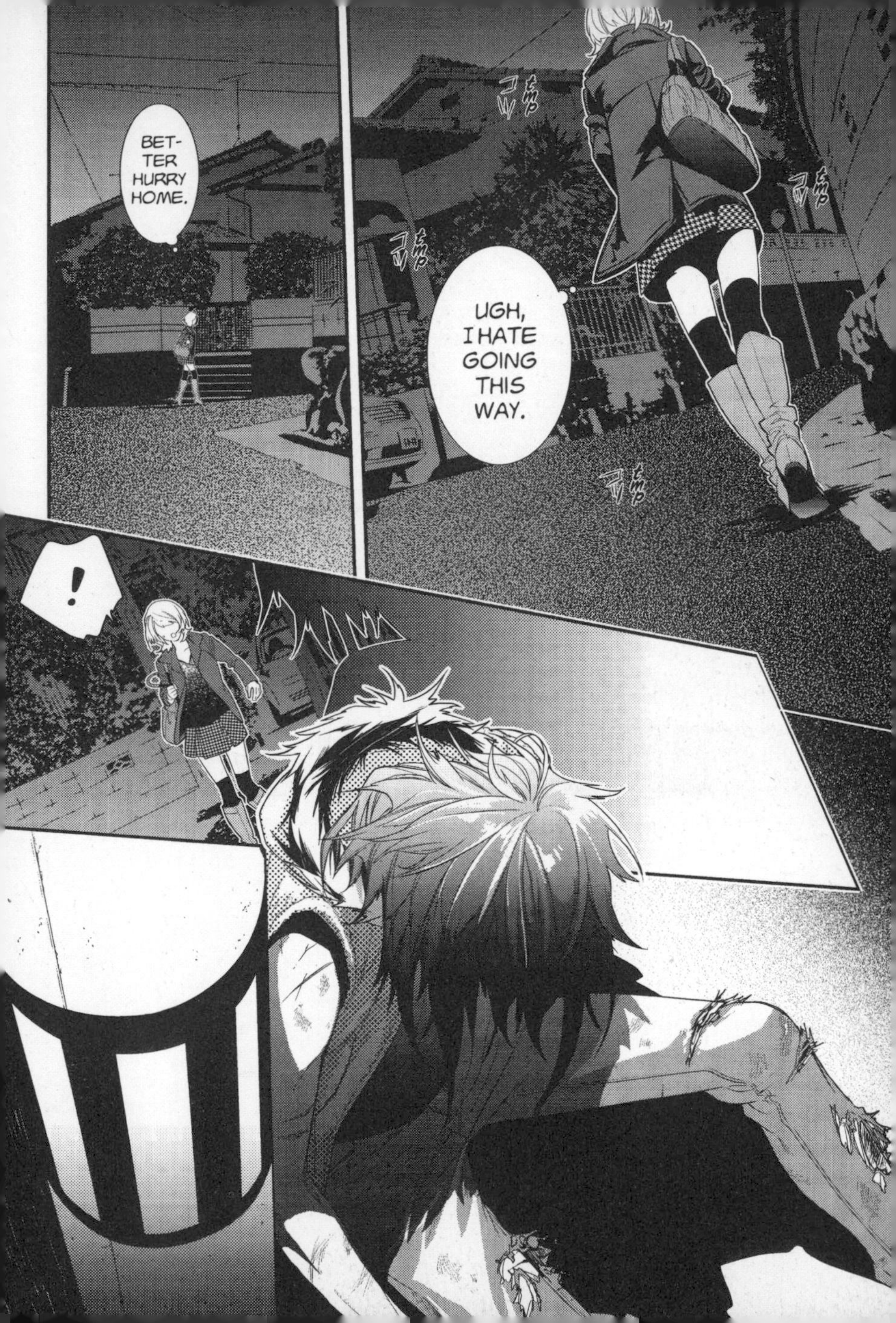
tmp
tmp
tmp
UGH, I HATE GOING THIS WAY.
tmp
BET-TER HURRY HOME.
!

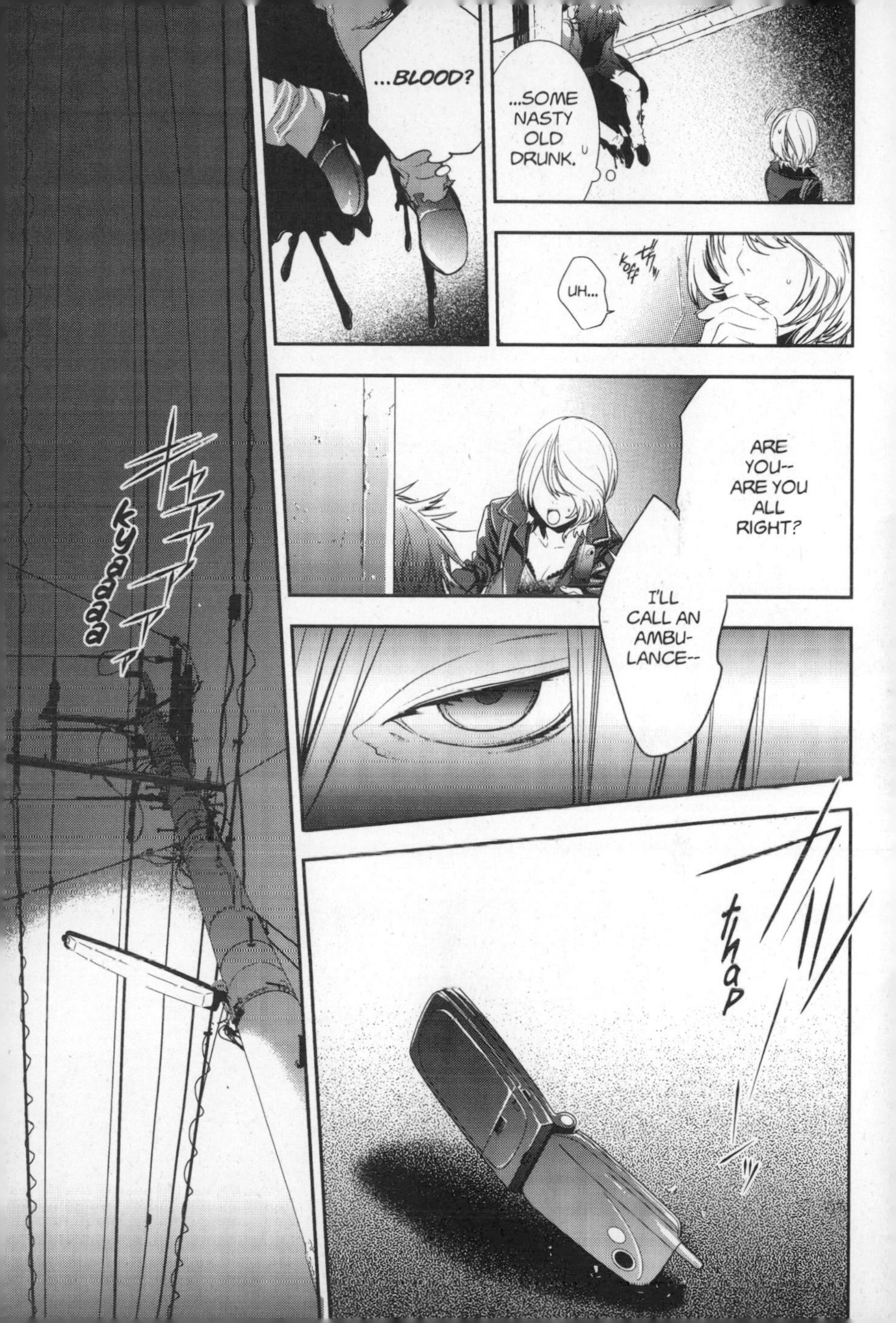
...SOME NASTY OLD DRUNK.
...BLOOD?
koff
UH...
ARE YOU-- ARE YOU ALL RIGHT?
I'LL CALL AN AMBULANCE--
thap
キャアアア
kyaaaaa

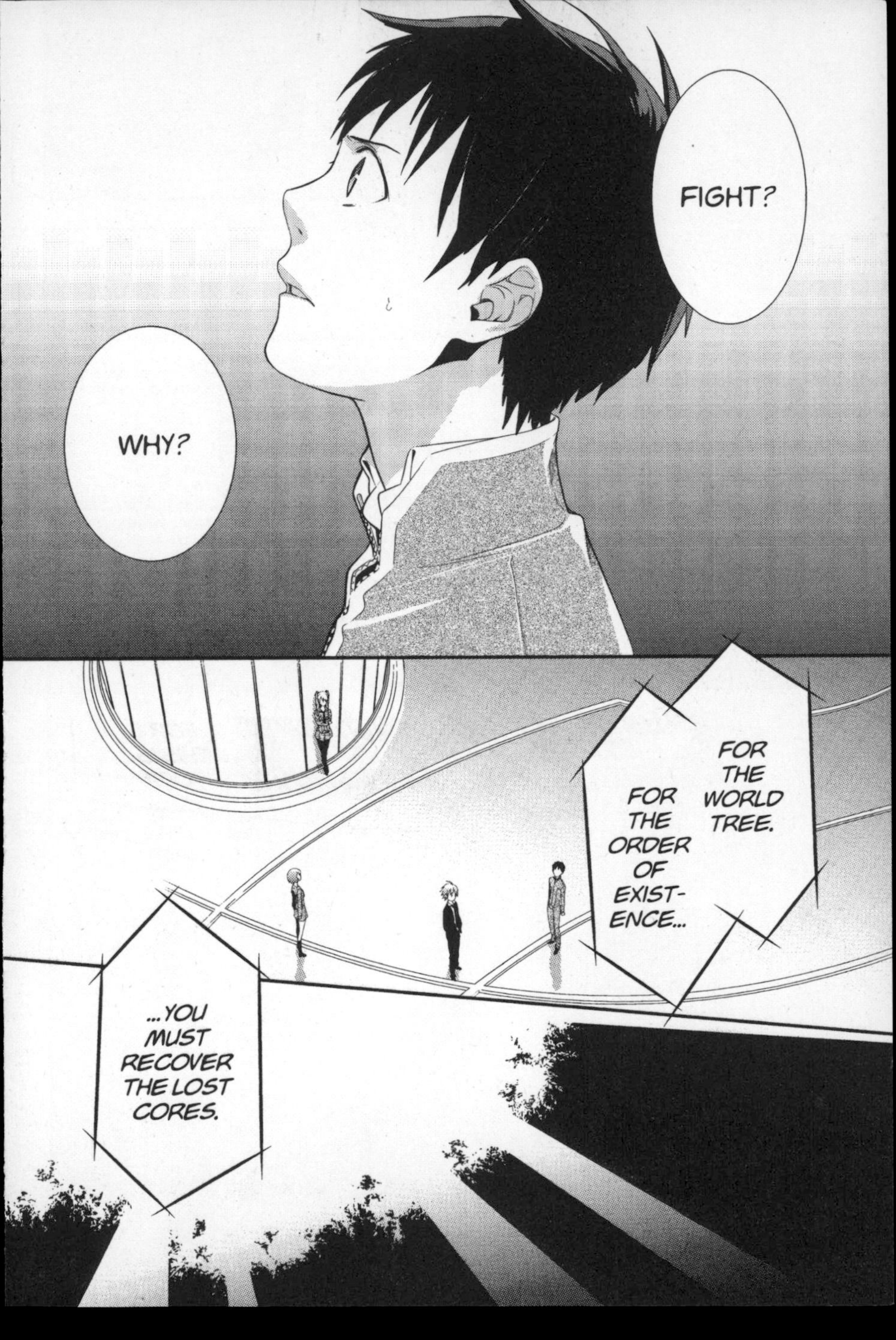
FIGHT?
WHY?
FOR THE WORLD TREE.
FOR THE ORDER OF EXIST-ENCE...
...YOU MUST RECOVER THE LOST CORES.

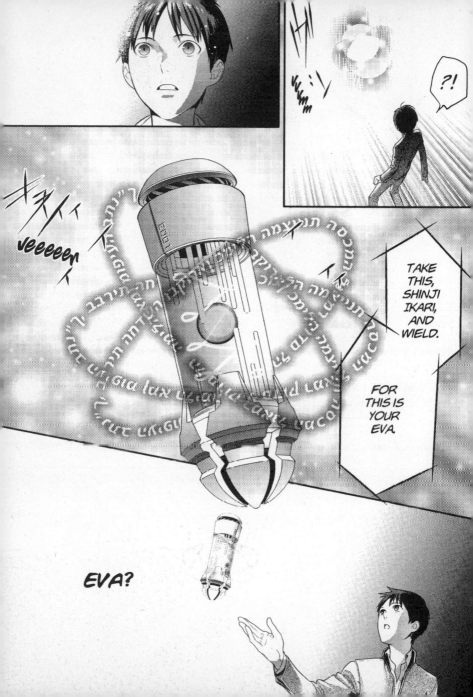

?!

veeeeer

TAKE
THIS,
SHINJI
IKARI,
AND
WIELD.

FOR
THIS
IS
YOUR
EVA.

EVA?

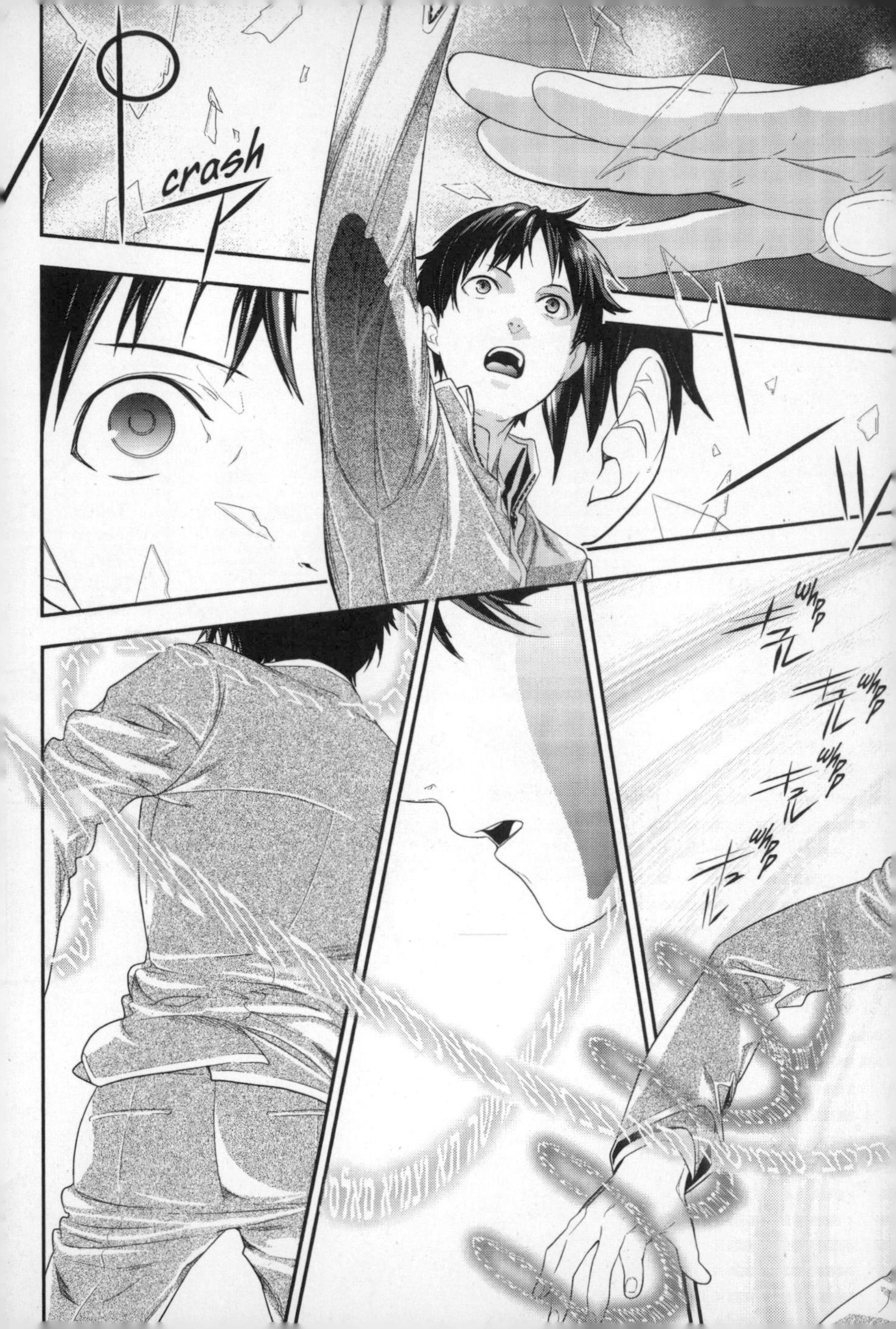
crash
whp
whp
whp
whp

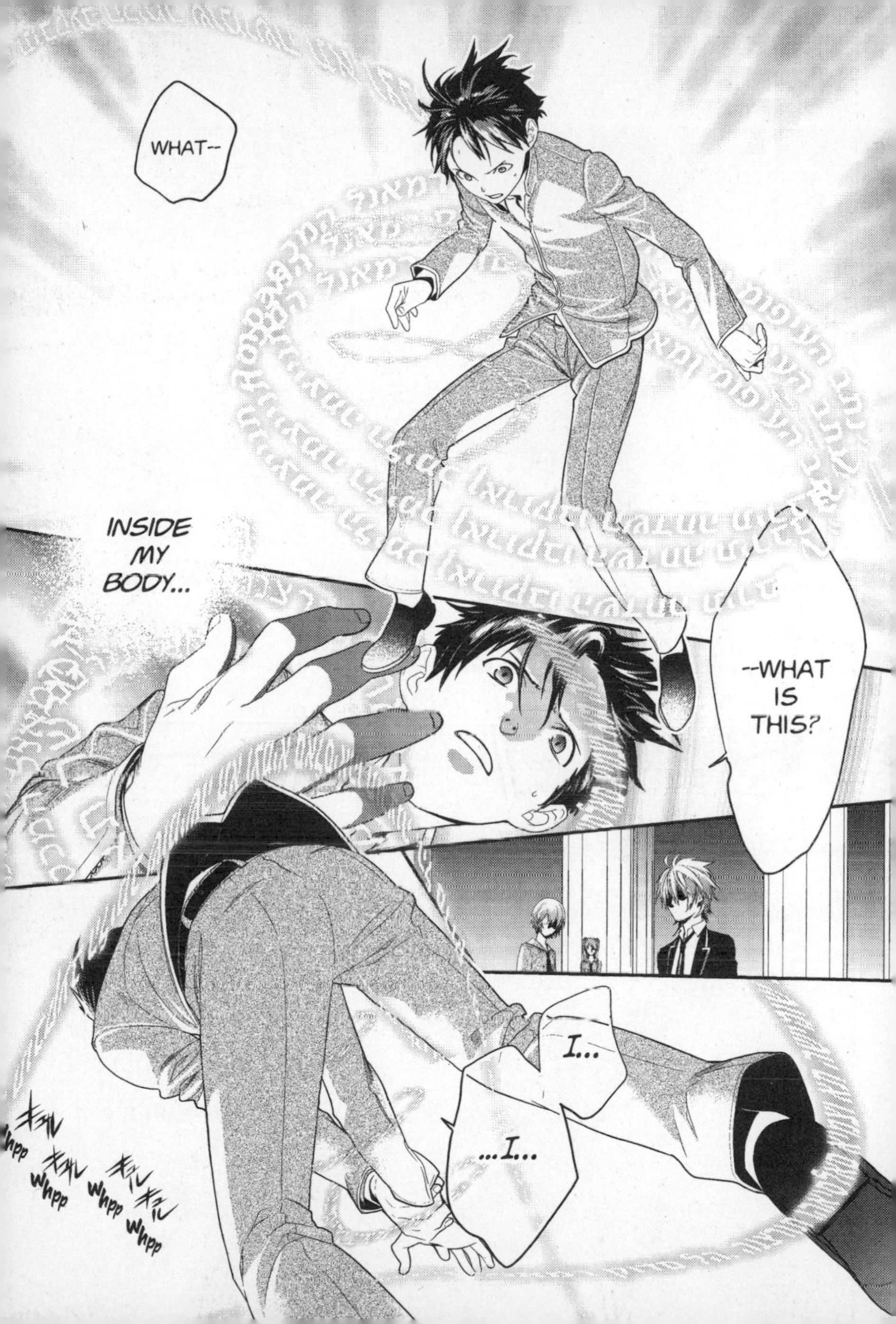
WHAT--
--WHAT IS THIS?
INSIDE MY BODY...
I...
...I...
Whpp Whpp Whpp Whpp

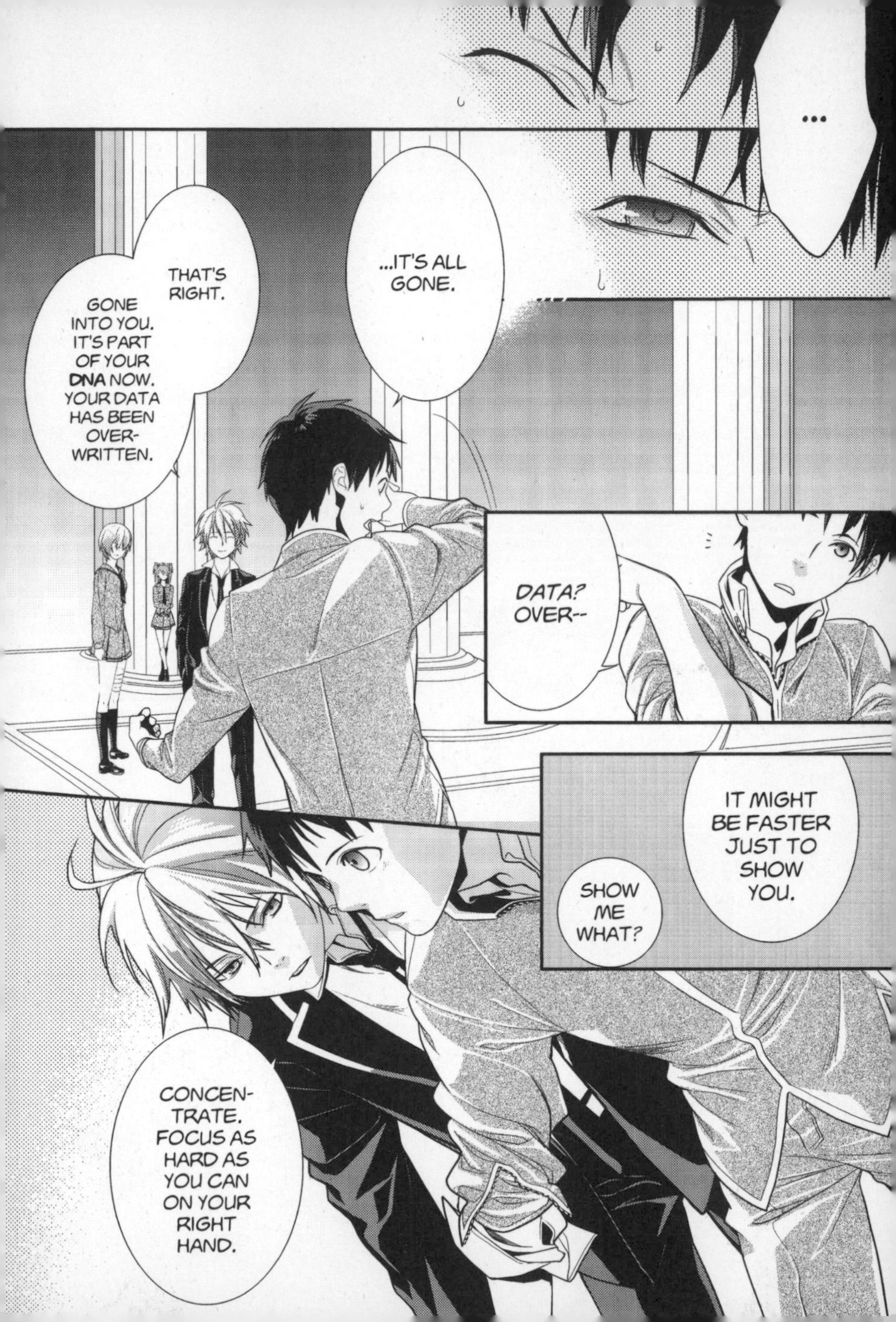
...
...IT'S ALL GONE.
THAT'S RIGHT.
GONE INTO YOU. IT'S PART OF YOUR DNA NOW. YOUR DATA HAS BEEN OVER-WRITTEN.
DATA? OVER--
IT MIGHT BE FASTER JUST TO SHOW YOU.
SHOW ME WHAT?
CONCEN-TRATE. FOCUS AS HARD AS YOU CAN ON YOUR RIGHT HAND.

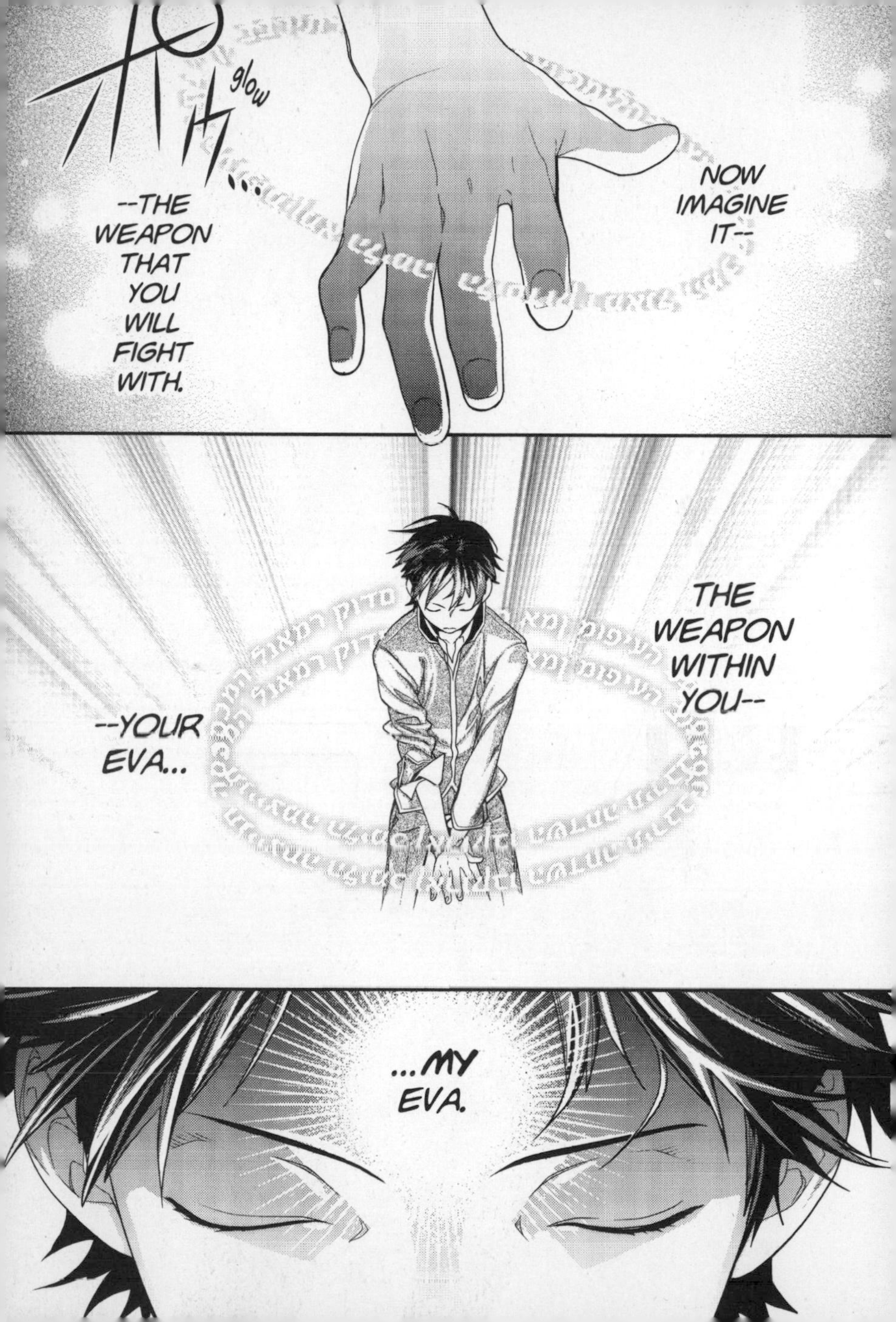
NOW IMAGINE IT--
glow
--THE WEAPON THAT YOU WILL FIGHT WITH.
THE WEAPON WITHIN YOU--
--YOUR EVA...
...MY EVA.

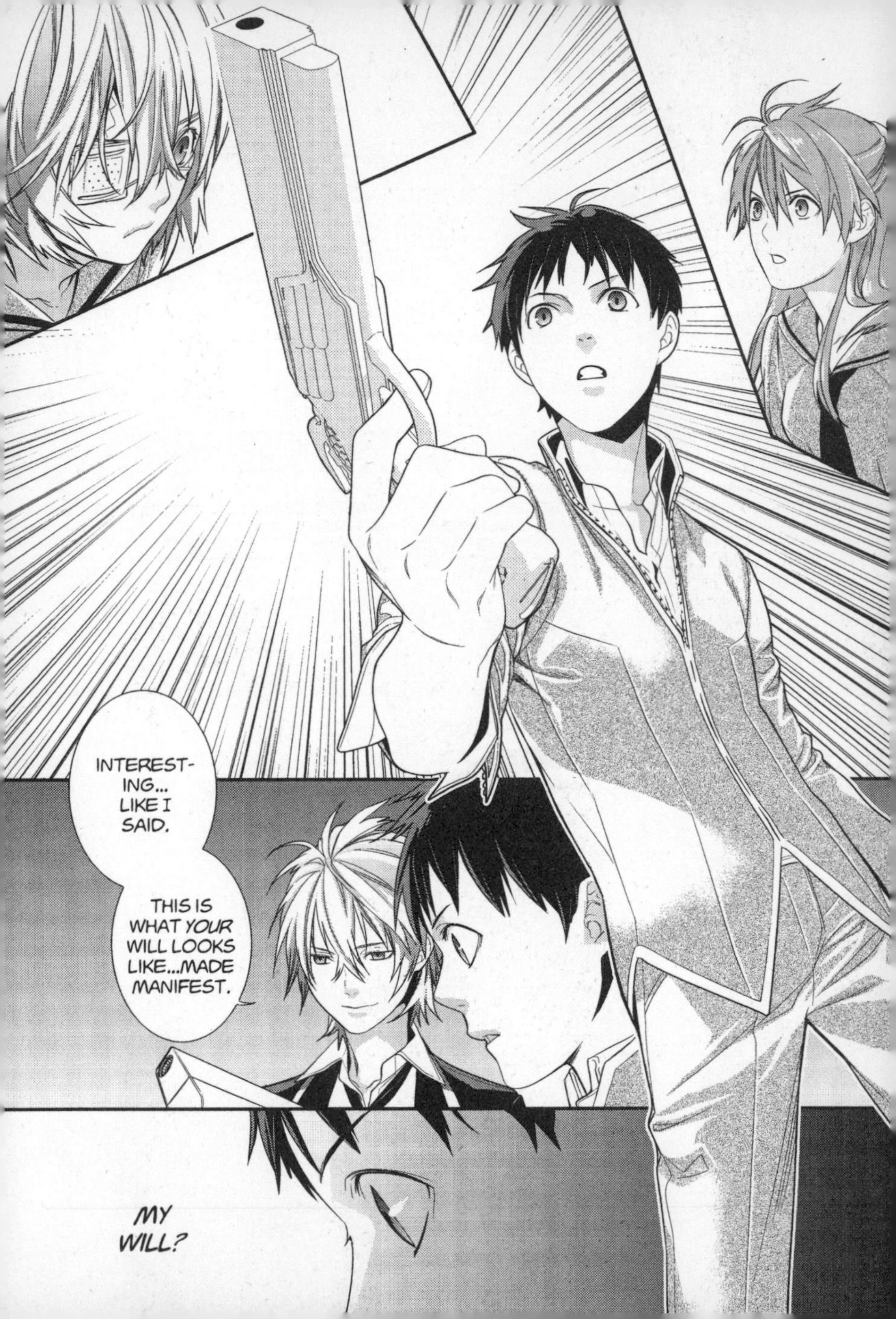
INTEREST-ING... LIKE I SAID.
THIS IS WHAT *YOUR* WILL LOOKS LIKE...MADE MANIFEST.
MY WILL?

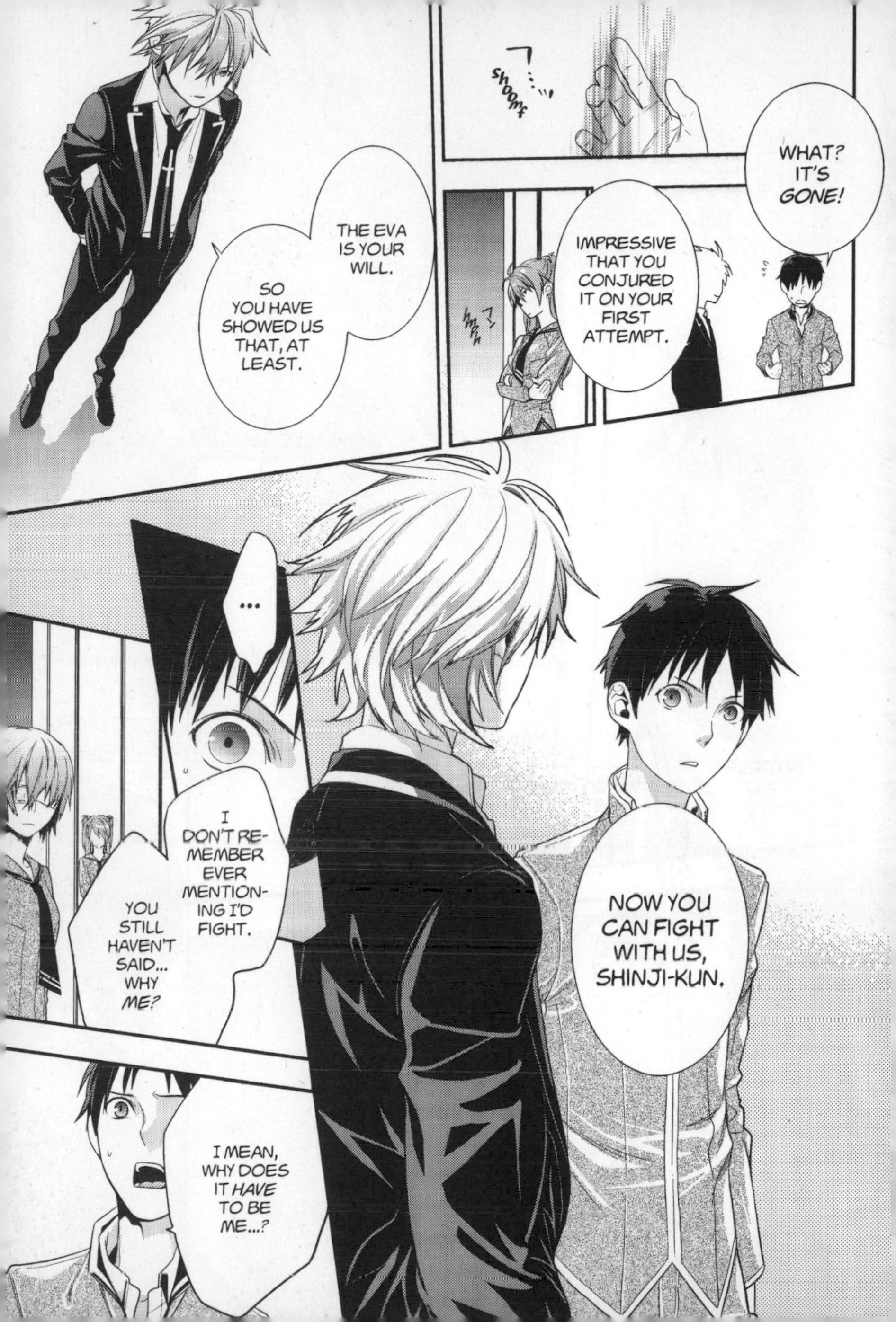
shoomf
WHAT? IT'S GONE!
IMPRESSIVE THAT YOU CONJURED IT ON YOUR FIRST ATTEMPT.
THE EVA IS YOUR WILL.
SO YOU HAVE SHOWED US THAT, AT LEAST.
NOW YOU CAN FIGHT WITH US, SHINJI-KUN.
...
I DON'T RE-MEMBER EVER MENTION-ING I'D FIGHT.
YOU STILL HAVEN'T SAID... WHY *ME*?
I MEAN, WHY DOES IT *HAVE* TO BE ME...?

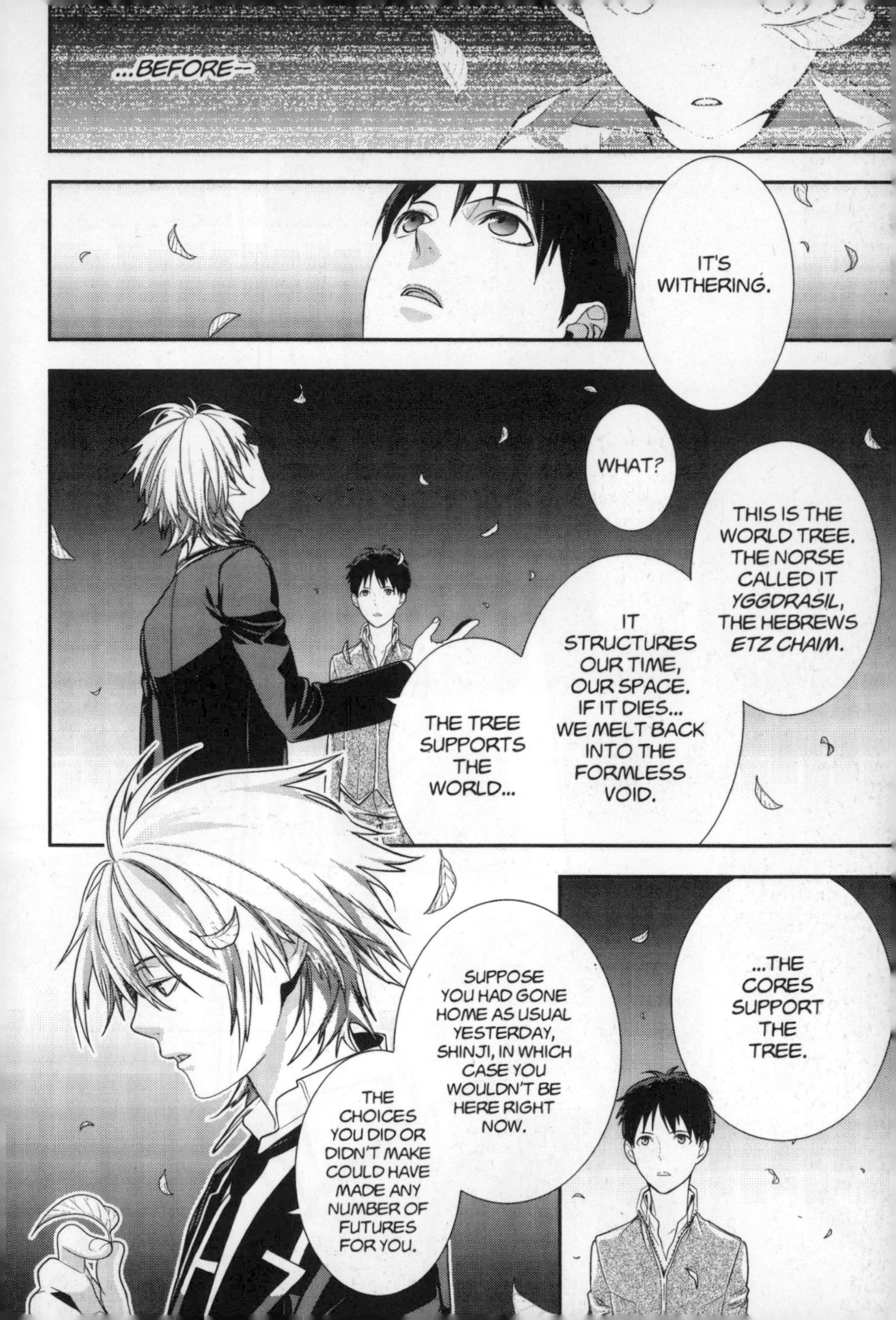
...BEFORE--
IT'S WITHERING.
WHAT?
THIS IS THE WORLD TREE. THE NORSE CALLED IT *YGGDRASIL*, THE HEBREWS *ETZ CHAIM*.
IT STRUCTURES OUR TIME, OUR SPACE. IF IT DIES... WE MELT BACK INTO THE FORMLESS VOID.
THE TREE SUPPORTS THE WORLD...
...THE CORES SUPPORT THE TREE.
SUPPOSE YOU HAD GONE HOME AS USUAL YESTERDAY, SHINJI, IN WHICH CASE YOU WOULDN'T BE HERE RIGHT NOW.
THE CHOICES YOU DID OR DIDN'T MAKE COULD HAVE MADE ANY NUMBER OF FUTURES FOR YOU.

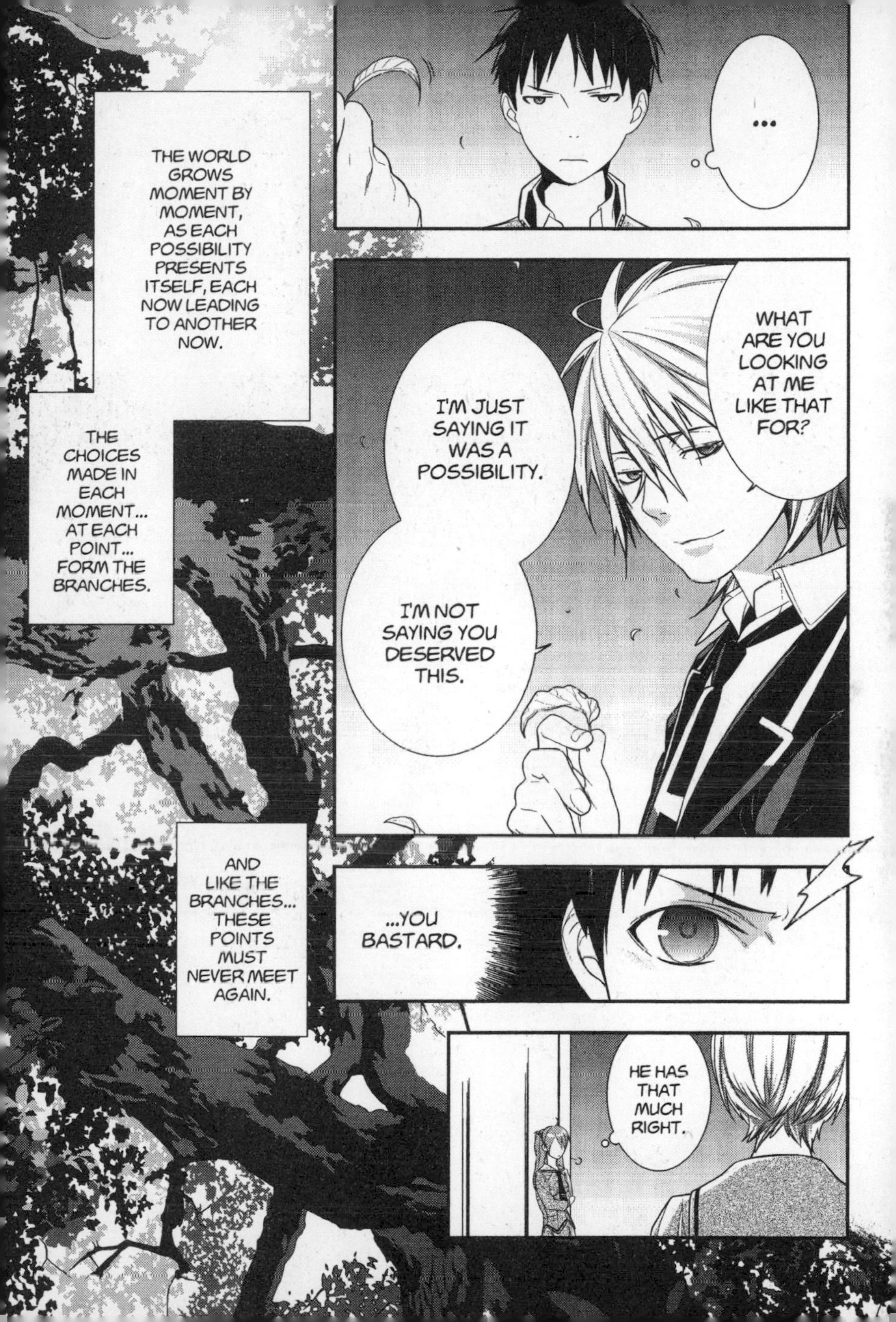
...
WHAT ARE YOU LOOKING AT ME LIKE THAT FOR?
I'M JUST SAYING IT WAS A POSSIBILITY.
I'M NOT SAYING YOU DESERVED THIS.
...YOU BASTARD.
HE HAS THAT MUCH RIGHT.
THE WORLD GROWS MOMENT BY MOMENT, AS EACH POSSIBILITY PRESENTS ITSELF, EACH NOW LEADING TO ANOTHER NOW.
THE CHOICES MADE IN EACH MOMENT... AT EACH POINT... FORM THE BRANCHES.
AND LIKE THE BRANCHES... THESE POINTS MUST NEVER MEET AGAIN.

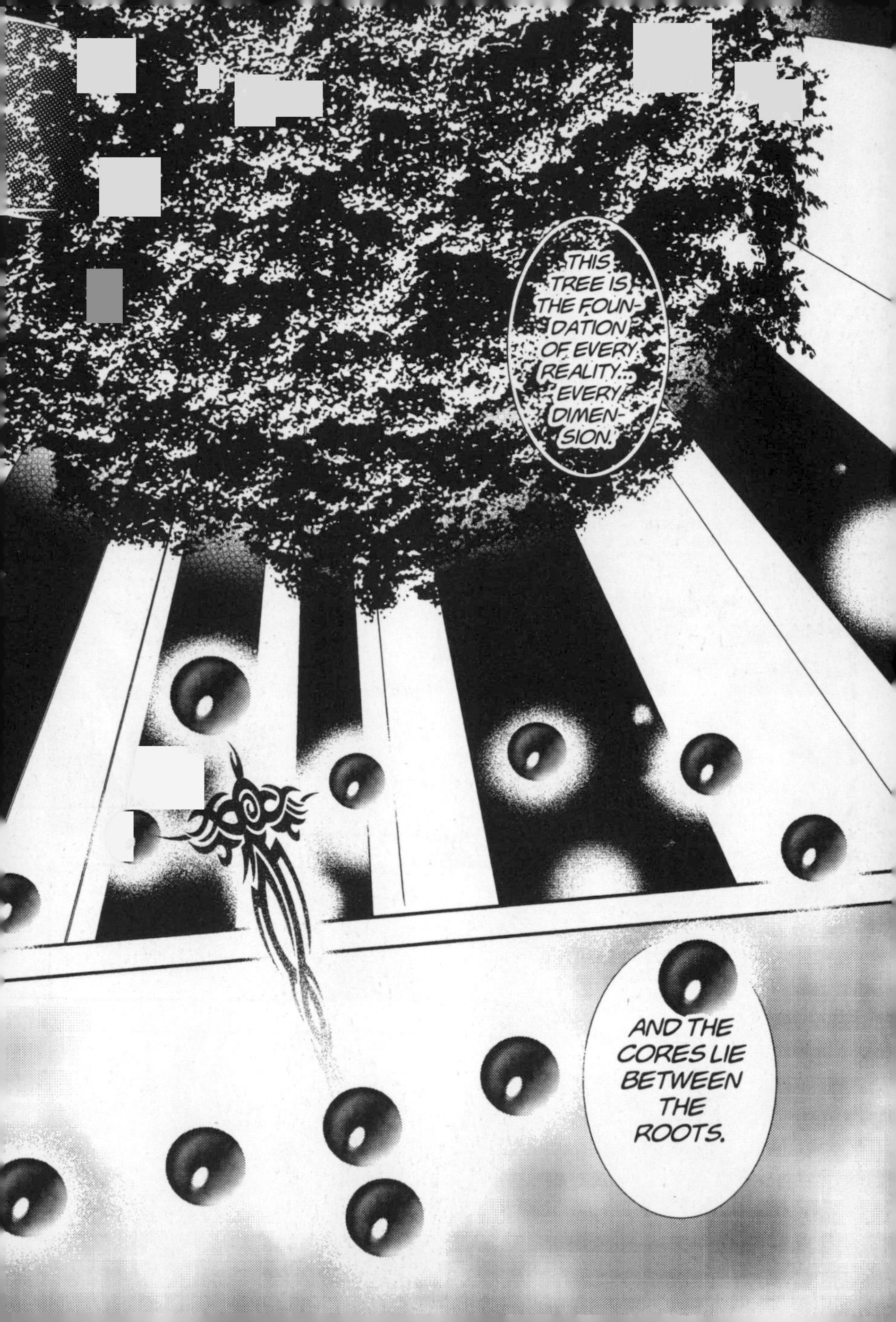
THIS TREE IS THE FOUN-DATION OF EVERY REALITY... EVERY DIMEN-SION.
AND THE CORES LIE BETWEEN THE ROOTS.

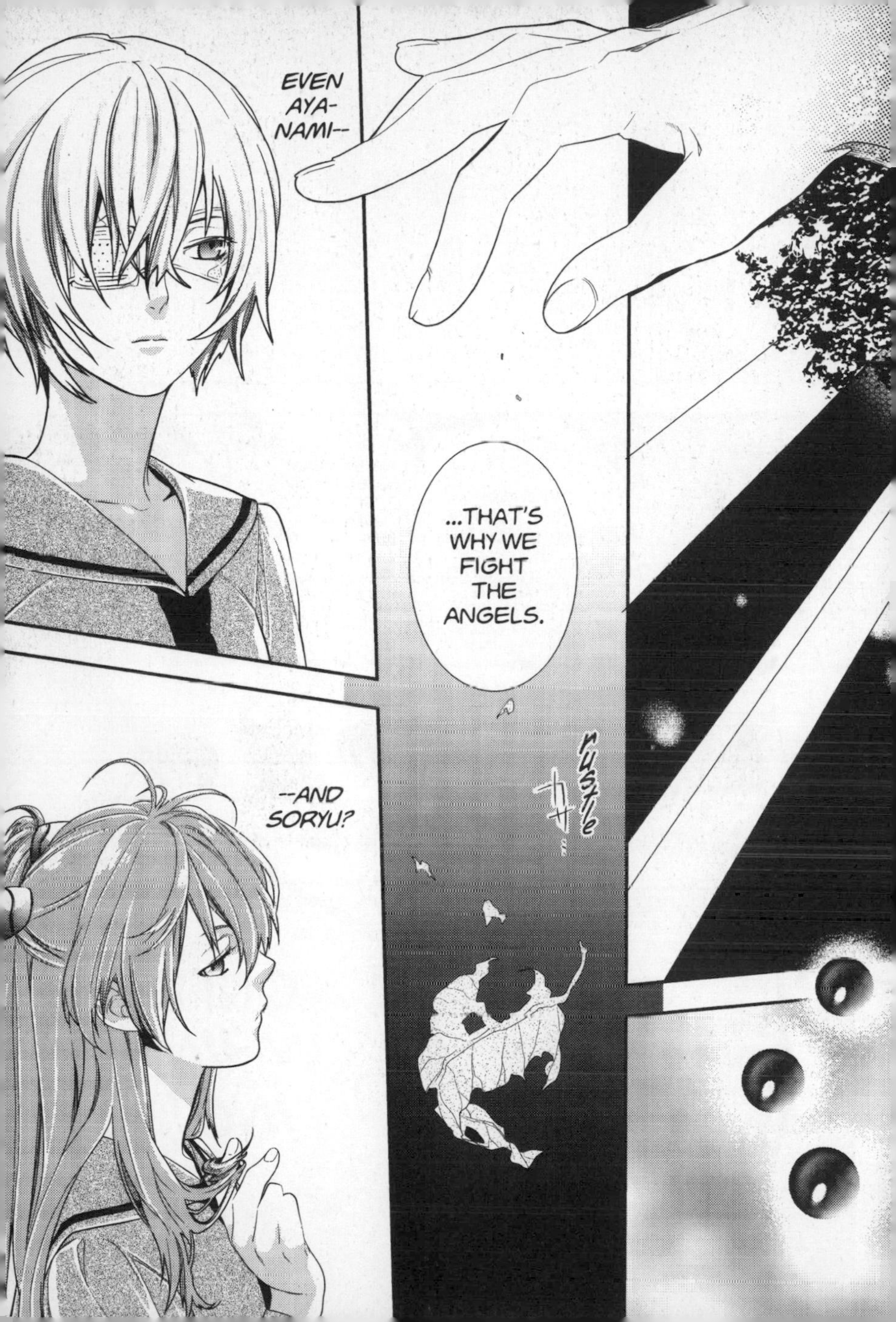
...THAT'S WHY WE FIGHT THE ANGELS.
rustle
EVEN AYA-NAMI--
--AND SORYU?

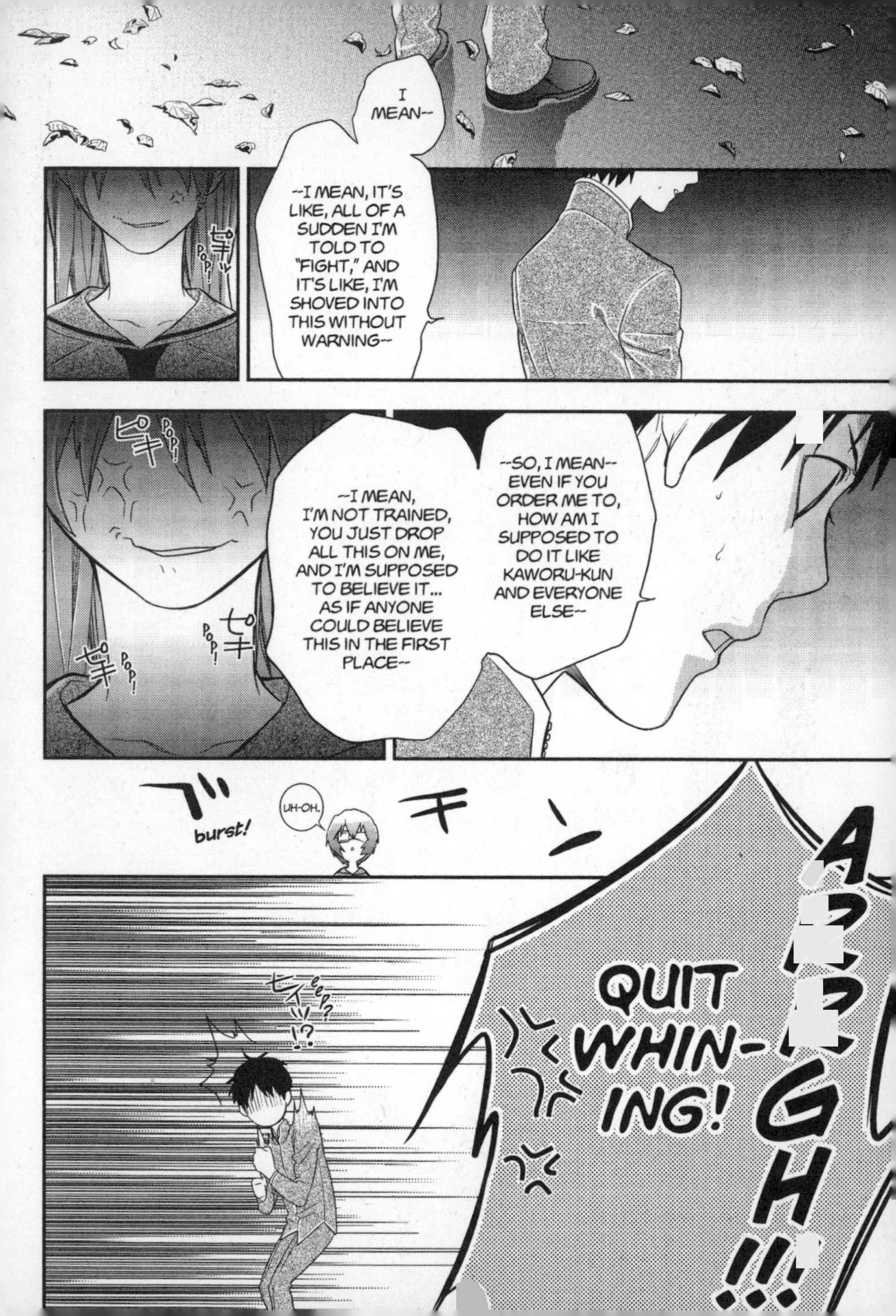
I MEAN--
--I MEAN, IT'S LIKE, ALL OF A SUDDEN I'M TOLD TO "FIGHT," AND IT'S LIKE, I'M SHOVED INTO THIS WITHOUT WARNING--
POP!
--SO, I MEAN-- EVEN IF YOU ORDER ME TO, HOW AM I SUPPOSED TO DO IT LIKE KAWORU-KUN AND EVERYONE ELSE--
--I MEAN, I'M NOT TRAINED, YOU JUST DROP ALL THIS ON ME, AND I'M SUPPOSED TO BELIEVE IT... AS IF ANYONE COULD BELIEVE THIS IN THE FIRST PLACE--
POP!
POP!
POP!
UH-OH.
burst!
QUIT WHIN-ING!
eep?!?

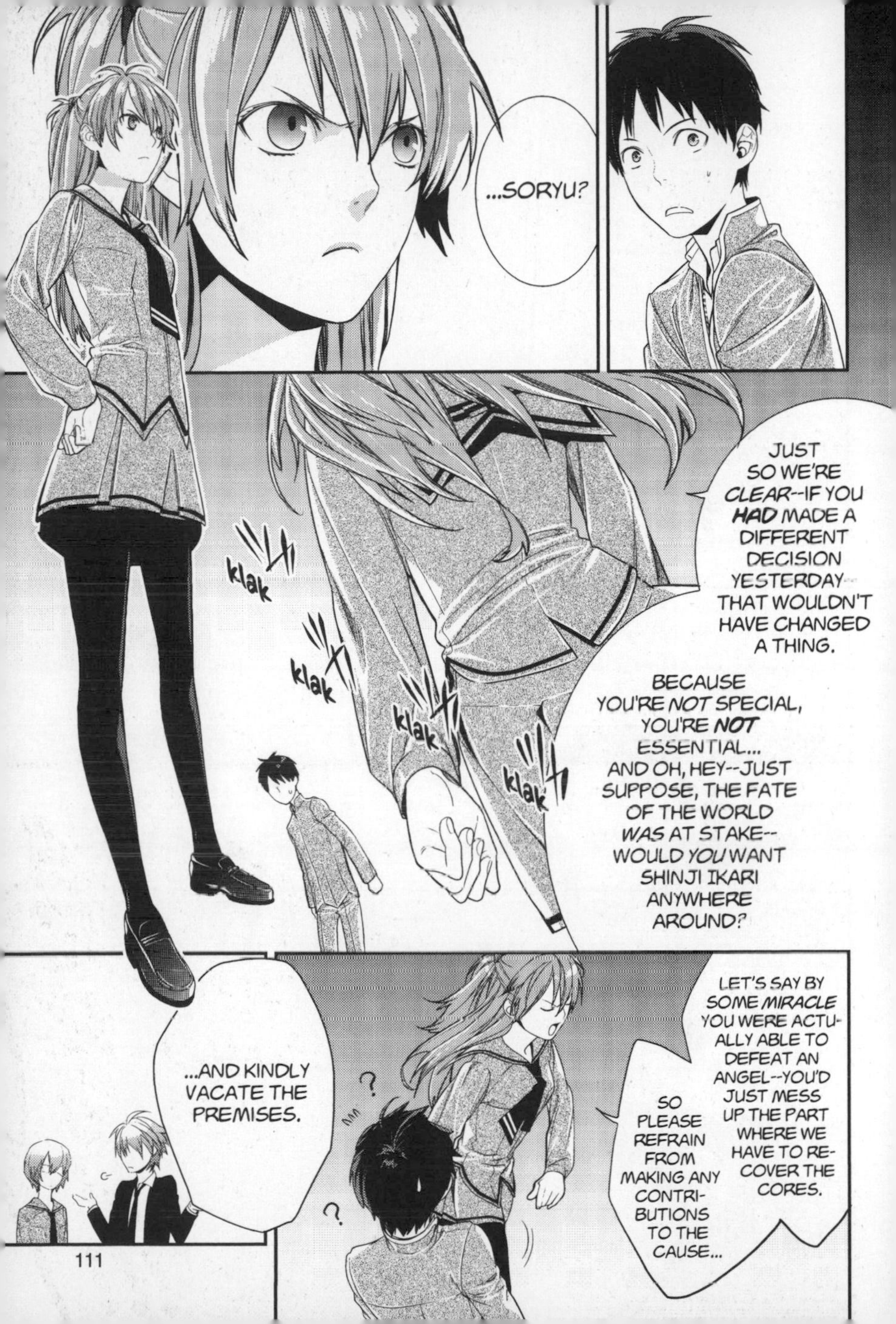

...SORYU?
JUST SO WE'RE CLEAR--IF YOU HAD MADE A DIFFERENT DECISION YESTERDAY-THAT WOULDN'T HAVE CHANGED A THING.
klak
klak
klak
klak
BECAUSE YOU'RE NOT SPECIAL, YOU'RE NOT ESSENTIAL... AND OH, HEY--JUST SUPPOSE, THE FATE OF THE WORLD WAS AT STAKE--WOULD YOU WANT SHINJI IKARI ANYWHERE AROUND?
LET'S SAY BY SOME MIRACLE YOU WERE ACTUALLY ABLE TO DEFEAT AN ANGEL--YOU'D JUST MESS UP THE PART WHERE WE HAVE TO RECOVER THE CORES.
SO PLEASE REFRAIN FROM MAKING ANY CONTRIBUTIONS TO THE CAUSE...
?
?
...AND KINDLY VACATE THE PREMISES.

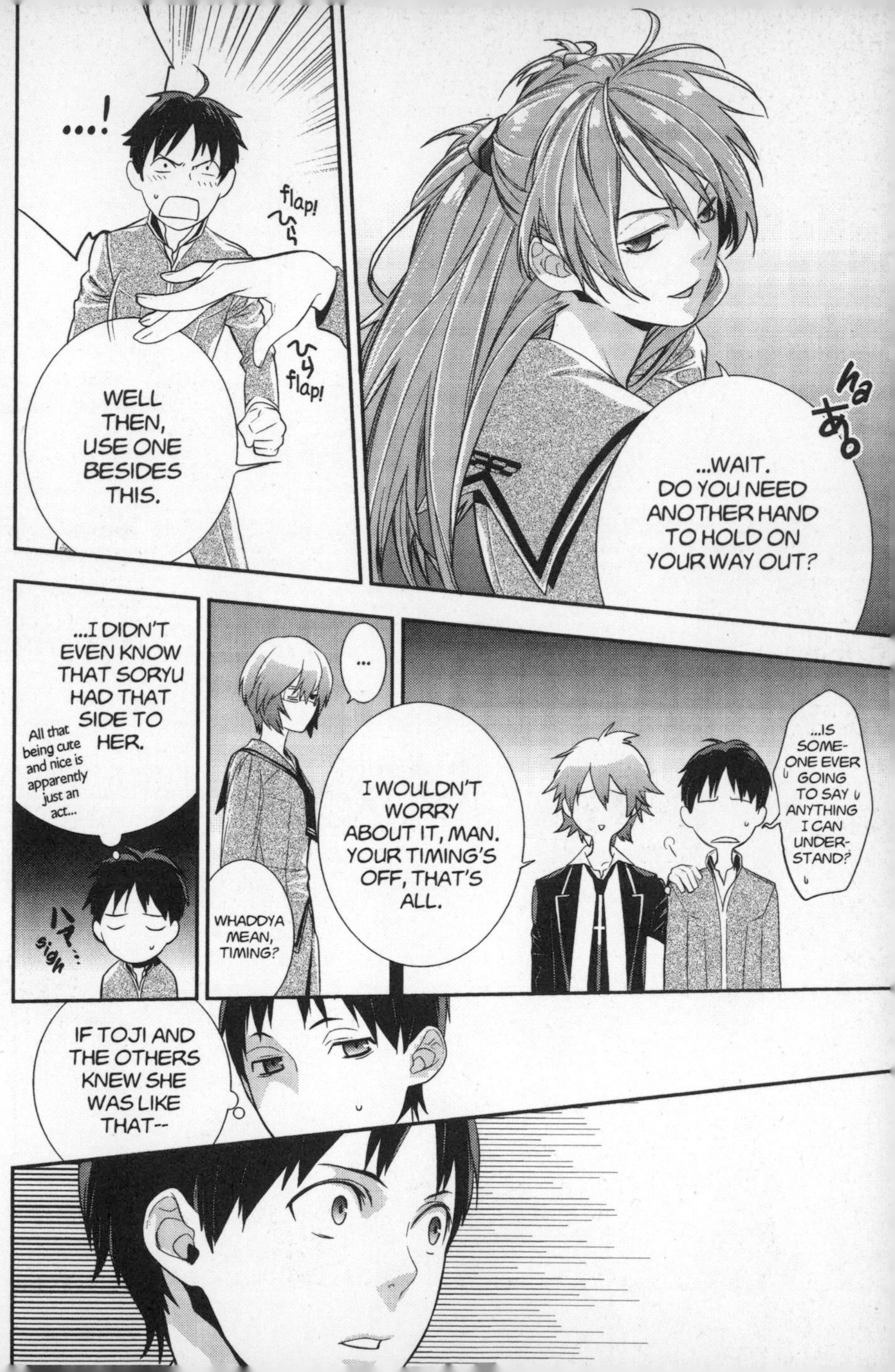
na あ。
...WAIT. DO YOU NEED ANOTHER HAND TO HOLD ON YOUR WAY OUT?
...!
flap!
flap!
WELL THEN, USE ONE BESIDES THIS.
...IS SOMEONE EVER GOING TO SAY ANYTHING I CAN UNDERSTAND?
I WOULDN'T WORRY ABOUT IT, MAN. YOUR TIMING'S OFF, THAT'S ALL.
...
WHADDYA MEAN, TIMING?
...I DIDN'T EVEN KNOW THAT SORYU HAD THAT SIDE TO HER.
All that being cute and nice is apparently just an act...
sigh
IF TOJI AND THE OTHERS KNEW SHE WAS LIKE THAT--

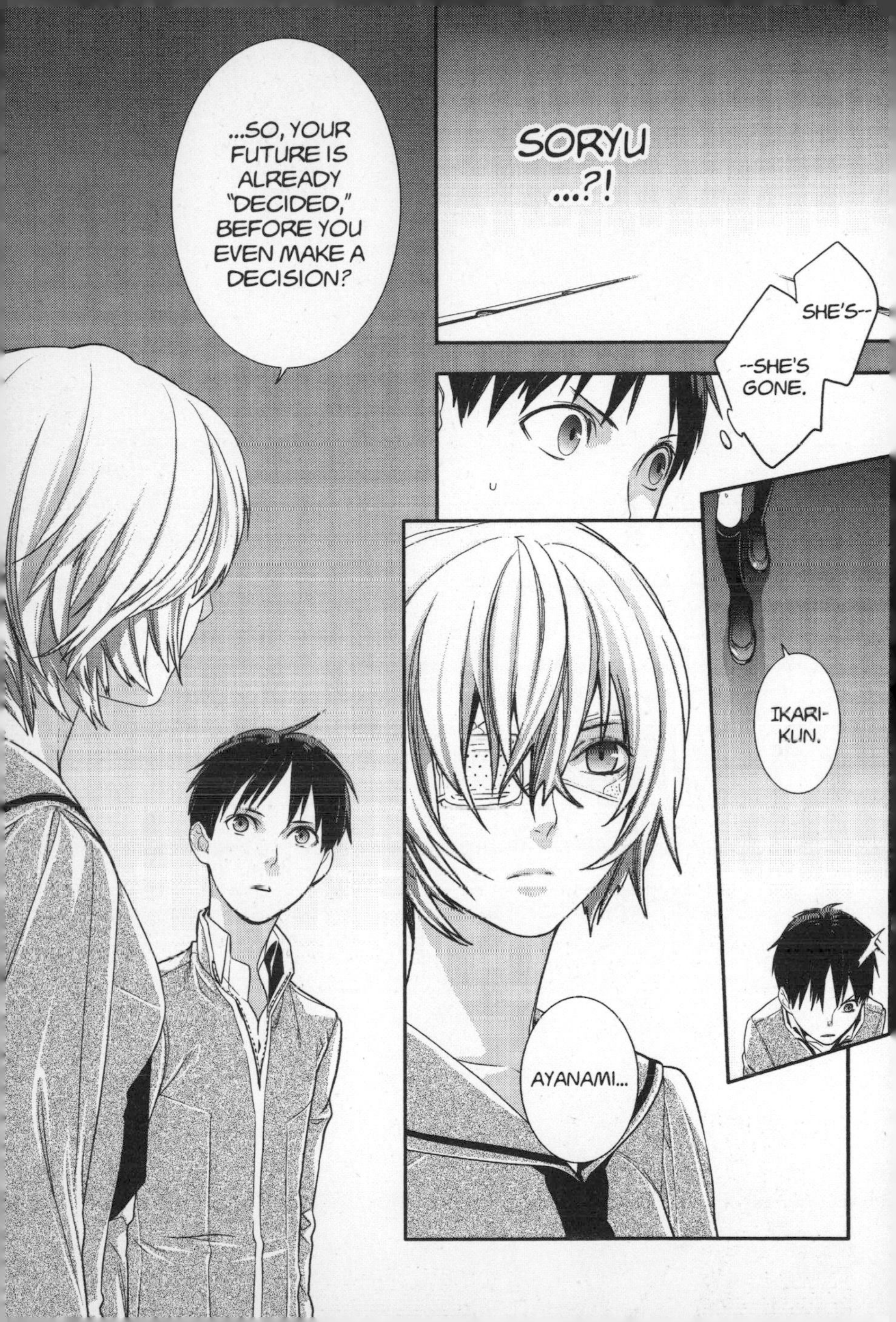
SORYU ...?!
SHE'S--
--SHE'S GONE.
IKARI-KUN.
AYANAMI...
...SO, YOUR FUTURE IS ALREADY "DECIDED," BEFORE YOU EVEN MAKE A DECISION?

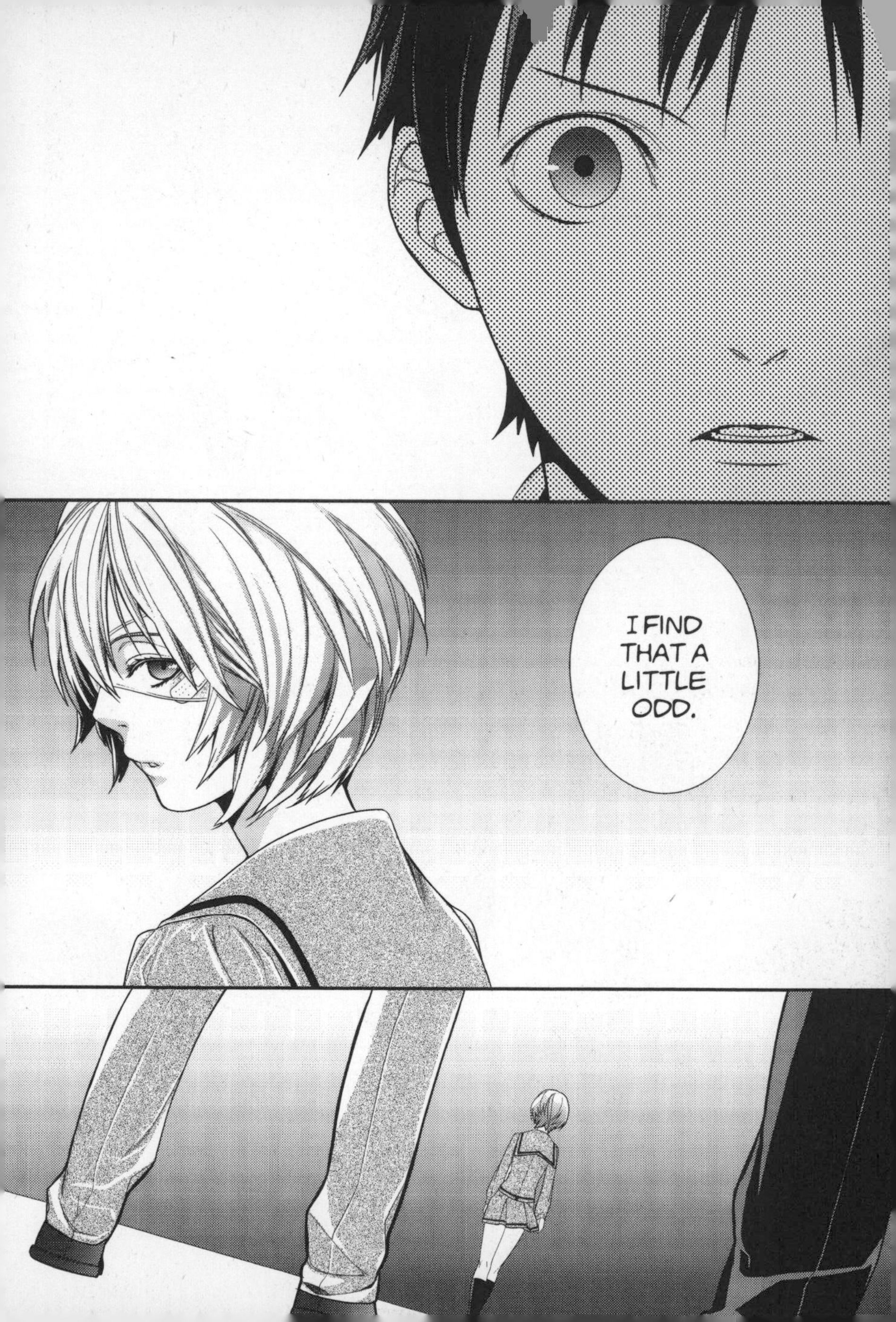
I FIND THAT A LITTLE ODD.

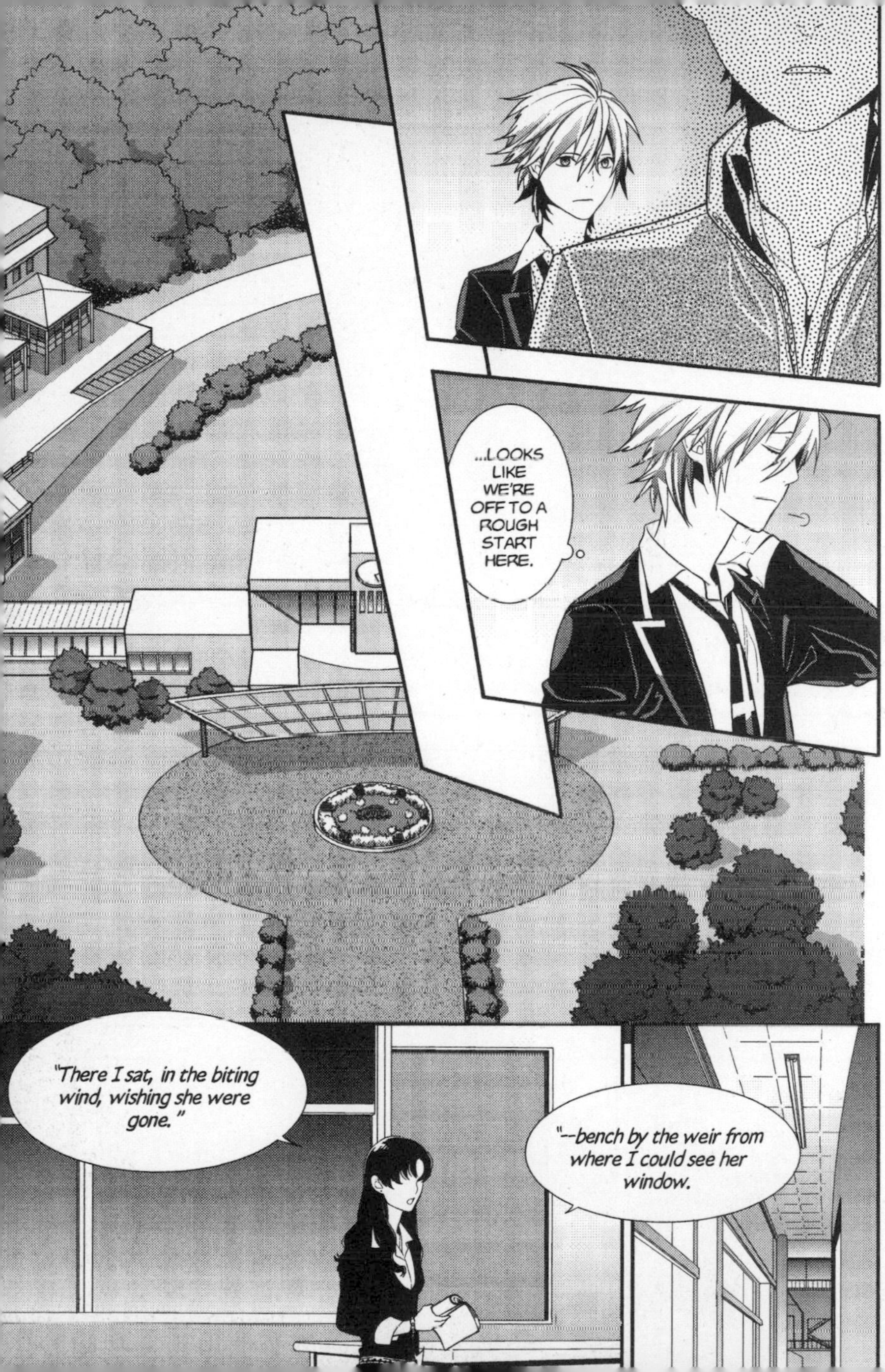
...LOOKS LIKE WE'RE OFF TO A ROUGH START HERE.
"--bench by the weir from where I could see her window.
"There I sat, in the biting wind, wishing she were gone."

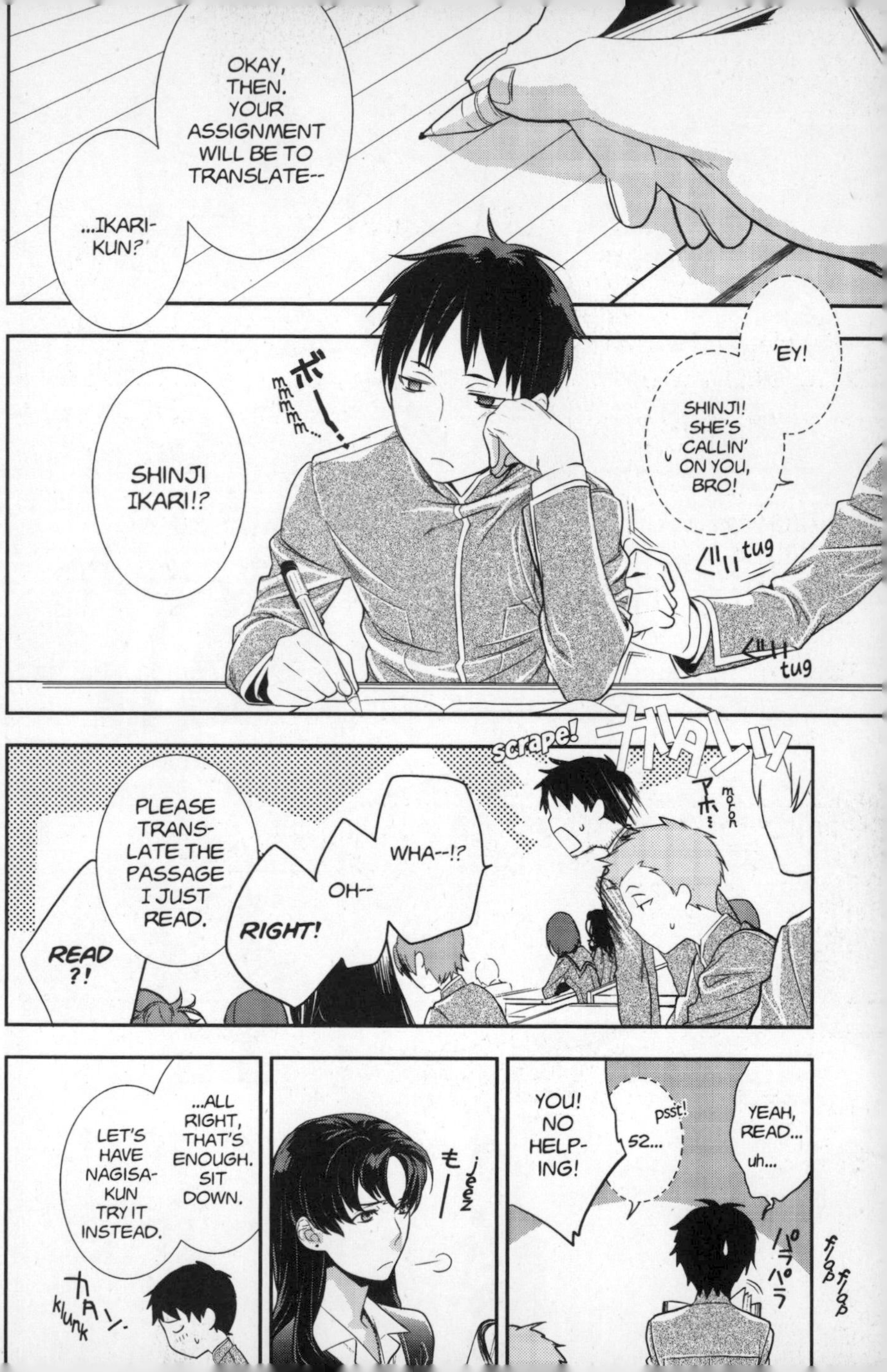
OKAY, THEN. YOUR ASSIGNMENT WILL BE TO TRANSLATE--
...IKARI-KUN?
'EY!
SHINJI! SHE'S CALLIN' ON YOU, BRO!
ぐい tug
ぐい tug
ボー! mmmmm...
SHINJI IKARI!?
ガタンッ scrape!
アホ… moron
WHA--!?
OH--
RIGHT!
PLEASE TRANSLATE THE PASSAGE I JUST READ.
READ?!
YEAH, READ...
uh...
psst!
52...
パラパラ flap flap
YOU! NO HELPING!
もー jeez
...ALL RIGHT, THAT'S ENOUGH. SIT DOWN.
LET'S HAVE NAGISA-KUN TRY IT INSTEAD.
カタン klunk

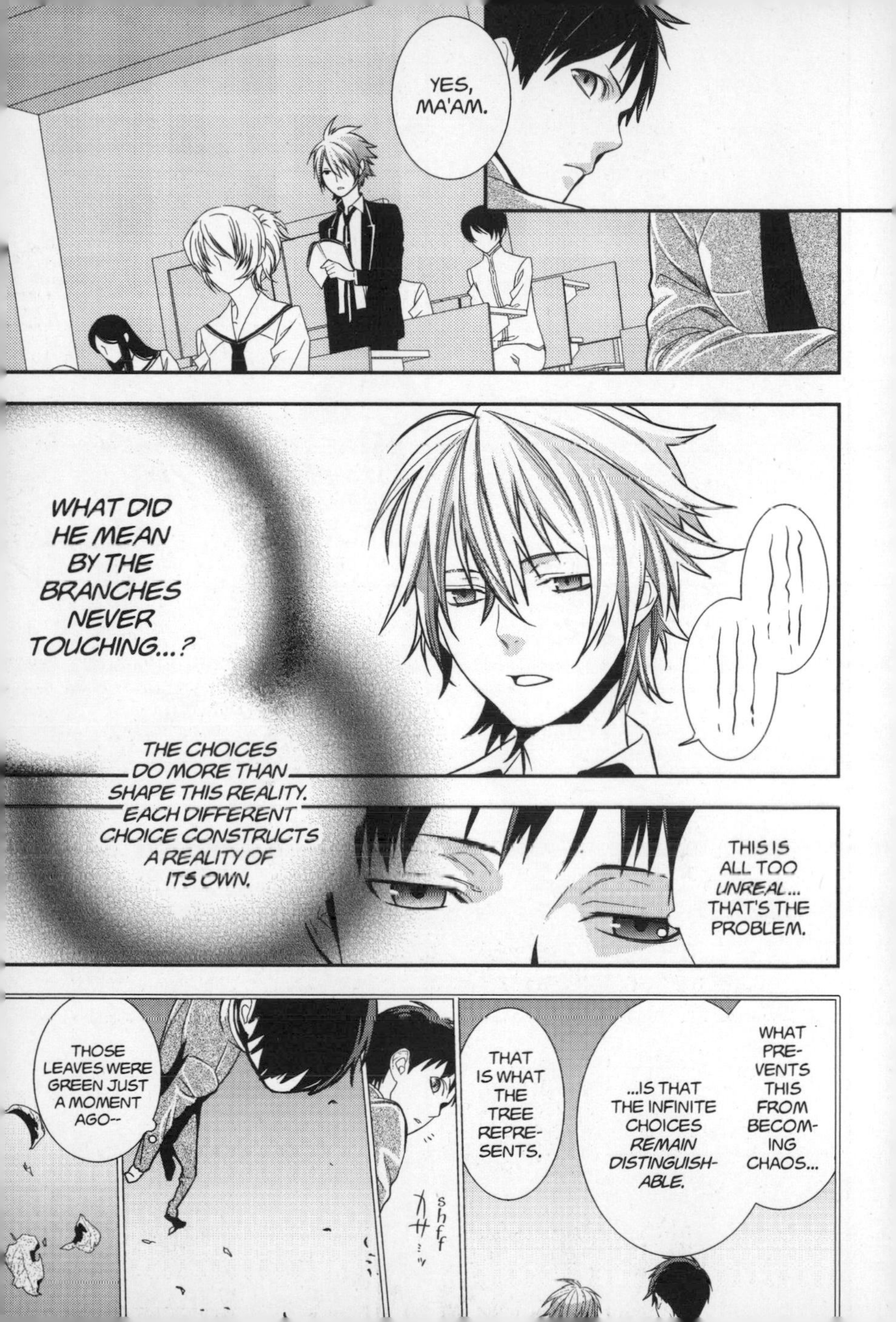
YES, MA'AM.
WHAT DID HE MEAN BY THE BRANCHES NEVER TOUCHING...?
THE CHOICES DO MORE THAN SHAPE THIS REALITY. EACH DIFFERENT CHOICE CONSTRUCTS A REALITY OF ITS OWN.
THIS IS ALL TOO UNREAL... THAT'S THE PROBLEM.
WHAT PRE-VENTS THIS FROM BECOM-ING CHAOS...
...IS THAT THE INFINITE CHOICES REMAIN DISTINGUISH-ABLE.
THAT IS WHAT THE TREE REPRE-SENTS.
THOSE LEAVES WERE GREEN JUST A MOMENT AGO--
shff

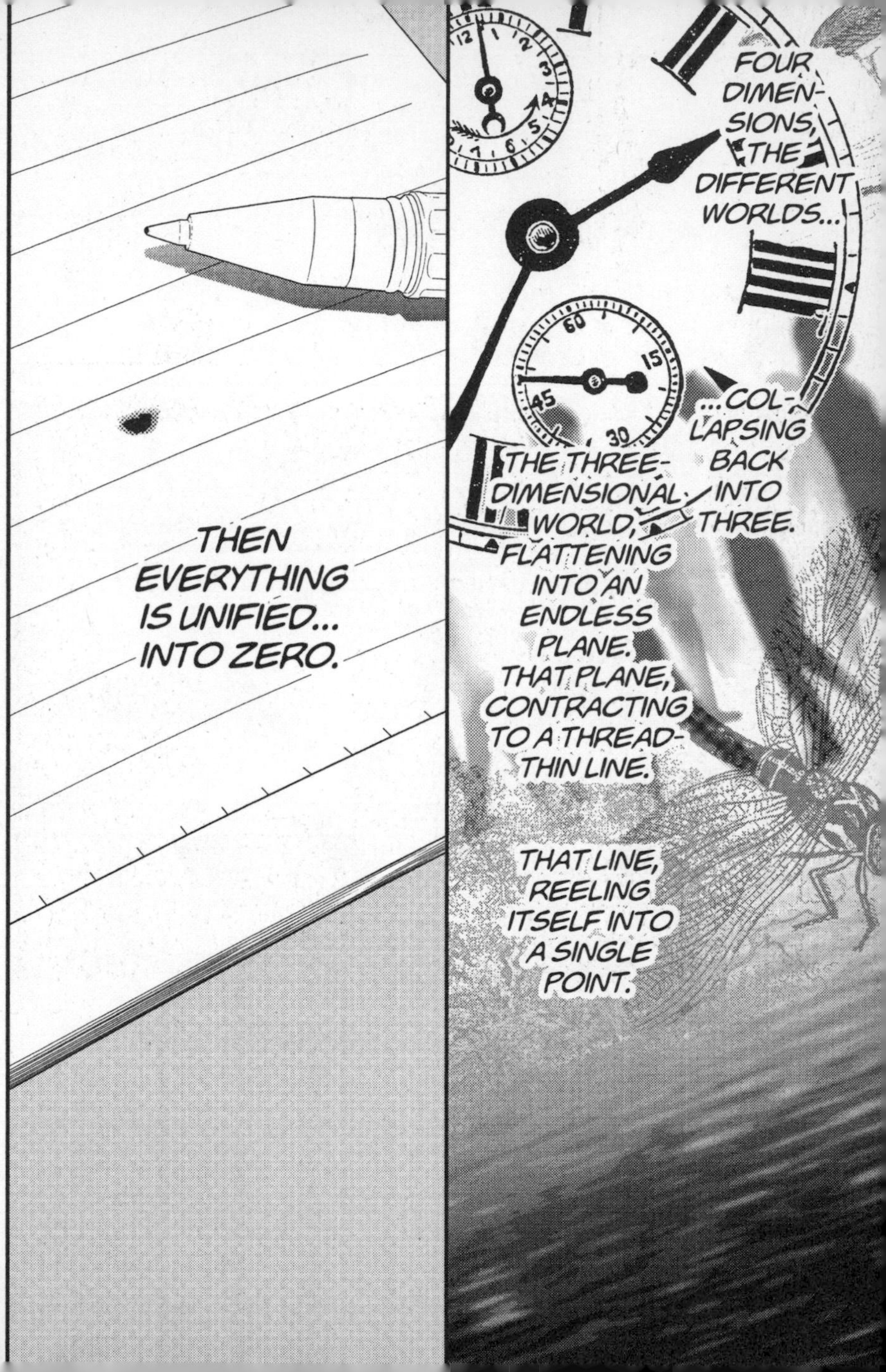
FOUR DIMENSIONS, THE DIFFERENT WORLDS...
...COLLAPSING BACK INTO THREE.
THE THREE-DIMENSIONAL WORLD, FLATTENING INTO AN ENDLESS PLANE.
THAT PLANE, CONTRACTING TO A THREAD-THIN LINE.
THAT LINE, REELING ITSELF INTO A SINGLE POINT.
THEN EVERYTHING IS UNIFIED... INTO ZERO.

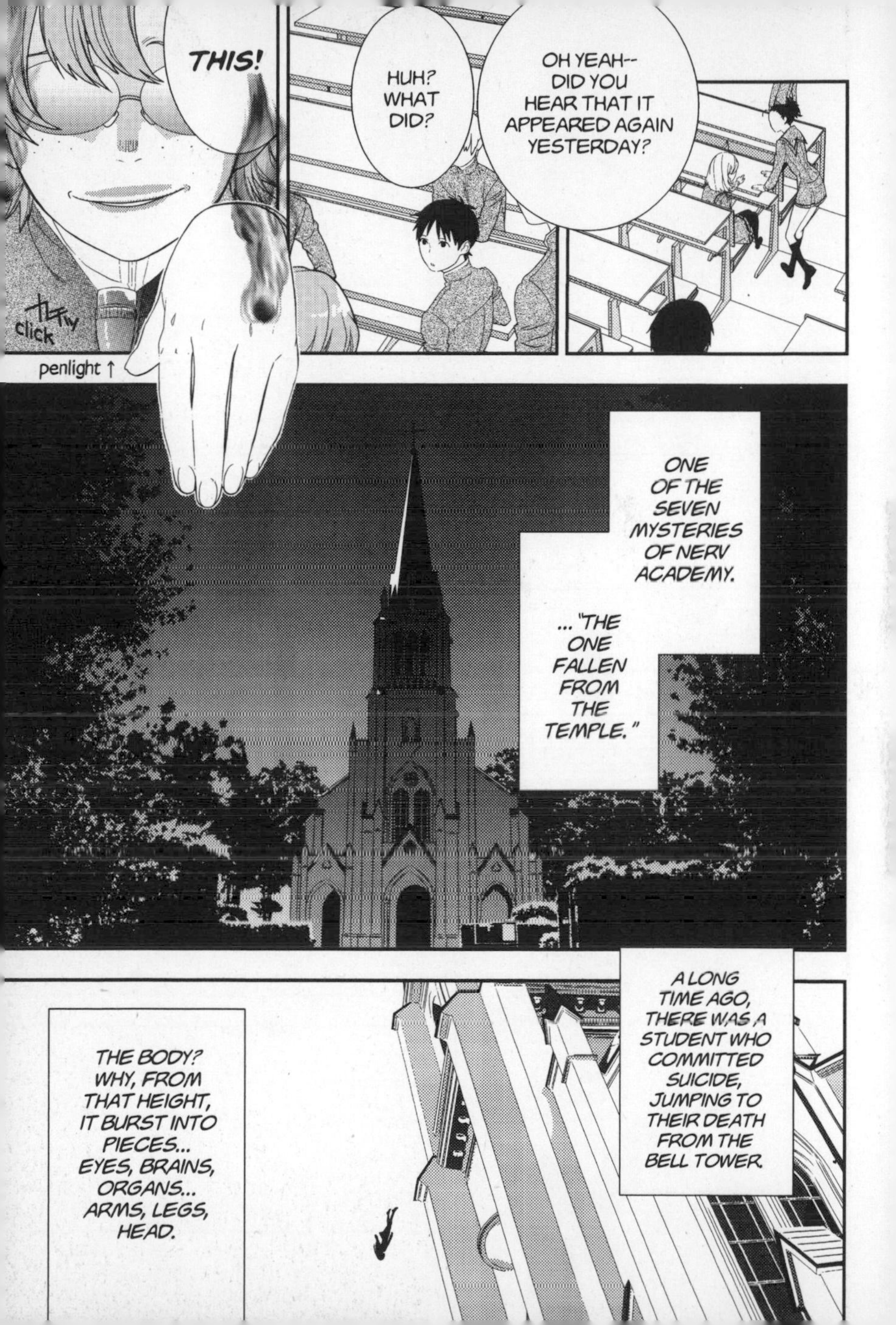
OH YEAH-- DID YOU HEAR THAT IT APPEARED AGAIN YESTERDAY?
HUH? WHAT DID?
THIS!
click
penlight ↑
ONE OF THE SEVEN MYSTERIES OF NERV ACADEMY.
..."THE ONE FALLEN FROM THE TEMPLE."
A LONG TIME AGO, THERE WAS A STUDENT WHO COMMITTED SUICIDE, JUMPING TO THEIR DEATH FROM THE BELL TOWER.
THE BODY? WHY, FROM THAT HEIGHT, IT BURST INTO PIECES... EYES, BRAINS, ORGANS... ARMS, LEGS, HEAD.

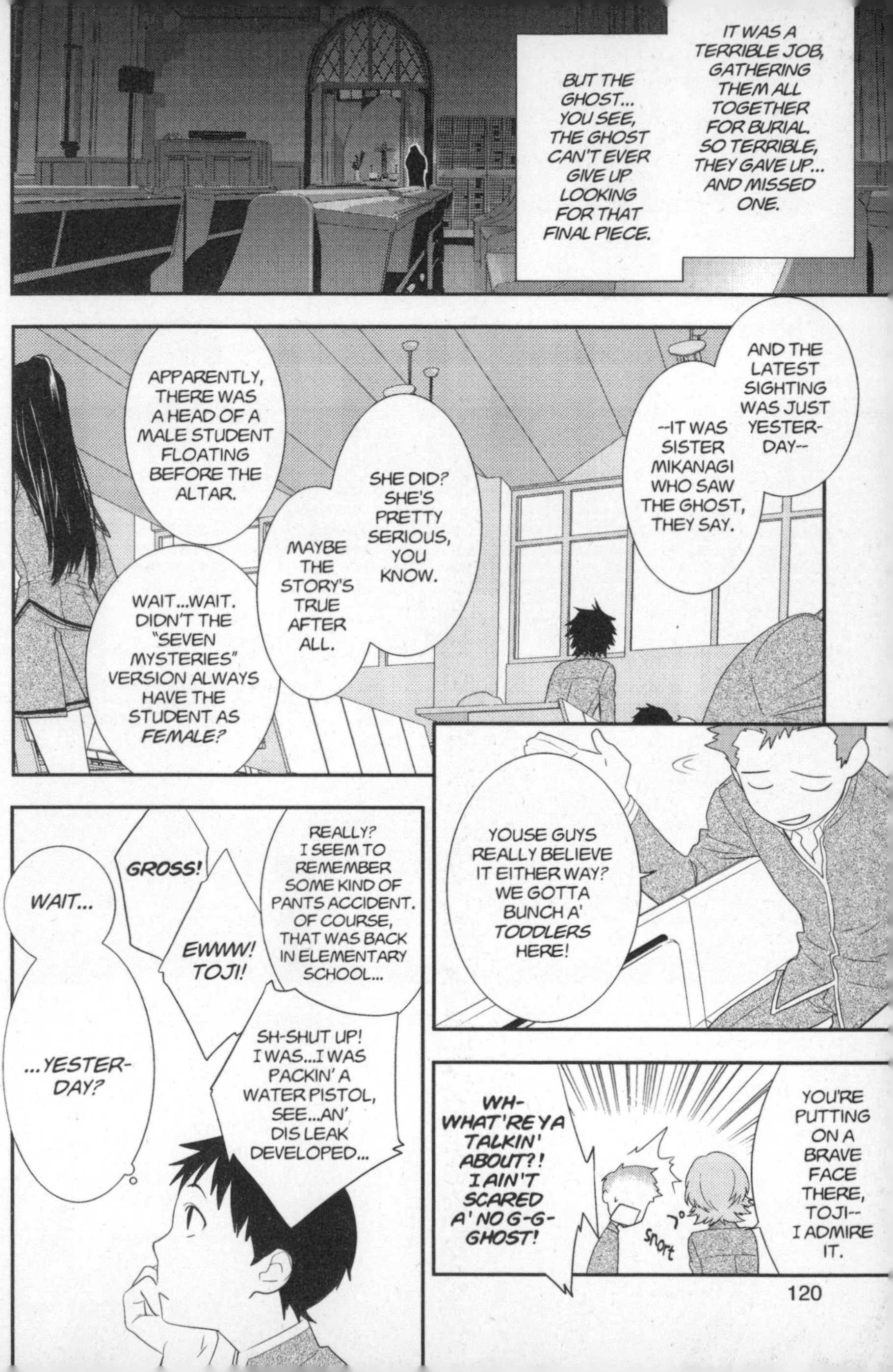
IT WAS A TERRIBLE JOB, GATHERING THEM ALL TOGETHER FOR BURIAL. SO TERRIBLE, THEY GAVE UP... AND MISSED ONE.
BUT THE GHOST... YOU SEE, THE GHOST CAN'T EVER GIVE UP LOOKING FOR THAT FINAL PIECE.
AND THE LATEST SIGHTING WAS JUST YESTER-DAY--
--IT WAS SISTER MIKANAGI WHO SAW THE GHOST, THEY SAY.
SHE DID? SHE'S PRETTY SERIOUS, YOU KNOW.
APPARENTLY, THERE WAS A HEAD OF A MALE STUDENT FLOATING BEFORE THE ALTAR.
MAYBE THE STORY'S TRUE AFTER ALL.
WAIT...WAIT. DIDN'T THE "SEVEN MYSTERIES" VERSION ALWAYS HAVE THE STUDENT AS *FEMALE*?
YOUSE GUYS REALLY BELIEVE IT EITHER WAY? WE GOTTA BUNCH A' *TODDLERS* HERE!
YOU'RE PUTTING ON A BRAVE FACE THERE, TOJI-- I ADMIRE IT.
WH- WHAT'RE YA TALKIN' ABOUT?! I AIN'T SCARED A' NO G-G-GHOST!
snort
REALLY? I SEEM TO REMEMBER SOME KIND OF PANTS ACCIDENT. OF COURSE, THAT WAS BACK IN ELEMENTARY SCHOOL...
GROSS!
EWWW! TOJI!
SH-SHUT UP! I WAS...I WAS PACKIN' A WATER PISTOL, SEE...AN' DIS LEAK DEVELOPED...
WAIT...
...YESTER-DAY?

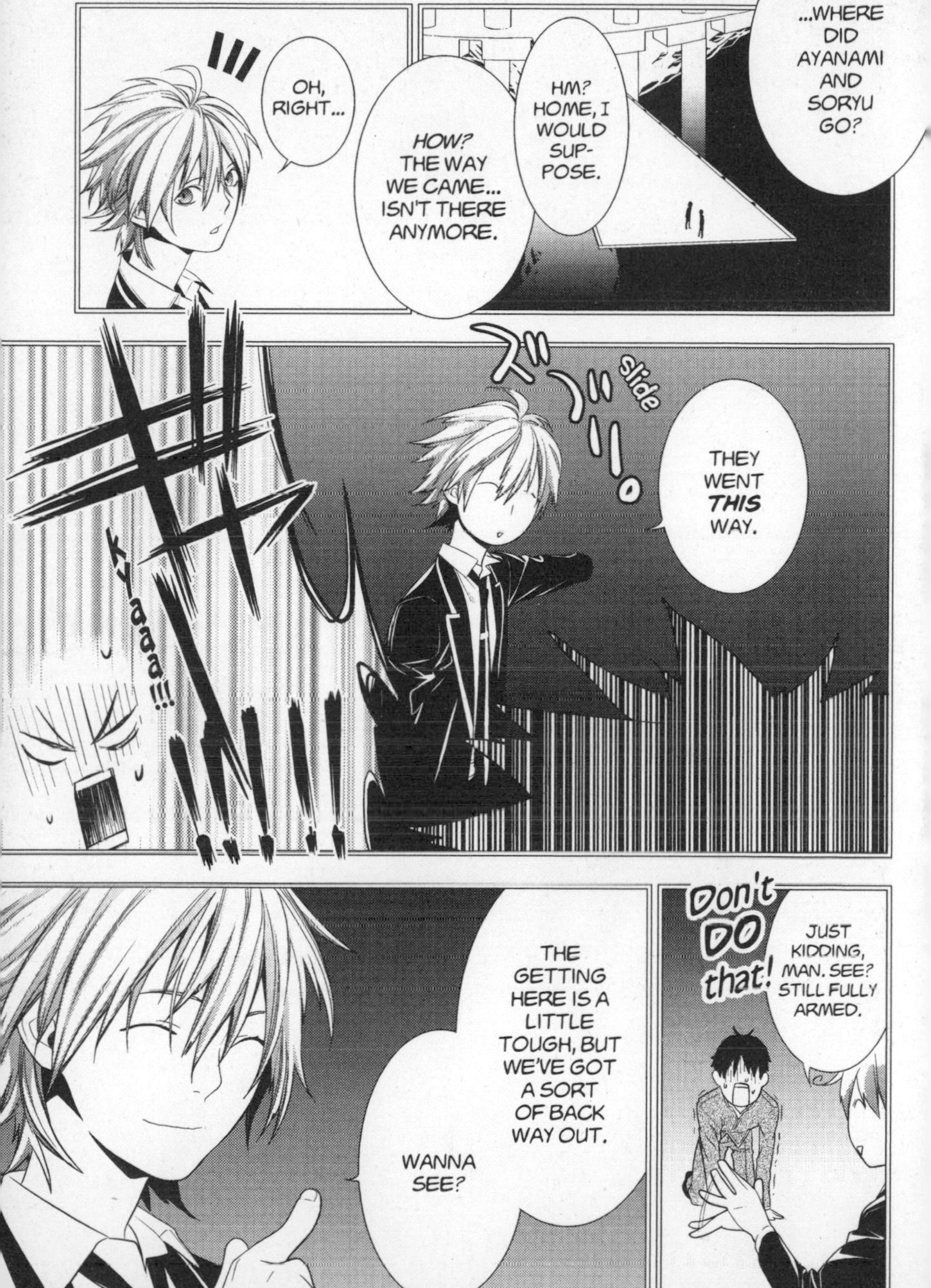
...WHERE DID AYANAMI AND SORYU GO?
HM? HOME, I WOULD SUP-POSE.
HOW? THE WAY WE CAME... ISN'T THERE ANYMORE.
OH, RIGHT...
slide
THEY WENT ***THIS*** WAY.
kyaaaa!!!
Don't DO that!
JUST KIDDING, MAN. SEE? STILL FULLY ARMED.
THE GETTING HERE IS A LITTLE TOUGH, BUT WE'VE GOT A SORT OF BACK WAY OUT.
WANNA SEE?

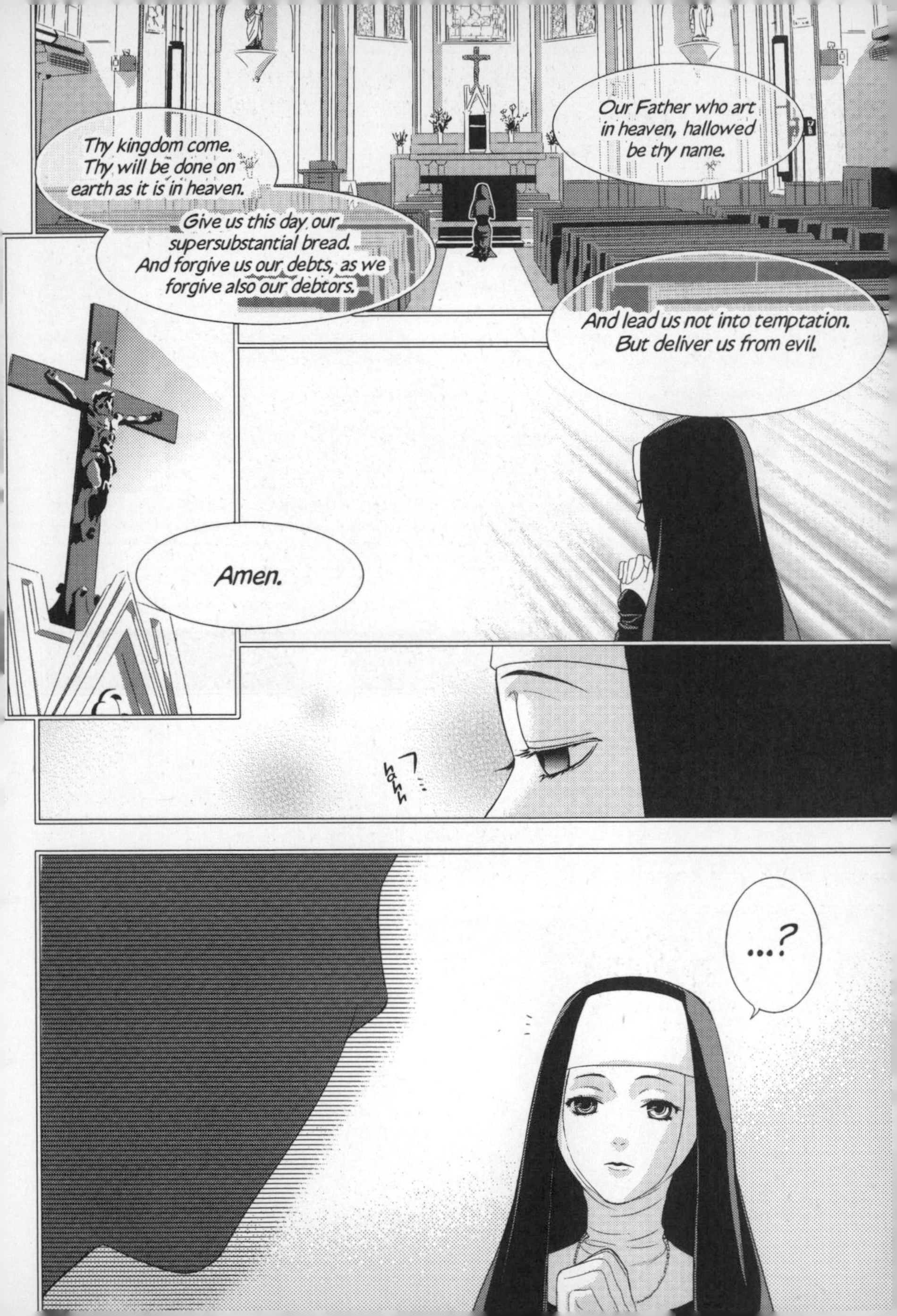
Our Father who art in heaven, hallowed be thy name.
Thy kingdom come. Thy will be done on earth as it is in heaven.
Give us this day our supersubstantial bread. And forgive us our debts, as we forgive also our debtors.
And lead us not into temptation. But deliver us from evil.
Amen.
...?

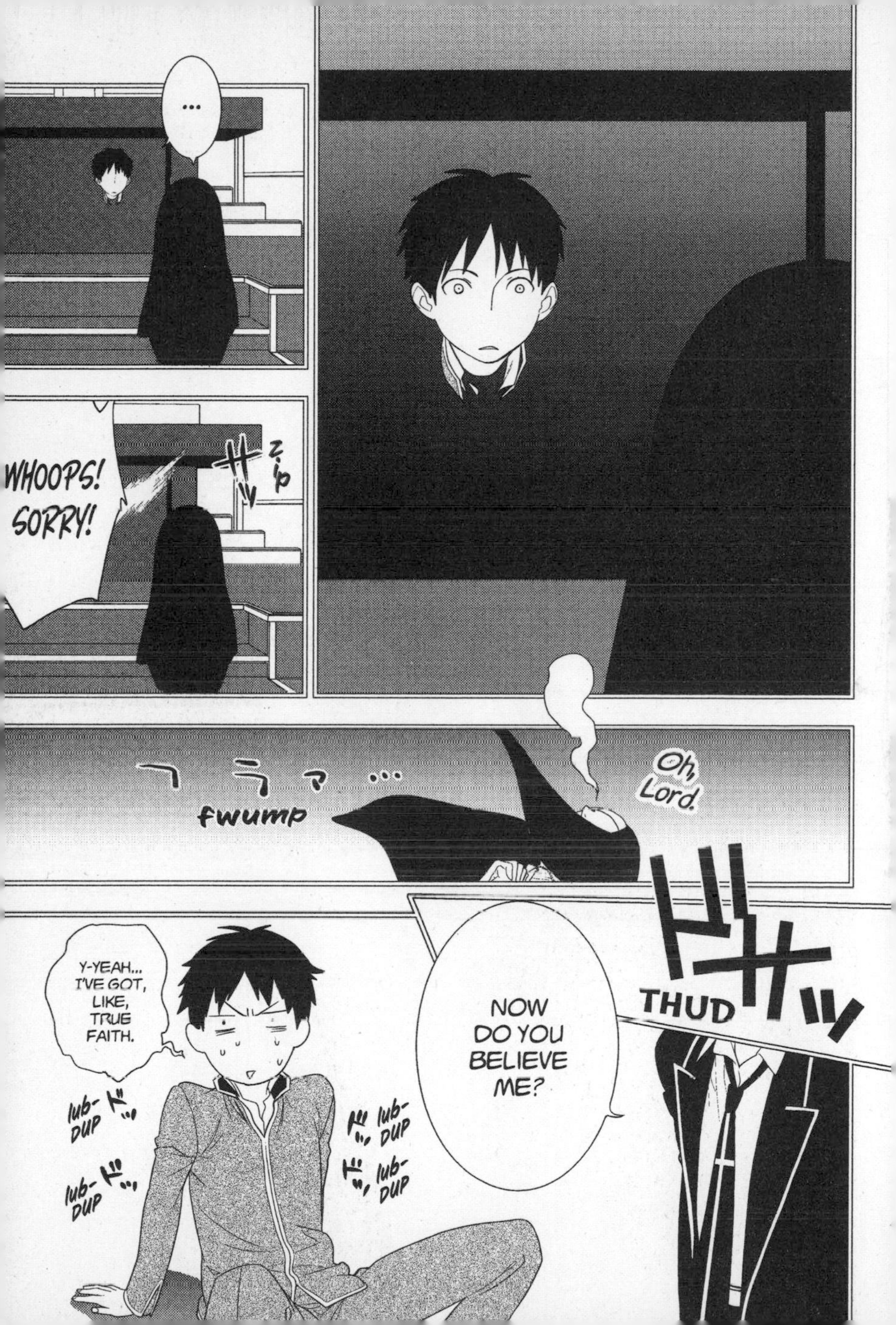
...
WHOOPS! SORRY!
zip
Oh, Lord.
fwump
THUD
NOW DO YOU BELIEVE ME?
Y-YEAH... I'VE GOT, LIKE, TRUE FAITH.
lub-DUP
lub-DUP
lub-DUP
lub-DUP

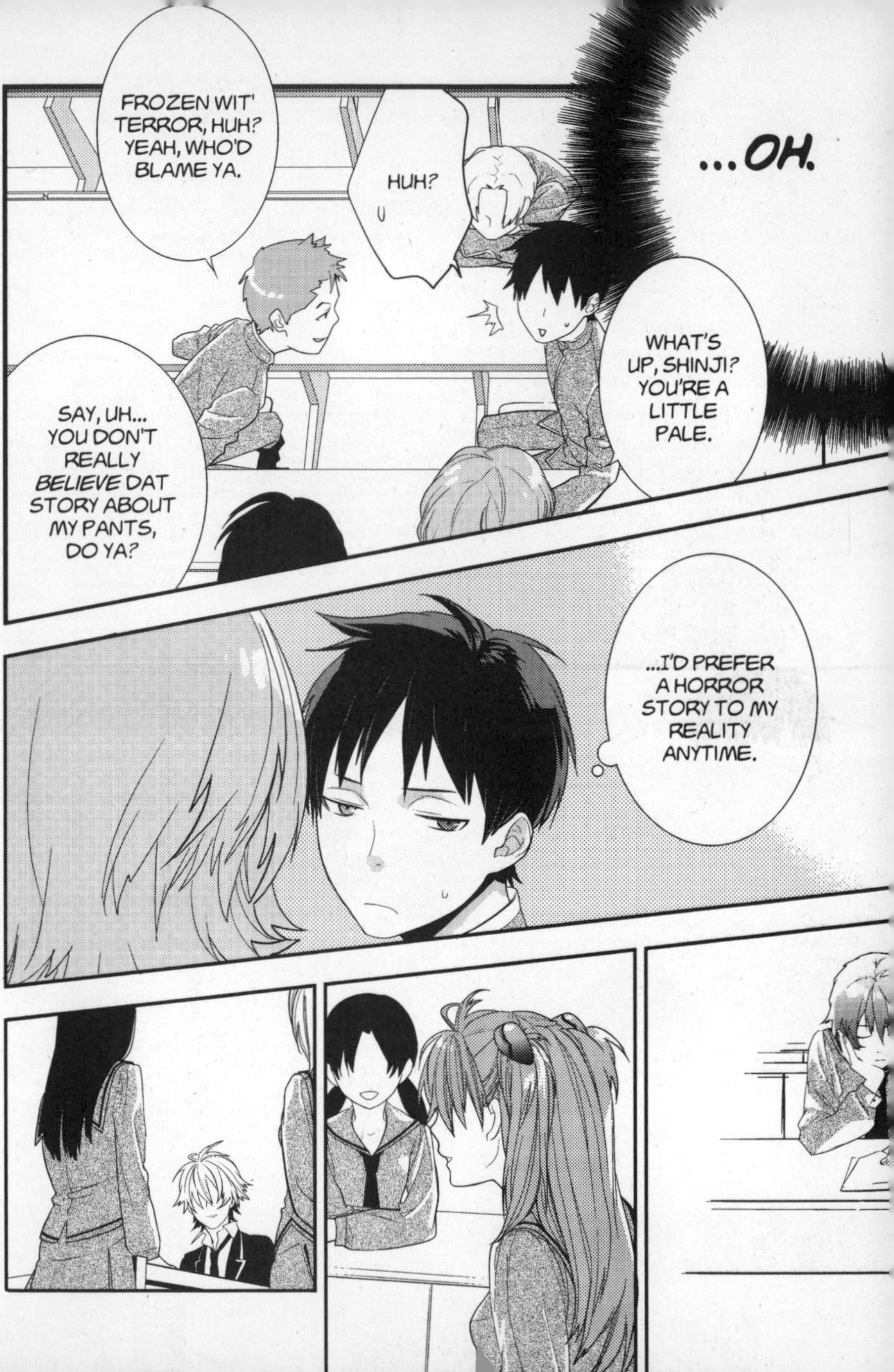
...OH.
WHAT'S UP, SHINJI? YOU'RE A LITTLE PALE.
HUH?
FROZEN WIT' TERROR, HUH? YEAH, WHO'D BLAME YA.
SAY, UH... YOU DON'T REALLY BELIEVE DAT STORY ABOUT MY PANTS, DO YA?
...I'D PREFER A HORROR STORY TO MY REALITY ANYTIME.

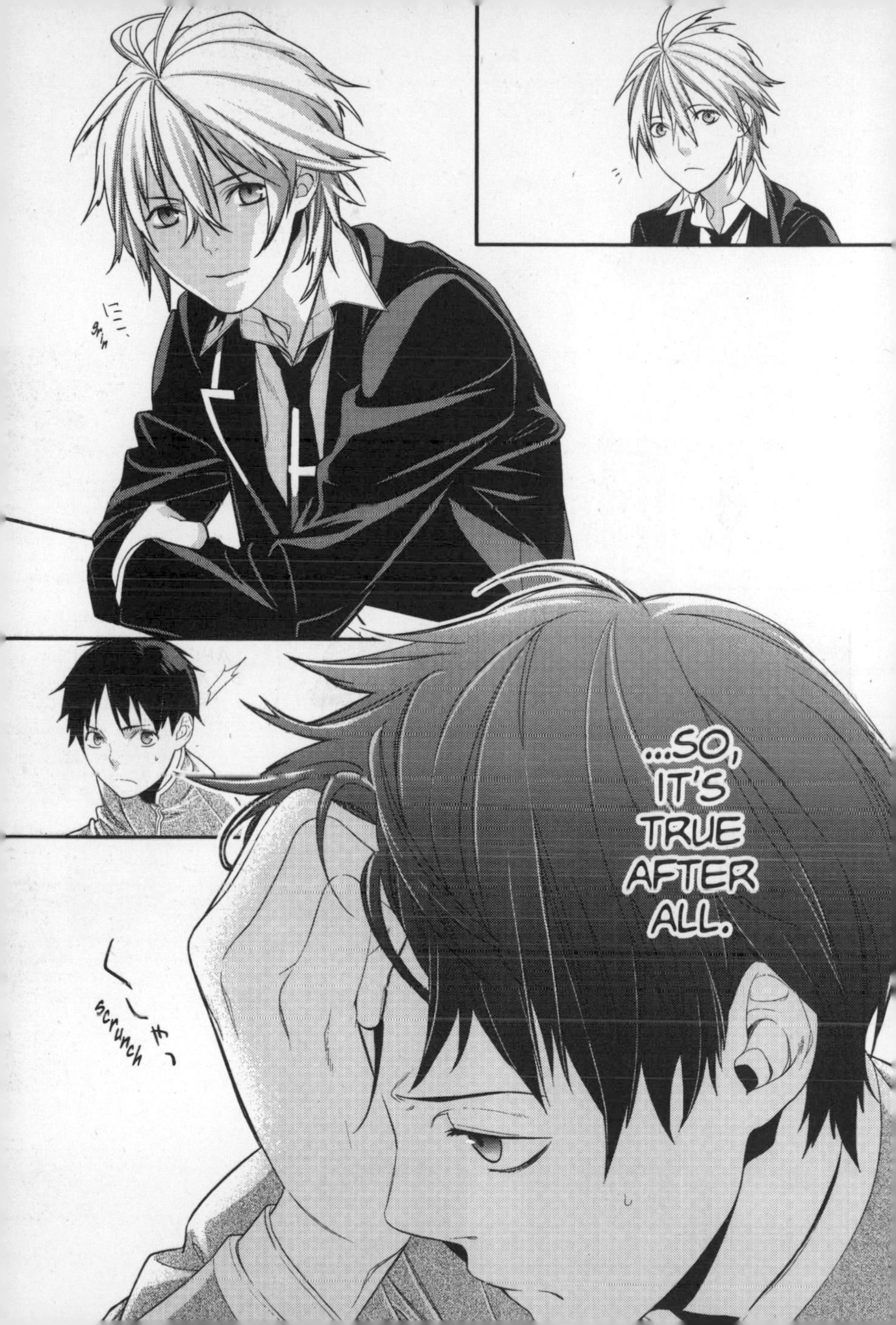
grin
...SO, IT'S TRUE AFTER ALL.
scrunch

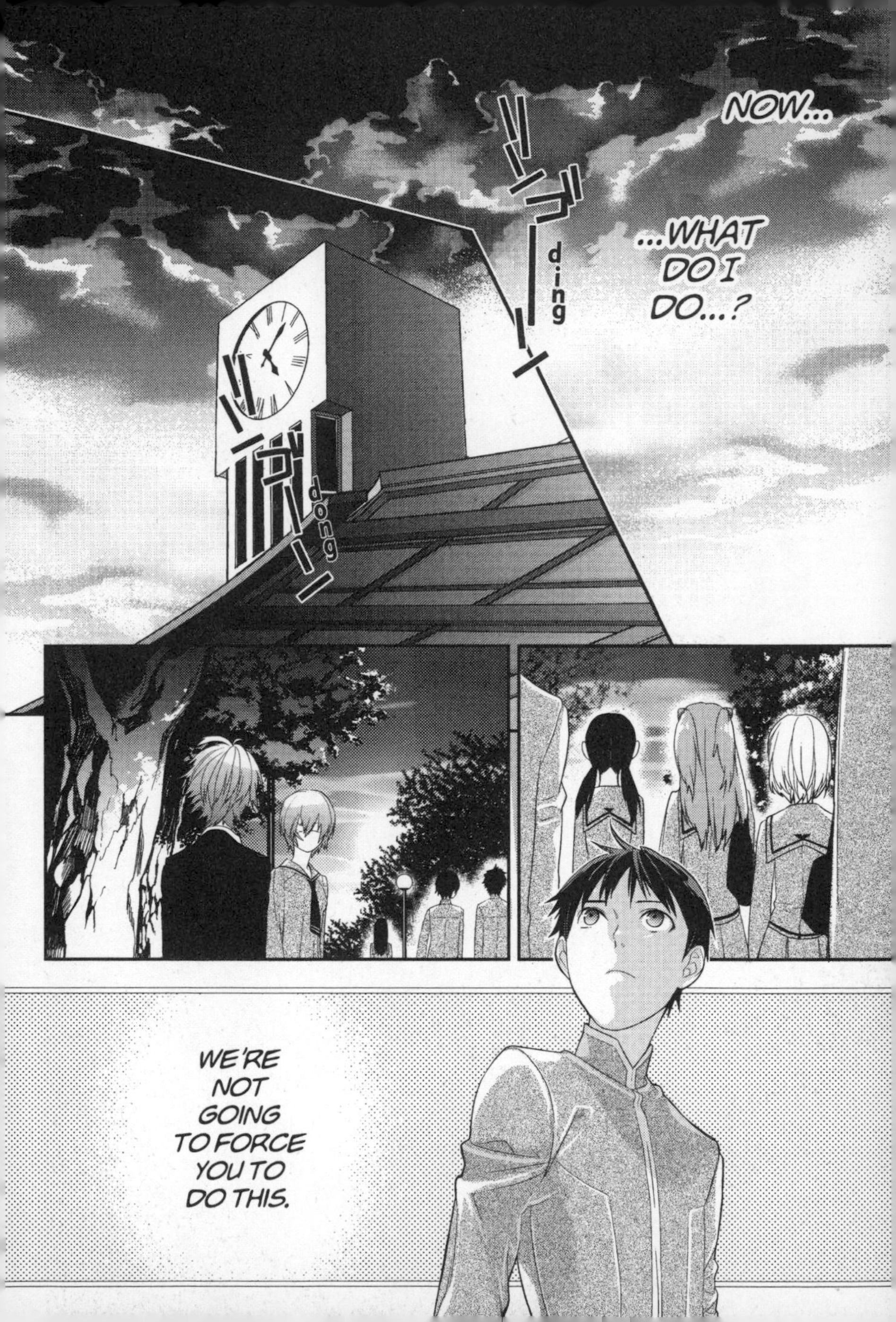
NOW...
...WHAT DO I DO...?
ding
dong
WE'RE NOT GOING TO FORCE YOU TO DO THIS.

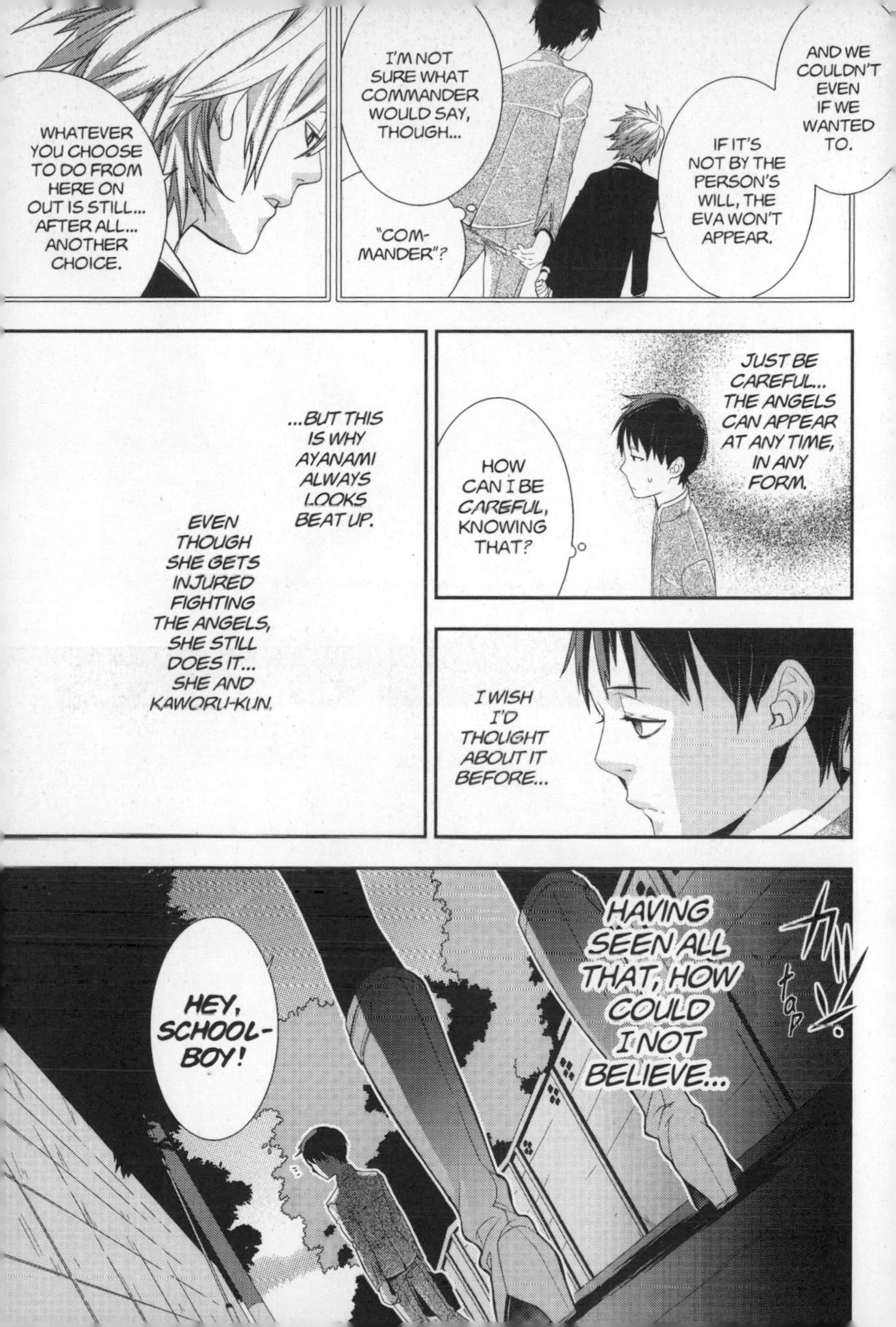
IF IT'S NOT BY THE PERSON'S WILL, THE EVA WON'T APPEAR.
AND WE COULDN'T EVEN IF WE WANTED TO.
I'M NOT SURE WHAT COMMANDER WOULD SAY, THOUGH...
"COM-MANDER"?
WHATEVER YOU CHOOSE TO DO FROM HERE ON OUT IS STILL... AFTER ALL... ANOTHER CHOICE.
JUST BE CAREFUL... THE ANGELS CAN APPEAR AT ANY TIME, IN ANY FORM.
HOW CAN I BE CAREFUL, KNOWING THAT?
I WISH I'D THOUGHT ABOUT IT BEFORE...
...BUT THIS IS WHY AYANAMI ALWAYS LOOKS BEAT UP.
EVEN THOUGH SHE GETS INJURED FIGHTING THE ANGELS, SHE STILL DOES IT... SHE AND KAWORU-KUN.
HAVING SEEN ALL THAT, HOW COULD I NOT BELIEVE...
tap
HEY, SCHOOL-BOY!

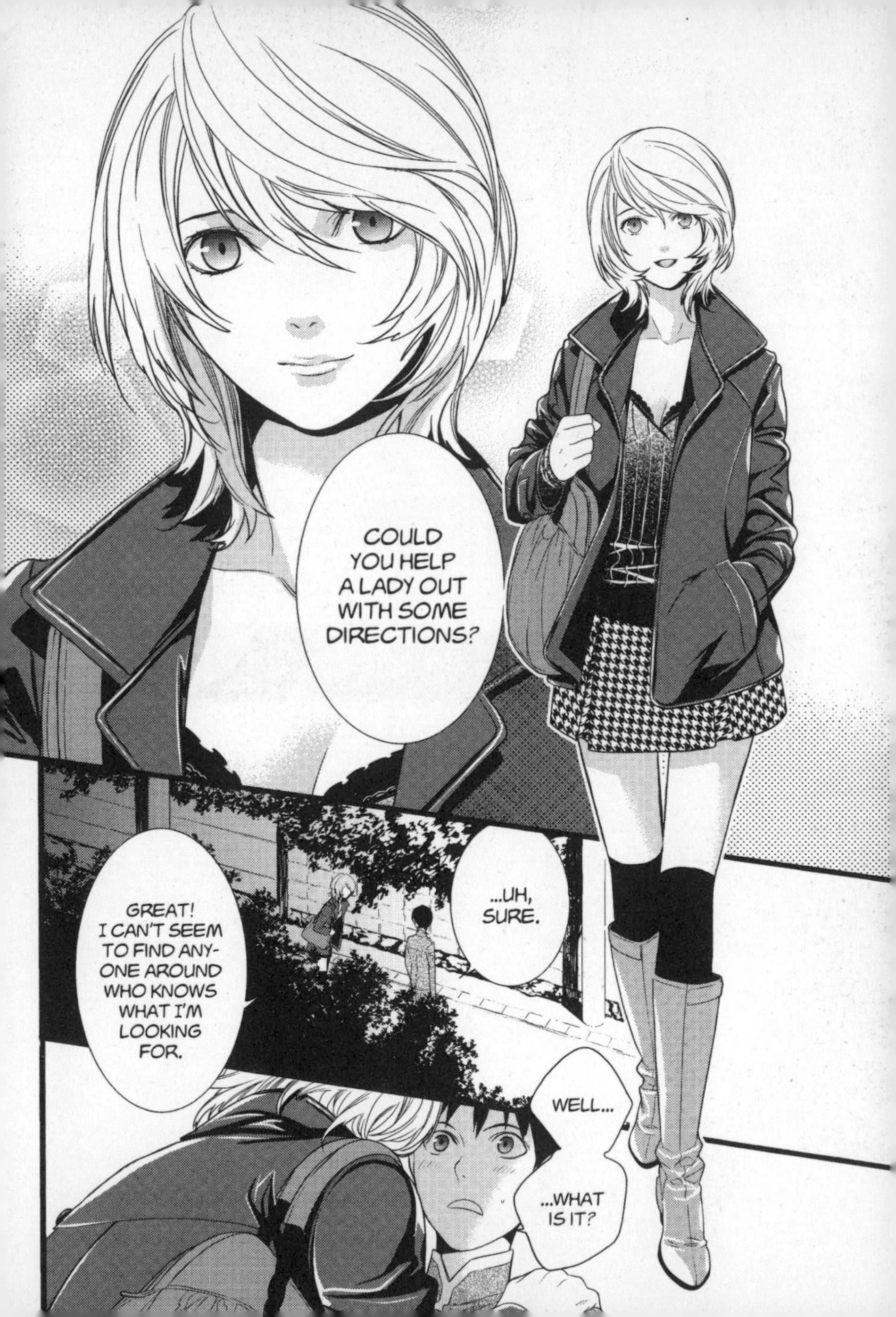
COULD YOU HELP A LADY OUT WITH SOME DIRECTIONS?
...UH, SURE.
GREAT! I CAN'T SEEM TO FIND ANY-ONE AROUND WHO KNOWS WHAT I'M LOOKING FOR.
WELL...
...WHAT IS IT?

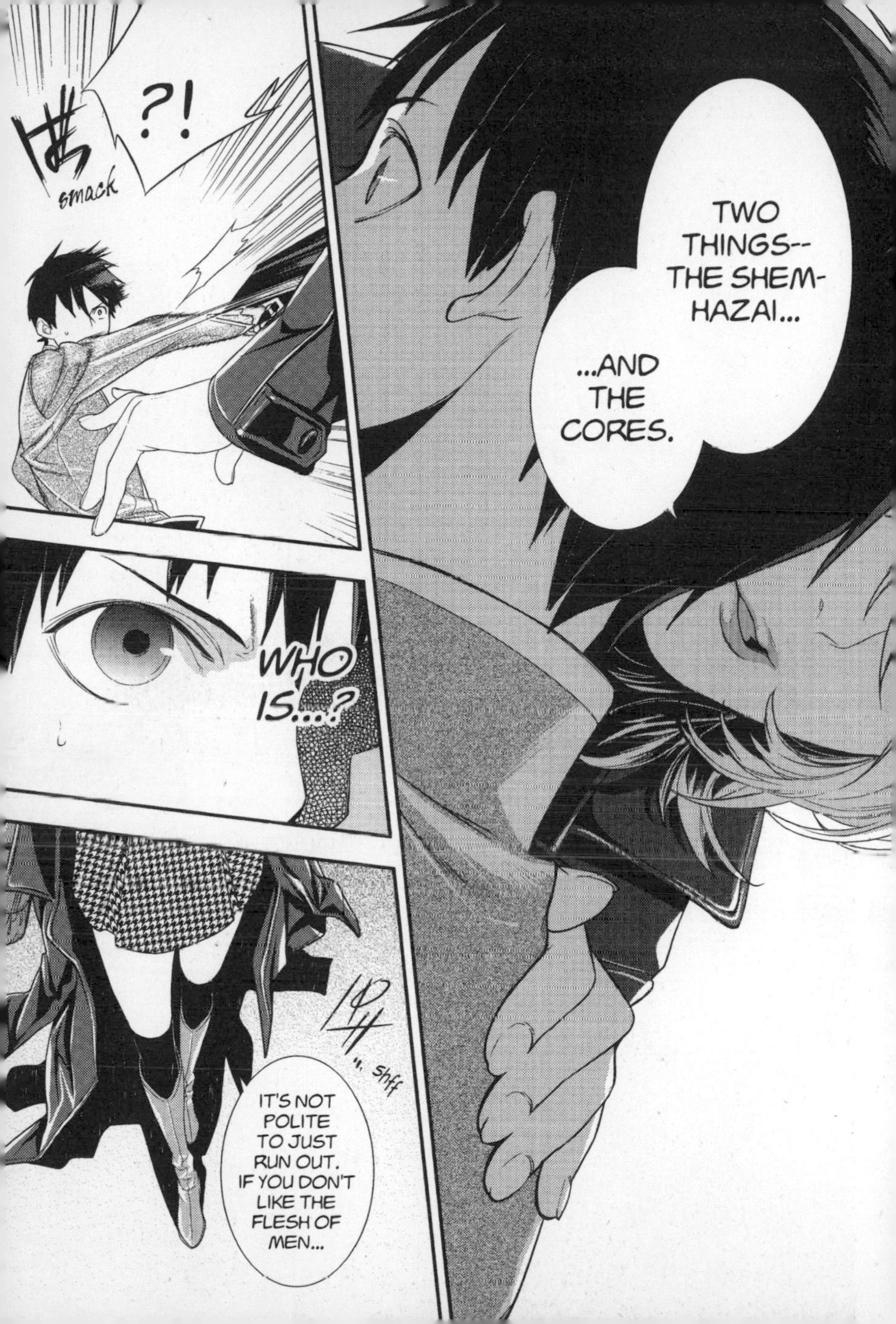
TWO THINGS-- THE SHEM-HAZAI...
...AND THE CORES.
?!
smack
WHO IS...?
shff
IT'S NOT POLITE TO JUST RUN OUT. IF YOU DON'T LIKE THE FLESH OF MEN...

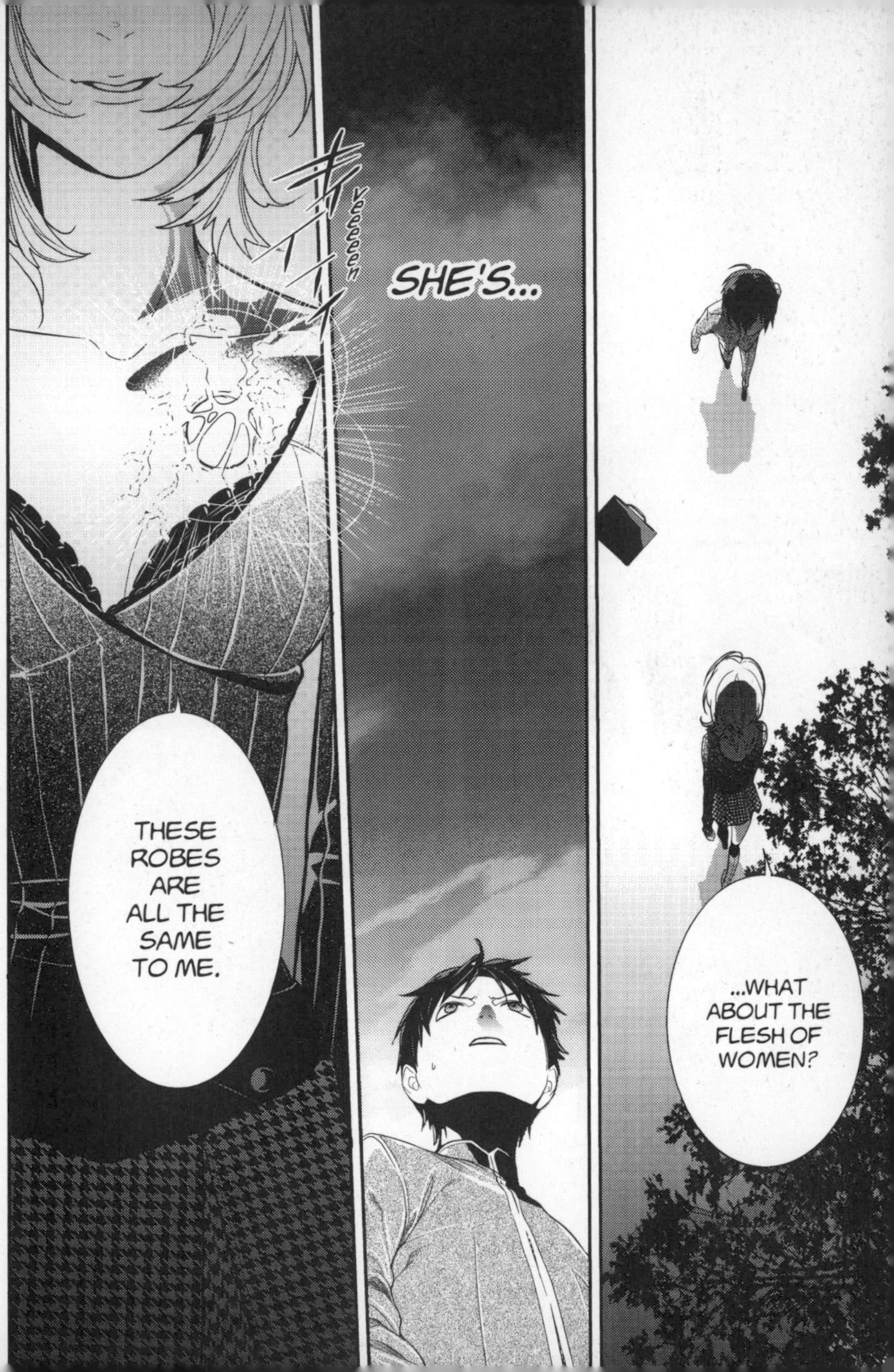
...WHAT ABOUT THE FLESH OF WOMEN?
SHE'S...
veeeeen
THESE ROBES ARE ALL THE SAME TO ME.

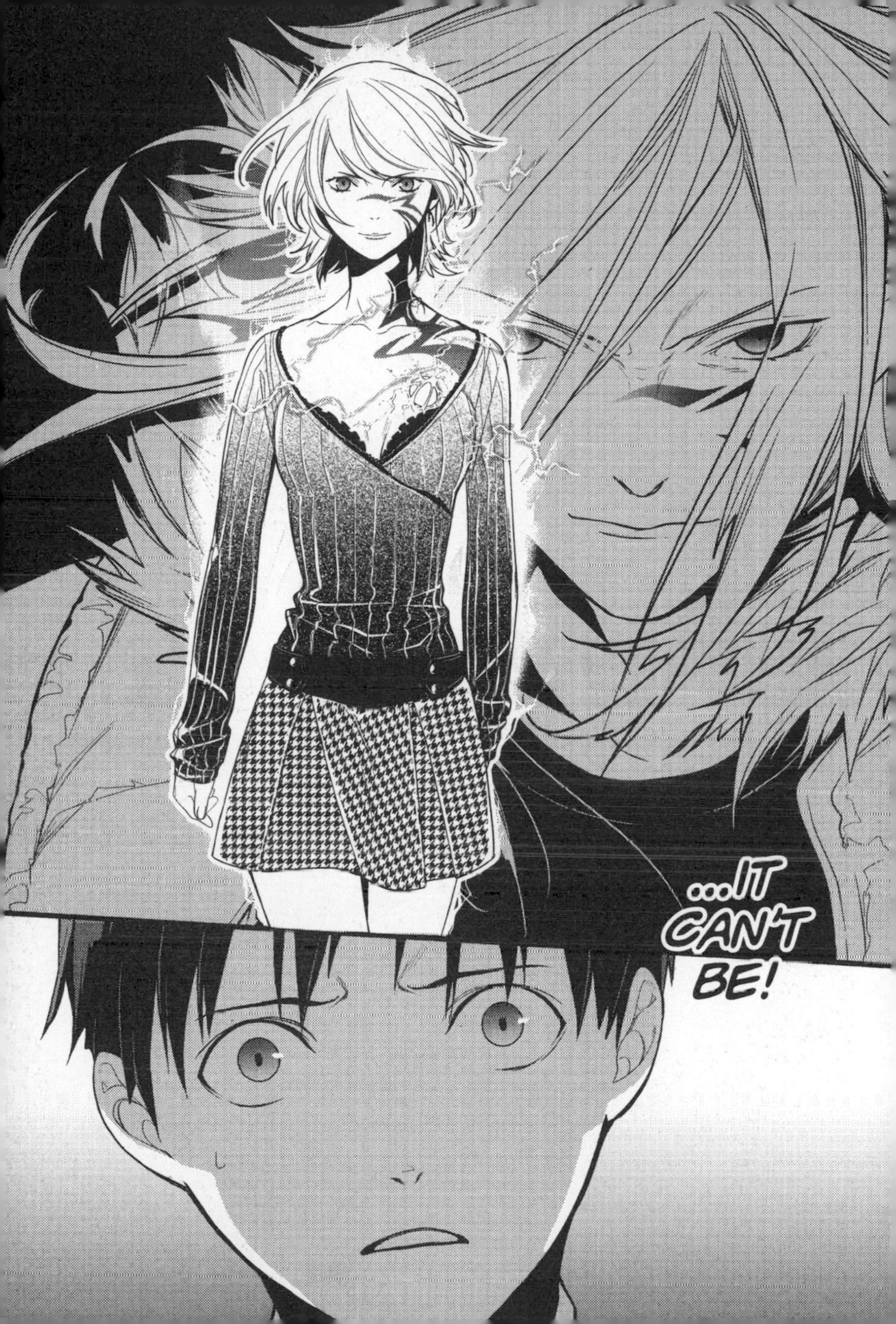
...IT CAN'T BE!

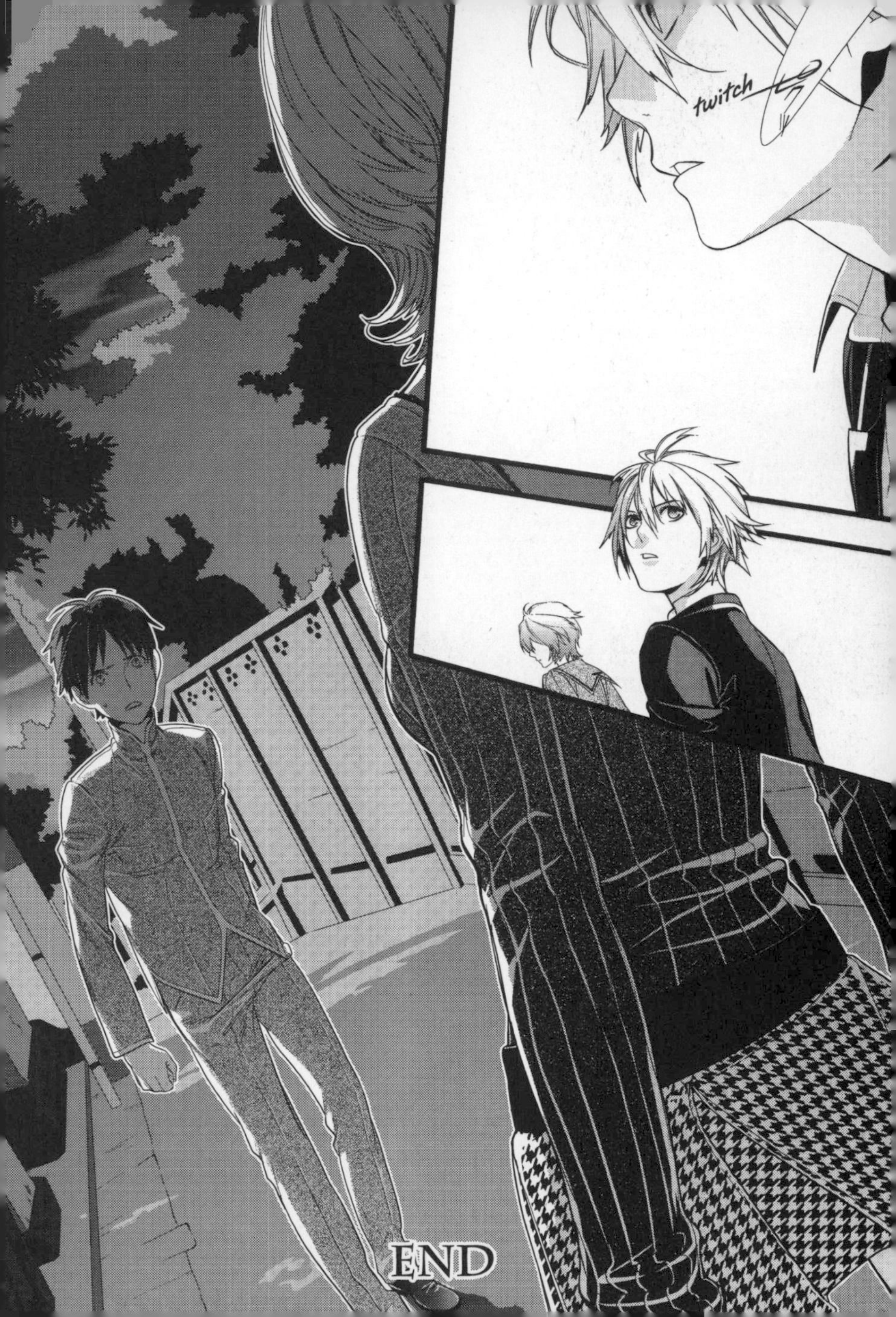
twitch
END

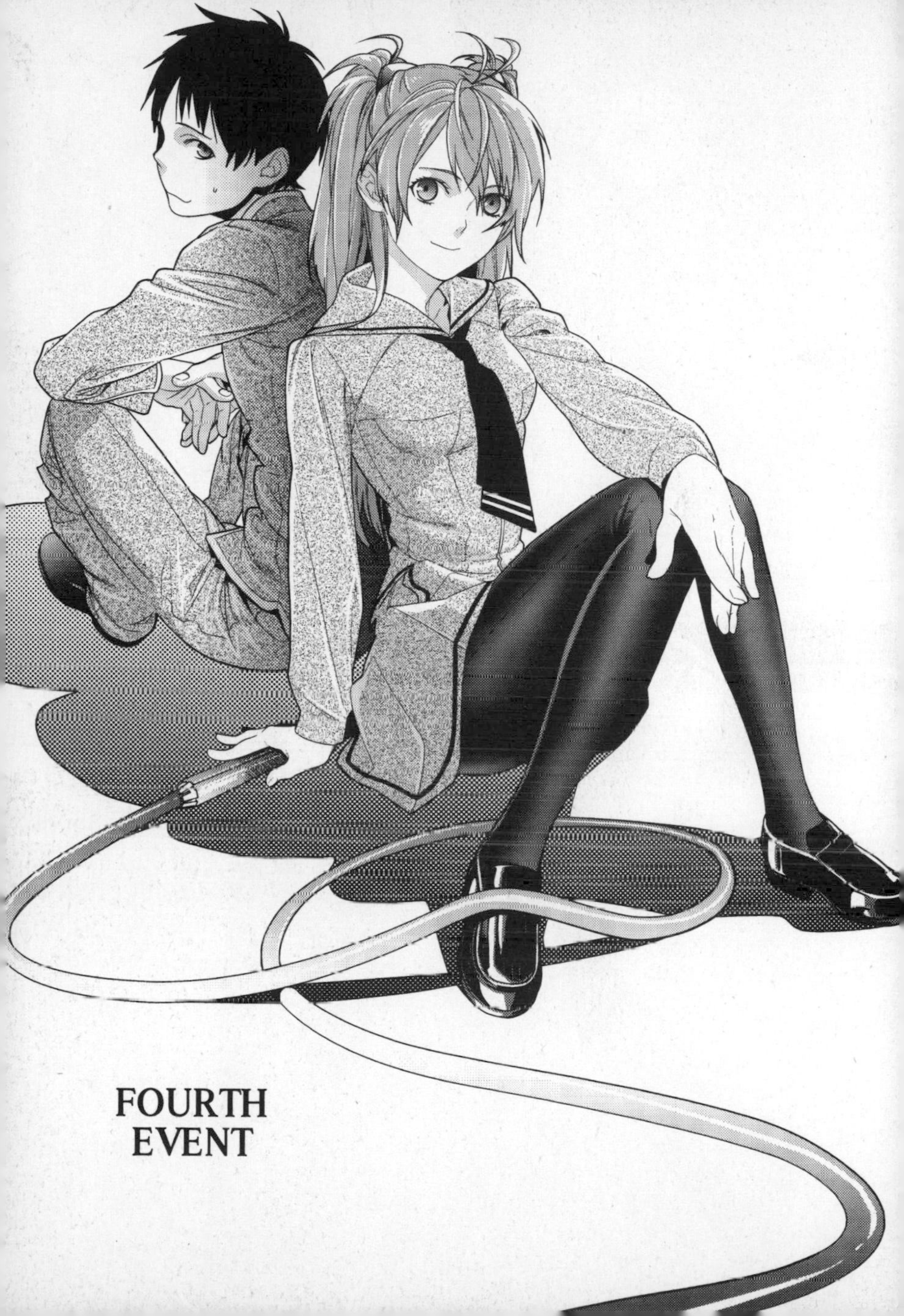

FOURTH EVENT

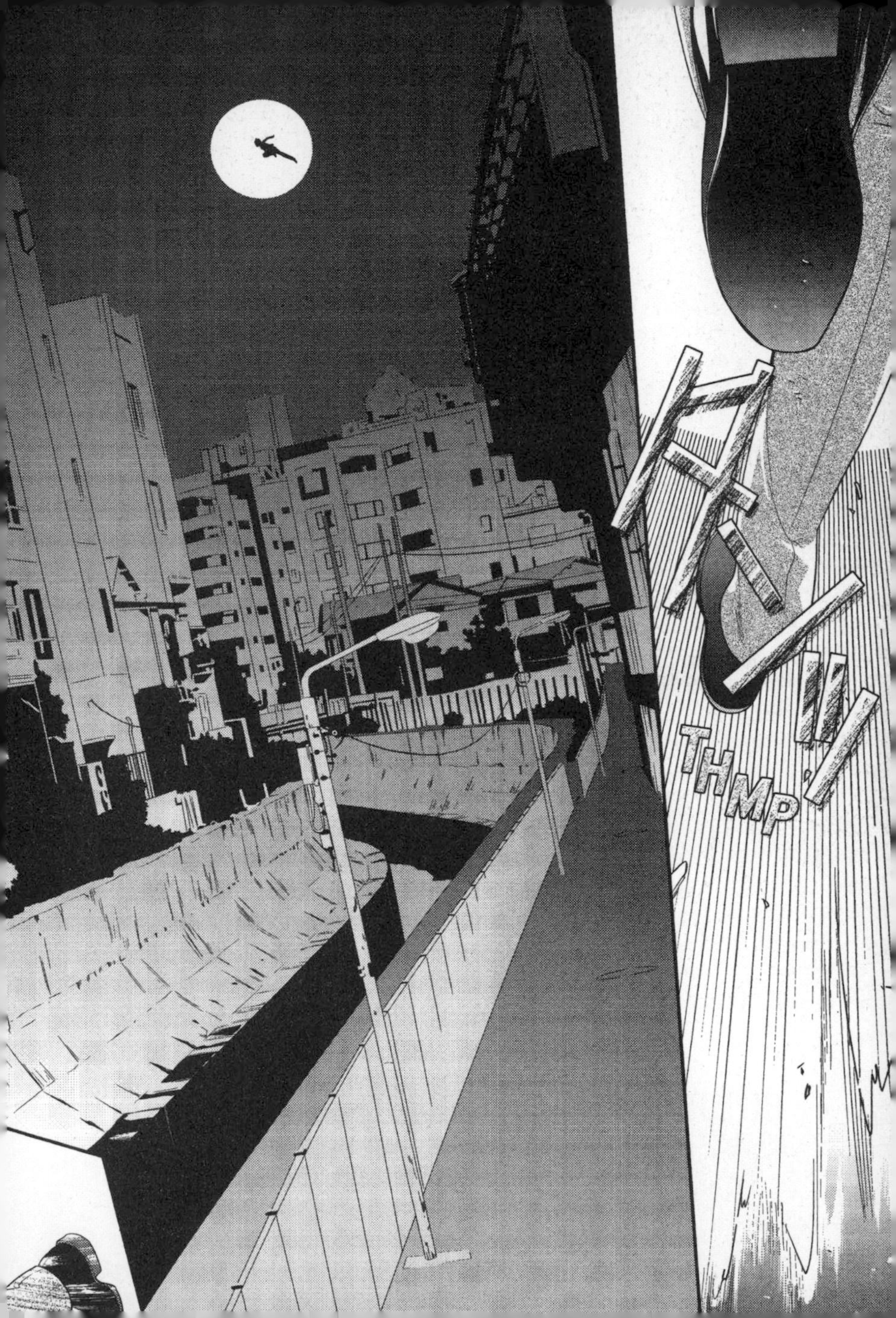
THMP

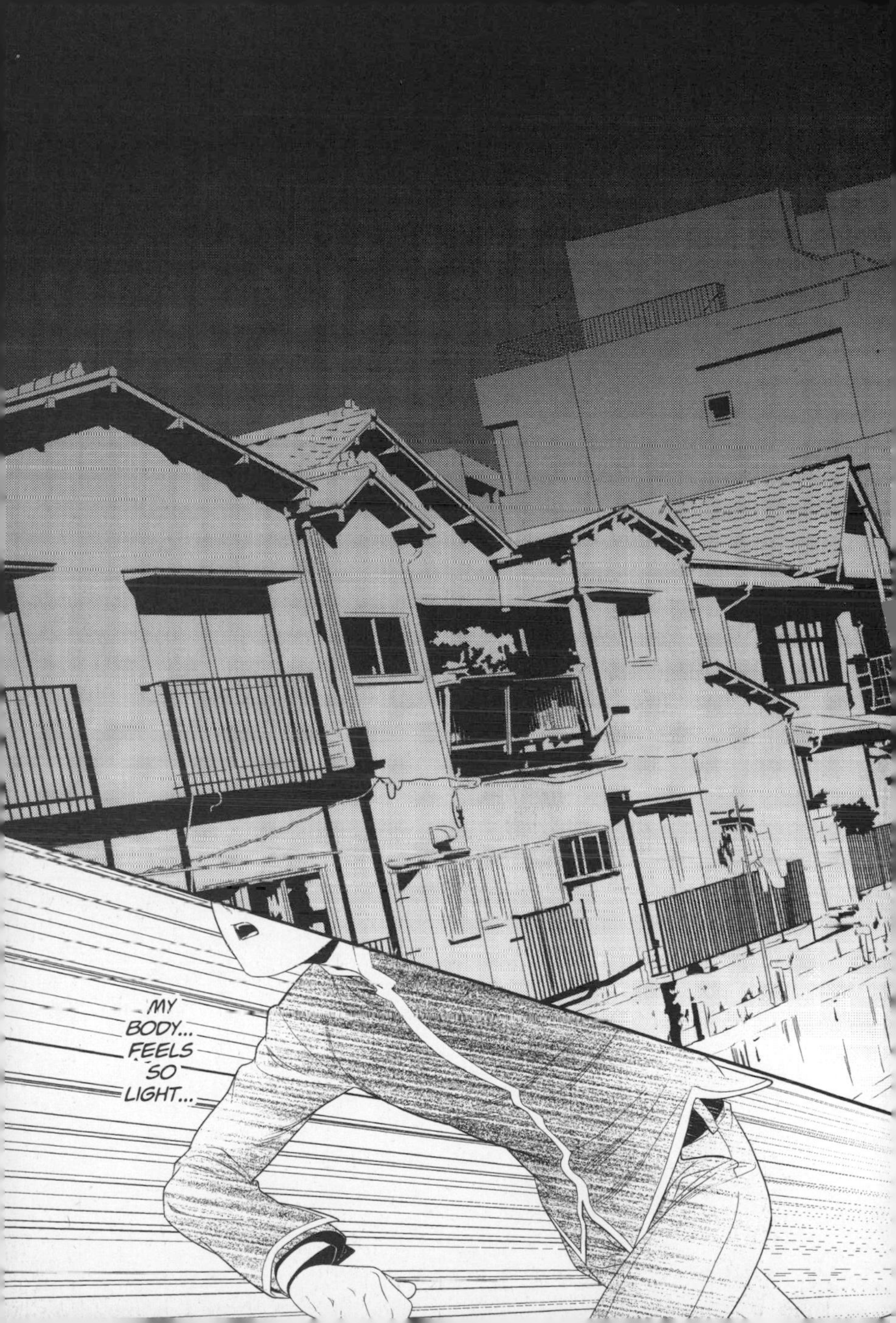
MY BODY... FEELS SO LIGHT...

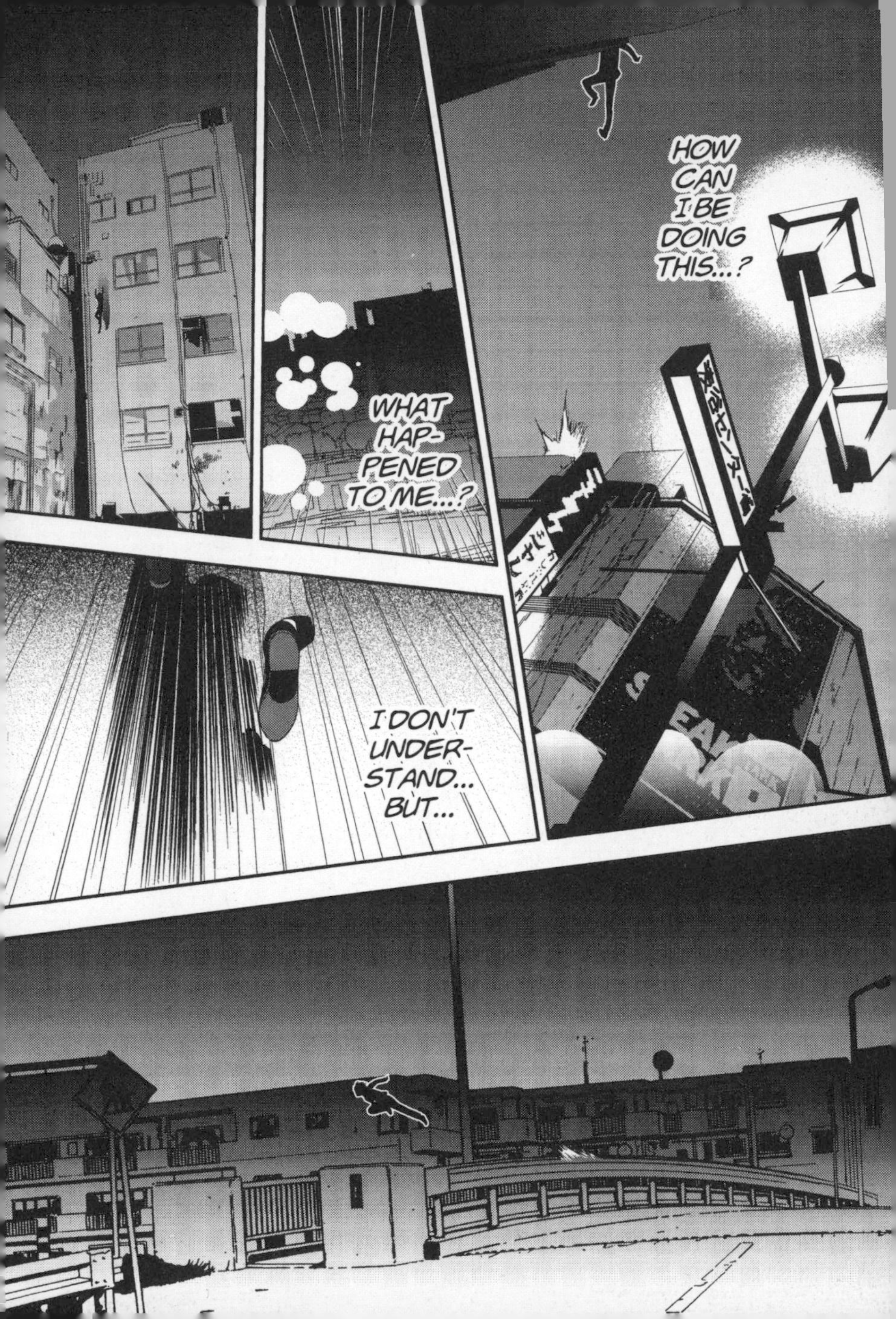
HOW CAN I BE DOING THIS...?
WHAT HAP-PENED TO ME...?
I DON'T UNDER-STAND... BUT...

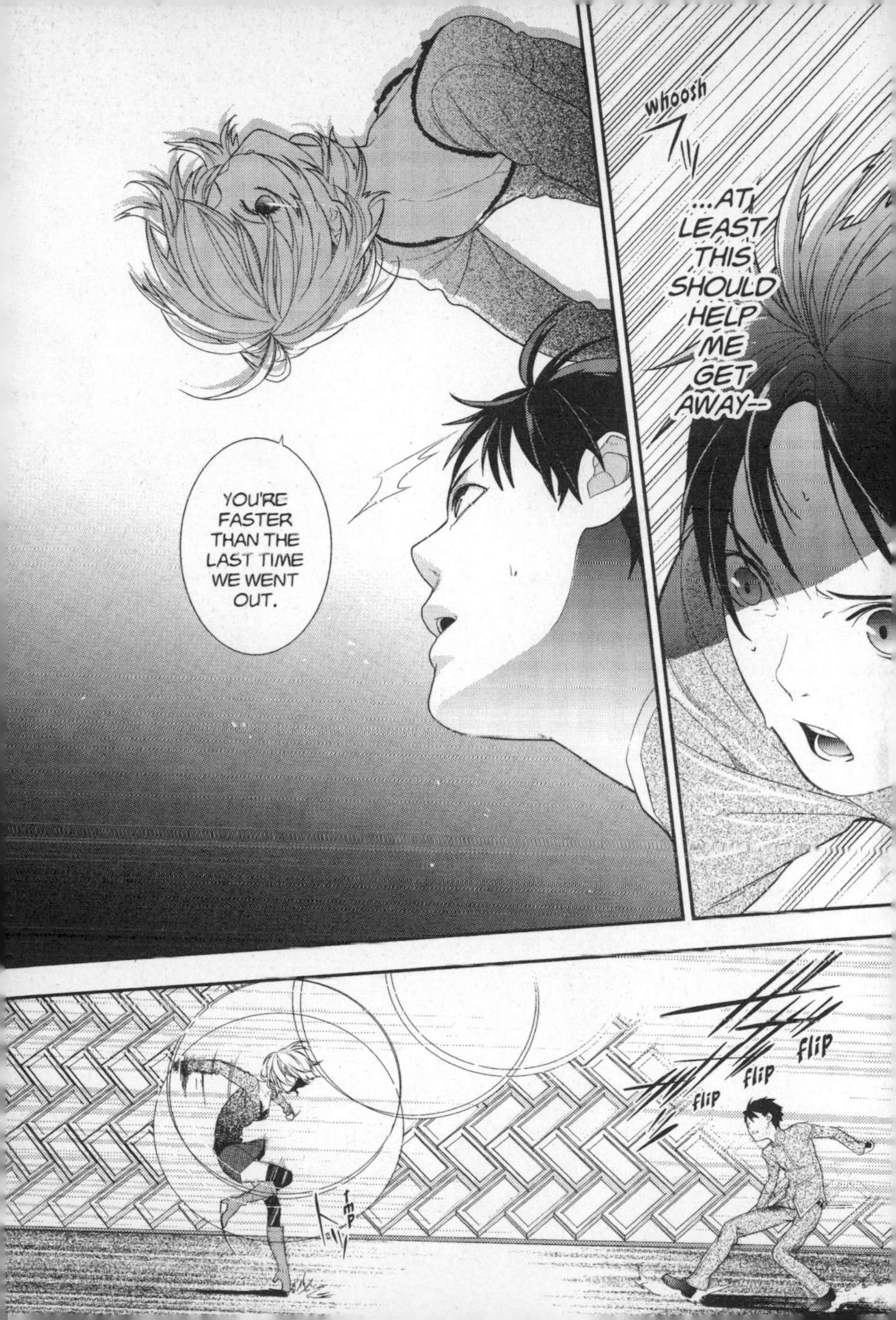
whoosh
...AT LEAST THIS SHOULD HELP ME GET AWAY—
YOU'RE FASTER THAN THE LAST TIME WE WENT OUT.
flip
flip
flip
tmp

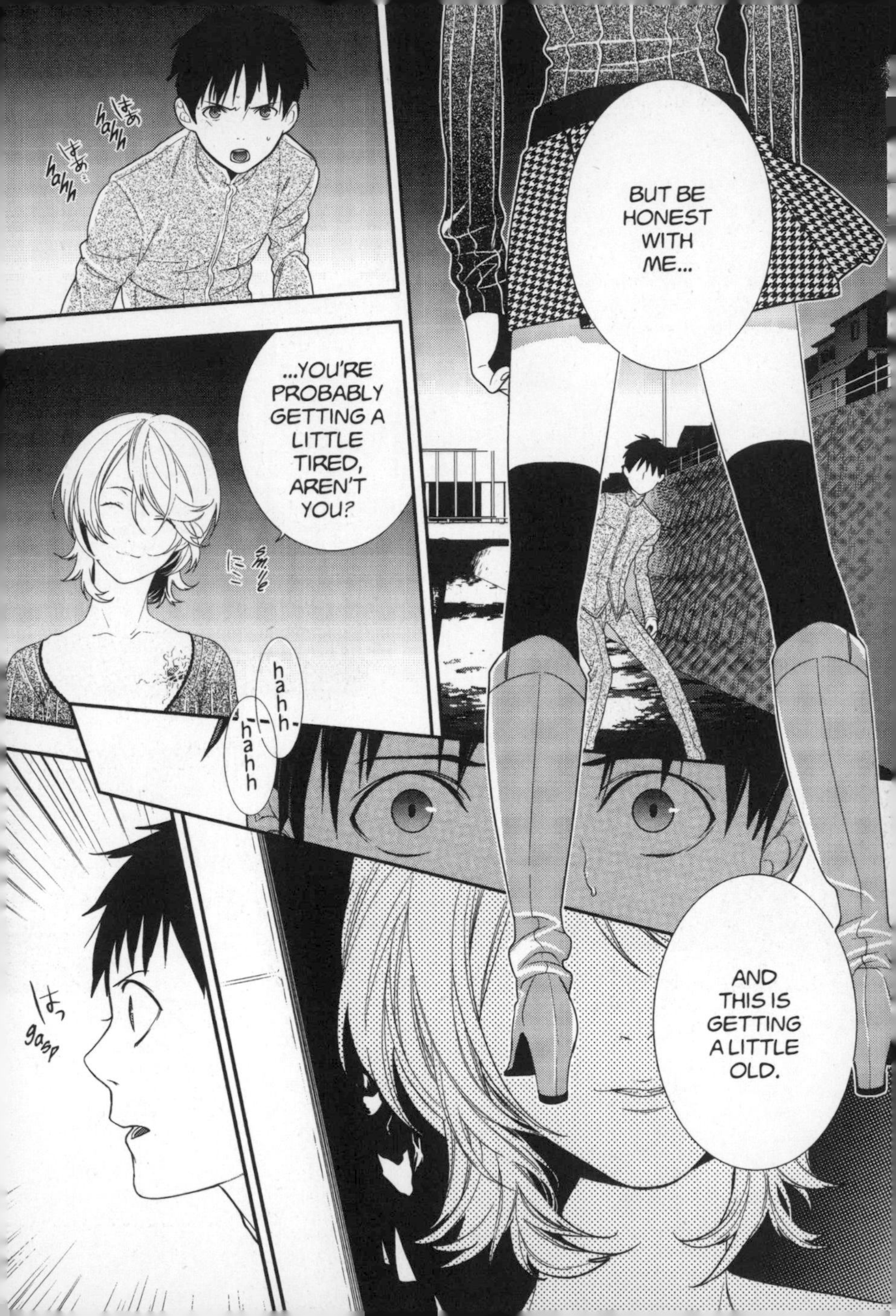
BUT BE HONEST WITH ME...
はあ hahh
はあ hahh
...YOU'RE PROBABLY GETTING A LITTLE TIRED, AREN'T YOU?
にこ
hahh-
hahh
AND THIS IS GETTING A LITTLE OLD.
はっ gasp

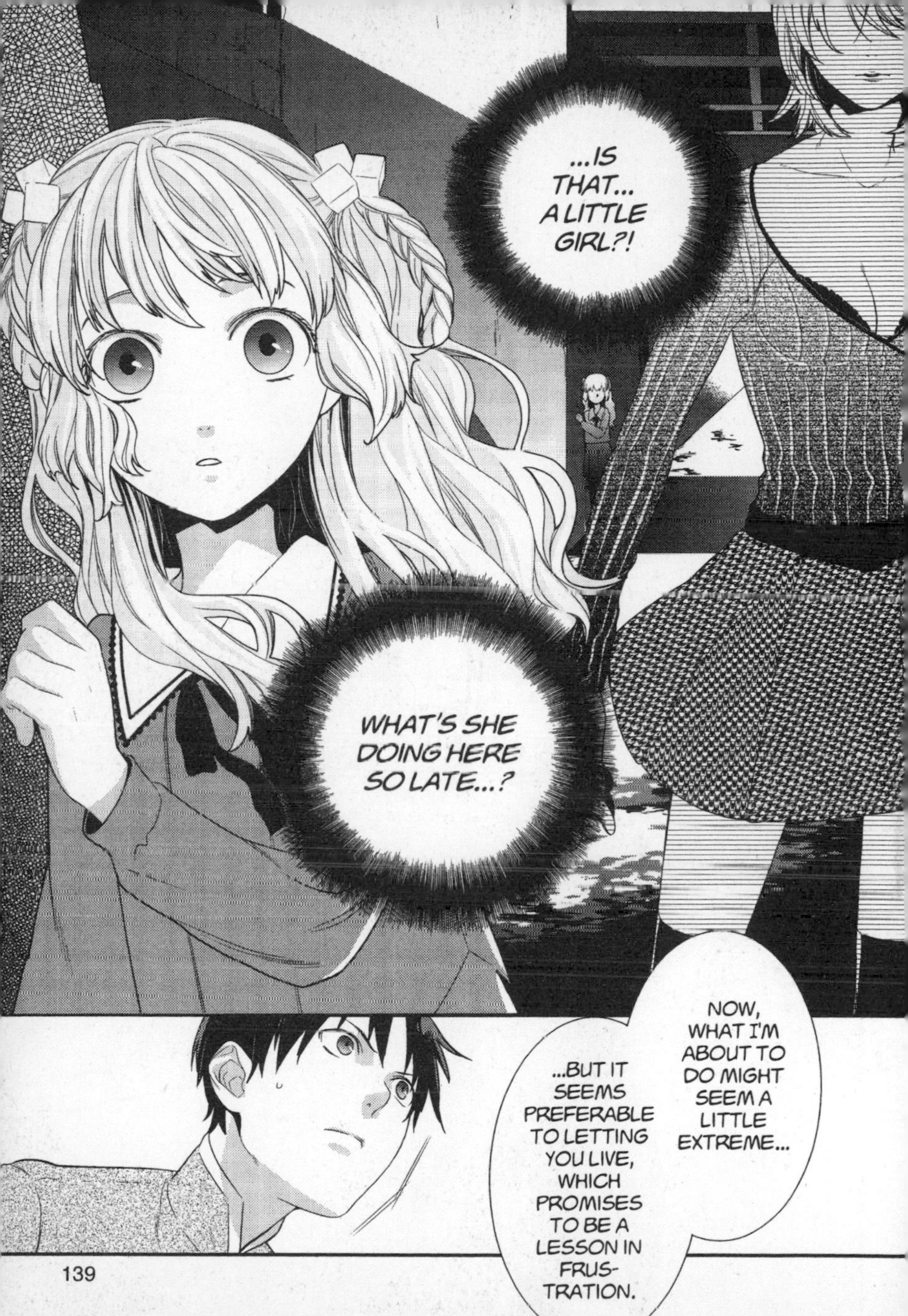
...IS THAT... A LITTLE GIRL?!
WHAT'S SHE DOING HERE SO LATE...?
NOW, WHAT I'M ABOUT TO DO MIGHT SEEM A LITTLE EXTREME...
...BUT IT SEEMS PREFERABLE TO LETTING YOU LIVE, WHICH PROMISES TO BE A LESSON IN FRUS-TRATION.

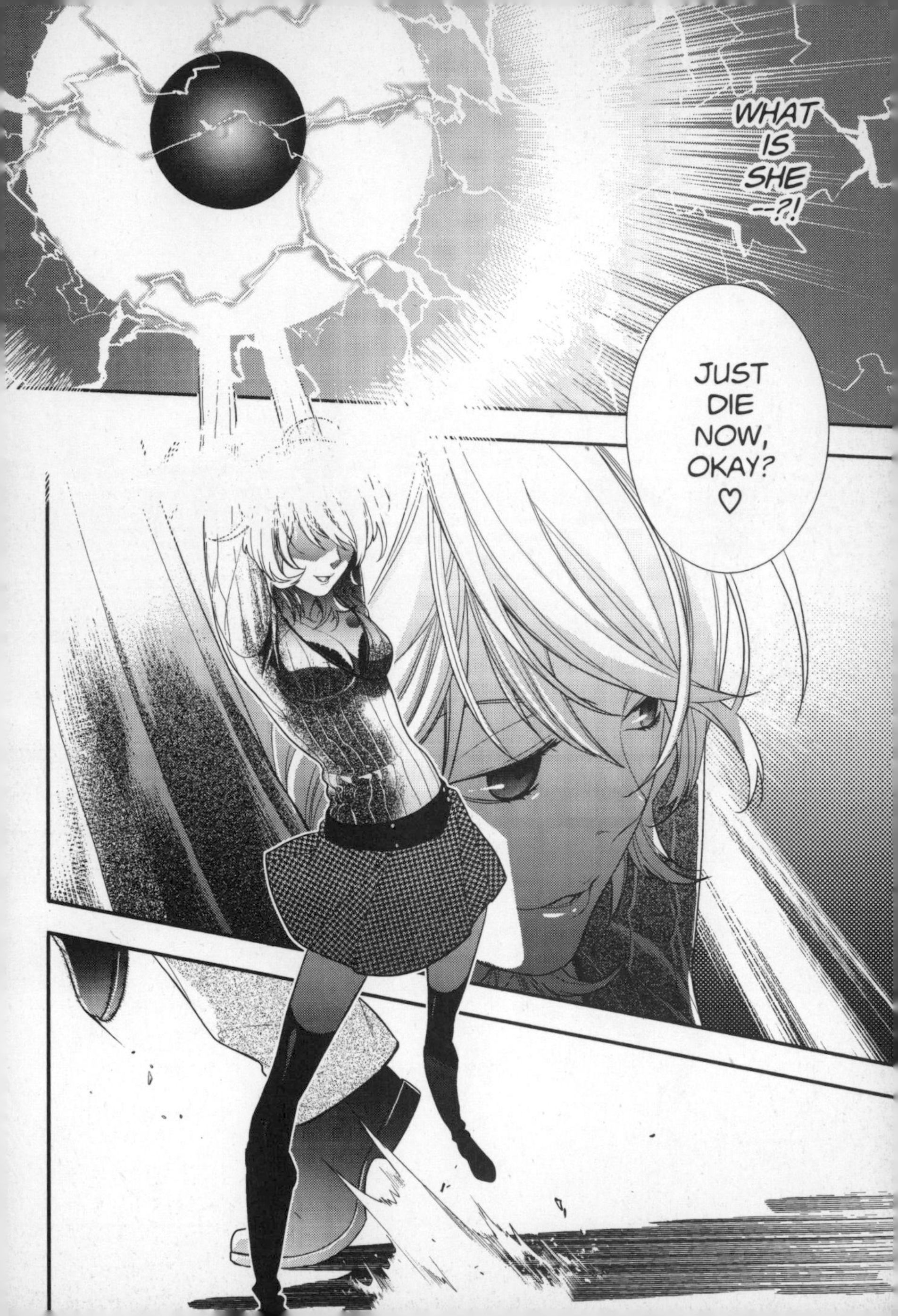
WHAT IS SHE --?!
JUST DIE NOW, OKAY? ♡

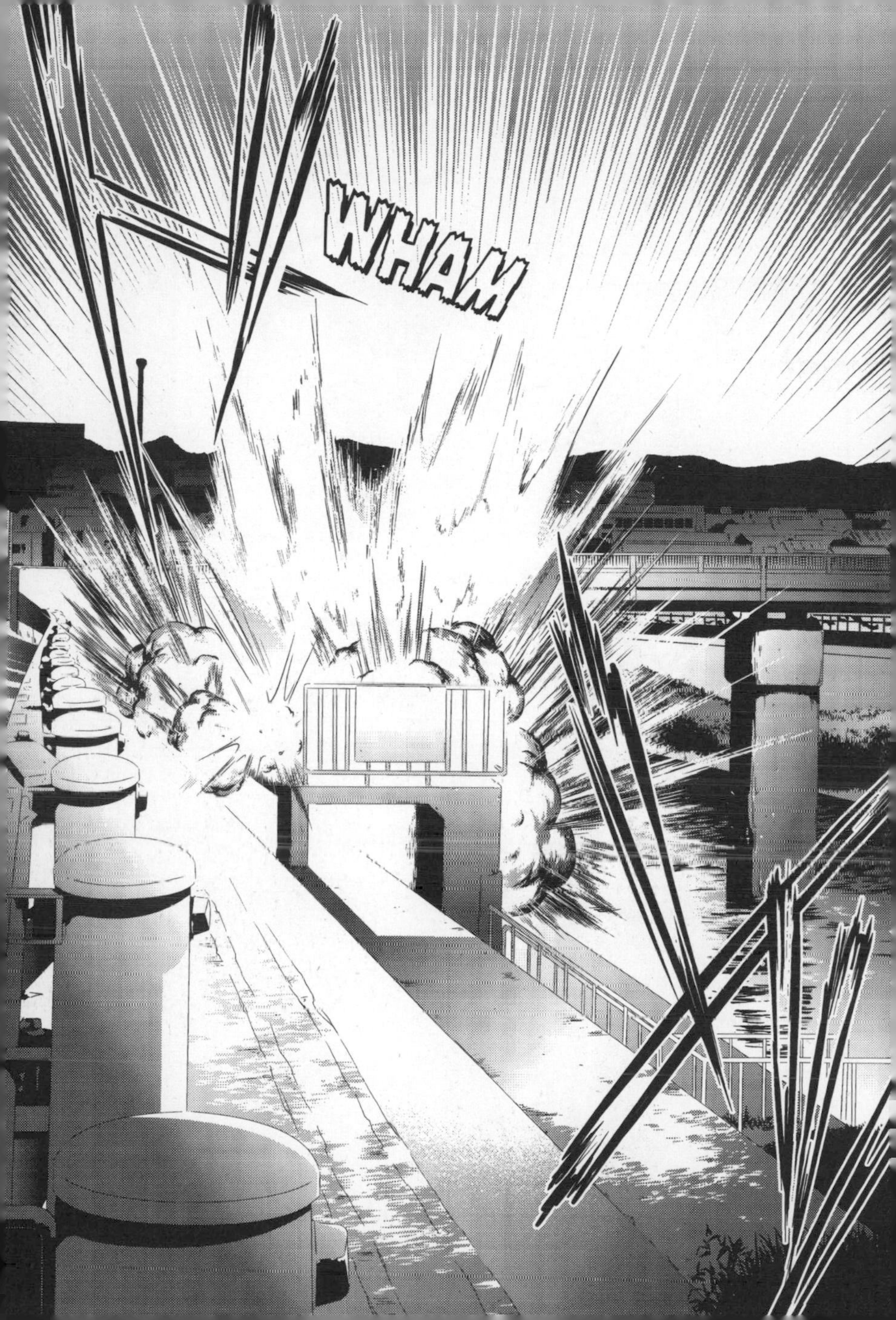
WHAM

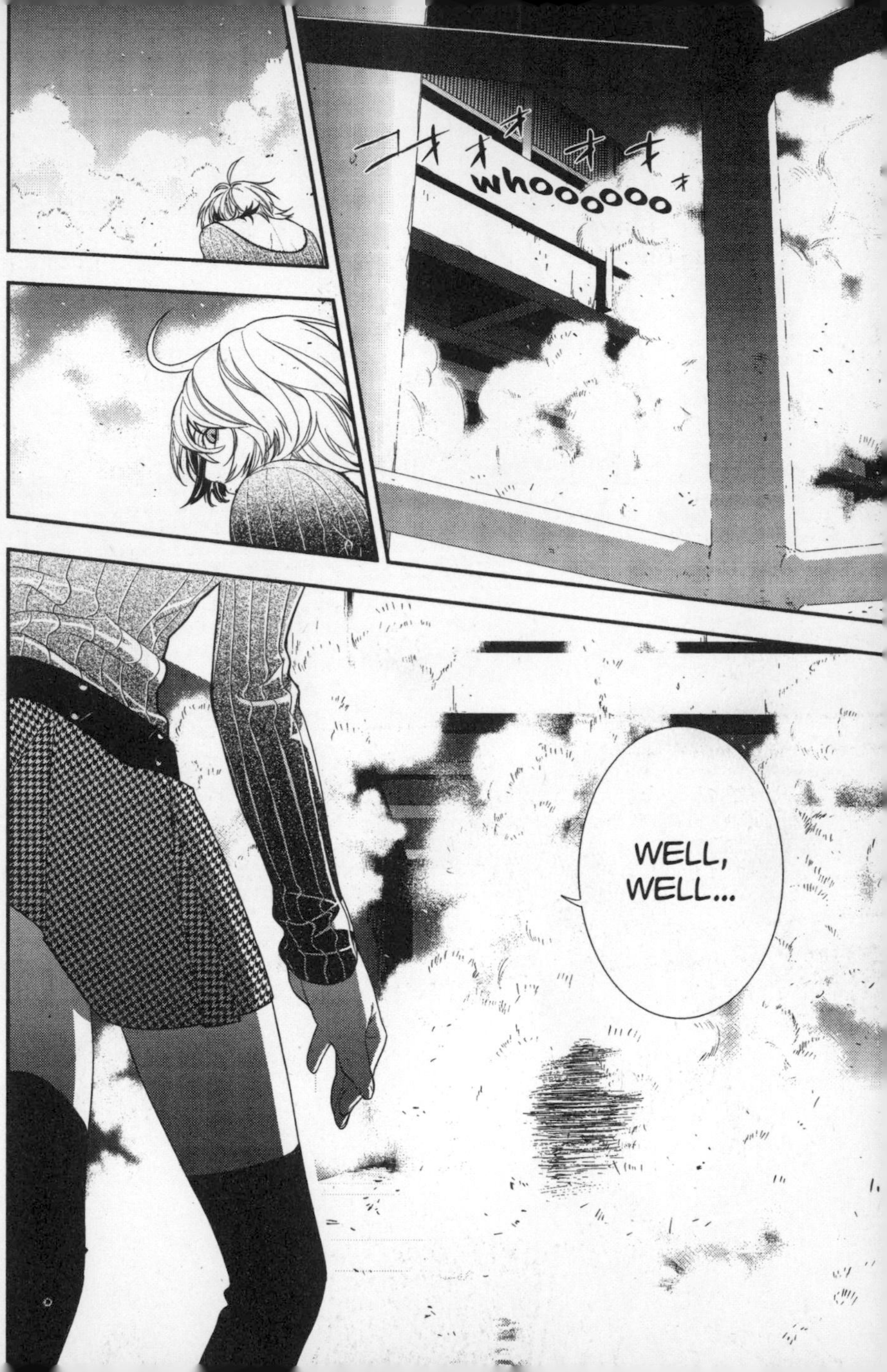
コオオオオオォ
whoooooo
WELL, WELL...

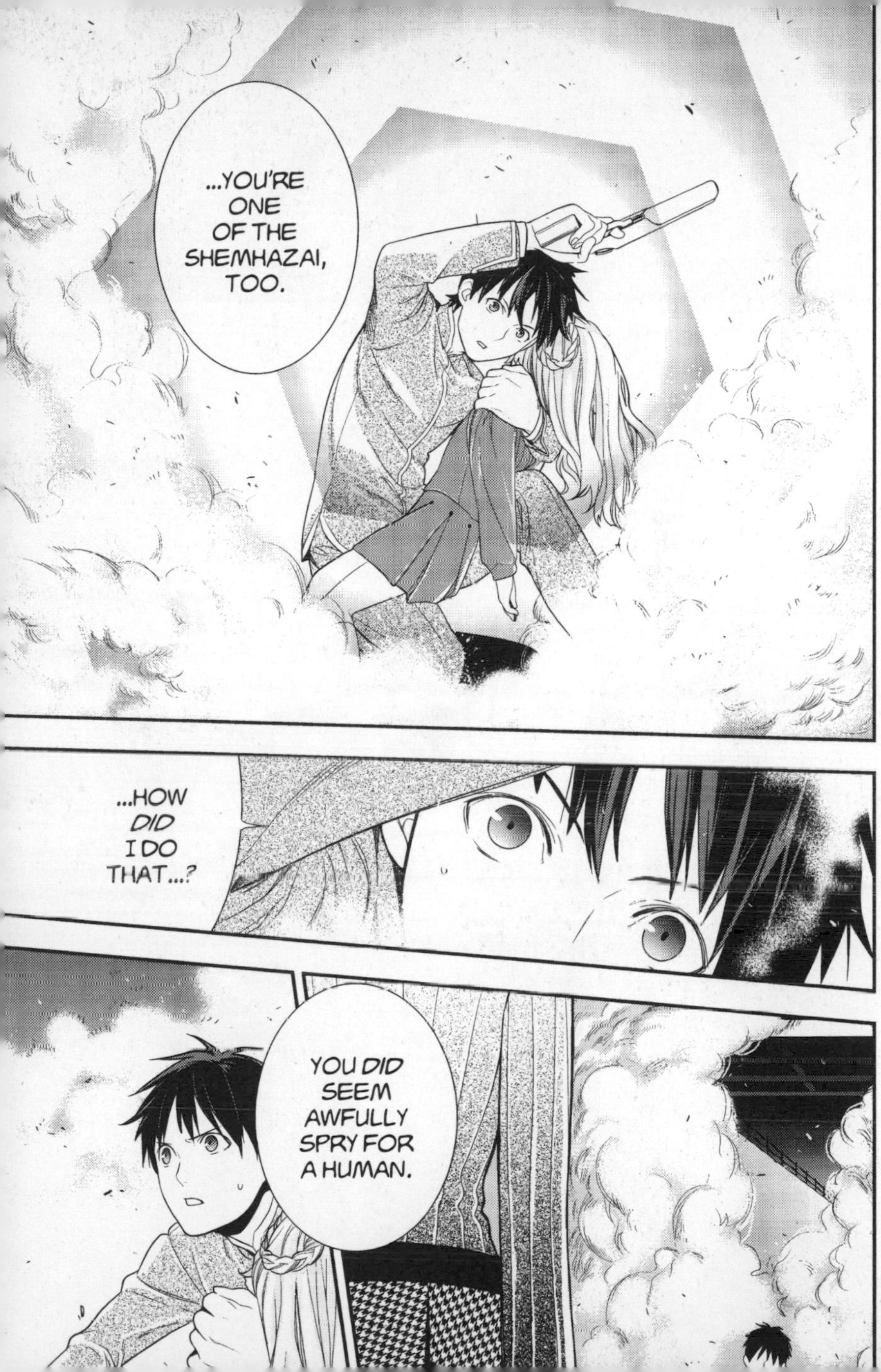
...YOU'RE ONE OF THE SHEMHAZAI, TOO.
...HOW *DID* I DO THAT...?
YOU *DID* SEEM AWFULLY SPRY FOR A HUMAN.

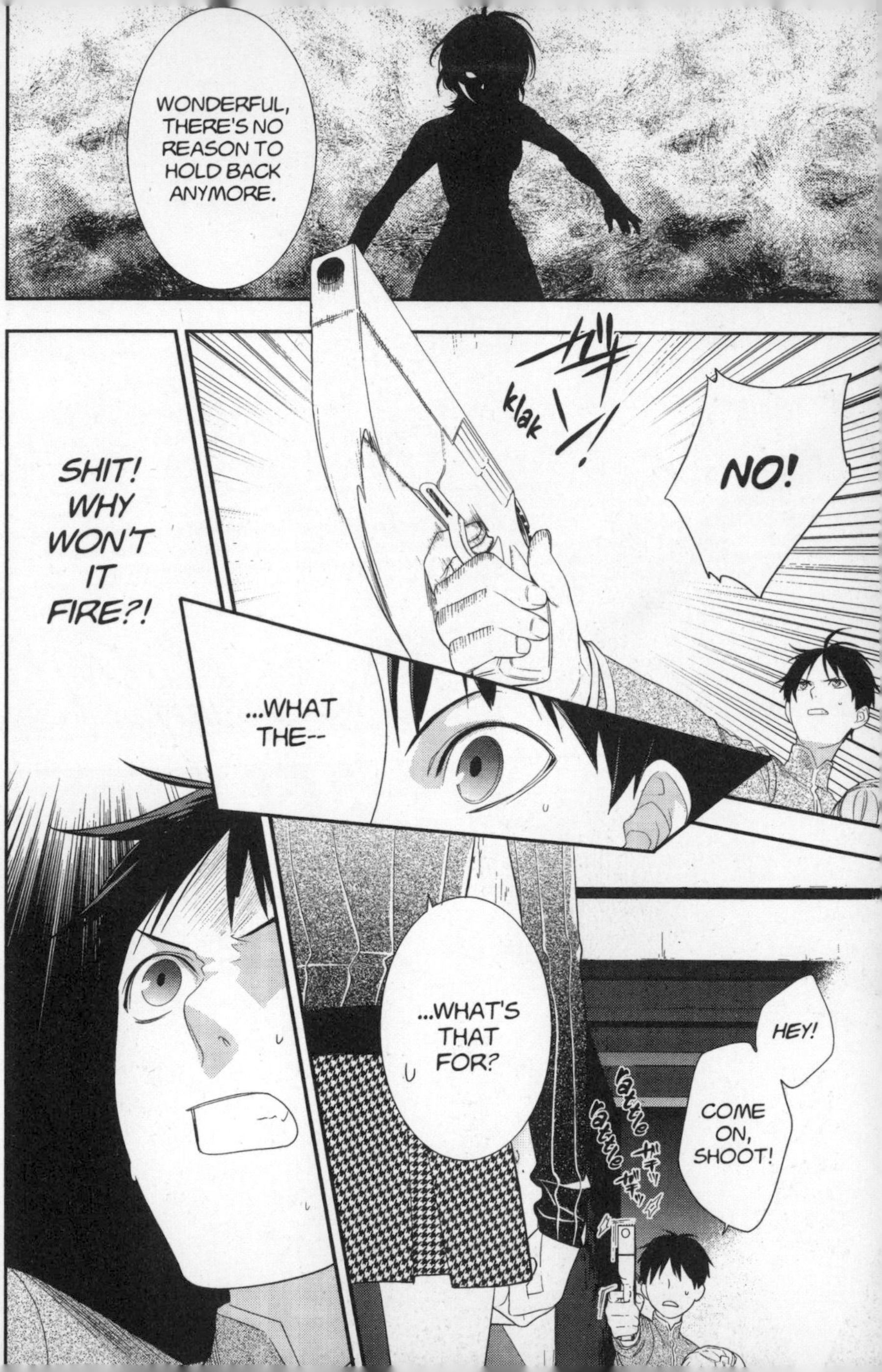
WONDERFUL, THERE'S NO REASON TO HOLD BACK ANYMORE.
klak
NO!
...WHAT THE--
HEY!
COME ON, SHOOT!
rattle rattle
...WHAT'S THAT FOR?
SHIT! WHY WON'T IT FIRE?!

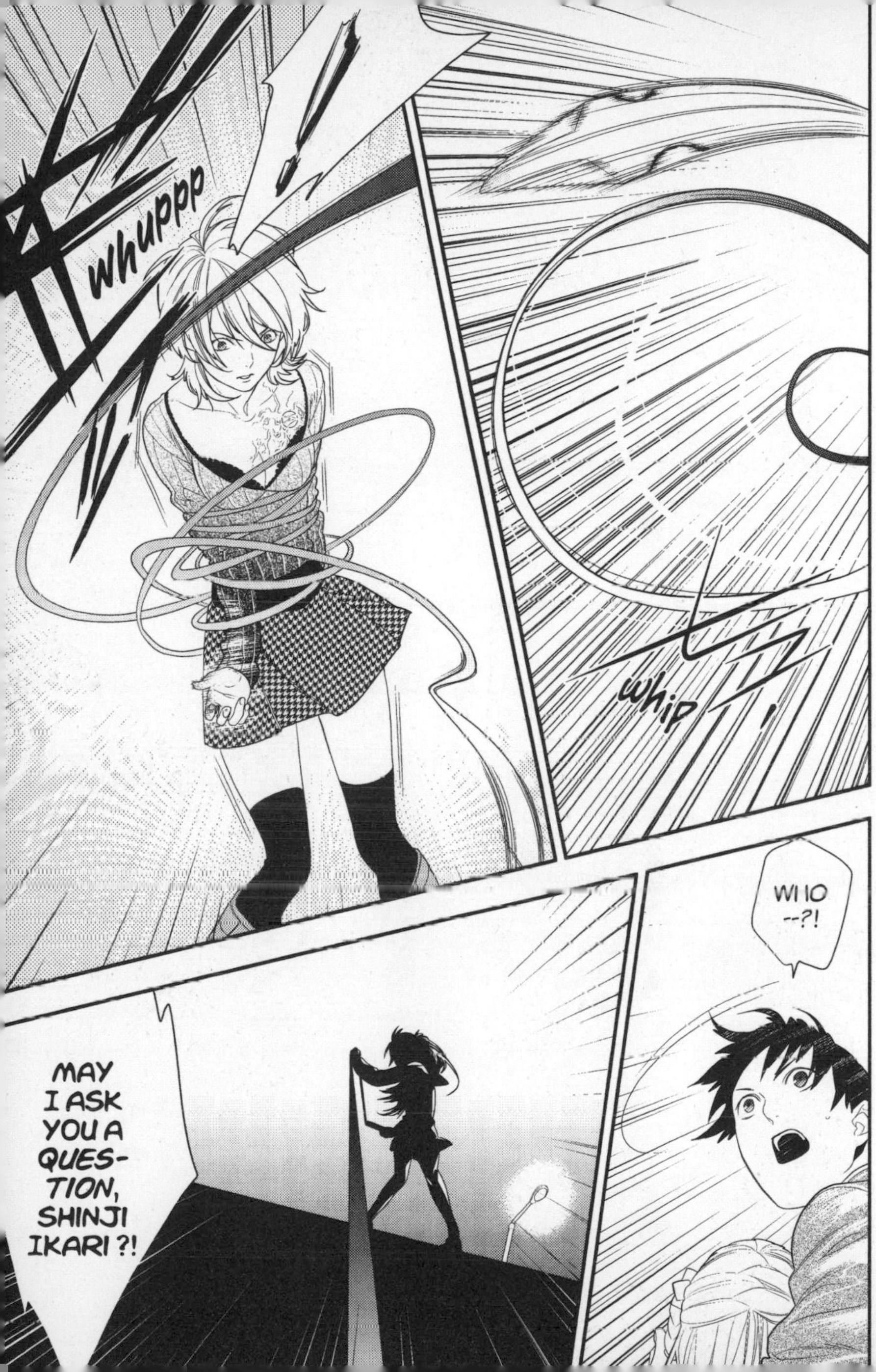
whip
whuppp
WHO --?!
MAY I ASK YOU A QUESTION, SHINJI IKARI ?!

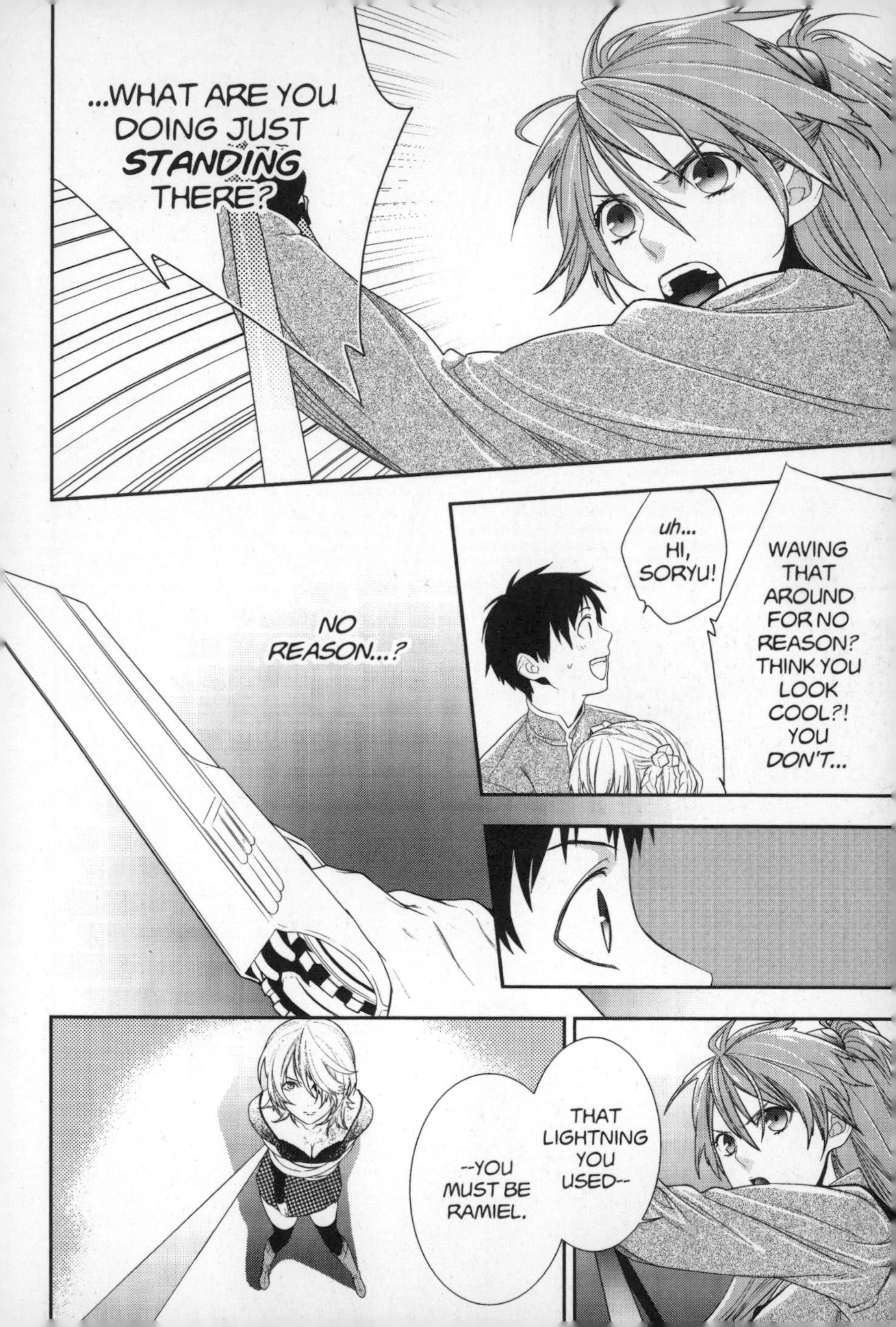
...WHAT ARE YOU DOING JUST STANDING THERE?
WAVING THAT AROUND FOR NO REASON? THINK YOU LOOK COOL?! YOU DON'T...
uh... HI, SORYU!
NO REASON...?
THAT LIGHTNING YOU USED--
--YOU MUST BE RAMIEL.

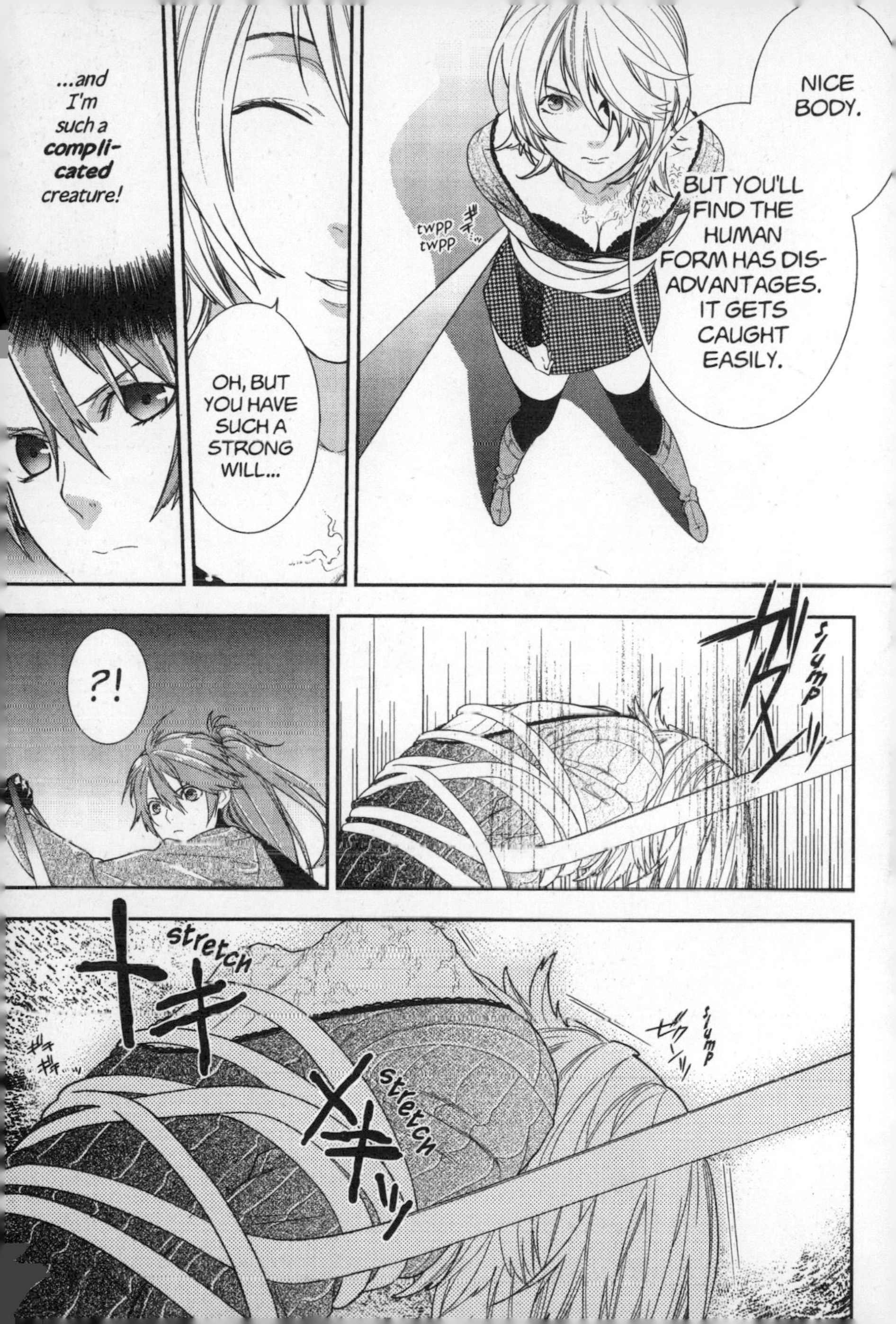
NICE BODY.
BUT YOU'LL FIND THE HUMAN FORM HAS DIS-ADVANTAGES. IT GETS CAUGHT EASILY.
twpp twpp
OH, BUT YOU HAVE SUCH A STRONG WILL...
...and I'm such a complicated creature!
slump
?!
stretch
stretch
slump

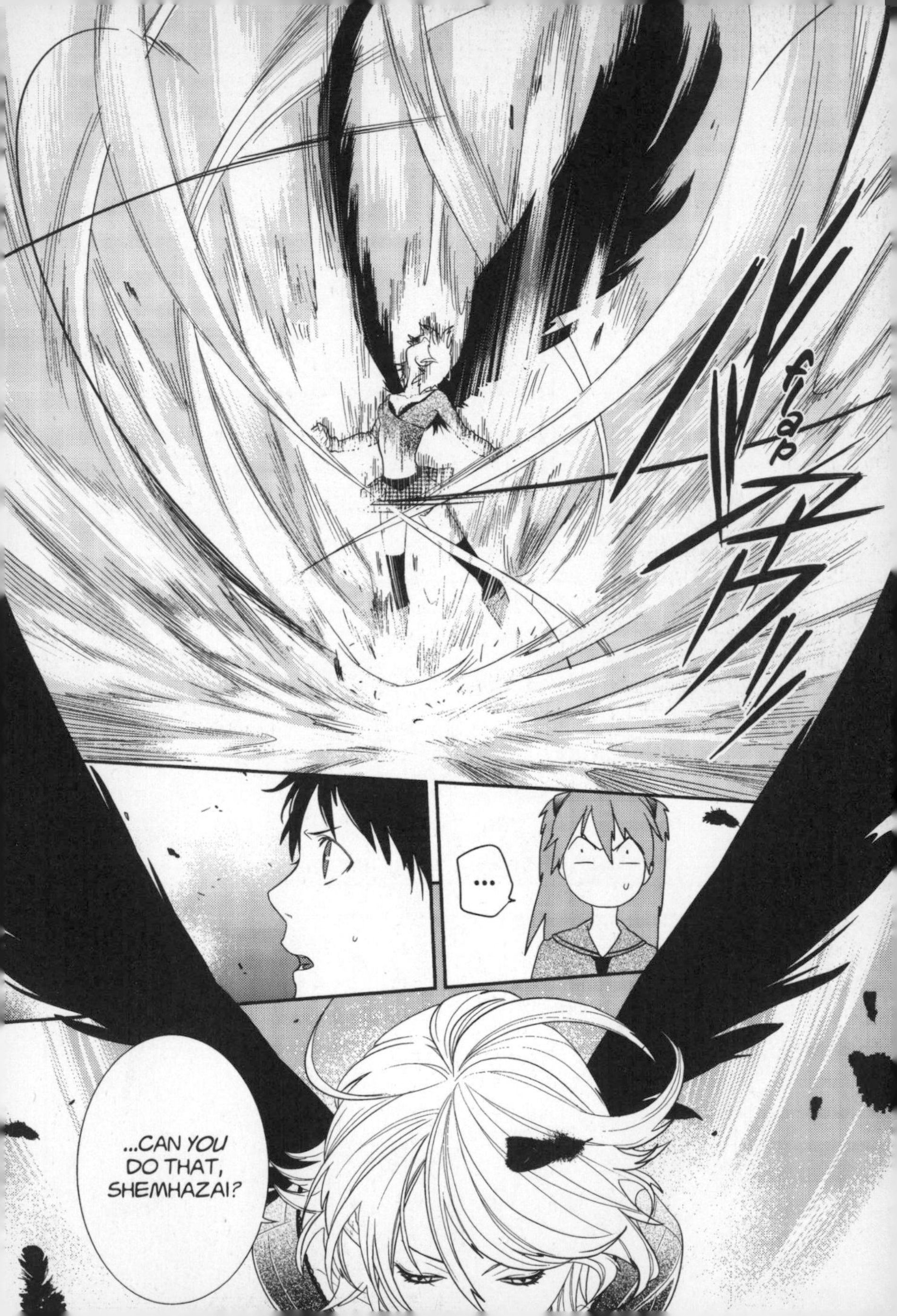
flap
...
...CAN YOU DO THAT, SHEMHAZAI?

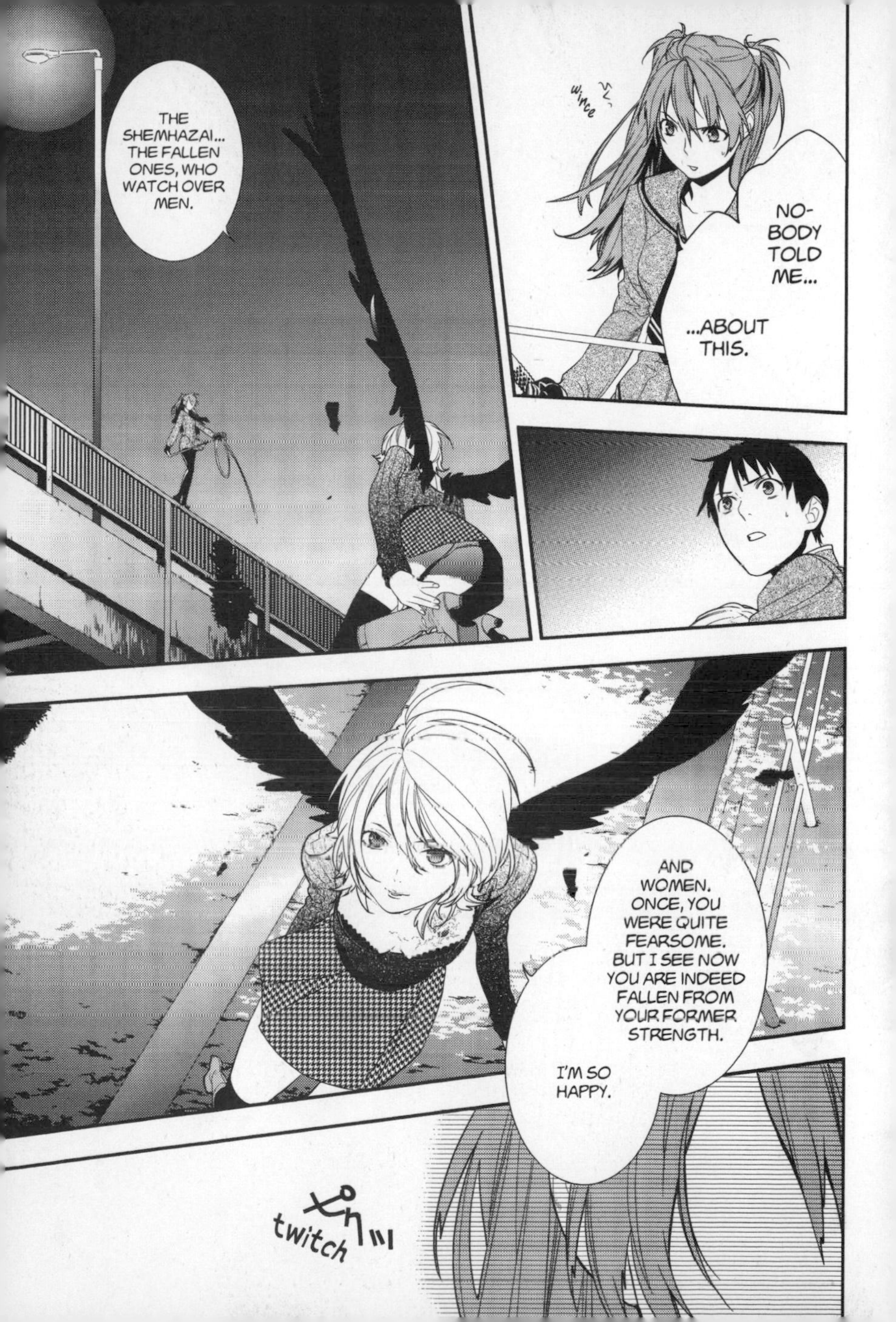
wince
NO-BODY TOLD ME...
...ABOUT THIS.
THE SHEMHAZAI... THE FALLEN ONES, WHO WATCH OVER MEN.
AND WOMEN. ONCE, YOU WERE QUITE FEARSOME. BUT I SEE NOW YOU ARE INDEED FALLEN FROM YOUR FORMER STRENGTH.
I'M SO HAPPY.
twitch

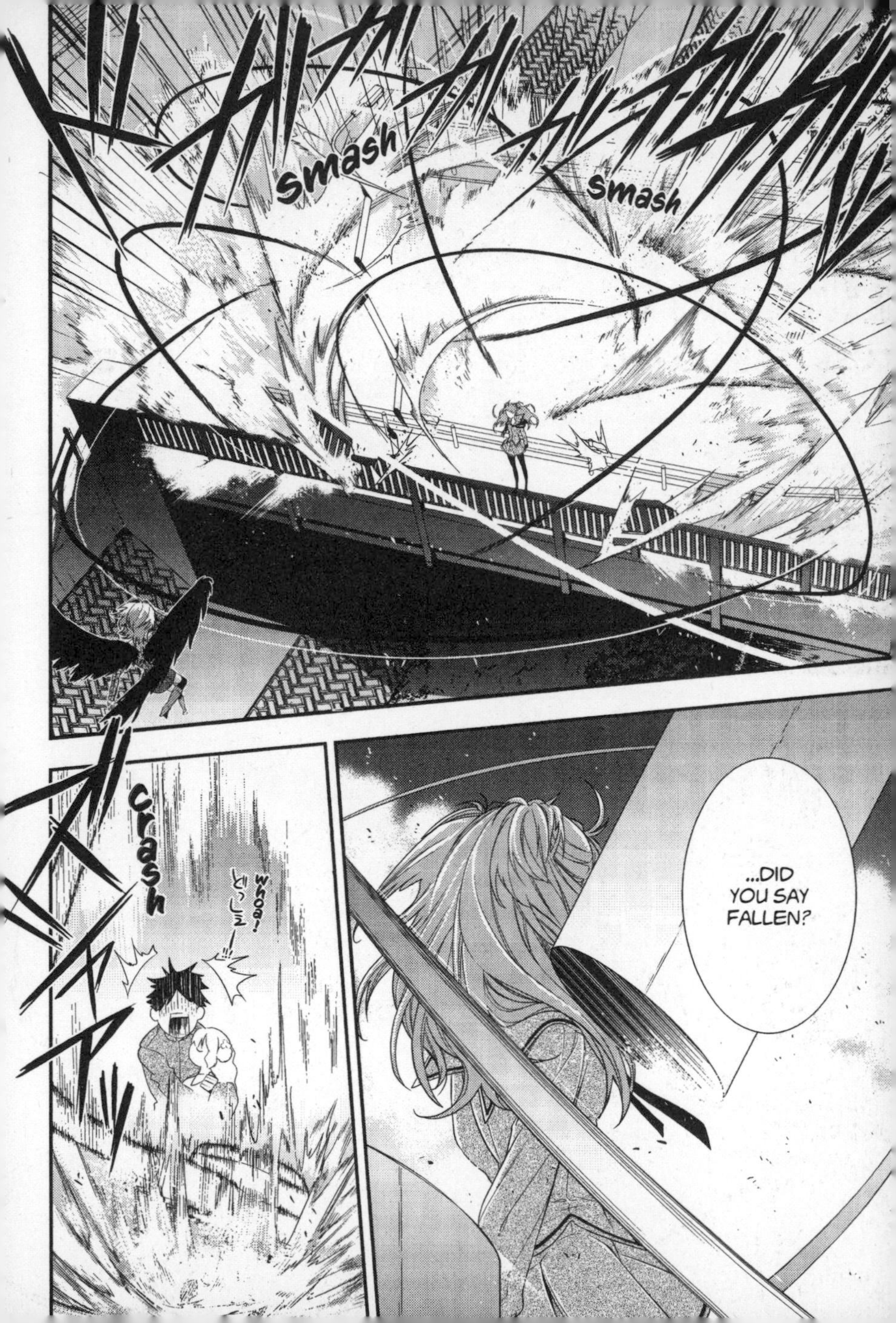
smash
smash
...DID YOU SAY FALLEN?
crash
whoa!
どっしぇー!!!

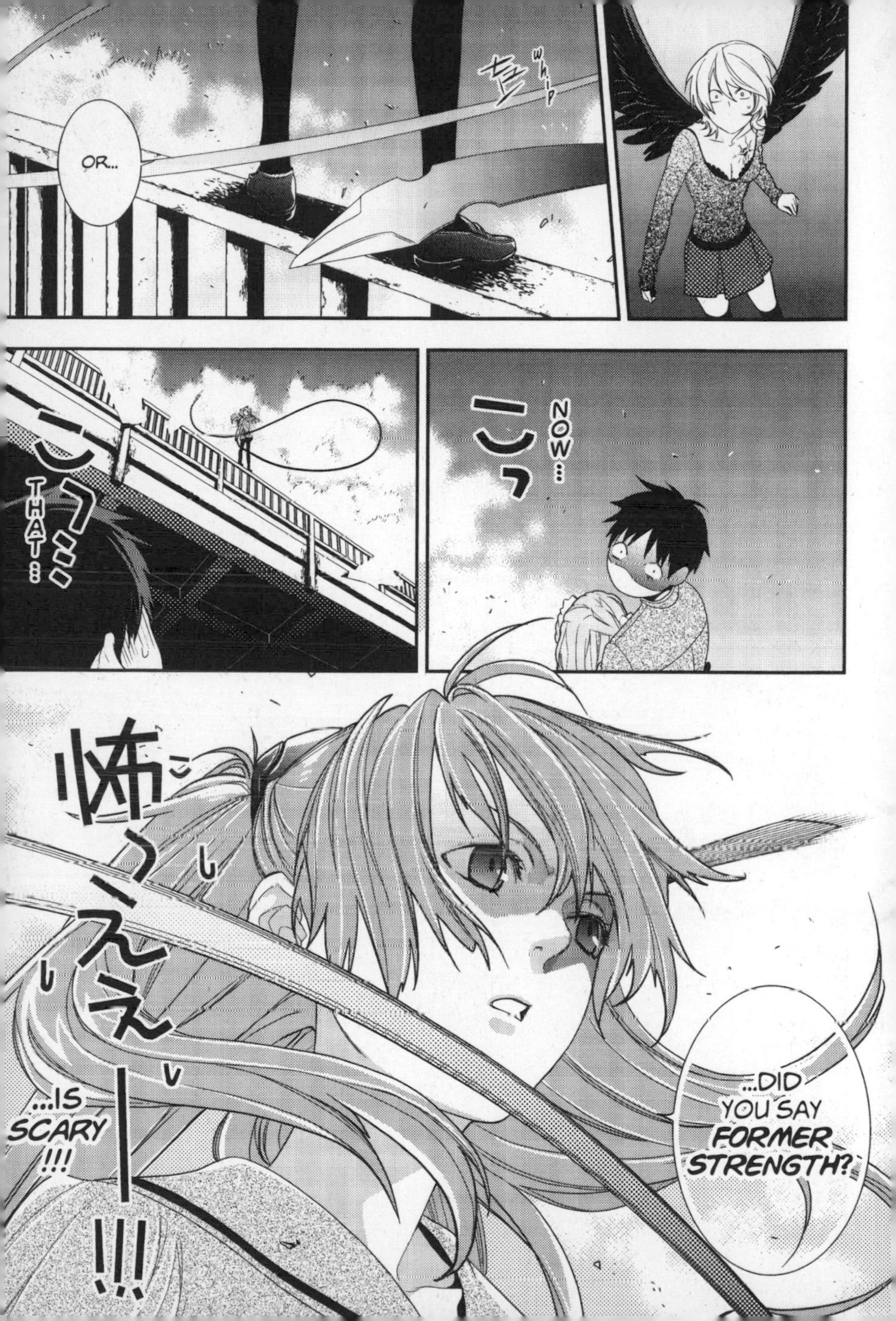

OR...
whip
NOW...
THAT...
...DID YOU SAY FORMER STRENGTH?
...IS SCARY!!!

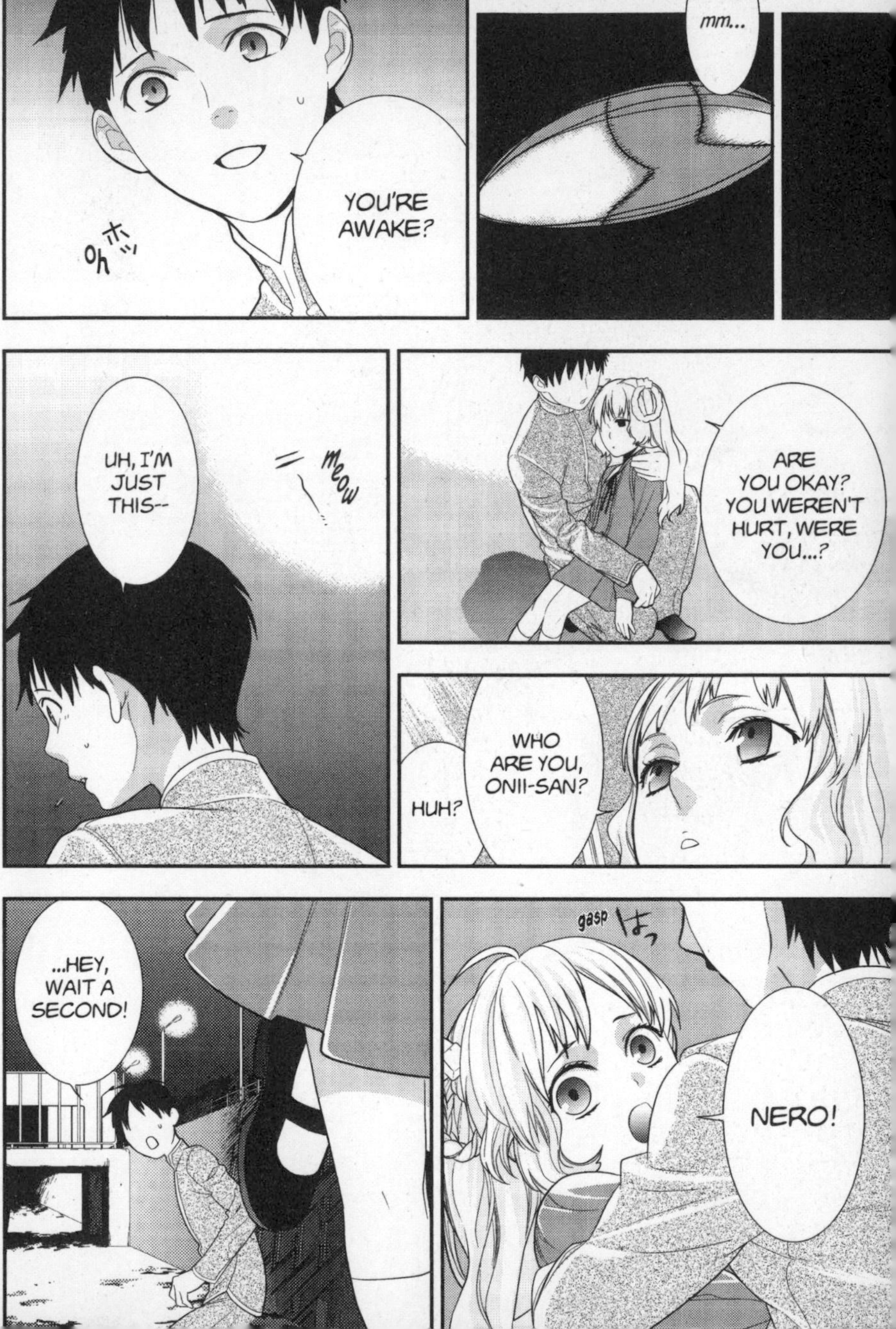
mm...
YOU'RE AWAKE?
oh ホッ
ARE YOU OKAY? YOU WEREN'T HURT, WERE YOU...?
WHO ARE YOU, ONII-SAN?
HUH?
UH, I'M JUST THIS--
meow
gasp はっ
NERO!
...HEY, WAIT A SECOND!

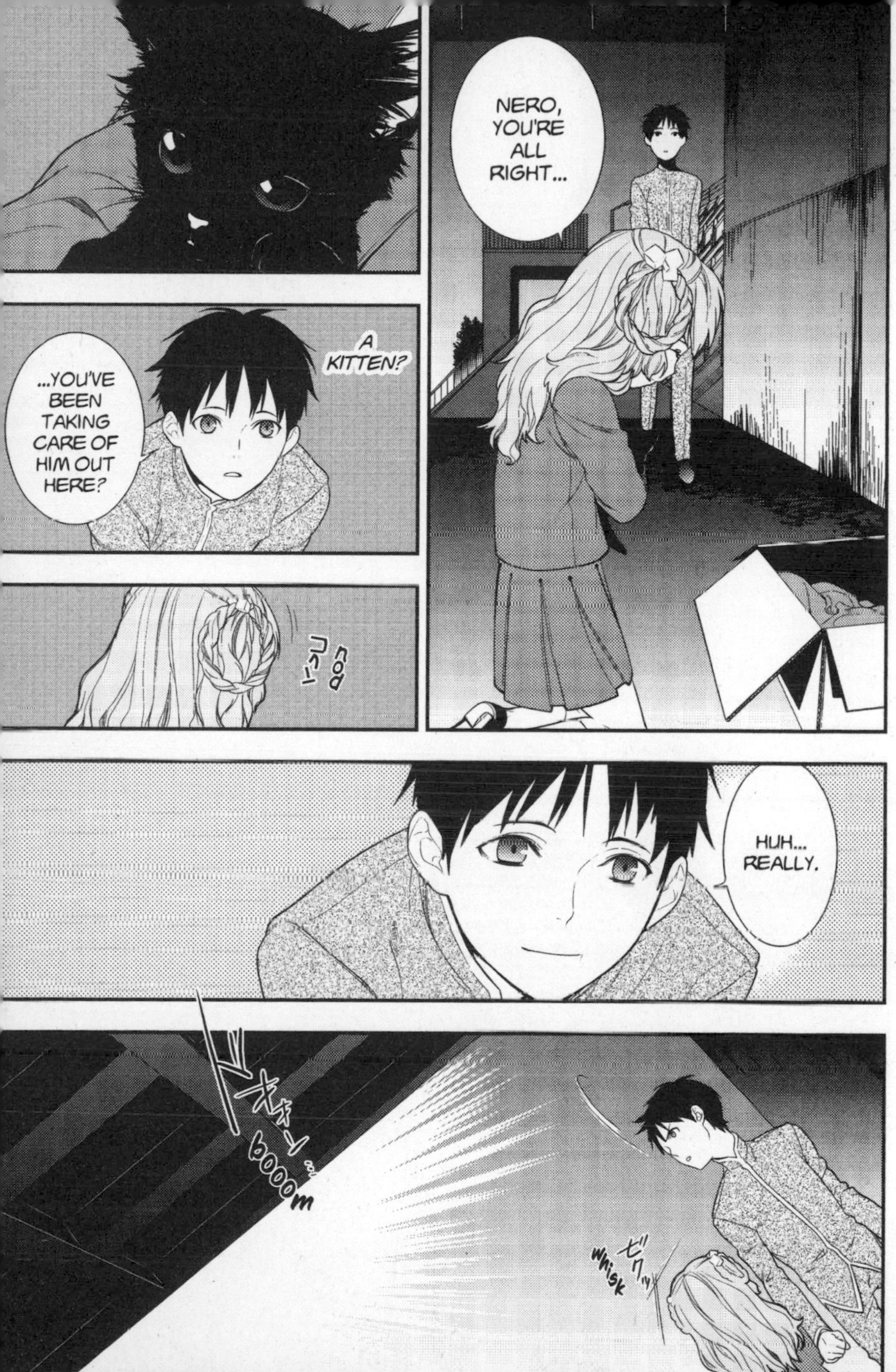
NERO, YOU'RE ALL RIGHT...
A KITTEN?
...YOU'VE BEEN TAKING CARE OF HIM OUT HERE?
コクン
nod
HUH... REALLY.
booom
whisk

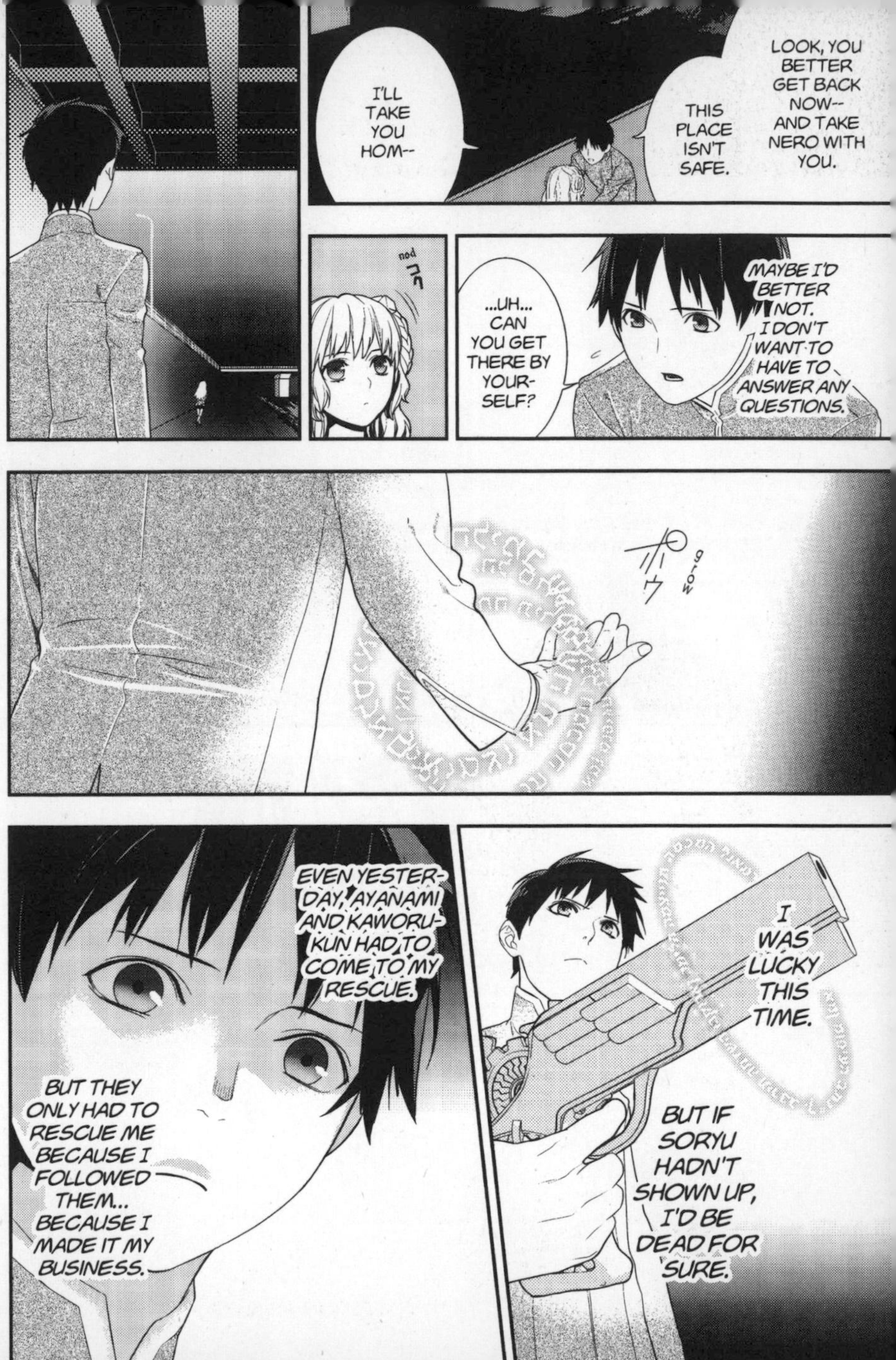
LOOK, YOU BETTER GET BACK NOW-- AND TAKE NERO WITH YOU.
THIS PLACE ISN'T SAFE.
I'LL TAKE YOU HOM--
MAYBE I'D BETTER NOT. I DON'T WANT TO HAVE TO ANSWER ANY QUESTIONS.
...UH... CAN YOU GET THERE BY YOUR-SELF?
nod
glow
I WAS LUCKY THIS TIME.
BUT IF SORYU HADN'T SHOWN UP, I'D BE DEAD FOR SURE.
EVEN YESTER-DAY, AYANAMI AND KAWORU-KUN HAD TO COME TO MY RESCUE.
BUT THEY ONLY HAD TO RESCUE ME BECAUSE I FOLLOWED THEM... BECAUSE I MADE IT MY BUSINESS.

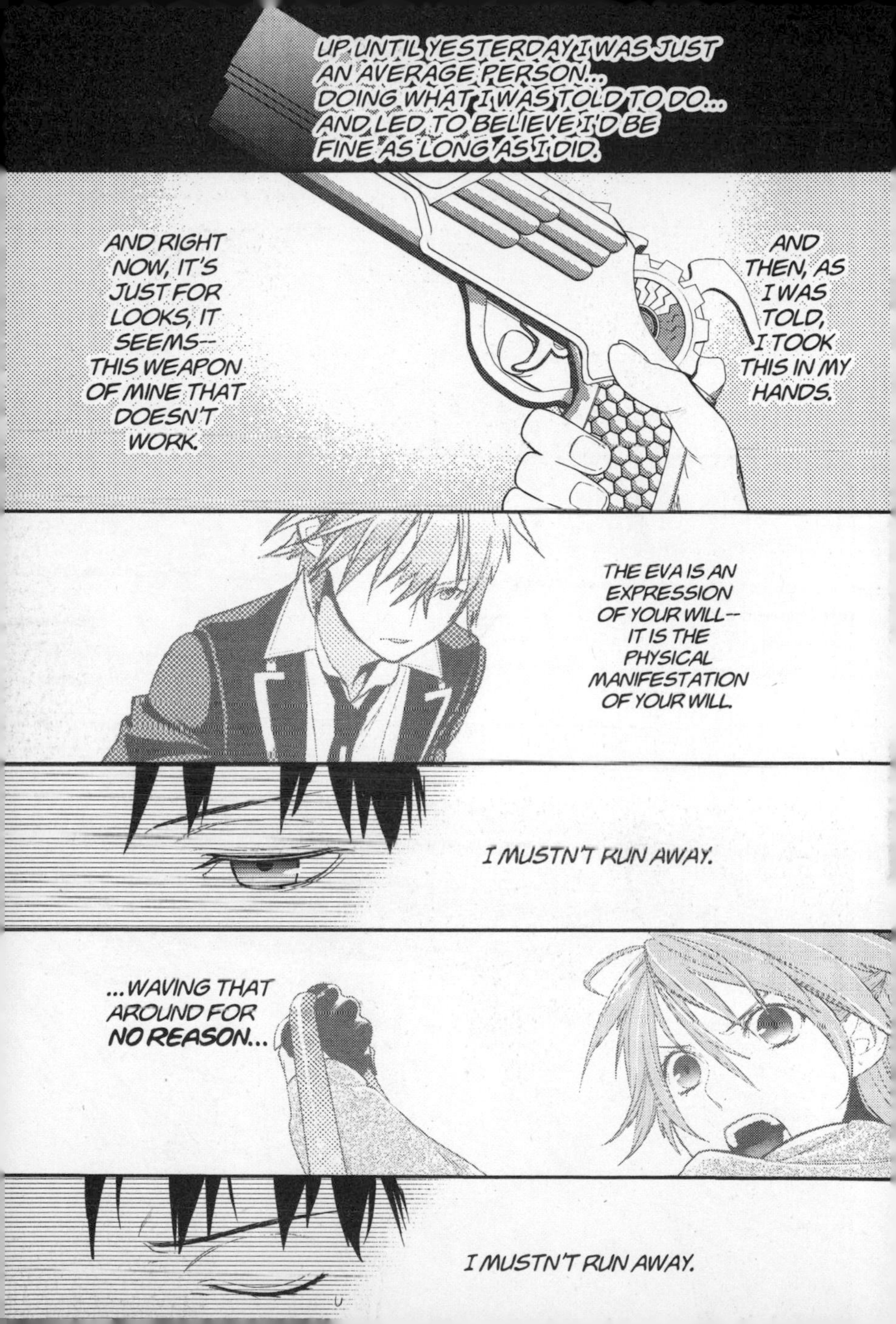
UP UNTIL YESTERDAY I WAS JUST AN AVERAGE PERSON... DOING WHAT I WAS TOLD TO DO... AND LED TO BELIEVE I'D BE FINE AS LONG AS I DID.
AND THEN, AS I WAS TOLD, I TOOK THIS IN MY HANDS.
AND RIGHT NOW, IT'S JUST FOR LOOKS, IT SEEMS-- THIS WEAPON OF MINE THAT DOESN'T WORK.
THE EVA IS AN EXPRESSION OF YOUR WILL-- IT IS THE PHYSICAL MANIFESTATION OF YOUR WILL.
I MUSTN'T RUN AWAY.
...WAVING THAT AROUND FOR NO REASON...
I MUSTN'T RUN AWAY.

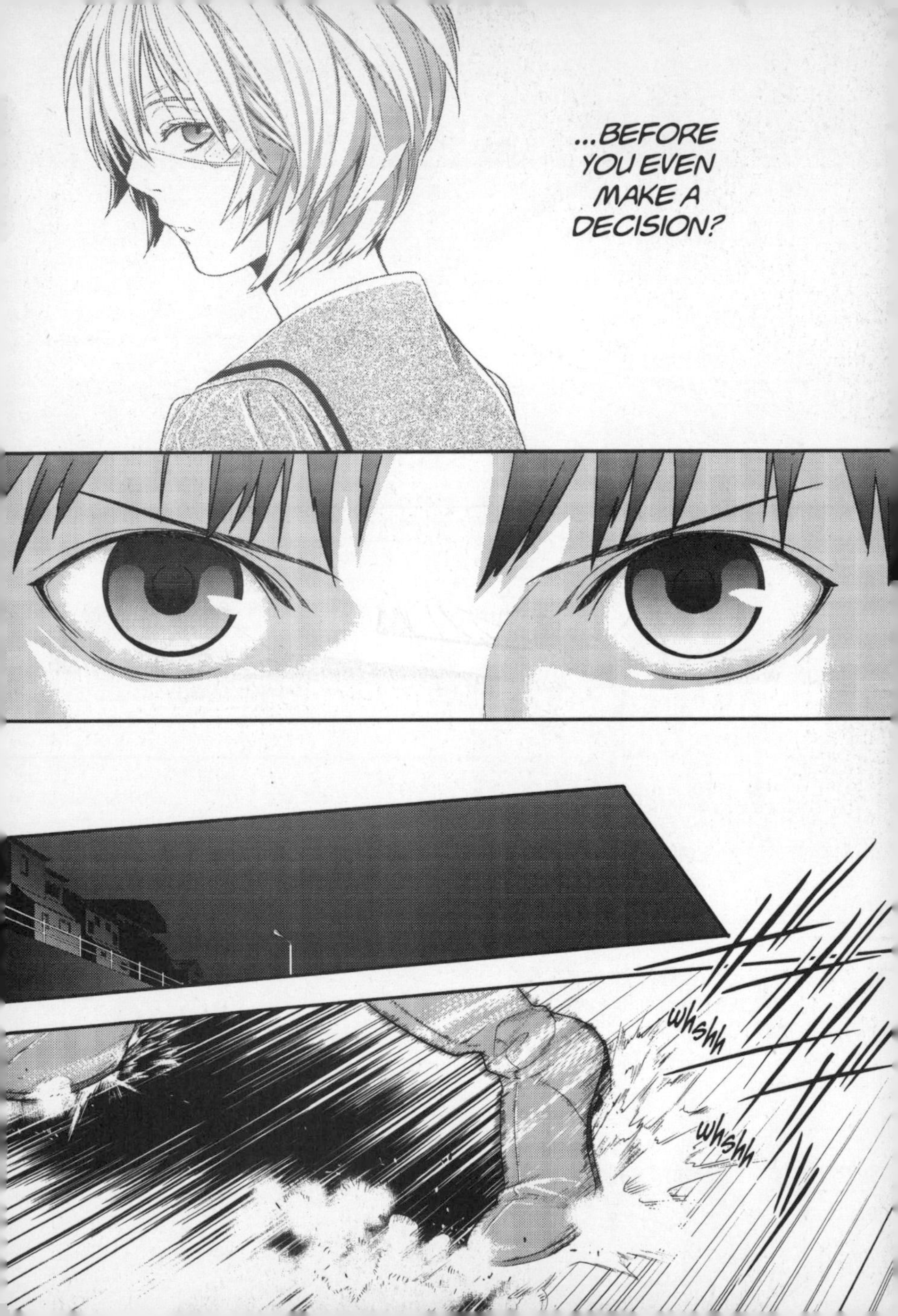
...BEFORE YOU EVEN MAKE A DECISION?
whshh
whshh

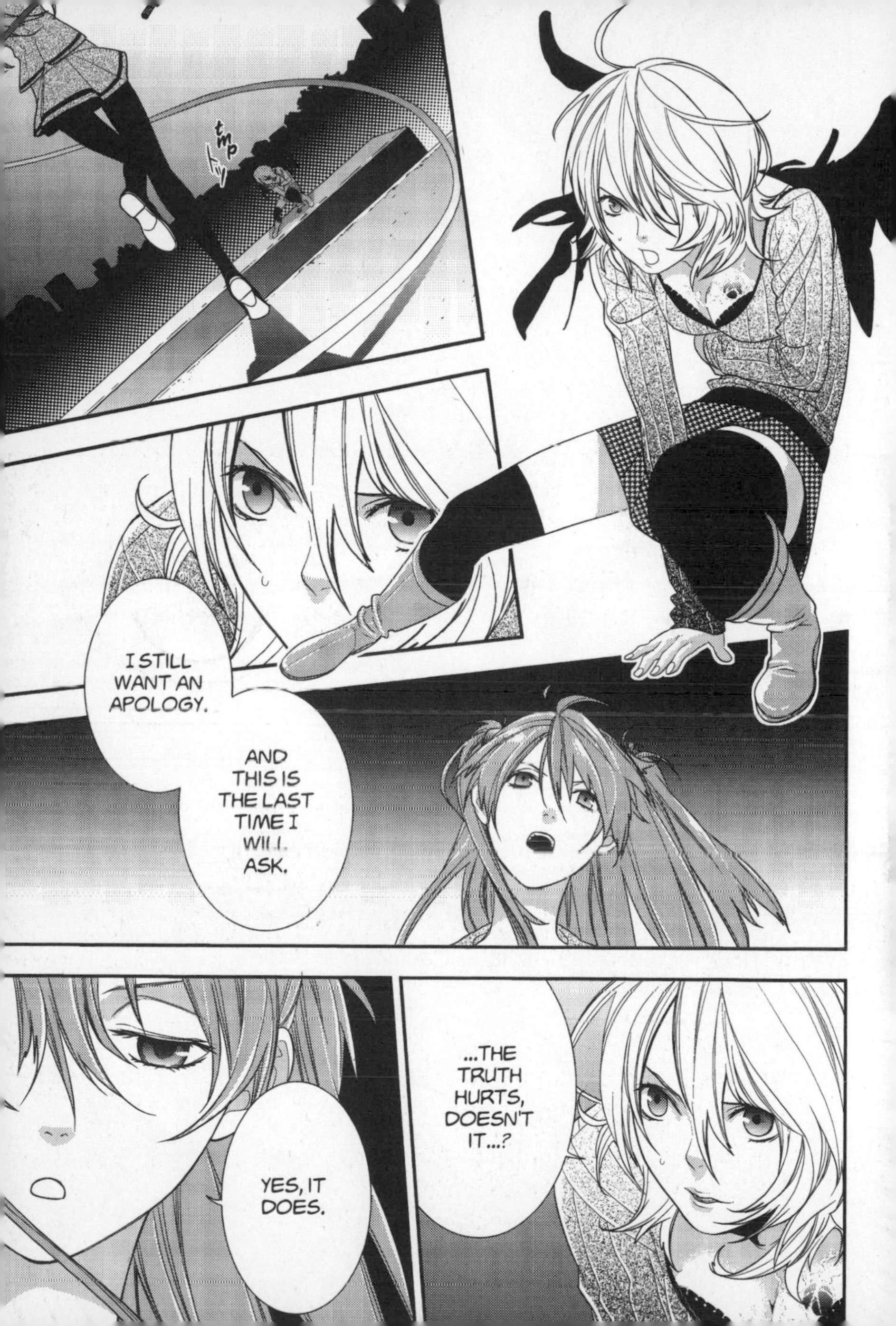
tmp
I STILL WANT AN APOLOGY.
AND THIS IS THE LAST TIME I WILL ASK.
...THE TRUTH HURTS, DOESN'T IT...?
YES, IT DOES.

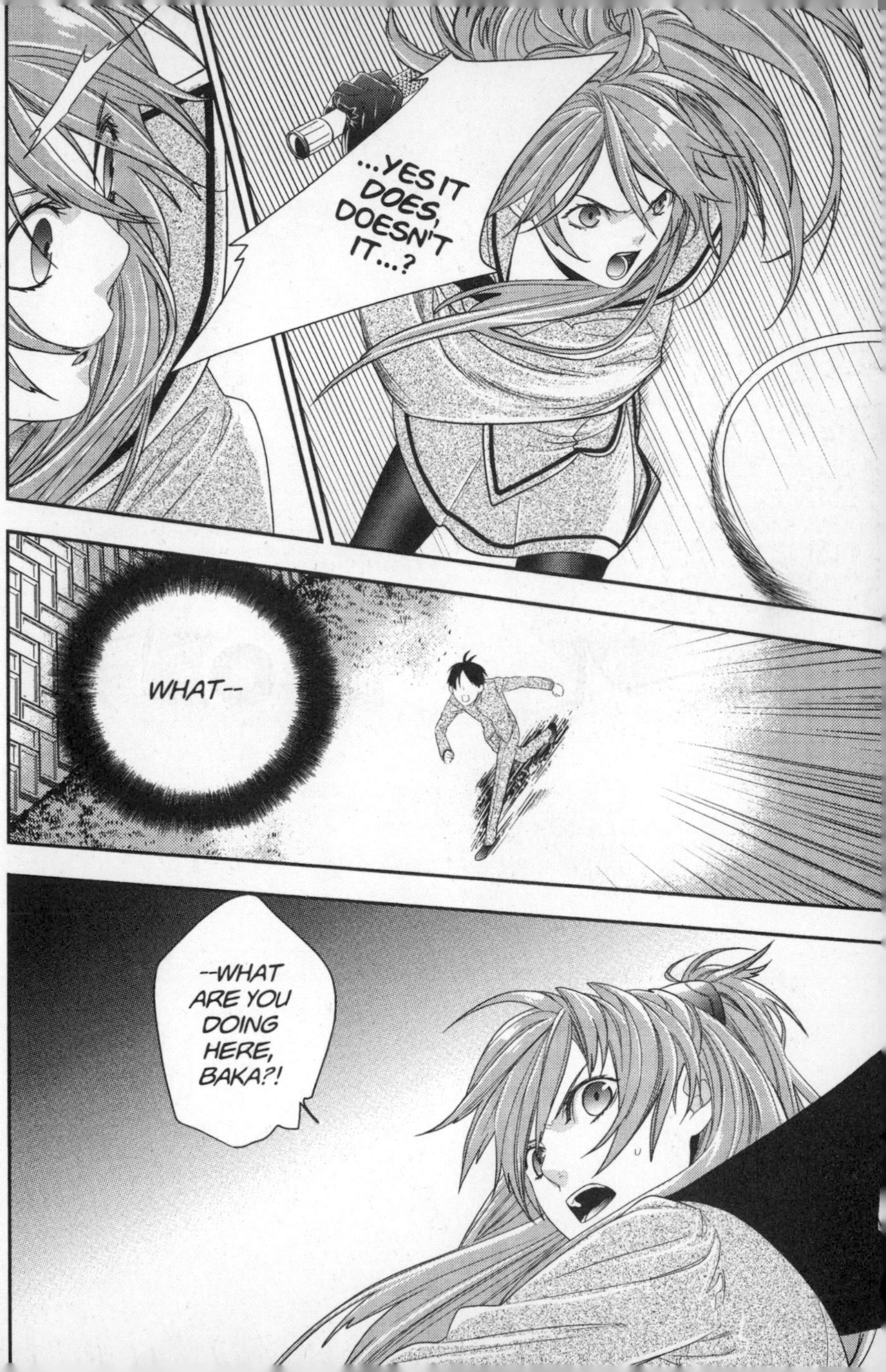
...YES IT DOES, DOESN'T IT...?
WHAT--
--WHAT ARE YOU DOING HERE, BAKA?!

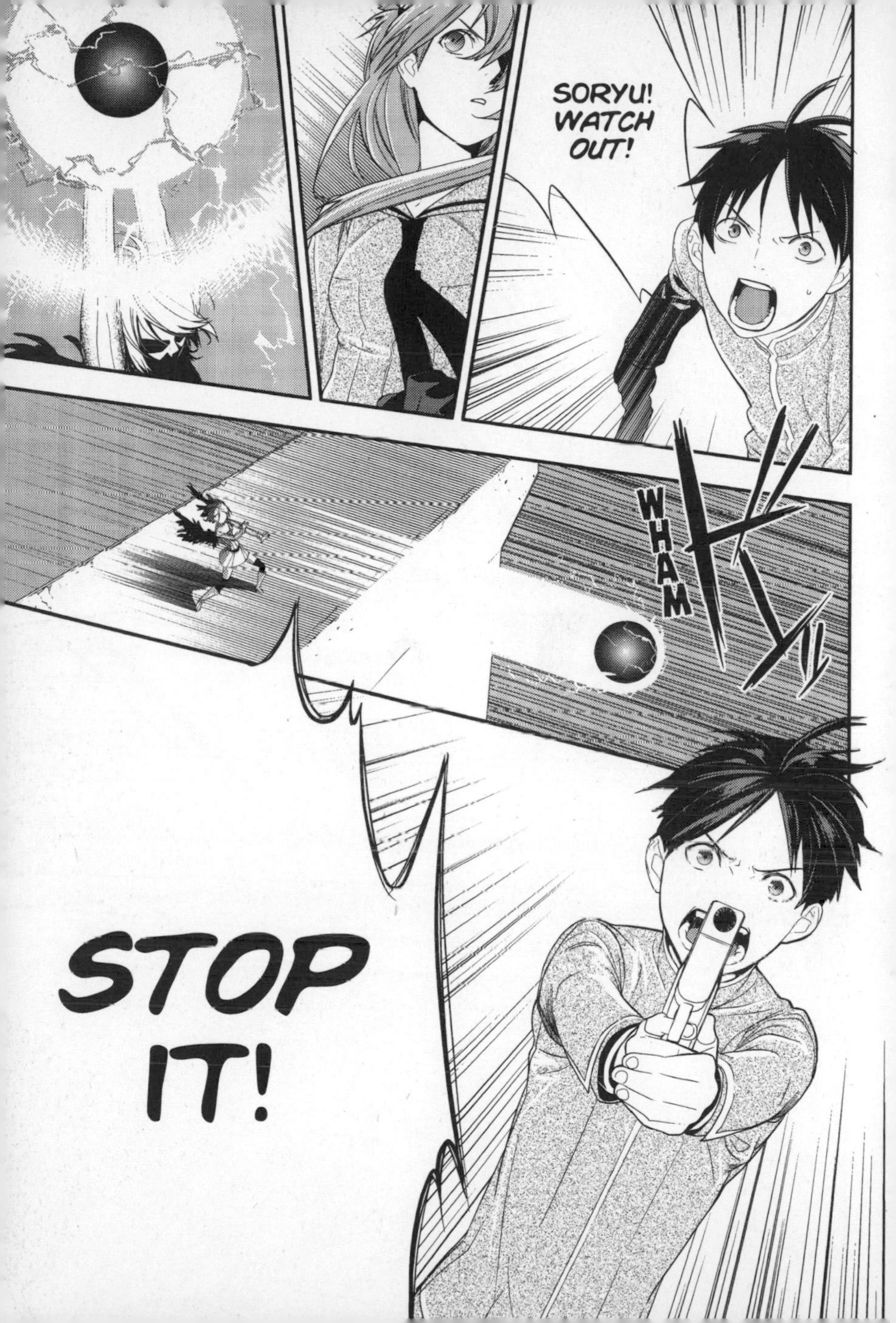
SORYU! WATCH OUT!
WHAM
STOP IT!

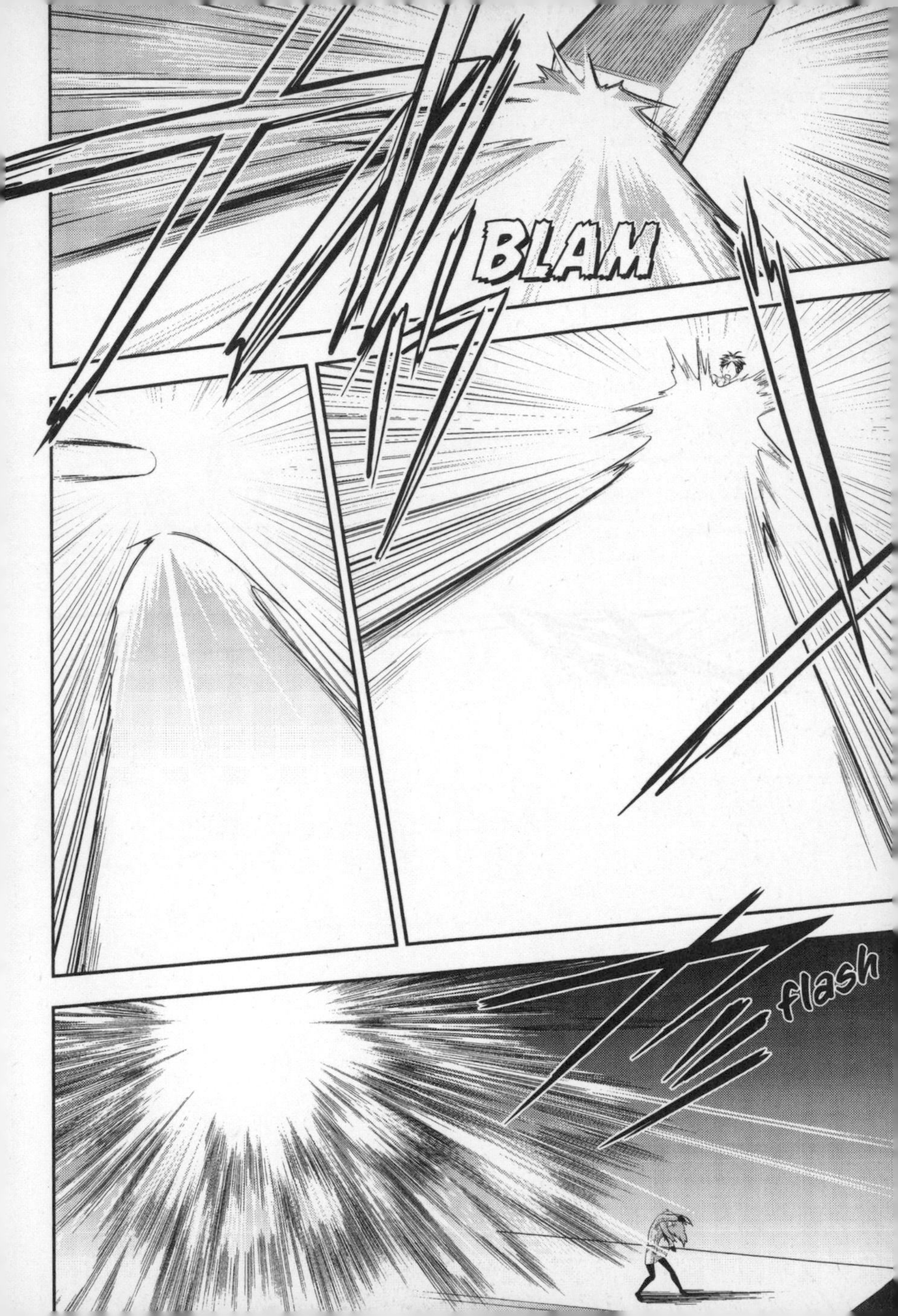
BLAM
flash

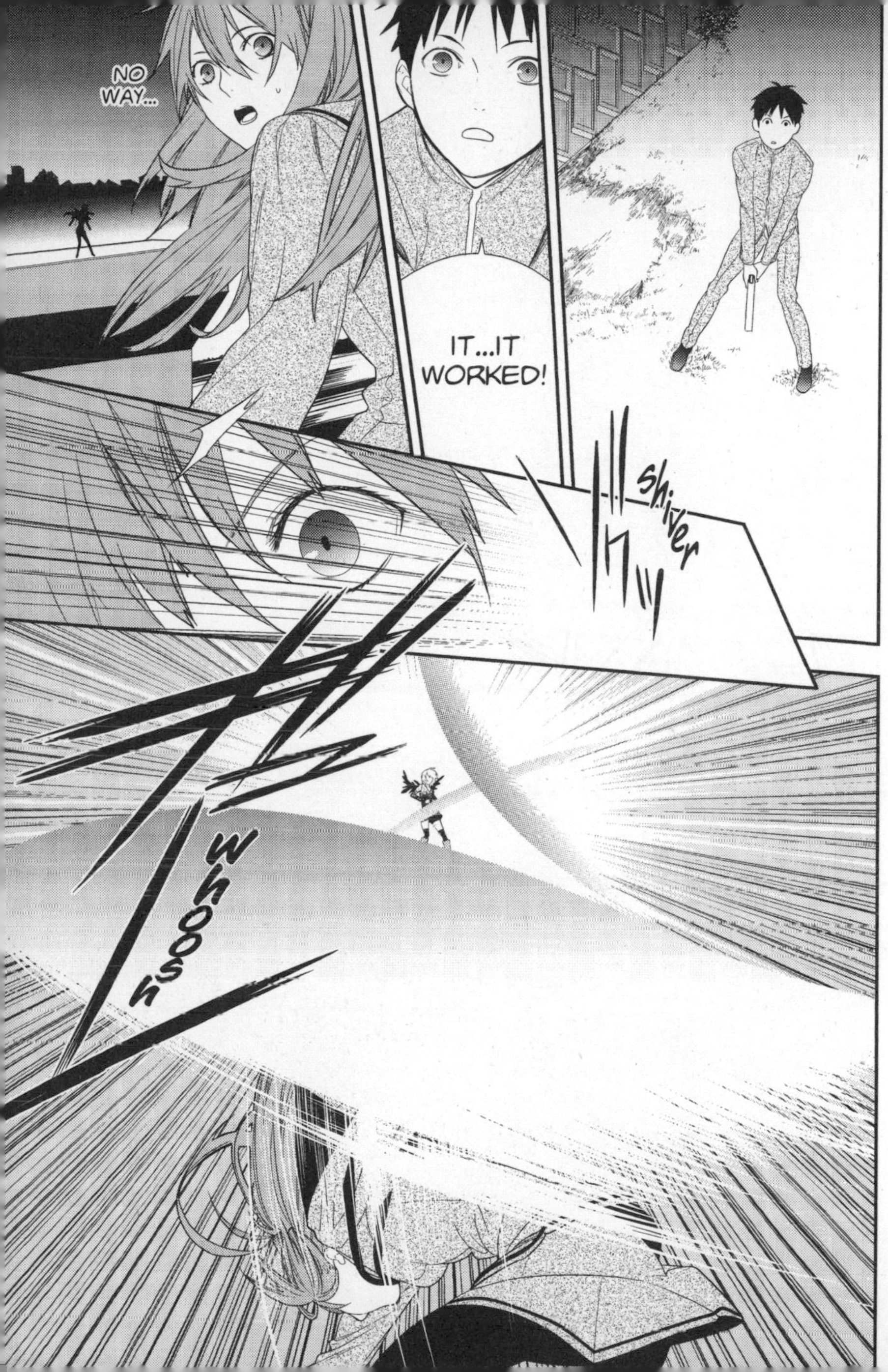
IT...IT WORKED!
NO WAY...
shiver
whoosh

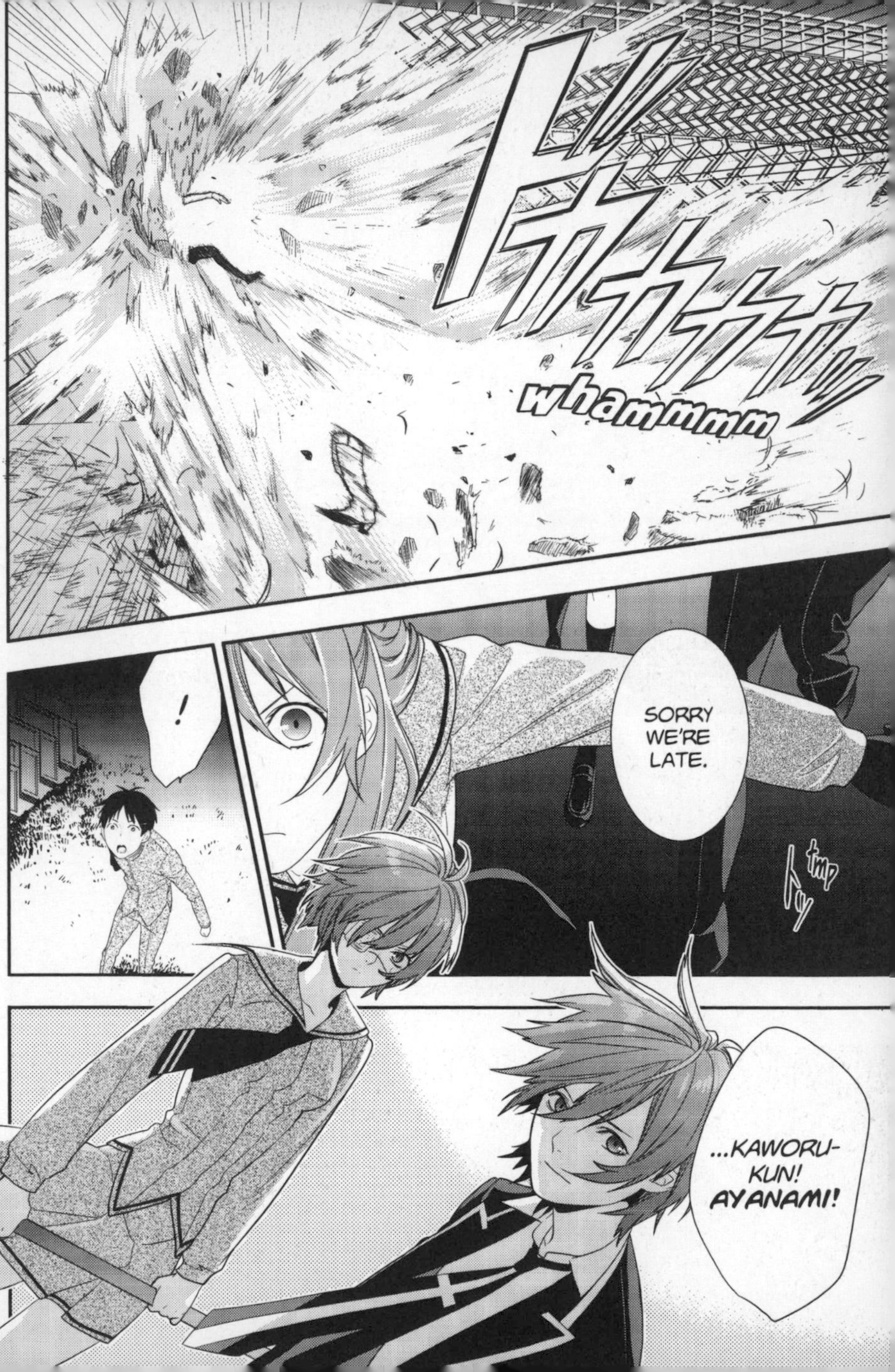
whammmmm
SORRY WE'RE LATE.
tmp
!
...KAWORU-KUN! AYANAMI!

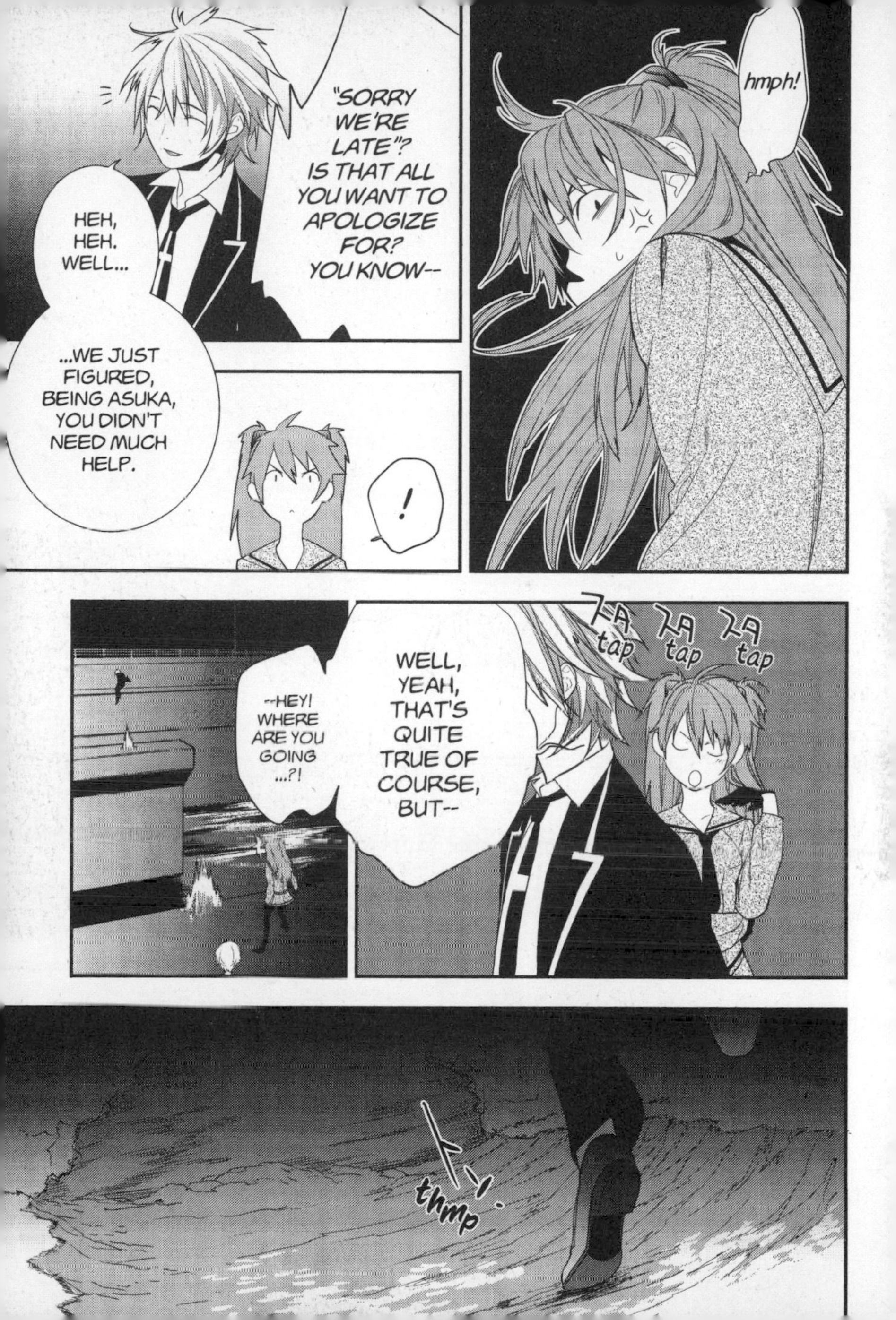
hmph!
"SORRY WE'RE LATE"? IS THAT ALL YOU WANT TO APOLOGIZE FOR? YOU KNOW--
HEH, HEH. WELL...
...WE JUST FIGURED, BEING ASUKA, YOU DIDN'T NEED MUCH HELP.
!
tap tap tap
WELL, YEAH, THAT'S QUITE TRUE OF COURSE, BUT--
--HEY! WHERE ARE YOU GOING ...?!
thmp

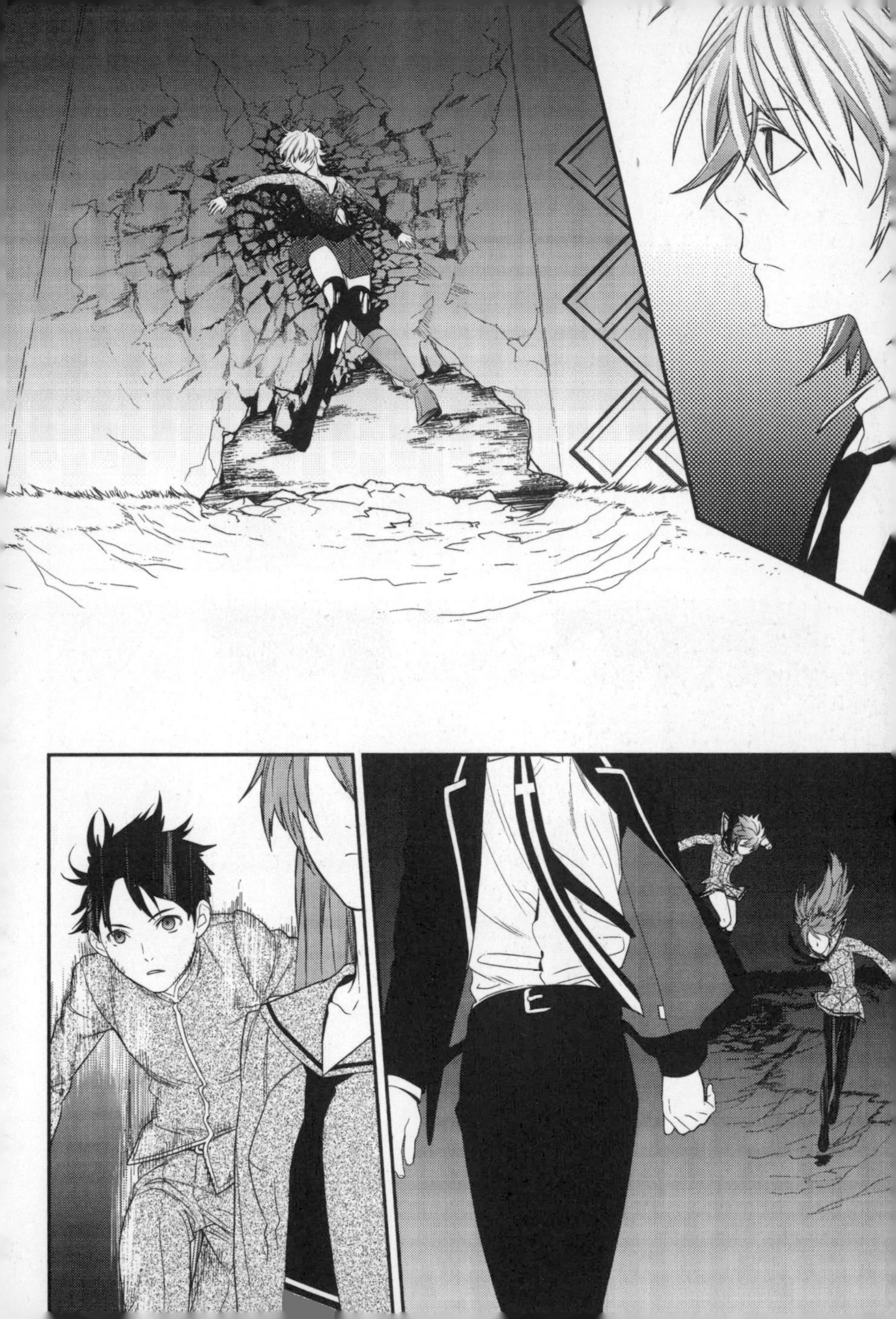

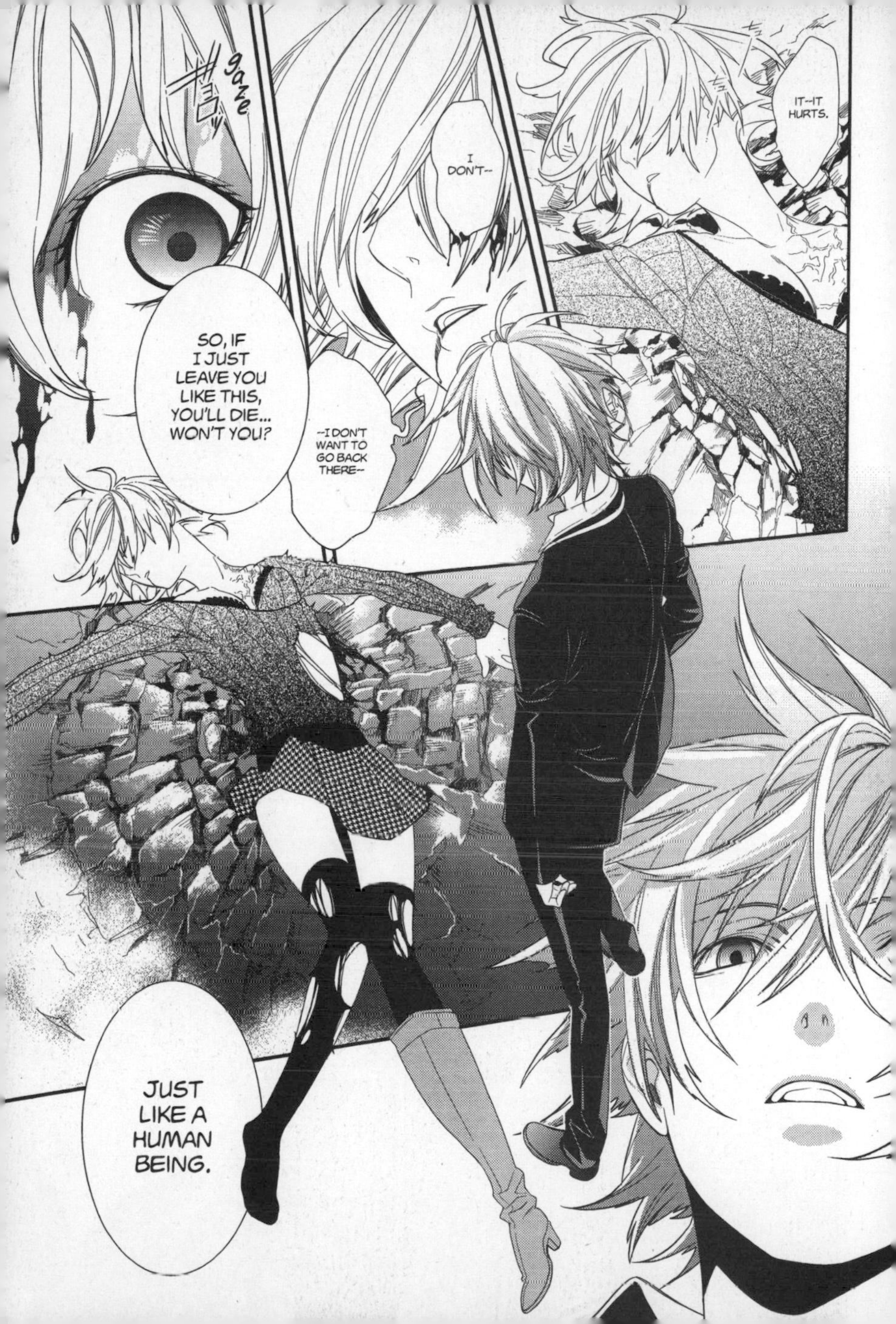
IT--IT HURTS.
I DON'T--
--I DON'T WANT TO GO BACK THERE--
gaze
SO, IF I JUST LEAVE YOU LIKE THIS, YOU'LL DIE... WON'T YOU?
JUST LIKE A HUMAN BEING.

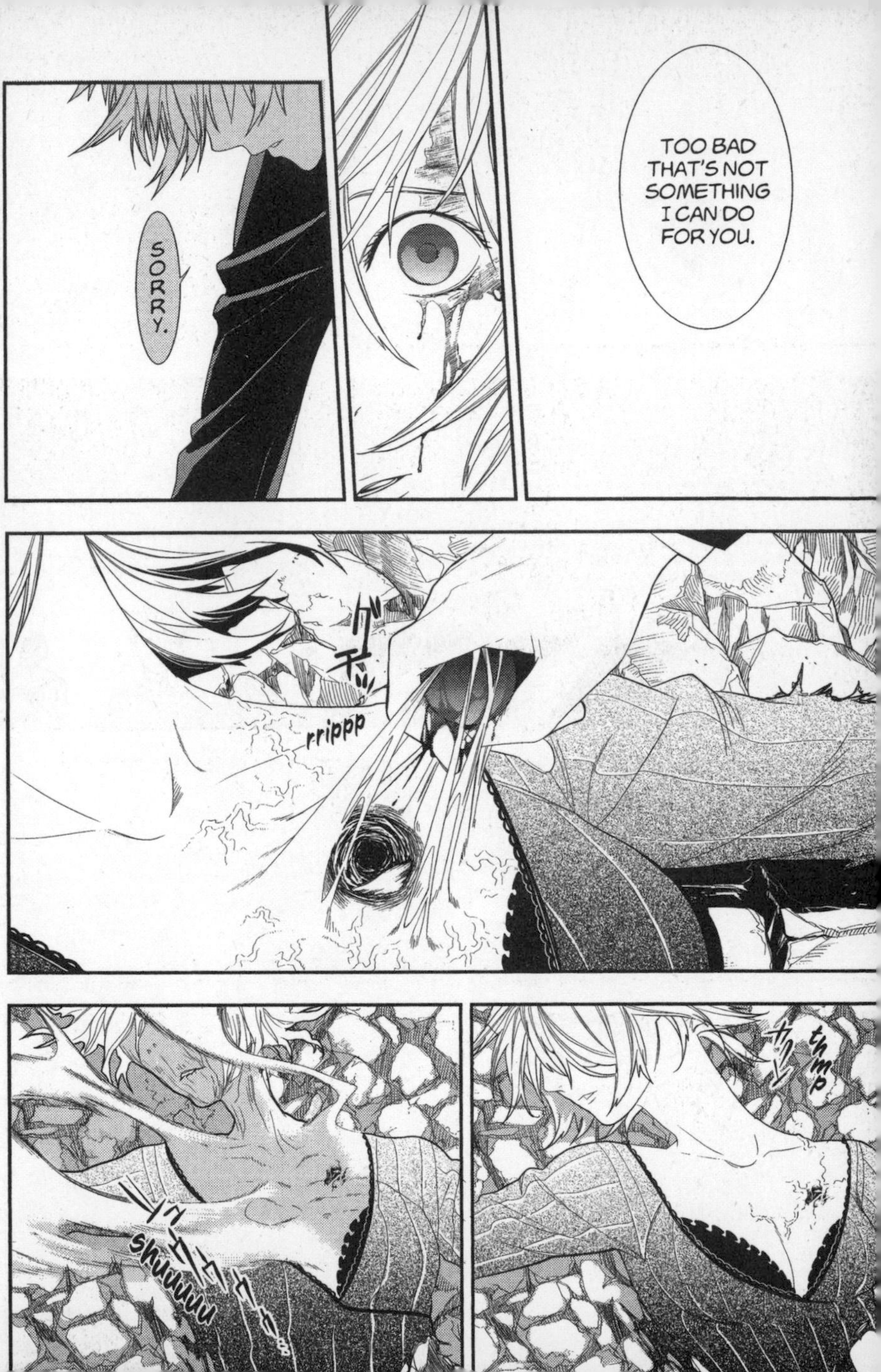
TOO BAD THAT'S NOT SOMETHING I CAN DO FOR YOU.
SORRY.
rrippp
thmp
shuuuuu

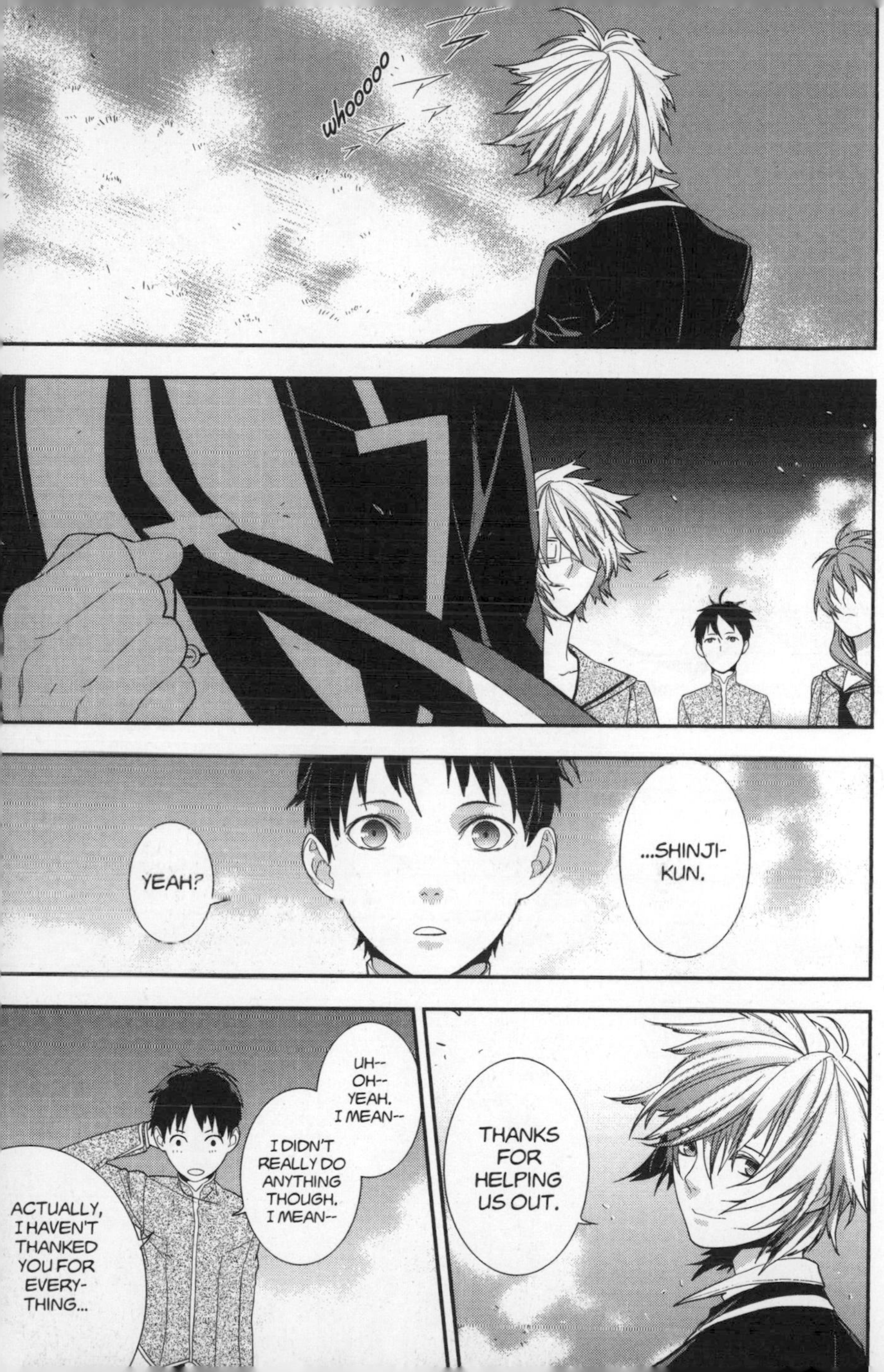
whoooooo
...SHINJI-KUN.
YEAH?
THANKS FOR HELPING US OUT.
UH-- OH-- YEAH. I MEAN--
I DIDN'T REALLY DO ANYTHING THOUGH. I MEAN--
ACTUALLY, I HAVEN'T THANKED YOU FOR EVERYTHING...

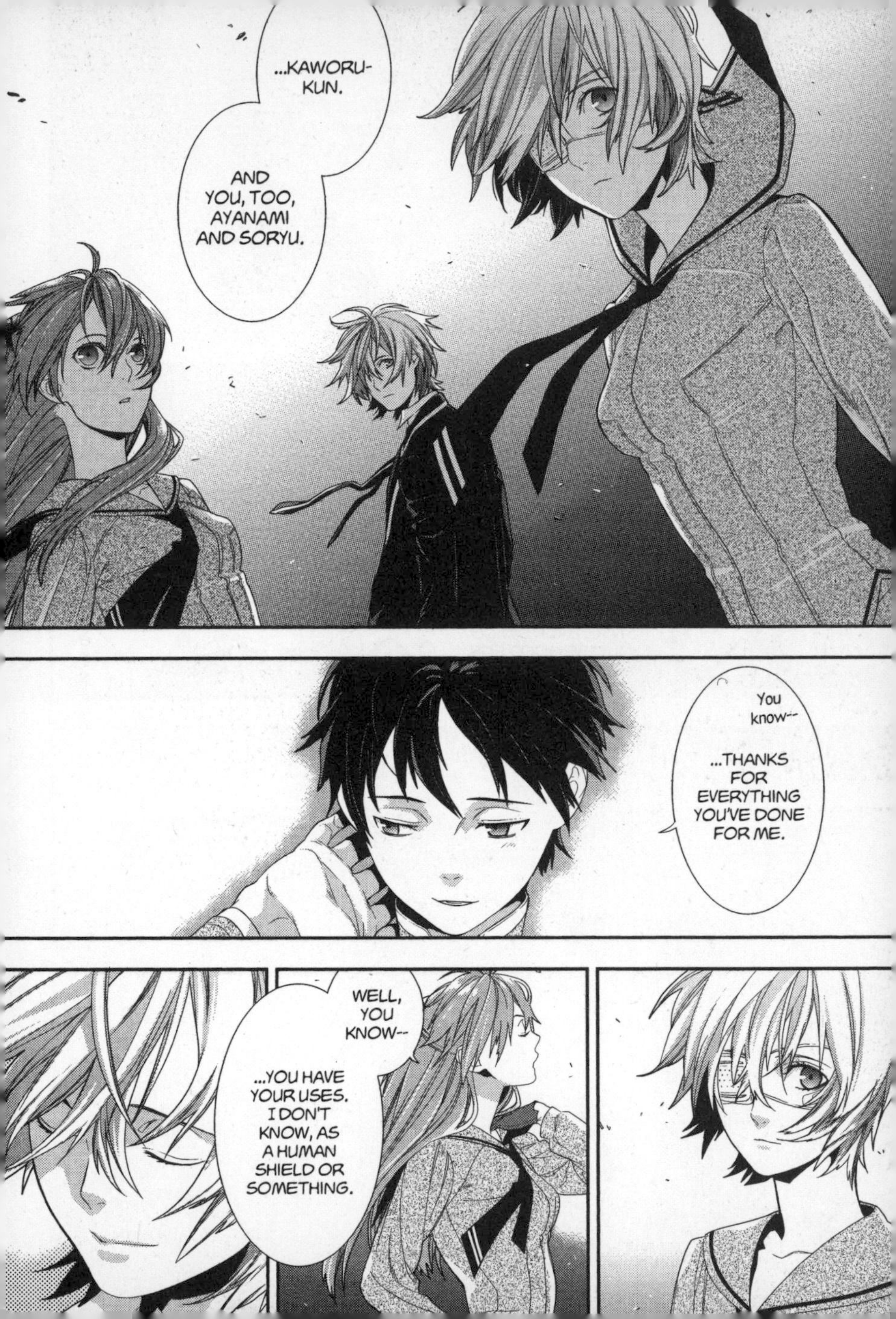
...KAWORU-KUN.
AND YOU, TOO, AYANAMI AND SORYU.
You know--
...THANKS FOR EVERYTHING YOU'VE DONE FOR ME.
WELL, YOU KNOW--
...YOU HAVE YOUR USES. I DON'T KNOW, AS A HUMAN SHIELD OR SOMETHING.

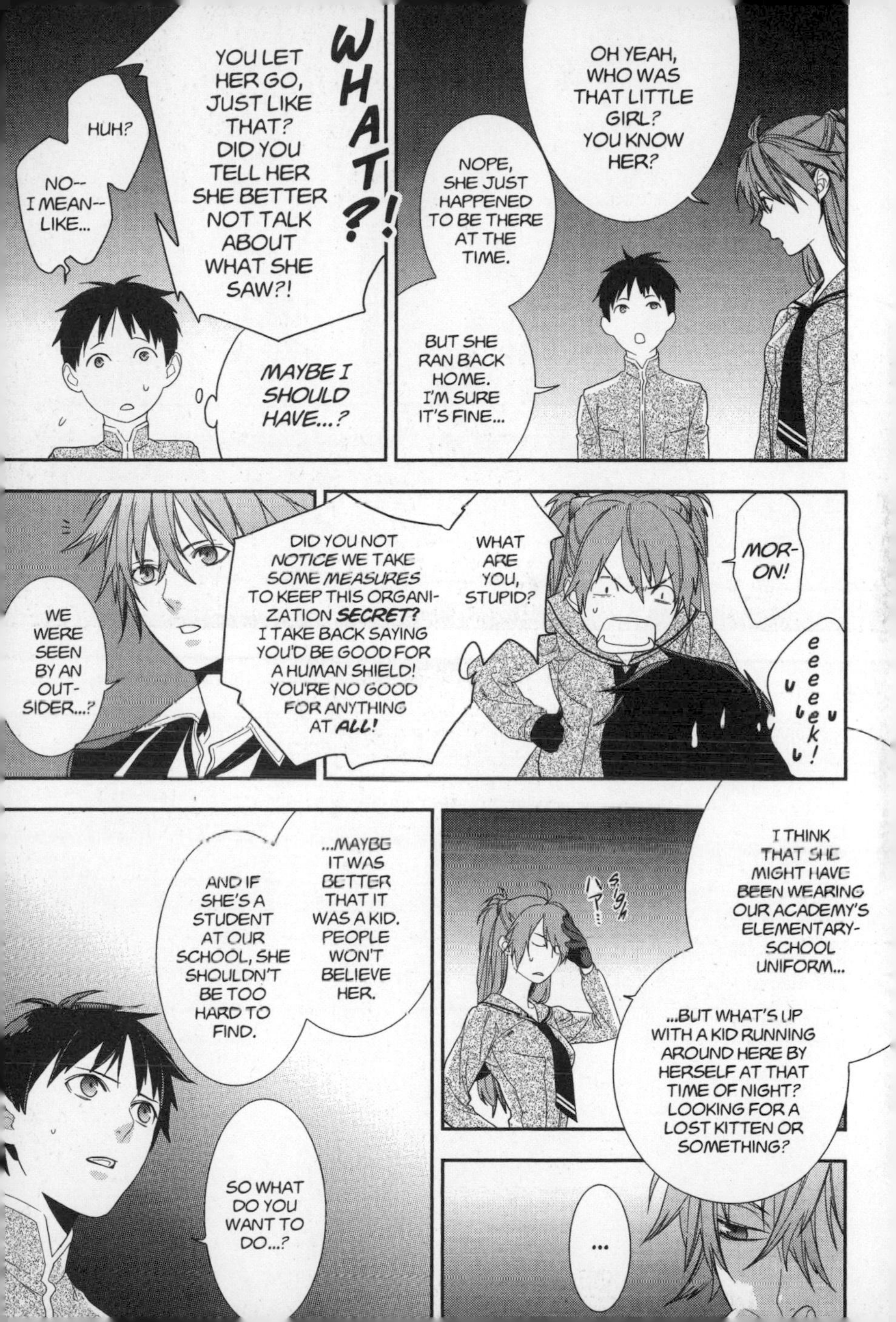
OH YEAH, WHO WAS THAT LITTLE GIRL? YOU KNOW HER?
NOPE, SHE JUST HAPPENED TO BE THERE AT THE TIME.
BUT SHE RAN BACK HOME. I'M SURE IT'S FINE...
WHAT?!
YOU LET HER GO, JUST LIKE THAT? DID YOU TELL HER SHE BETTER NOT TALK ABOUT WHAT SHE SAW?!
HUH?
NO-- I MEAN-- LIKE...
MAYBE I SHOULD HAVE...?
MOR-ON!
eeeeeek!
WHAT ARE YOU, STUPID?
DID YOU NOT NOTICE WE TAKE SOME MEASURES TO KEEP THIS ORGANIZATION SECRET? I TAKE BACK SAYING YOU'D BE GOOD FOR A HUMAN SHIELD! YOU'RE NO GOOD FOR ANYTHING AT ALL!
WE WERE SEEN BY AN OUTSIDER...?
I THINK THAT SHE MIGHT HAVE BEEN WEARING OUR ACADEMY'S ELEMENTARY-SCHOOL UNIFORM...
ハァ…
sigh
...BUT WHAT'S UP WITH A KID RUNNING AROUND HERE BY HERSELF AT THAT TIME OF NIGHT? LOOKING FOR A LOST KITTEN OR SOMETHING?
...
...MAYBE IT WAS BETTER THAT IT WAS A KID. PEOPLE WON'T BELIEVE HER.
AND IF SHE'S A STUDENT AT OUR SCHOOL, SHE SHOULDN'T BE TOO HARD TO FIND.
SO WHAT DO YOU WANT TO DO...?

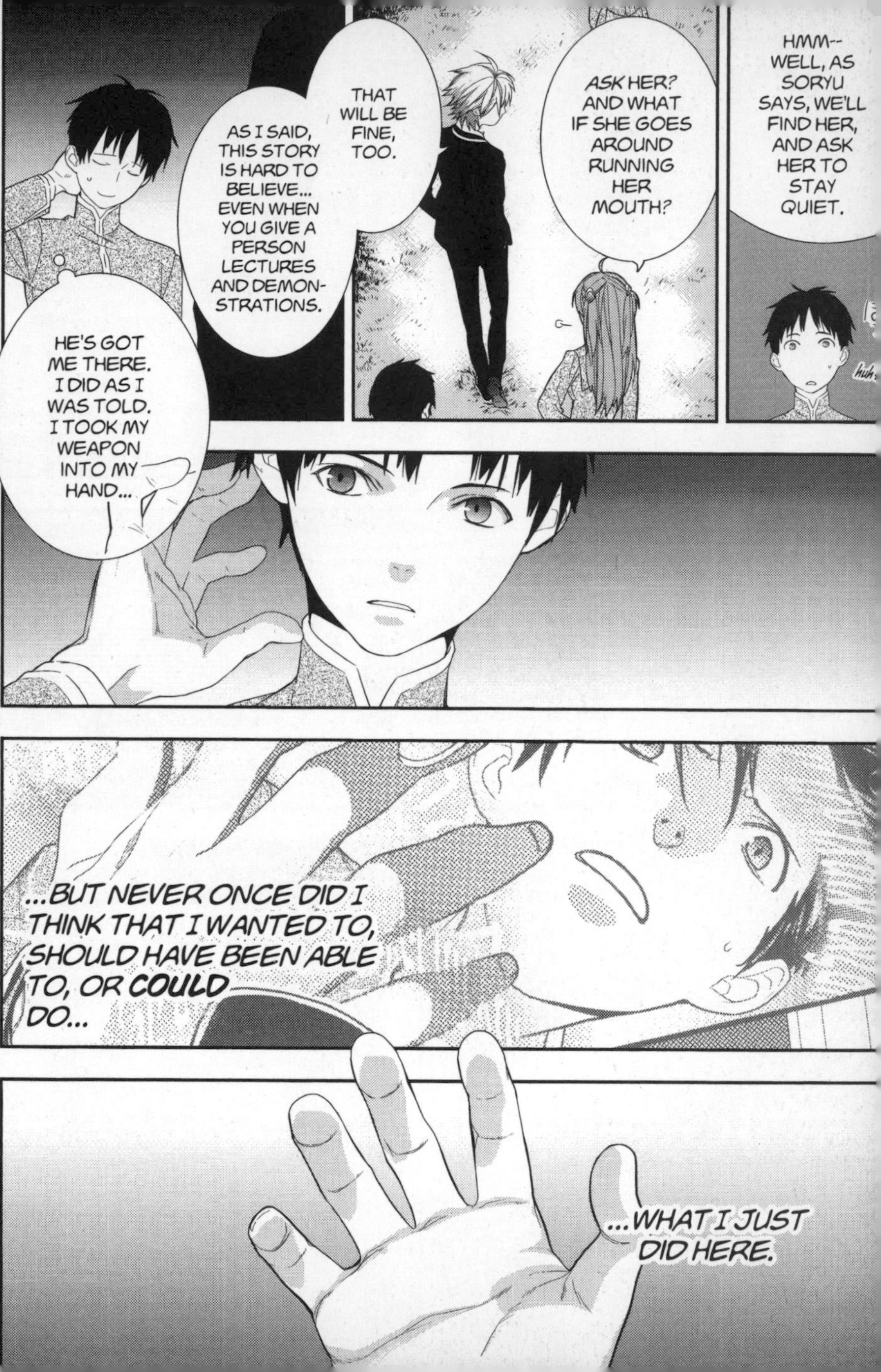
HMM-- WELL, AS SORYU SAYS, WE'LL FIND HER, AND ASK HER TO STAY QUIET.
huh
ASK HER? AND WHAT IF SHE GOES AROUND RUNNING HER MOUTH?
THAT WILL BE FINE, TOO.
AS I SAID, THIS STORY IS HARD TO BELIEVE... EVEN WHEN YOU GIVE A PERSON LECTURES AND DEMON-STRATIONS.
HE'S GOT ME THERE. I DID AS I WAS TOLD. I TOOK MY WEAPON INTO MY HAND...
...BUT NEVER ONCE DID I THINK THAT I WANTED TO, SHOULD HAVE BEEN ABLE TO, OR COULD DO...
...WHAT I JUST DID HERE.

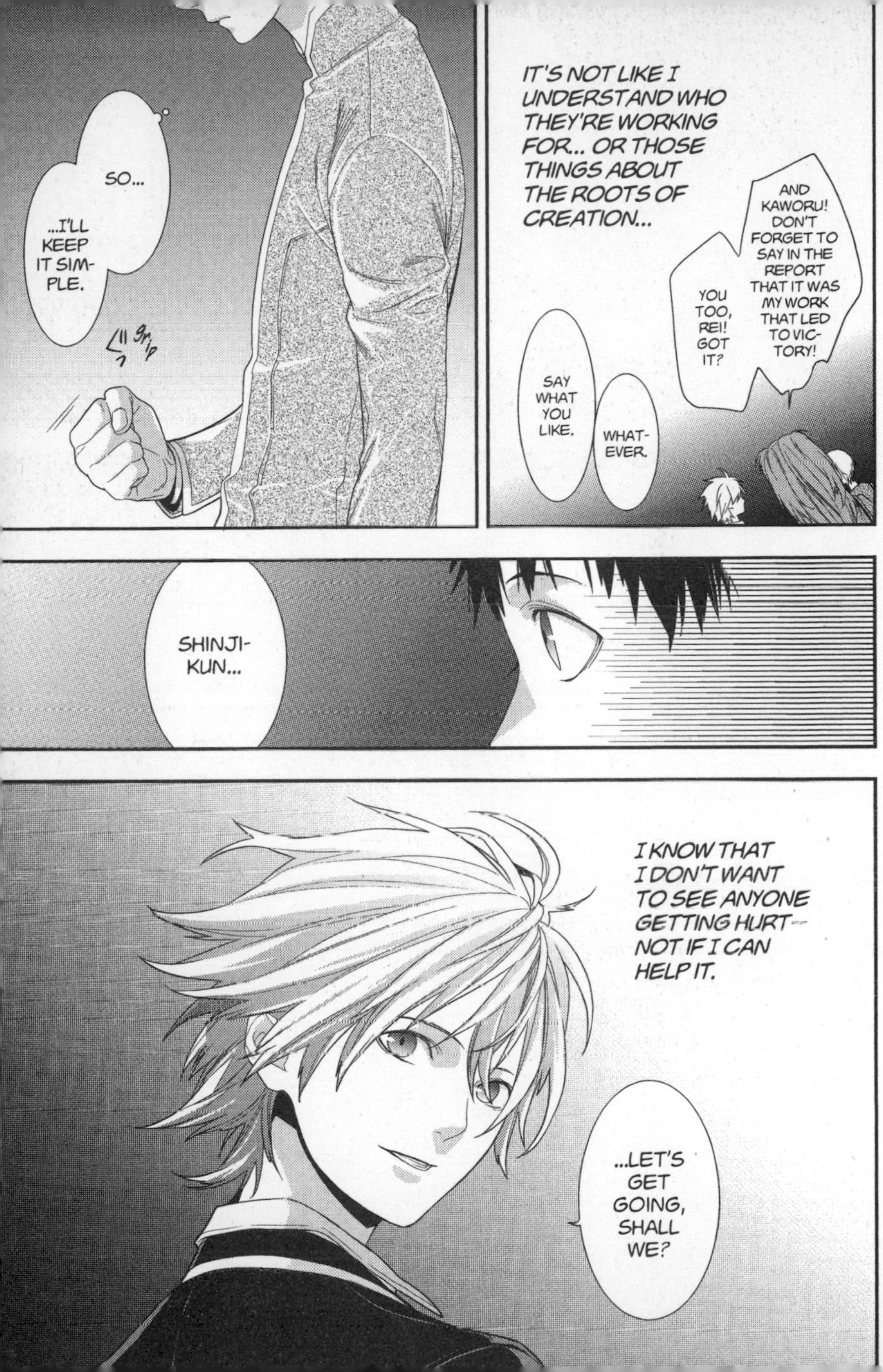
IT'S NOT LIKE I UNDERSTAND WHO THEY'RE WORKING FOR... OR THOSE THINGS ABOUT THE ROOTS OF CREATION...
AND KAWORU! DON'T FORGET TO SAY IN THE REPORT THAT IT WAS MY WORK THAT LED TO VIC-TORY!
YOU TOO, REI! GOT IT?
WHAT-EVER.
SAY WHAT YOU LIKE.
SO...
...I'LL KEEP IT SIM-PLE.
grip
SHINJI-KUN...
I KNOW THAT I DON'T WANT TO SEE ANYONE GETTING HURT-- NOT IF I CAN HELP IT.
...LET'S GET GOING, SHALL WE?

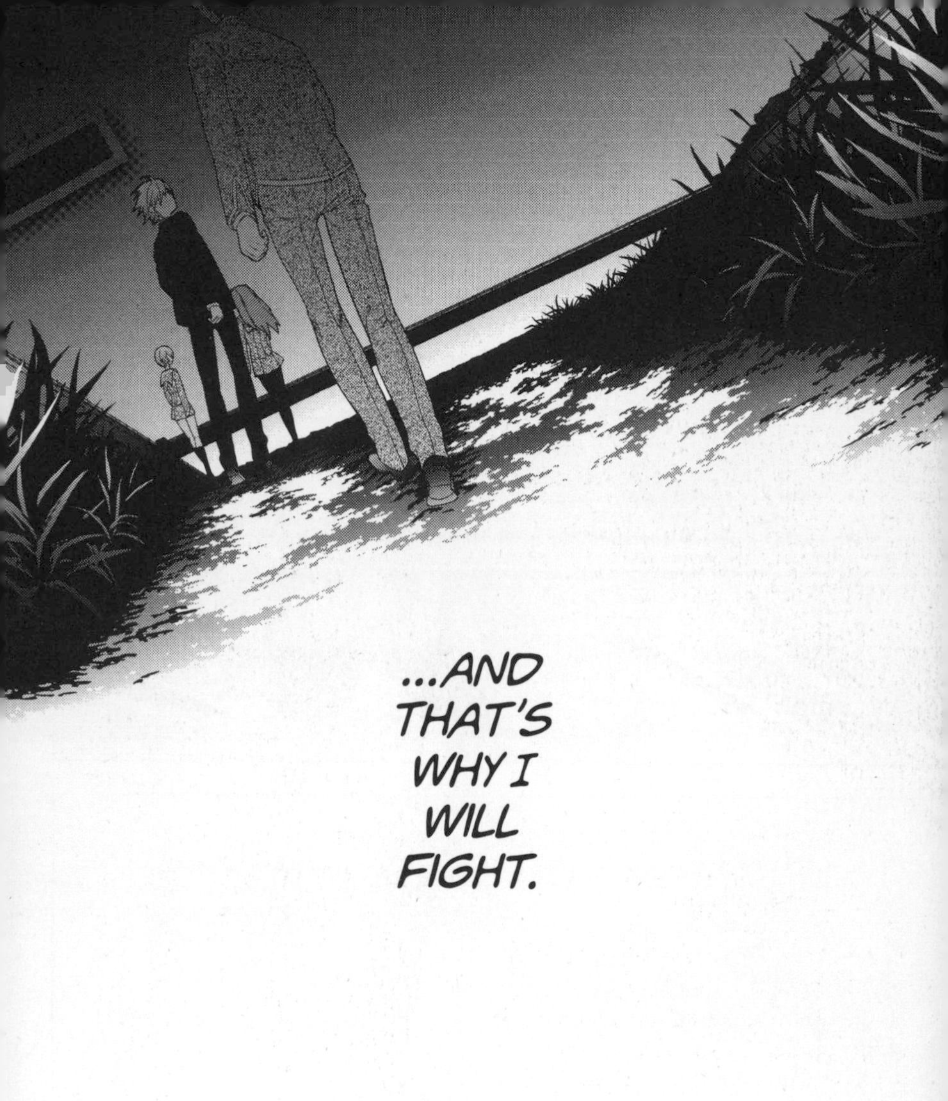
...AND THAT'S WHY I WILL FIGHT.

END

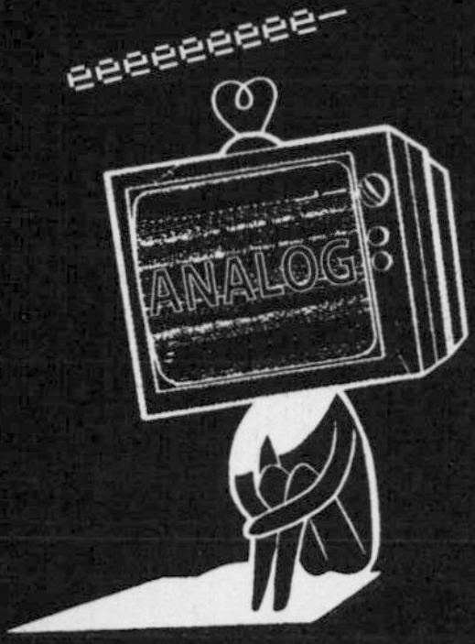
eeeeeeeee—
ANALOG

AFTERWORD

And I had thought it was uncool to ride the wave of the times—but it paid off.

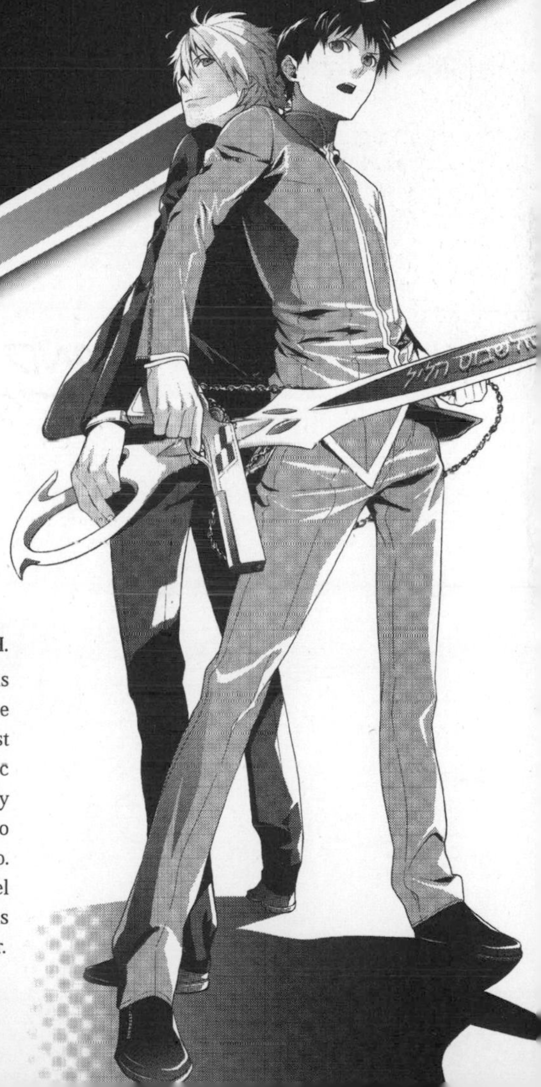

MINGMING

A CAPRICORN, BORN ON JANUARY EIGHTH.

DISCLAIMER: This version of *Evangelion* is fiction and has almost nothing to do with the actual, existing *Evangelion*. This is my first serialized story. This is my first graphic novel. I am thankful from the bottom of my heart that I've gotten this far, and thankful to all of you who decided to pick this book up. Even though this is, as I said, only a parallel *Evangelion*, I hope that we can enjoy this journey together until the very last chapter.

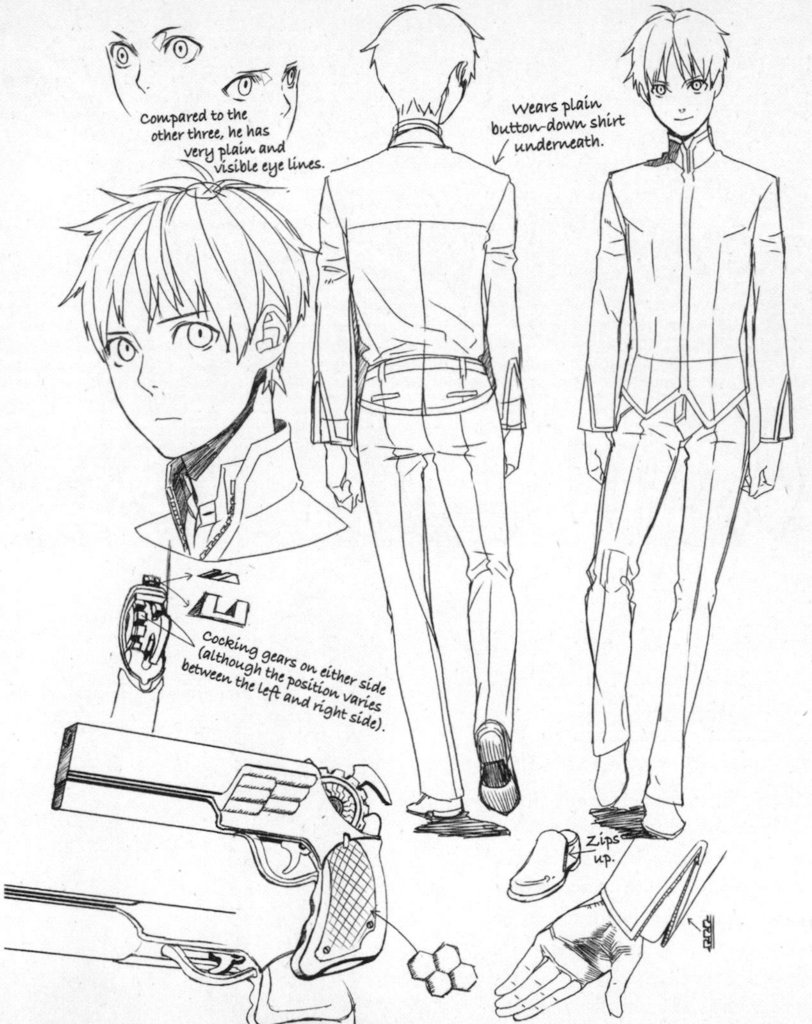
Compared to the other three, he has very plain and visible eye lines.
Wears plain button-down shirt underneath.
Cocking gears on either side (although the position varies between the left and right side).
Zips up.

Shinji Ikari

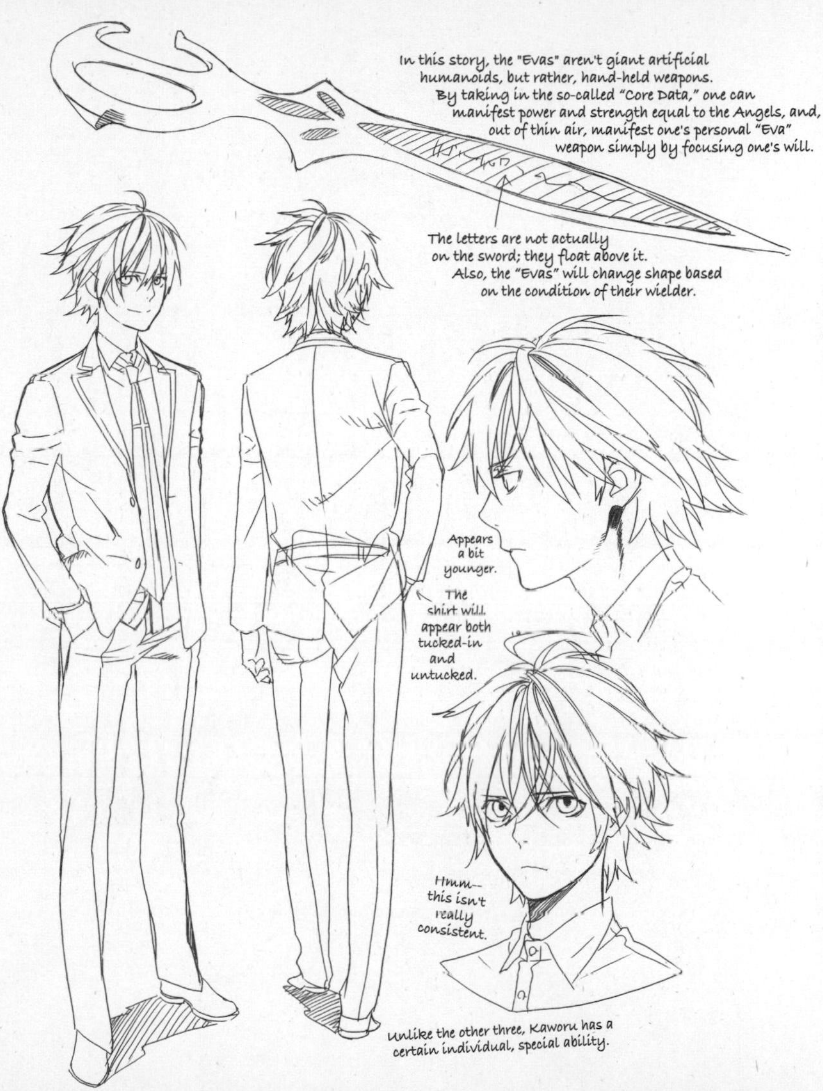
In this story, the "Evas" aren't giant artificial humanoids, but rather, hand-held weapons. By taking in the so-called "Core Data," one can manifest power and strength equal to the Angels, and, out of thin air, manifest one's personal "Eva" weapon simply by focusing one's will.
The letters are not actually on the sword; they float above it. Also, the "Evas" will change shape based on the condition of their wielder.
Appears a bit younger.
The shirt will appear both tucked-in and untucked.
Hmm— this isn't really consistent.
Unlike the other three, Kaworu has a certain individual, special ability.

Kaworu Nagisa

MINGMING'S GRAFFITI

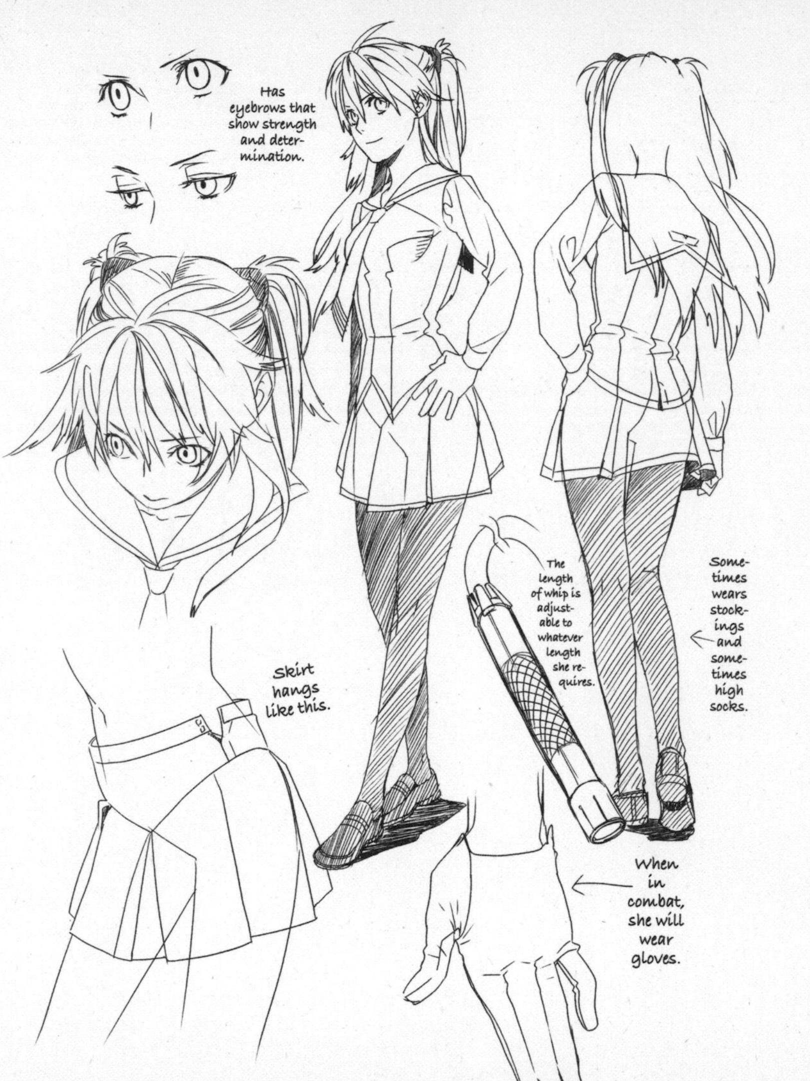
Has eyebrows that show strength and determination.
The length of whip is adjustable to whatever length she requires.
Sometimes wears stockings and sometimes high socks.
Skirt hangs like this.
When in combat, she will wear gloves.

Asuka Langley Soryu

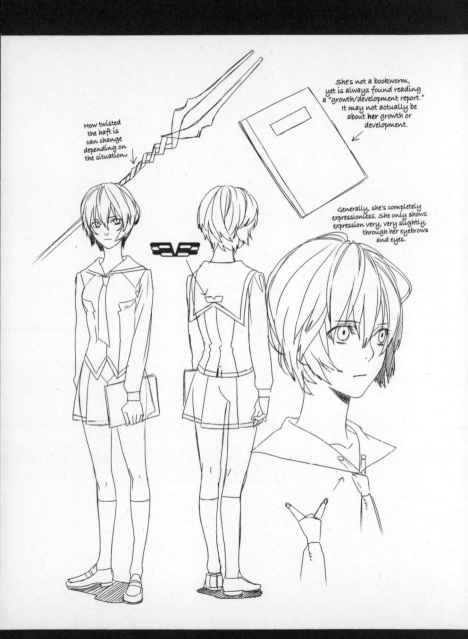

How twisted the haft is can change depending on the situation.

She's not a bookworm, yet is always found reading a "growth/development report." It may not actually be about **her** growth or development.

Generally, she's completely expressionless. She only shows expression very, very slightly, through her eyebrows and eyes.

Rei Ayanami

DESIGNER
STEPHEN REICHERT

EDITOR
JEMIAH JEFFERSON

PUBLISHER
MIKE RICHARDSON

English-language version produced by **Dark Horse Comics**

NEON GENESIS EVANGELION CAMPUS APOCALYPSE Volume 1

First published in Japan as NEON GENESIS EVANGELION GAKUEN DATENROKU Volume 1. © Mingming 2008 © GAINAX · khara. First published in Japan in 2008 by KADOKAWA SHOTEN Publishing Co., Ltd., Tokyo. English-translation rights arranged with KADOKAWA SHOTEN Publishing Co., Ltd., Tokyo, through TOHAN CORPORATION, Tokyo. This English-language edition © 2010 by Dark Horse Comics, Inc. All other material © 2010 by Dark Horse Comics, Inc. All rights reserved. No portion of this publication may be reproduced or transmitted, in any form or by any means, without the express written permission of Dark Horse Comics, Inc. Names, characters, places, and incidents featured in this publication either are the product of the author's imagination or are used fictitiously. Any resemblance to actual persons (living or dead), events, institutions, or locales, without satiric intent, is coincidental. Dark Horse Manga™ is a trademark of Dark Horse Comics, Inc. All rights reserved.

Published by
Dark Horse Manga
A division of Dark Horse Comics, Inc.
10956 SE Main Street
Milwaukie, OR 97222

darkhorse.com

**To find a comics shop in your area, call the
Comic Shop Locator Service toll-free at 1-888-266-4226**

First edition: September 2010
ISBN 978-1-59582-530-8

1 3 5 7 9 10 8 6 4 2
Printed at Lebonfon Printing, Inc., Val-d'Or, QC, Canada

MISATO'S FAN SERVICE CENTER

c/o Dark Horse Comics • 10956 SE Main Street • Milwaukie, OR 97222 • evangelion@darkhorse.com

Greetings from the editor of the English-language edition of *Neon Genesis Evangelion: Campus Apocalypse*. Welcome to this manga—and welcome also to its fan art and letters column, Misato's Fan Service Center. While this letters column shares its name with the lettercol in Dark Horse's other manga series based on *Neon Genesis Evangelion*, the charming *Shinji Ikari Raising Project*, that book has an editorial team that is the inverse of this one!

My name's Jemiah (pronounced Juh-MEE-uh), and my first exposure to the vast and gorgeous world of *Evangelion* came at the hand of benevolent dictator—er, that is, regular manga editor, Carl Gustav Horn—when he invited me along in a group of coworkers to see the new big-screen version of the saga, *Evangelion: 1.0 You Are (Not) Alone* at the chichi Living Room Theaters in downtown Portland. Now, I had been interested in *Evangelion* for years by that point—the series is a favorite amongst my friends who are anime enthusiasts—but I kept putting off my own entrée into the series, having been warned that it would "take over [my] life." Truer words were rarely uttered. I loved the movie, and promptly blazed my way through the original anime series, finally staggering away with a smoking crater where my brain used to be, blasted clean away by a grenade of sheer awesome.

I've been an anime and manga fan since ye olden days of the 1980s (!!! Yes, we actually had TV way back then) and would get up at 4:30 in the morning to watch *Voltron* and *Robotech*, and the occasional run of *Nausicaä of the Valley*

of the Wind when it showed up on HBO. My love for the medium continued into adulthood, where I discovered the ambitious noir stylings of *Cowboy Bebop* and the melancholy, disturbing cyberpunk of *Serial Experiments: Lain*. But nothing could have truly prepared me for *Evangelion*: the richly drawn characters, the impossible stakes, the honesty about human feelings, and the staggering audacity of That Ending. I couldn't get enough!

Thus, when this series was offered to me, I jumped at the chance. I'm still new to the editorial field, mostly having worked as an assistant for the last few years, but I have definitive ideas about what's good, what's not-so-good, and what's OMG-brilliant. I look forward to going on this journey with you readers; take up your crosses, your pistols, and your schoolbooks, because it's time for the Campus Apocalypse to begin!

Hey! Write in! Send your letters, fan art, and photos to the address listed above! There's a very good chance you could win some rare *Evangelion* swag from the coffers of Carl Horn, as well as having your work printed in these very pages!

See you all in Volume 2!

—Jemiah

NEON GENESIS EVANGELION
THE SHINJI IKARI RAISING PROJECT

Stunning, hotheaded Asuka Soryu has been friends with Shinji Ikari since they were little. And she always assumed they'd stay together—until the day the beautiful, brilliant Rei Ayanami showed up in class! When Shinji starts to get curious about Rei, Asuka needs to figure out if she wants to be just friends with Shinji, or something more. But why are so many people keeping an eye on these relationships?

Volume 1
ISBN 978-1-59582-321-2 | **$9.99**

Volume 2
ISBN 978-1-59582-377-9 | **$9.99**

Volume 3
ISBN 978-1-59582-447-9 | **$9.99**

Volume 4
ISBN 978-1-59582-454-7 | **$9.99**

Volume 5
ISBN 978-1-59582-520-9 | **$9.99**

Volume 6
ISBN 978-1-59582-580-3 | **$9.99**

Volume 7
ISBN 978-1-59582-595-7 | **$9.99**

EACH VOLUME OF *NEON GENESIS EVANGELION* FEATURES BONUS COLOR PAGES, YOUR *EVANGELION* FAN ART AND LETTERS, AND SPECIAL READER GIVEAWAYS!

DARK HORSE MANGA
darkhorse.com

AVAILABLE AT YOUR LOCAL COMICS SHOP OR BOOKSTORE
TO FIND A COMICS SHOP IN YOUR AREA, CALL 1-888-266-4226

For more information or to order direct: • On the web: darkhorse.com • E-mail: mailorder@darkhorse.com • Phone: 1-800-862-0052 Mon.–Fri. 9 AM to 5 PM Pacific Time.

Kosuke Fujishima's Oh My Goddess!

$10.99 each!

Winner of the 2009
Kodansha Award! Discover
the romance classic that's
America's longest-running
manga series!

For more information or to order direct: • On the web: darkhorse.com

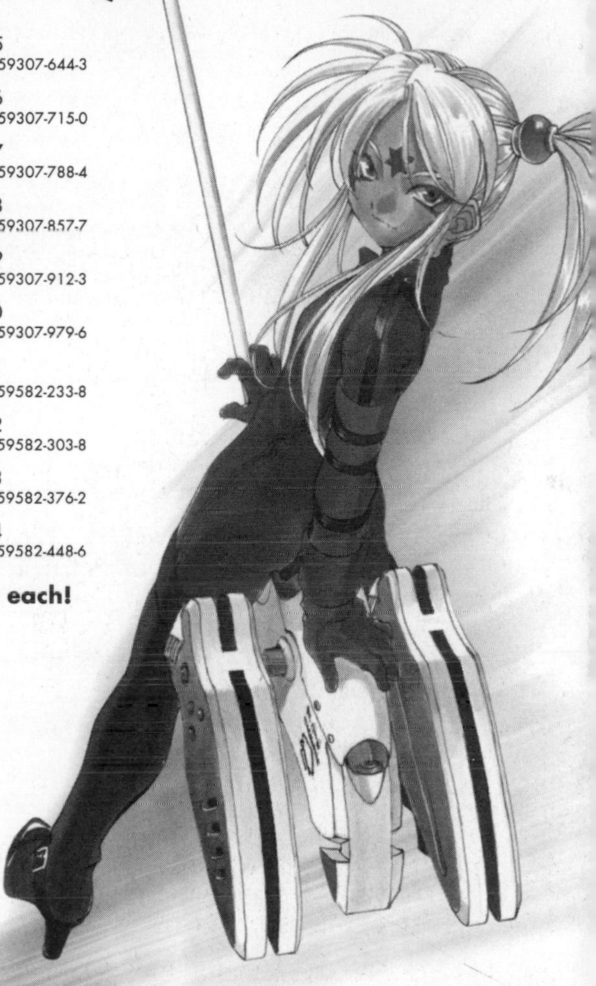

the KUROSAGI corpse delivery service

黒鷺死体宅配便

If you enjoyed this book, be sure to check out *The Kurosagi Corpse Delivery Service*, a new mature-readers manga series from the creator of *Mail*!

Five young students at a Buddhist university find there's little call for their job skills in today's Tokyo . . . among the *living*, that is! But their studies give them a direct line to the dead—the dead who are still trapped in their corpses, and can't move on to the next reincarnation! Whether you died from suicide, murder, sickness, or madness, they'll carry your body anywhere it needs to go to free your soul! Written by Eiji Otsuka of the notorious *MPD-Psycho*!

Volume 1:
ISBN 978-1-59307-555-2

Volume 2:
ISBN 978-1-59307-593-4

Volume 3:
ISBN 978-1-59307-594-1

Volume 4:
ISBN 978-1-59307-595-8

Volume 5:
ISBN 978-1-59307-596-5

Volume 6:
ISBN 978-1-59307-892-8

Volume 7:
ISBN 978-1-59307-982-6

Volume 8:
ISBN 978-1-59582-235-2

Volume 9:
ISBN 978-1-59582-306-9

Volume 10:
ISBN 978-1-59582-446-2

$10.99 each!